For Marge —
Good wishes —

[signature]

12/7/05

Readers' comments:

"My Lessons with Kumi has given me a plethora of methods to use when I teach, perform and work with private clients. We could all use Colgrass' book as a 'how-to' manual for living. Many, many thanks."
Cheryl Weiss, Performance Enhancement Coach and Voice Teacher, Tucson, Arizona

"After reading Colgrass' marvelous book, I'm connecting easier with my radio guests and listeners, and the stress of difficult management decisions is all but gone. I even conquered my old nemesis, fear of heights, and climbed a tall pyramid!"
Anette Damgaard, Assistant Manager, Danish Broadcasting Corporation

"What a novel approach to a self-help book. I can enjoy reading it just for the story alone, with or without the exercises. This book has just been added to the required reading list for students at the New England Conservatory who are performing in community outreach concerts."
Kenneth Radnofsky, Professor of Music, New England and Boston Conservatories

"I feel I can recommend this book to other lawyers for its many suggestions on how to 'face the terrors' of this business (like speaking in public) and generally to help them improve their professional performance."
Guilherme Lacombe de Goes, Senior Partner, Gianini, Perelo & Lacombe de Goes, Barristers & Solicitors, Sao Paulo, Brazil

"As with the creation of a play, life is a series of opportunities to get things right. By combining his teaching tale with his manual of techniques and exercises, Michael Colgrass allows us to imagine how we might use these tools to shape our life into a story we would want to tell."
Jens Kohler, Stage and Screen Actor, Los Angeles

My Lessons With Kumi

How I learned to perform with confidence
in life and work

Michael Colgrass

Real People Press

MY LESSONS WITH KUMI:

HOW I LEARNED TO PERFORM WITH CONFIDENCE IN LIFE AND WORK

©Copyright 2000 by Michael Colgrass

Cover art: John Martin
Cover design: David Saltmarche/See Spot Run Inc.
Photos: Arnold Matthews
Illustrations: Michael Colgrass
Editor: Steve Andreas
Book design: Ulla Colgrass

Library of Congress Cataloging-in-Publication Data

Colgrass, Michael.
    My Lessons With Kumi: How I learned to perform with confidence in life and work / by Michael Colgrass.
        p. cm.
    Includes bibliographical references and index.
    ISBN 0-911226-40-0
    1. Self-help techniques. I. Title.

BF632 .C57 2000
158.1--dc21   99-088119

For Ulla and Neal

Contents

Notes & Exercises

1

SEE YOUR NOSE ON A MOUNTAINTOP

...*A NEW TOY TO PLAY WITH*

"Imaginative people trick their brains all the time. That's how they accomplish their dreams. And brains love it. They're in the game-playing business. They'll play games with you if you don't give them something to do."

I drove through the mountains of northwestern Montana for over an hour before turning off onto a rutted road darkened by old pines. As the jeep whined and bumped its way up through the forest I began to wish I was back in New York. But Allan's words kept ringing in my mind: "Give it a chance. If it doesn't work, it doesn't work."

Near the top of the mountain I found a small cabin nestled in a cluster of fir trees. My stomach fluttered slightly as I got out of the jeep and looked around.

"Hello, anybody there?" I said. The front door stood half open and I peered into a large space with a fireplace at one end. A rough-hewn wooden table stood by a sink near a big window overlooking the valley. In the center of the room a wiry little man was hanging upside down with his arms crossed over his chest. His feet were locked in foot straps attached to a high bar. He said, "You must be Nicholas."

I wondered if I should try to bend over to match his position.

"Yes, we talked on the phone about stage fright."

His voice sounded like metal scraping gently on granite. "You'd like to have stage fright?"

"No, I'd like to get rid of it."

"Why get rid of something useful?"

"Stage fright's useful?"

"It brought you to me."

I couldn't think of anything to say.

"Take a room in Bear Canyon tonight. Dream about what you want for yourself and come back tomorrow."

This was too weird for me. What was I talking to, a bat? And what did he mean "dream" tonight? To think about what I want, or to somehow control my dreams? My night dreams happen by themselves, and daydreaming is pure fantasy world. What I really wanted was my job back to be paid to experiment with my computer video ideas, but that was beyond the powers of Mr. Kumi. So I'd made this whole trip for nothing. I decided to go back to New York and work it out on my own.

I wound my way down the mountain in second gear. My throat was constricted and I had to open my mouth to breathe. I stopped the jeep, got out and retched violently. The forest was still. I wiped my mouth and sat down on a bed of pine needles.

No job, no marriage and a son who still blames me for the divorce. Is that what I'm going back to? Marion is the one light on the horizon. She understands, and Charles likes her. She thought coming here was a good idea.

A beam of sunlight slanted through the trees and shone on a gossamer circle of silk threads. In the center sat a spider in predatory stillness. I watched for any sign of movement, but saw only the eerie undulating of the web.

"Somebody might get you first," I whispered.

I got back in the jeep and drove very slowly down the mountain. Once on the highway I thought about New York. I was good at my job and it was wrong for them to let me go. Still—much as I hated to admit it—maybe it wasn't only to save money that Globalcom dropped me. I don't always relate easily to people, I guess. Sometimes I wondered why I wasn't persuasive enough to make people listen. The truth is, in the back of my mind every day I wanted to express my ideas with confidence. In meetings, one-on-one— even on the phone—it was hard for me to speak naturally and maintain my composure. And public speaking was worst of all. I guess I'd been no better in communicating with Andrea.

Thinking through this litany, I knew I couldn't go back to being that person. Something had to change. I pulled into a bed & breakfast and took a room for the night.

The next morning I returned to Kumi's cabin, ready for more or less anything. The sun was just beginning to streak the sky. The door to his house was still open but he wasn't there. I wondered vaguely if he was just playing with me or had lost interest.

I walked around outside the house and saw him near a large lichen-covered rock formation gazing over the mountain vista to the southeast. Strips of snow laced the upper granite crevices of the near mountain and a sprinkling of pines sloped down into a valley of aspens and cottonwoods. On the horizon was a huge snow-capped mountain turning pink in the changing morning light.

I walked over and stood for a minute watching Kumi.

Without looking at me, he said, "See that mountaintop?" I followed his eyes and looked at the snow-capped peak.

"See yourself at your best, standing over there in all your strength."

I took a deep breath to cover my irritation. I'm a practical person and haven't time for touchy-feely stuff. "I don't see myself, I just see the mountain."

"Touch your nose and then see it on the peak," he said, pointing to the mountain.

Allan had warned me that some of Kumi's ideas might seem a little off the wall. I tried to follow his instructions even though I felt awkward.

"My nose on the peak?"

"Yes."

"You mean, like a dot or big, or what?"

"Any size you like."

I put my hands on my hips and looked at my shoes for a moment. "Why are we doing this?"

"You're from New York, aren't you?"

"Yeah."

"I met a guy from Brooklyn once who said to me, 'Kumi, I figure one of two ways—either I figure what the hell, or I figure the hell with it.' So, figure either way."

I resisted a smile. His eyes twinkled. The muscles in my jaw begin to relax and I threw my wind breaker on the grass. Once again I felt my nose —it was cold—and tried to place it on the mountaintop. Gradually a faint outline started forming before my eyes, almost as if I were sculpting it on the sky.

"How's it going?"

"It comes and goes."

"But you're getting an image?"

"A little, yeah."

"Now do the same with your face and body."

I touched my cheeks and the bones of my face.

"I don't see anything."

"Take your time."

"Can I close my eyes?"

"Sure."

I took a deep breath and closed my eyes, still feeling my face.

"I'm not seeing anything."

"You don't have to *really* see it, just *imagine* you're seeing it."

Suddenly I saw a transparent image of part of my face and then it went away.

"How do I hold onto it?"

"*Feel* it being over there, watch it moving."

Oddly enough, it was easier for me to feel the image first, then see it. Bit by bit, as I touched my body, parts of my torso and limbs appeared vaguely on the horizon. The picture faded in and out but I was getting pieces of it.

"Take the part of you that's easiest to see and make it brighter."

I looked at him and back at the mountain. I closed my eyes and saw my left ear and my hairline. I imagined painting my ear a bright orange, then my face, nose and mouth. Gradually the whole face became brighter, then disappeared.

"Can we stop a minute?"

I let out a big sigh and rubbed my head.

"I think it'd be easier to climb that mountain than see myself on it."

"You'll get it. It's just new for you."

I scanned the landscape and drank in the fresh pine breeze.

"Try less hard this time. In fact, don't try at all, just feel any part of the image of yourself that comes most naturally into view."

I looked back up at the mountain peak. A thin outline of head and shoulders began to form. I don't know if they were mine, but I imagined they were. I was breathing more naturally and felt less tense.

"Okay."

"Now make the picture larger. See it on a big screen."

The idea of a screen helped, as if I were watching myself in a movie. Suddenly I heard my voice and saw a vague image of my mouth.

"Yeah, okay…"

"Make the image brighter as you move the screen toward you."

I felt my image moving toward me, from the mountaintop, but I wasn't sure what I was seeing.

We continued playing in this way for some time, brightening and darkening parts of the picture, making them larger and smaller, testing to see which contrasts would make the image most vivid. For me, larger and brighter felt best and made it easier to imagine. I was getting more interested in the exercise as I began to see portions of my body in color. But part of me was still resisting the exercise, because I saw no sense in doing it.

"Are you moving in the picture, or still?"

"Still, like a photo."

"Give it motion."

"It won't move."

"Move your arms and then see them moving over there," he said nodding to the mountain.

I flexed my fingers, then my arms, and marched in position, then tilted my head back and forth. As I felt these motions I saw these parts of the image move, but the picture faded in and out of focus.

"Now, recall a time when you did a fantastic job on something and remember how that felt. See yourself feeling that way."

"I can't think of anything fantastic I've ever done."

"Take your time. Aeschylus said, 'Everything divine is effortless.'"

"Well, I'm not Aeschylus, whoever that is."

Suddenly I recalled the first time I got an on-line video relay with a clear picture and no break-up in the sound. I was elated and my colleagues at Globalcom gathered around. I saw, faintly in the distance, the smile I had on my face that day. My body relaxed as I enjoyed the image.

"Now move that picture closer to you, and then closer still, and then faster and faster and rush it into your body."

"How do I do that?"

"Just do it."

I fixed on the smile, the crinkle around my eyes and the flush in the cheeks. I concentrated as hard as I could to hold the image. As I moved that picture closer to me my heart began to pound. I felt the image "enter" my body with a jolt.

"Do it again."

I got back whatever image I could and repeated the exercise, feeling a strong rush as it traversed space and slammed into my body.

"Again."

I repeated this action a number of times, getting different parts of the picture in view with each repetition. I felt like I was ready to fly off the edge of the mountain I was standing on.

"Ohh...can we stop now?"

I leaned back against a rock, closed my eyes and rubbed them. My eyelids felt heavy as I massaged my temples. When I opened my eyes the mountains were purple and half shaded by cumulus clouds. I looked at my watch—ten-thirty. We'd been at this for two-and-a-half hours!

I looked around for Kumi and saw him carrying logs into the cabin. I went over to help him.

"May I ask what that was all about?"

"Did you enjoy it?"

"I'm not sure."

"How do you feel when you see yourself like that?"

"I feel, uh...unusual. I've never done it."

"Does it feel comfortable or uncomfortable?"

I had to think for a minute. "The act of doing it is really strange, but the feeling that comes from it is...well, not bad, actually. I'm just not sure why we did it."

"Imagine a time when feeling confident will be useful to you. Like for an interview or exam or any test situation where you need a high level of concentration and energy."

"Well...I'm giving a talk in two weeks that I'm kind of dreading. It's at my college reunion. An old friend of mine got an award and they want me to say a few words about him. I'd like to feel good when I'm doing that—you know, confident. But no one's going to be there to get me into the right frame of mind, so what's the point?"

"Imagine that it's two weeks from now and you're at the place where you'll talk. Feel yourself being there now."

"Feel it how?"

"See the surroundings through your own eyes, hear people talking, feel the atmosphere, use your imagination."

This felt odd to me, but odd seemed to be the name of the game here. All this imaginary stuff reminded me of being a kid, living in a fantasy world. But why not? So, I imagined a large room probably in some restaurant, with about a hundred people sitting at tables set for dinner. Maybe I'd be back at a speaker's table with a microphone, glasses and a pitcher of water. I got the old feeling of being with one or two of my college buddies and actually began to see them, mentally exchanging their shirts and jeans for suits and ties.

"Okay, I'm there. So now what?"

"Imagine that you will be speaking to these people shortly. But before you do, take a moment and see yourself on that mountain peak, talking exactly the way you want—a large, radiant picture of yourself, in color, speaking in a rich voice, feeling the way you feel when you're at your very best— and then pull that picture into you as you did before."

"I don't know how radiant I can make it."

"Do what you can."

"So, I'm in the future, at the reunion dinner, and still remembering the mountain?"

"Right."

"And I'm hearing the voice I'm going to use in my talk?"

"Yes. Also, see yourself talking."

"From the mountain?"

"From the mountain."

"This is weird—my sermon from the mount!"

"Sure it's weird. Go ahead."

I planted myself at the event and retrieved, as best I could, the picture and feeling of myself on the mountaintop. Then I heard my voice, which was easy. I suddenly realized I had done something similar to this before — imagined myself at future events—but those images just came to me involuntarily and they weren't always pleasant. This was the first time I had ever *consciously* created the picture of a future event in my mind, especially seeing myself in it. The impression I was getting now of being at my college re-union two weeks ahead of time was so strong that I even felt my new dress shoes on my feet.

"I'm wearing a suit and tie," I said aloud.

"How do you feel?"

"Okay. I feel there the way I feel here."

"Good. We're planting that feeling in your future. Now give your talk—in that future space."

"I don't know yet what I'm going to say."

"Give the gist of it."

I looked at the vague image of the crowd I imagined around me and began making up a speech. Although I heard myself speaking aloud in that room, I was silent here in front of Kumi. When I finished I looked at him.

"So, how was it?" he asked

"This feels really strange to me."

"That's natural—you've never done it. Just tell me how the speech went."

Thinking about my speech as if I'd already done it felt oddly pleasant. "Actually, I felt a little nervous. But it went okay. I got through it."

"Is that how you normally feel when you give a talk?"

"Oh, I don't give talks very much. But no, I choke up when I have to speak in public."

"You mean you *used* to choke up. Now you have a *new* way to feel about it, and that new feeling is planted in your future, waiting for you. It's nice to know you can walk into that room two weeks from now and feel only a *little* nervous, isn't it?"

"Well, yeah, but how do I know that? After imagining it for only a few minutes?"

"Imagining things is how you make them happen. That's what I'm teaching you. When you fully immerse your mind in the act of doing something—seeing it, hearing it, feeling it—that's as good as doing it. Your brain doesn't know the difference."

"Well, I think my brain would."

"See this lemon," he said, holding out his empty hand. "I'm going to cut it with this knife." He pretended he was cutting a lemon with a real knife. A good acting job. Then he took half of the lemon and held it to his mouth, making a loud sucking sound. My mouth felt the fresh tang of lemon and I salivated.

"Tasty, huh?"

"Yeah, but you tricked my brain."

"I tricked your brain or you tricked your brain?"

"Well, I'm not sure who did it, but…"

"Imaginative people trick their brains all the time. That's how they accomplish their dreams. And brains love it. They're in the game-playing business. They'll play games with you if you don't give them something to do."

I nodded. "That's true."

"Brains need to be directed, because they can go wayward or get lazy. So we're going to make sure your brain remembers this good feeling of giving the speech in two weeks. You're going to reinforce its memory by practicing this exercise every day between now and speech-time. And just to make sure you practice it, you're going to remind yourself now to practice it tomorrow, and the next day, and the next day, and so on. So, right now I want you to see yourself practicing this exercise at home every day, and again just before giving your speech."

I sighed. "This is work."

"Yes, it's work"

"Okay. So, now you're asking that I be here with you and see myself at home practicing."

"Right."

"Yeah, I do have to get this straight, you know. You've had me flying around everywhere so much I'm not sure where I am anymore."

Kumi laughed in a funny high-pitched "hee-hee" voice, like a child, and patted me affectionately on the back. "Don't worry, you're doing fine. Go ahead."

I got the feeling of being in my Riverside Drive apartment. Then I half saw, half felt myself there and heard my voice practicing my speech. I noticed that practicing the speech in this way I felt hardly any of the old anxiety. I got the impression that my face looked more confident so I must have been seeing myself, and as I watched it I felt calm. Kumi looked at me, nodding his head as if he could see the results just by watching me.

"I hope it's still there two weeks from now," I said.

"If you practice it will be, and it'll get better. Ultimately, you want to see more than just yourself giving a speech—you want to see the rest of your life."

"I'm doing well if I can see the rest of the week."

"Practice making images in your mind every day and you will see farther and farther into the future. You said you recently lost your job."

"Yes."

"What did you do?"

"I developed video-conferencing software for a large computer firm."

"So who're you working for now?"

"Myself."

"Do you see where that's going?"

"Not really."

"Well, now's the time to start. You're part of a large army of displaced workers who have to figure out how to make it on their own. I want you to visualize every day: long-term for your goal, making images of what you want in your future, and short-term for creating alternatives in your daily life. And *feel* these images fully in your body, as if they are already occurring experiences. Are you willing to do that?"

I felt a flicker of irritation and looked away. A bird circled and called out sharply, "We-chew—kek, kek, kek, kek, kek." Suddenly it dived, turned a series of somersaults, tumbling over and over in a flurry of feathers, then swooped up and disappeared over the trees.

I looked at Kumi. He was staring at me with his eyebrows raised in a questioning position.

"I'll try," I said.

"Try?"

"Alright, I'll do it."

"Ahhh. Now take a moment and imagine other situations where visualizing like this might be helpful to you."

I remembered when I got fired in March and how upset I felt. Not only at being betrayed by my boss but because I'd failed to express myself as I should have. I keep hearing Streicher saying, "I think we've gone far enough with on-line conferencing." At the time I was working on creating large, high quality computer video images for businesses wanting to hold live meetings on the Internet. "After all," Streicher said, "we don't really need pictures to communicate." Yet he was the one who always said, "There's nothing like seeing the person you're negotiating with."

Replaying the event in my mind, I wondered why I hadn't pointed out that contradiction. The reason is *I didn't see it at the time because I was so hurt*. Is it possible I might have come out of that encounter feeling different than I did—

better, more resourceful—and that playing it over in my mind these past months could have been less painful? Maybe this exercise could be applied to my relationship with my son, Charles, who had just started university. Perhaps I could help him with his physics without getting into an argument.

"Successful people see themselves five, ten times their normal size in bright colors, performing wonders—like they're watching themselves in a movie," Kumi said.

"How do you know?"

"Because they tell me. I asked a professional basketball player once how he got so good at his free throws. He said he practiced with an imaginary ball. I asked him why and he said, 'Because it always goes in.'"

I grinned and nodded. "And seeing yourself succeeding always works?"

"If you believe in it and do it repeatedly. You recall your successes to get back that good feeling. Many people sabotage themselves by remembering their failures and worrying about repeating them. They bring back all the bad feelings that come with those memories. To make it even worse, they say to themselves, 'It's not going to go well,' which guarantees that it won't. You get what you predict."

"But how do I know I can do it when I really need it?"

"Creating pictures in your mind is a skill like any other. The more you practice it the better you become. You visualize numbers and equations, don't you? That's part of your work."

"Yeah, but that's different."

"Different how?"

"You're asking me to visualize *myself*, and to see situations in my life I've never seen before. That's hard for me."

"Practice by recalling pleasant images. Like a favorite game you had as a child, a teacher you liked, a graduation day."

Suddenly I saw in my mind a big pail of water full of green apples that we were dunking for at a birthday party in my basement. I must have been nine years old. I also remembered getting a stomachache eating too many of those green apples.

"Or a favorite movie or television program."

Now a whole slew of images came flooding in.

"I knew a guy who said he could never get an image in his mind," Kumi said. "I asked him what he enjoyed most as a kid and he said his fire truck—and bang, the picture of this red foot-long six-wheeler flashed in full color right in front of him. Now he says he can make an image of anything he wants and then step into the image and feel himself doing it."

"That doesn't mean he'll get it."

"But he knows how it feels to have it—it's within reach. Then he's inspired to go for it."

"What if he makes an image of something and steps into it and finds it's wrong for him?"

"He makes a new image."

"Like an actor working on a scene—step in and out of it until you get it right."

"Yes."

"But it takes a long time to learn that."

"Not when you make it a daily ritual. Do a little bit at a time. Going too fast for a full bright picture is as frustrating as trying to lift a heavy weight for the first time. The happiest memories will be the easiest to recall."

One of the happiest days for me was the day Charles was born. And Andrea looked so beautiful. Recalling those early happy days of our marriage is almost unbearable. Maybe that's why I don't want to visualize past success or happiness, because when you don't have it anymore it's too painful to think about.

"Kumi, has it ever occurred to you that maybe some people just don't visualize?"

"All people visualize, because visualizing is part of the brain's daily business. But many people are simply not in the habit of paying attention to these images. They don't know they're being influenced by them. They think their behavior is being directed by forces outside themselves. Such people need to learn how to see the pictures that are flashing in their minds in order to understand the effect those images are having on them. Your behavior is directly influenced by your internal imagery, Nick, but you may not always be aware of the images your brain is following. Are you seeing pictures that inspire and help you, or are you watching doomsday films? If you don't make your own images, you'll let others make them for you. Outstanding people don't leave their internal imagery to chance—they *choose* what they want to see, creating pictures that make them feel strong and resourceful. In effect their life is a work created by them."

I had mixed feelings about this idea. I'm not exactly a fatalist, but I have always felt that things "happen to you." Is it possible that I could actually make things happen in my life instead of just waiting for them to happen, come what may? If I accepted the idea that I make my own life then I'd be admitting I created the condition I'm in, and I didn't want to admit that. On the other hand, if I created my present situation maybe I could also create a new one that was better.

"Why do some people seem to visualize themselves and their lives automatically while I have to work so hard at it?"

"Maybe their parents were very visual and they picked it up from them. Or maybe it just came to them naturally. Our senses are like our limbs—some people have strong arms, others strong legs, depending how much they use them. You're used to recalling emotions and hearing dialogue in your head, but not at visualizing yourself and others close to you."

"Then why do I see numbers clearly in my mind?"

"Maybe because you feel no emotion about them. Emotions tend to cloud the imagery in our minds. And human situations are full of emotion."

"Are you saying I shouldn't feel?"

"Of course you should feel, but you also need to learn how to *detach* from your feelings when it's appropriate. That's one of the advantages of visualizing, it helps you gain objectivity in your life. You're in the habit of letting your emotions overwhelm you, and then imagery is very difficult, if not impossible."

Again, I felt the swell of emotions from my last meeting with Streicher.

"So what do I do?"

"You practice."

I looked at the mountain peak, which was now a brownish gold.

"But when you imagine a better life or a perfect performance aren't you really kidding yourself? My presentation or a life situation will just go the way it'll go."

"No. It will go the way you *make* it go. Ask yourself, How do I want it to go? Then see and feel it going that way and memorize that feeling by playing back that picture over and over. Your brain gets the message and plays it back to you when you need it. I assure you, that's how people succeed. It's not enough to know the theory about how visualizing works —you must practice and develop it as a skill so you have it when you need it. Replay in your mind your successful events and erase your failures. Actually, it's better to say *keep* the memory of the failures because you can learn from them but, for the moment, reduce them to tiny black and white snapshots and file them away, for reference when useful."

Kumi and I worked for another day on variations of the visualization exercise. When I left I felt more at ease. Except perhaps for a slight uneasiness at having nothing major to argue about. I still didn't understand how you could make something happen by just imagining it. Especially if that meant seeing it in your mind.

Bumping my way down the treacherous road to the highway, I wondered what confidence was anyway. Why do we need it? I'm always amazed when a sports announcer says that a top athlete "lost his confidence." Michael Jordan? Martina Hingis? How can a champion lose confidence? Kumi says it doesn't make any difference who you are. Confidence is the condition of your senses—pictures that are bright, sounds that are rich, feelings that give you energy. Your senses reflect your beliefs and your beliefs are influenced by your senses. If you win the lottery the world looks bright, if a friend dies the sky goes black. He's implying I can change my behavior by training my senses to respond in new ways. Is it really possible to change just by doing a few exercises, especially at the age of forty-five? But he didn't say it was easy, in fact he said I had to work at it every day until I got the hang of it, and then remember to use it. It'd be a lot easier to just stock up on valium, but I've learned that doesn't work for long. So, for the moment, here I was, working at seeing myself on mountaintops.

When I got back to New York I followed Kumi's instructions and practiced visualizing in my apartment. But New York was noisy. So I had to work to make my images even bigger and brighter to focus on them. I did them first thing in the morning when I was fresh. Kumi said it was a good way to kick-start the day. And also a good thing to do at night to program my unconscious just before going to sleep.

I always tried to see myself at my best. (There's that word "try" again that Kumi doesn't like. But, dammit, this is an *effort* for me, and I *am* trying.) I recalled what past successes I could, going all the way back to my childhood. I found that if I started with the *feeling* of a memory (but not so much that it blocked out the image) it was easier to get a picture or partial picture of it. Kumi says that's because feeling is one of my strong senses. Sometimes I'd recall the words someone spoke because recalling dialogue is easy for me. When I play back Marion's voice in my mind it's much easier for me to get an image, or a partial image, of her.

I asked Kumi why he kept insisting that I look at the mountaintop to visualize. He said the eyes are "wired" to the senses. When I look up, I activate the visual part of my brain. I asked what scientific proof he had of that and he said, "None." He encouraged me to question it and prove it to myself. So I experimented looking up, down and sideways when visualizing and I discovered something curious. If I look up to my left I tend to *recall* images, and when I look up to my right I seem to more easily *construct* new ones.

<table>
<tr><td>(my left)
**I see the past
over here**</td><td>(my right)
**I see the future
over here**</td></tr>
</table>

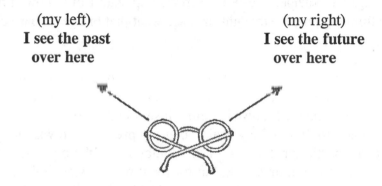

Visualizing through my not-so-rose-colored glasses.

I may be on to something here, but I need more time to try it out. And I want to see how it works for other people.

I also notice that pictures come into my mind more naturally when I connect them to things I really enjoy hearing or touching or smelling or tasting. Just hearing the words "Peking duck" puts that taste in my mouth and I see Sai Woo's on Mott Street. I guess I've had these images in my mind all those years and just never noticed them. But negative thoughts also bring back images. Now that I think of it, that's probably what my father did because he always seemed to be looking at the darker side of life. Some people think he gave himself the cancer that killed him. And he was the person I grew up imitating!

After a few days of practice, I didn't know if I was actually visualizing myself better or if I just thought I was, but the exercises were feeling more natural. I wavered between thinking I was making some progress and wondering if I wasn't just wasting my time—and money. I had to admit I was feeling a new energy. But then a lot of it seemed too simple—even simple-minded. Make an image and change my life? How about the situation I'm born into? How about the natural limitations of the human mind? To me, the idea of imagining a better life was always a kind of "pie in the sky" attitude, not accepting things the way they really were.

But if I want to change maybe I have to start by pretending. If I believe something long enough I might actually start doing it. If negative thoughts and feelings have helped create the screwed up state I'm in now, I might as well try thinking positive thoughts and see what that brings. What've I got to lose?

Two weeks later I felt ready to give my speech. I had imagined it every day as a pleasant event and so I was literally "looking forward" to it. On the day of the reunion dinner I followed Kumi's instructions and did another visualization session to "remind my brain" that my presentation was the primary event of this particular day. All of this might seem like overkill for such a small thing as a five-minute talk, but for me it was no small thing.

At the reunion I was seated at a table with my old college prof and two or three others who would also say a few words. When my turn came, Mr. Lombard introduced me. As he spoke my name I got that funny feeling in my stomach that always creeps up on me when I'm about to speak in public and I wondered how I'd do. Then, to my surprise, I saw my mountain peak and stepped up to the microphone and smiled comfortably at all my college friends.

(My notes on this visit with Kumi are on page 268)

2

ZZ-ZZT!

...GIVE YOURSELF A CHARGE

"Your state of mind is a choice. You can see life darkly and decide you're a victim, or you can pay attention to the rich moments in your life and other people's lives and use those good feelings and images to help you create the outcome you want."

Looking out the window of the plane on my return trip to the Rockies, I remembered what Allan had said about Kumi.

"He's part Inuit   you know, Eskimo."

"Eskimo!"

"He was born in the Arctic. His mother was Inuit and his father was a Norwegian explorer icebound for a winter in the town where Kumi grew up. He never knew him."

"How'd he ever get to Montana?"

"How does anyone ever get to Montana? It's the land of the Free Spirit. He's a kind of a Buddha meets Daniel Boone."

That description appealed to Marion. She's a free spirit herself. You have to be, to survive as an artist in New York. She's a singer-actor and has done off-Broadway and some film. Somehow she has drawn me into the world of the arts. It's all new to me, but I find it fascinating. I also find her fascinating, probably because we're so different. She went to Stanford and studied English lit, history, theater and dance, and ended up with a catch-all degree in the humanities. I, on the other hand, am a single-track guy who studied physics and math and am most happy locked away in a room someplace working out a computer program. How she ever got attracted to me I don't know. When she says I'm solid and dependable, those could be euphemisms for boring. But if I'm ever to come out of my shell, she's the one to help me.

I recalled our conversation at a Thai restaurant on West Seventieth Street. She was eager to know about my meeting with Kumi.

"He's interesting, but he's kooky. I honestly don't know what to make of him. One minute I'm spellbound by him and the next I'm ready to turn around and go home."

"Hmm. Do you think he has what you want?"

I sat back and looked at her—green eyes, freckles, and what they call carrot-colored hair. Irish genes, she says.

"Maybe, but I feel uncomfortable. He's not like me at all."

She raised her eyebrows and tilted her head.

"Well, I guess nobody is," I said. "He does have a sense of humor though."

"Then he's ahead of most people," she said. "Is he expensive?"

"A couple of days' visit comes to a little over twenty-five hundred, including the flight."

"That's a lot of money."

"It's a little more than half what I get for repairing a video system, which takes about forty hours. Then I have my severance and unemployment."

"But you still have the mortgage on the condo. And Charles' college."

Which begs the unasked question, What right do I have to spend this money on myself? What did I do to deserve it?

"Do you have many of those video repair jobs?"

"I'm putting out the word."

"How many more visits are you going to make to Kumi?"

"I don't know, maybe one or two. I can only take so much of this stuff."

Her elbow was on the table with her chin cupped in her hand, looking at me.

"So what's that I see brewing behind those eyes?" I said.

"I'm glad you're going. I just don't want you to get lost up there in the mountains and forget where home is."

These thoughts were interrupted as my plane touched down in Montana. The pre-dawn flight to Minneapolis with a connection to Kalispell got me to Montana early in the afternoon. Two hours later I got to that obstacle course that leads up to Kumi's cabin, arriving exhausted.

Kumi came out to the jeep and handed me an orange. I looked at our mountain range and then walked over to a cluster of trees and sat on a rock. The fresh smell of the green-black pines took away my fatigue.

I saw a beautiful little bird, plump like a chicken with reddish-brown and white speckle, the color of ancient rock shield. It was walking around aimlessly, cackling and beating its wings in the air. "I never saw a bird like that," I said.

"That's a white-tailed ptarmigan, a kind of grouse. A pine marten just ate all her young."

"What's a pine marten?"

"Like a weasel."

"So what'll she do now?"

"Lay more eggs."

"It doesn't seem fair."

"Fair! What's fair got to do with it? Ptarmigan are great survivors. They can adjust to anything. They turn white as snow in the winter and the color of the cliffs in spring. She'll do okay. But that marten will have to watch out for the fox, and the fox for the wolf. That's the way it is."

We went inside and I sank into a deep sleep on the couch. When I opened my eyes it was dusk. I smelled soup. We ate in silence, listening to the wind rustle branches on the roof of the cabin.

"Did you bring your sleeping bag? I've got a place for you right there in the corner."

We washed the dishes and sat down by the fireplace with a cup of tea. Kumi put some aspen logs on the grate and lit the pinepole kindling.

"So, how'd your talk go?"

"Not bad, but I had to concentrate every minute to keep from getting nervous. I did the visual exercises every day."

Kumi squinted at me.

"Well, almost every day. And I did them right before I gave my talk, just like you said."

"So?"

"When I stood up to speak my head was clear and I didn't have any memory slips, which is an improvement. In fact, I got more applause than any of the other speakers."

"That's not what this is all about. You're not competing with others, you're working to improve your*self*."

I watched a piece of bark curling in the fire.

"Well, my mouth did go dry a couple of times and I felt a fluttering in my stomach. I thought this visualizing was supposed to take care of all that."

"You want everything at once."

"You mean there's more?"

"We've barely scratched the surface. Did you bring your tape recorder?"

I tapped the Sony in my shirt pocket.

"Sit in this chair. How long is the tape?"

"Fifty minutes each side."

"Good. Take a deep breath and squeeze your fingers together like this."

He touched his thumb to his first finger, like he was holding a piece of thread. His thumbnail pressed into the fleshy pad of his finger. I felt uneasy and thought, Now what?

"Is this yoga?"

"No."

"Well, what are we going to do?"

"I'm going to teach you how to change the world and find eternal happiness. What else?"

"Okay." I chuckled and imitated his finger squeeze.

"Both hands," he said. "Now, take a deep breath…and recall a loving moment from your life, one of the happiest.

I watched the moon out his window. But a flood of unhappy memories came over me.

"I can't find one."

Kumi reached over and separated my fingers. "As soon as one comes, touch your fingers together again."

I sighed. Here we go again, looking for Nirvana. If I had happy memories I wouldn't be here. Suddenly I remembered walking in a field with my father when I was a child. His hand is around my shoulder and I smell his pipe. I nodded my head.

"Squeeze the fingers," he said. "Use your thumbnail."

I pressed both thumbs and fingers together.

"In this memory, look around you…listen to the sounds… notice the feeling of your body…the smell of the air…"

I saw the shadows in the trees and felt the heat of the sun. Our shoes made a rustling sound in the tall grass. I was surprised I could recall all that. "Uh-huh."

"Squeeze your fingers." He paused a moment and then went on. "As you continue to enjoy the feeling of this memory, notice the location of that feeling in your body. Many feel a difference in temperature somewhere in the mid-section, chest or neck, but for you it may be elsewhere."

Find the location of a memory in my body? If anyone had been watching me now I would have been too embarrassed to go on. Then I remembered Marion doing some kind of a yoga meditation exercise where she touched her fingers together in a similar way. Gradually a warm feeling loomed up along my breast plate just below the clavicle.

"When you locate that feeling in your body, notice its size and shape and mark its borders in your mind."

I decided to go along with these strange requests just to see where it would take me. I was amused at the idea of measuring the length of a feeling in my chest. Then I noticed to my surprise that the warm feeling seemed to be roughly an oval about eight inches long and four inches wide.

"Now, very slowly, allow the borders of this feeling to spread out over your body, like liquid spreading slowly over a table top."

At first nothing happened, then I felt the warmth moving downward into my stomach, then sideways into my ribs. I nodded my head to let him know it was happening.

"Now allow the feeling to spread throughout your torso… into your shoulders …your arms and hands…your legs…up into your neck, head and face…"

A part of me wanted to resist this, but Kumi's voice was so soothing I found myself just going along with it. I felt as though a warm liquid was filling out my body, and every limb and organ it touched just seemed to sink softly under the weight. Although I was relaxing deeply—almost in a kind of trance—I was conscious of everything that was going on.

"…and as the feeling of that loving moment fills out the last inch of your body, I'm going to ask you to do something very nice for yourself…*double the feeling*…and *squeeze* the fingers…" He paused.

The idea of doubling the feeling was a kind of shock. As I pressed my thumb-nail into my finger, the warmth of my father's presence and the surround-ings of the sunny field intensified. I felt a glow throughout my body.

"…and as you continue to enjoy that feeling, you may recall the memory of a particular child or animal you very much enjoy…be with this child or animal now, see its eyes, listen to the sounds it makes, and feel its touch, notice its smell…"

I felt the presence of Tarby, the black cocker spaniel I had as a boy, and how he liked to nuzzle my leg at night. My right arm was touching his fur.

"…and when the feeling of this memory is at its strongest…*squeeze the fingers…*"

Kumi paused for a few moments and then went on.

"…and as you continue to enjoy that feeling, you may recall a favorite place in nature…notice the season of the year…and the colors…the shadows…the things that are moving and the things that are still…the sounds…the feeling of the temperature on your body…the smell of the air…"

I saw and smelled the ocean on Long Island and heard the waves crashing on the beach. I tasted salt and felt the buoyancy of the water and the warmth of the sun on my back as I swam.

"…and…*squeeze the fingers…*"

He paused again.

"…and as you continue to enjoy that…recall a time when you did an outstanding job on something…it may have been a little thing, like picking just the right gift and seeing the person's pleasure at receiving it…or a big thing, like successfully completing a course or creating something you were proud of…"

Some years ago I needed a very large table that would accommodate all my computer equipment, but I couldn't find the right shape anywhere. I asked a carpenter friend, but he was too busy at the time and suggested I build it myself. He showed me a few basic principles, told me where to get the wood and I built a beautiful nine-by-six foot L-shaped pine table into the corner. I feel enormous pride every time I look at it. After building it, I knew I could do things I'd never done before if someone just showed me how.

"…and, when that memory is fully with you…*squeeze the fingers…*"

He paused again.

"...and now let's review these feelings...the happy moment...and *squeeze*...that endearing child or pet...and *squeeze*...your favorite nature spot...and *squeeze*...that resourceful moment...and *squeeze*...

"...and perhaps other moments are coming into your mind that are remarkable and deeply satisfying, and which give you a feeling of joy or of deep calm, and as you allow these memories to continue to come to you...*squeeze the fingers*...

"Rest a while and think about these things you've just recalled...and when you're ready, taking all the time you need, and at your own pace, you can begin to return to your normal, everyday state."

Gradually my body seemed to "wake up," though I had not been asleep. My mind had been crystal clear and I remembered everything Kumi had said. I felt refreshed and energetic, and very much at peace. I don't now how long I sat there before Kumi spoke again

"Stand up and walk around," he said.

I walked outside. The air had an almost vanilla-like smell of pine bark. The night was chilly, clear and still, and the stars were so close I could almost touch them. Gradually the horizon lit up and began to move, like a silk curtain laced with a hundred-million green and yellow lights undulating gently in a breeze. It almost made me dizzy to look at it, like I was on a boat in the sea. I touched the railing of the porch to keep my balance.

"The northern lights," Kumi said. "You're lucky. This sight is rare for Montana. In the Arctic, you can almost hear them whisper, like spirits riding with the lights in the sky."

He held up his hand, pressing his thumbnail into the pad of his forefinger and made a short buzzing sound, like the touching together of two live electrical wires.

"Zz-zzt!"

"Zz-zzt!" I said and took in a panoramic view of the sky as I pressed my thumb into my finger. The warm feelings and images I had just recalled came back to me.

"Whenever you see something beautiful, that's your cue to squeeze the fingers. Even little things: "My, what a nice tie, Nicholas." *Zz-zzt!* You see a sky full of stars. *Zz-zzt!* You get a great idea. *Zz-zzt!*"

I said "Zz-zzt" and thought of Marion and the warm feeling of being with her. She was the one who encouraged me to start my own business with new forms of video-conferencing, and also to undertake this adventure in Montana.

"Every single day I want you to find a quiet spot, recall one more inspiring memory from your life, and squeeze your fingers, adding that memory to those we've revived tonight. If you like, you can play back the tape of my voice to get started. In a month you will have recalled thirty more inspiring memories, plus new ones you've added from daily life. Imagine how many good feelings you will have collected by the end of the year.

"Picture where you will practice this at home and see yourself doing it now."

I saw the easy chair in my apartment.

"And promise me—promise *yourself*—you will do it every day, no matter what."

"I don't know that I can keep a promise I make to myself."

"What would have to happen before you could?"

I didn't want to say you have to respect yourself before you can keep a promise to yourself.

"It's one thing to make a commitment in the moment and another to keep it when the time comes."

"You mean you've never committed yourself to anything and stuck with it, not ever?"

I recalled my third year in college when I wanted to throw in the towel, but somehow kept going instead. And those long hours in the middle of the night when Charles was a baby, when I took my turn giving him his bottle and changing him.

"It'd be easier if I knew you were going to be there with me."

"Then imagine I'm there with you."

I tried to hold on to my stubbornness, but felt it slipping away.

"Okay. I…promise."

I awakened the next morning to the sound of birds. I padded over to the window and looked at my mountain peak, swathed in the aurora of morning light. The sky was vermilion and the lower part of the mountains was barely perceptible through the morning mist. A chipmunk hopped onto the window ledge and eyed me with curiosity before picking up a pine cone. "I'm new here," I said.

I walked outside. The air smelled of burnt aspen from last night's fire. Kumi was piling up firewood. I walked among the trees to see if I could figure out how many birds were part of this morning's chorus. Suddenly the singing stopped, except for one solo bird. I whistled back at it but it didn't respond.

When I returned to the cabin, Kumi was making breakfast. "You like wheat bran?" Kumi said. "Here's some fruit." He added water to skimmed milk powder and stirred it in a large pitcher. Hot herbal tea was steeping in the pot. I was very hungry and had hoped for my usual bacon and eggs with toast and coffee.

"Think you'll survive without caffeine and saturated fat?" he said with a wry smile.

"Where do you get your water?" I asked.

"A cistern under the house. The spring run-off gives enough for almost the whole year, when I'm lucky."

"About the only time you count on luck, right?"

"I'll take whatever I can get."

During breakfast I thought about the previous evening. I knew he wouldn't say anything about it until I asked. "Kumi, tell me more about what we did last night."

"I taught you a signal you can use when you need it."

"A signal."

"Zz-zzt! To bring back good feelings." He held up his fingers.

"When would I need it?"

"You tell me."

I thought for a moment. "To deal with a tense situation?"

Kumi looked at me.

"Or before an important business meeting," I said.

"Or when you're about to give a speech? Zz-zzt!" he said. He held up his fingers and looked at me with a smile.

I pressed my thumbnails into the pads of my first fingers and—somewhat to my surprise—a feeling of well-being drifted over me.

"Imagine you'd done this before talking at your class reunion. How would things have been different?"

I recalled the evening. "I don't know."

"Well, guess."

"Maybe I would've felt a little more at ease."

"The finger squeeze is the other half of the visualizing exercises we did last time. With the images you *see* yourself as being confident, with the squeeze you *feel* yourself being confident. The images bring good feelings and the feelings bring good images. You have it two ways."

I poured myself another cup of tea. I could have used some caffeine, but the hot liquid was at least soothing.

"The idea is to create a kind of resource memory bank," he said, "where you can make instant deposits and withdrawals."

"Do you get interest on those deposits?" I said.

"In fact you do. Every time you do a job well, or have an experience that's exciting or moving or humorous, you can add that feeling to your memory bank by simply squeezing the fingers. Inspiring events might occur at any time, and the squeeze signal is an easy way to assemble them and store them."

"But events are so fleeting—they come and go in a flash," I said.

"Exactly. And you can put a hold on them in a split second with this simple touch, and no one even knows you've done it. And then you can recall the memory with equal ease when you need it."

"Why use both hands? Isn't one enough?"

"In case one hand's holding something you can use the other."

"And you say this really works?"

"Of course it works. I saw it work for you just now. You've heard of Pavlov's dog. The dinner bell brings back the memory of food and the dog salivates; your finger squeeze brings back the memories of happiness and comfort and you relax."

"Sounds too easy."

"Look at how easily you develop a negative memory. Something bad happens and bang, you think about it for twenty years. Think of the Squeeze also as a form of self-defense—your armory of resourceful feelings to fend off the invasion of the negative. We live in the age of information, much of it violent. For many of us, our myths are created by television, where superficial news reports and titillating entertainment is the norm. In this culture it's all too easy to develop the perception that the world is nothing but earthquakes and floods, arson, drugs, corruption, rape and war. If these are the images and feelings you send to your brain, don't be surprised when you get disturbing messages back. That's the way neurology works."

I got up from the table and looked out the window. I wondered where all last night's stars had gone.

"Are you suggesting I've actually programmed myself to feel negative. Why would anybody want to do that?"

"You do what you're used to."

"And you think you can change that."

"Yes."

"I disagree. People think they change, but they just fall right back into their old habits. That's nature."

"Nonsense, that's programming."

"Well, if you leave the world and go sit on a rock someplace you can afford to be theoretical. I choose to be practical."

"Hee, hee, hee," he said in that child-like laughter and slapped his palm on the table. "An old man living in a dream world, am I?"

"That's how you strike me sometimes."

"Look, Nick," he said, carrying the dishes to the sink, "I'm not suggesting you turn off the world, or that you turn off the TV. I'm saying that, in the face of the onslaught of events that vie for our attention, it's all the more important to be able to *filter* what comes into your brain so you can place world events, and yourself, in perspective. Your state of mind is a choice. You can adopt other people's interpretations of the world or you can create your own. You can see life darkly and decide that you're a victim, or you can pay attention to the rich moments in your life and other people's lives and use those good feelings and images to help you create the outcomes you want. Your immediate desire is to create for yourself a state of mind where you can perform at your best, no matter what the conditions. And that's what the squeeze is designed to help you do."

I found myself going back and forth on accepting and resisting Kumi's ideas. Maybe I was just suspicious of "new age miracles." But I do like the little guy. He's just so different from anyone I've experienced before. Marion's feelings are mixed too. She wants me to improve myself, but she's getting a little antsy about my always taking off to the mountains. The way I see it, if this stuff has any value it will prove itself to me. Just do the exercises and see what happens.

For the next two days we took leisurely walks and talked little. Kumi seemed to realize that it would be wise to back off a little and give me some space. Meanwhile I had decided I'd just go along with his ideas and see where they lead. After all, what can it hurt? I'm in the mountains for a few days and then I go home. It's not like I'm committed.

For some reason I got immersed in nature, a sort of natural state of mind I probably picked up from Kumi. We squeezed our fingers so often I didn't even realize I was doing it. One afternoon Kumi asked me to lie on the grass and watch the sky. At first I was bored, then gradually my limbs felt as though they were filling with water and I was sinking into one of the clouds, floating over the landscape. After a while, I could no longer tell if it was the earth or the clouds that were moving.

Kumi had a way of leaving me alone at such moments, yet giving the feeling he was nearby, watching over me. This allowed me to forget the world, and my internal conversations with myself would completely fade away. After three days, the pain in my lower back, which a doctor had told me was "stress-related," and for which I might need an operation, was barely noticeable.

After this weekend of deep relaxation I felt a little more ready to face New York. While packing my gear, I recalled Kumi's eye movements, which I had made a point of watching when I wasn't in a trance. My first lesson with him was about visualizing—the eye position for that was *up*. In the last few days, our work was primarily about *feeling* and I noticed that Kumi's eyes were almost always *down*.

If, as Kumi says, our eyes are wired to our senses, could it be that we have a specific eye position for each sense?

Experimenting with myself, I noticed that I feel emotion more easily when I look down to my right. Eyes down to my left makes me feel like talking to myself. This is one of my favorite eye positions. Now that I think of it, I was looking down a great deal of the time on this visit, what Marion calls, "searching for a lost object." But by the second day I think I was looking down to the *right* most of the time, and I wasn't talking to myself. Does this mean I can turn off my internal dialogue just by looking down to the right? I could check that when I practice squeezing the fingers. I'm getting excited about this eye stuff—and it's all mine. I'm not going to tell Kumi about it until I see if it really works. Kumi may be a dreamer, but I'm a scientist. I need evidence.

(my left—my right)

Talking to myself   **Feeling**

How My Eyes Work

On the plane to Minneapolis a young woman sat next to me. She would have been pretty, but her face was tight and pale. We were delayed on take-off and started talking. She was a buyer for a grain company and had just attended a conference. She said she hoped I didn't think she was an alcoholic if she had a few quick drinks immediately after take off. "I'm absolutely petrified of flying," she said.

At first I thought, "You've got your problems and I've got mine." Then it struck me that maybe I could help her.

"Excuse me, I know this little game that's kind of nice to play when you feel tense." She expressed interest and suddenly I realized I was on the spot. Could I really help her, or would I make a fool of myself? What would Kumi think of my using his techniques to meet women on airplanes? I rationalized that I was practicing by teaching her a skill. Then I heard Kumi's voice— "...figure either what the hell, or the hell with it."

I demonstrated how to squeeze the fingers, imitating Kumi's low, sooth ing voice. First, I had her take a nice deep breath. Then to recall a series of wonderful experiences and spread the good feeling throughout her body, as Kumi had done with me. She squeezed after each memory. I watched her face go from pale to a healthy glow, as her facial muscles relaxed and a little smile settled into place.

When the flight captain said we were cleared for take-off, his words had no apparent effect on her. As we taxied and took off, her expression didn't change. Finally, after about thirty minutes she stirred, turned to me and said, "Oh, thank you," and went to sleep. It worked! I could even teach it to somebody else!

As we prepared for landing she woke up. I held my fingers up and said "Zz-zzt!" She did the same and smiled. I noticed with pride that she kept her eyes open as we touched down in Minneapolis. Then she turned to me and said, "I'll never forget this," and gave me her name and address. I continued on to New York and never saw her again.

(My notes on the Zzt-Squeeze are on page 275)

3

JACK NICHOLSON ON THE ROCKS

...CREATE A WHOLE GANG OF COACHES

"It only takes a second to establish a phobia. A snake falls out of the tree in front of you, you magnify it in your mind to the size of a house and, bang, you've got a phobia! So, you do an exercise in which you shrink the snake back down to normal size, step way back so you can see it at a safe distance, laugh at the whole thing and you're back to where you were before the snake fell out of the tree."

The room was dark and Marion's image appeared on the screen of a twenty-one inch monitor. She was standing next to me in jeans and a white shirt.

"That's us!" she said.

"Yup, that's us. You're making your debut on the Net."

Marion did a little dance and sang a tune, watching herself on the screen.

"But why bother doing all this on the Net when you can already do it using direct video hook-up?"

"Because it's cheaper. You'll be able to audition live from your own living room without expensive equipment. But I'm still not satisfied. I want to make a quantum leap in live image transmission. I just don't know what it is yet."

For the next few weeks I had jobs installing a video-conferencing system for an advertising agency and repairing another one for a brokerage firm. I did the finger squeezes every day and actually found myself using it one morning while demonstrating video-relay to a group of business students at New York University.

Usually the first thing I do when I have to give a class is look at the clock, wishing it was over. To get through it, I just rattle off what I know until my time is up. While I addressed the class this one morning a young man in the front row continually yawned and looked at his wrist watch. I felt a growing agitation toward him and began losing my concentration. My usual response would have been to get mad at him, but that has never been productive. Instead, I pressed my left thumbnail into my forefinger. My breathing deepened and Kumi's cabin flashed in my mind. Then I said, "I don't know about all of you, but I think eight in the morning is a hell of an hour to tackle computers." They laughed and my yawner smiled and sat up in his chair. I told them about the most boring teacher I'd ever had who read everything from notes. "I would never do that. Instead I fascinate you with internal variables, hexadecimal representations and terminal sequences in feed files." Laughter again. "Wouldn't I be an exciting blind date?"

Maybe I was starting to loosen up and feel a little more confident. But with Marion it was a different story. Since my divorce I'd been wary of committing myself to anyone. She was sensitive to this and didn't pressure me. At the same time, she was beginning to wonder what I was doing with my life, and I had no answers.

On the last day in New York before returning to the mountains we went to an off-Broadway matinee performance of a new production of "Moby Dick." I wondered how they were going to get a giant whale on stage and was astonished at their solution. The stage set was a boat and we—the audience— were the whale! The actor playing Ahab had the perfect balance between anger and fear in his eyes when he looked at us and yelled in fury, "Moooo- by Dick!" The set designer used our imagination to create Ahab's torturer, because she knew each person in the audience would imagine the thing he or she fears most.

Afterward, we sat on a bench in Riverside Park overlooking the Hudson River and talked about my visits to Kumi and where it was all leading.

"I just wonder what your goal is, Nick?"

"To get what I need."

"Which is?"

"A feeling of control over my life. I don't want to find myself in the rapids again, grappling for a life jacket."

"That's a little vague."

"I thought you liked the idea of my going to Kumi."

"I just think you should have a plan."

"I'm waiting to see what'll happen."

"What if nothing happens?"

Marion is very goal-oriented. She always has an outcome set for herself and when she reaches it she sets another one. I guess that comes from being an artist. I got a job with a corporation right out of college and never had to think about personal goals. I just followed someone else's lead. The idea that I could actually start designing my own life at age forty-five was very frightening.

"Marion, I'd appreciate it if you just didn't push too hard right now."

She got up and walked across the asphalt walkway and stood at the railing, looking at the water. The early evening sun was red in the west and cast her in black silhouette against the sky. In the distance a steamer was moving out to sea. At that moment I felt the distinct possibility that I was losing Marion.

On the flight the next day I tried to sort out my thoughts, but I couldn't come to any solutions. So I decided to review the things I'd done with Kumi so far. I'm feeling a little better about giving presentations, but I'm still not sure when I'm communicating effectively, on stage or off. How does somebody ever know that? How do you get that kind of objectivity, a perspective on yourself? If I could do that I might be able to understand what's going on between Marion and me.

I was transfixed by the eerie gold of the tamaracks which framed the road up to Kumi's cabin. Their needles also coated the ground like a blanket which gave the effect of driving into a fairy tale forest. At the top, when I stepped out of the jeep the high mountain air hit my lungs, I stared at the orange and yellow trees mixed with green pines. I heard squirrels scurrying in the bushes. "Can I join this party," I said.

In the yard in front of Kumi's cabin I saw three rocks—large, medium and small—forming a triangle about fifteen feet from each other. To my recollection they had not been there before. I walked over and sat down on the large rock.

"You found it." Kumi's voice jarred me out of my reverie.

"Oh, hi," I said. He was wearing a red jacket. "Found what?"

"It took some time to move that thing," he said, pointing to the big rock.

"Yeah. It's in a good place for seeing the valley. What are those other rocks for?"

"They're good for seeing other things," he answered.

I walked over to the medium-sized rock, looking around to see what perspective that would give.

"Now you can see the rock you were just sitting on," he said.

"Yeah..." I said.

"Now go back and sit on the big rock again."

I walked over and sat on it.

"Looks different now, doesn't it?" he said.

"I can't see it. I'm sitting on it."

"Exactly. Would you like some soup?"

I knew better than to say anything more at the moment. Talking to Kumi could sometimes be like verbal shadow boxing, so I just decided to shut up. We ate a delicious soup made from vegetables and herbs. He served it with his homemade bread. "You could open your own restaurant with this combination, Kumi. Except your location is a little off the beaten track." He smiled and looked out the window.

After eating I was sleepy and snoozed on the couch. When I opened my eyes, Kumi was making tea. I followed him outside, carrying my cup.

He walked over to the big rock and stood there. "Here I am, addressing an audience" he said, gesticulating like he was talking to a large group. "'Ladies and gentlemen, how are you today, I'm fine, blah, blah, blah' whatever you say in these talks."

I had to smile at his imitation of me giving a speech.

"Now I wonder how I look and how my voice sounds when I'm giving this speech. So I step over here." He walked over to the medium rock. "From here I look back at the large rock, where I'm talking. Here at this medium rock, I am now the world's greatest coach, whoever I want to be. As the coach, I watch and listen critically to me speaking over there, and make my suggestions." Then he walked back to the big rock. "Now I am the speaker again and I try out what my coach advised." He mimicked a person moving and speaking with conspicuously improved control.

"You mean, you do all that yourself, go back and forth between being the speaker and the coach?"

"Right."

"Well, if that were possible I wouldn't need a live coach. I wouldn't need you, for example."

"After I've shown you something once you shouldn't need me. But later on, when you're working on your own, you may wish that your coach was present so you could ask questions and fine-tune your work. That's what this exercise does for you. However, sometimes you can coach yourself on something for the very first time just using your imagination."

"How?"

"I'll show you in a minute." He looked at the small rock. "Now I'm going to add another position. I wonder what the *audience* thinks about my speech, so I go over here." He walked over to the small rock and assumed a stance of indifference.

"Here I'm a member of whatever audience is relevant to the occasion. As this person, I may not know you or be knowledgeable about the subject you're talking about. I see you standing over there, giving a speech. How does your speech come across to me? By standing at this little rock you know how the listener is responding to you, because, when standing here, you *are* him."

Then Kumi returned to the large rock. "Now you make any changes you think you need to make to satisfy your audience's needs, turning to your coach for help when necessary." He glanced at the medium rock. "You go back and forth between all three rocks until you have seen this performance from everyone's perspective and are satisfied that you understand what needs to be changed."

He stepped away and gestured for me to do it. I thought for a moment and then walked over to the large rock and stood there, remembering my talk at the class reunion. I could hear my voice in my head:

So when I graduated from college I thought I had it made. I got a good job, good salary, met my wife and we had a son. I had no idea that halfway into my career I'd be out of a job and divorced. So what did I learn from that? I'm not a philosopher, but that experience taught me that there is no real security in life, except inside yourself.

Kumi gave me a few minutes to establish this position. Reviewing my speech brought back the feelings I had when speaking that night.

"Now choose the coach you want."

I was beginning to feel tired. I felt a little silly about the idea of walking between rocks out in the wilderness and playing games with imaginary coaches.

"I frankly don't see how this is going to change anything, Kumi."

"That's a natural reaction when you haven't done it yet."

I didn't know how to answer that one, so I decided to just go through the exercise quickly and be done with it. Then I thought of my favorite actor, Jack Nicholson. I like the easy-going, jocular manner he always seems to have. What would he say about my talk?

"See your coach over there by the medium rock," Kumi said.

Gradually I got an image of Nicholson standing there, looking at me like he was waiting. Kumi gestured toward the medium rock and I stepped over to it, taking the coach position as Nicholson. I took a minute to get the feeling of being him and then and looked back at the big rock. I saw myself there with my suit and tie in front of the microphone, and the white tablecloth over the long table. I looked at Kumi.

"So, what do you think your coach would say about your talk."

I took a chance that I might look silly and talked to myself the way I thought Nicholson would. "Aw, c'mon, Nick, for godsake let go and enjoy yourself." I even sounded like him! Acting like Nicholson, I sauntered over to the big rock and smoothed out "Nick's shoulders," which looked tense. "And smile a little bit, you're greeting your friends, having a good time."

I was really getting into it now as I walked back to the medium rock, chewing imaginary gum and assuming Nicholson's jaunty gait. "Now, try it again, kid," I said, addressing me at the big rock in his offhand way. Now I saw myself speaking differently, with more of a casual manner. I nodded and returned to the big rock and, becoming me again, did what I'd just watched myself do. As myself, I let go of my shoulders, which I had been hunching without realizing it, and found myself speaking in a slightly deeper, more relaxed voice. It felt better.

"When you're ready, go to the audience position," Kumi said.

I looked at the small rock, and walked over to it. When I turned around and watched myself speaking at the big rock from this new position as an audience member, I noticed one thing right away—while addressing the audience I had been looking either down at my notes or at the people closest to me. Standing out here as the listener I felt excluded. So, I waved to the speaker and raised my eyebrows as if to say, "I'm here too—talk to *me*."

Then I went back to the "speaker's rock" and looked back at this listener at the small rock and automatically raised my head and stood erect, looking out over the whole audience. I breathed more deeply as I did this. I had been slouching and didn't realize it.

I looked at Kumi. "This is remarkable. How did I know what the coach would say, or what a spectator would think?"

"You just know. It's like we have a thousand cameras running inside us all the time recording everything we do, and we can play back any moment of any event we want, and from any perspective. See yourself now from an overhead camera."

At first I didn't know how to do this. Then I remembered a scene from one of my favorite Hitchcock movies, "North by Northwest," where Cary Grant is running out of the UN Building and we're seeing him from way up on the roof of the building. He looked about the size of an ant. I saw myself in the same way, and noticed how insignificant my nervousness seemed from way up in the air.

"And from a camera down there in the grass."

As Kumi "placed cameras" all around me I found ways to see myself from these different angles. The picture wasn't always crystal clear, and sometimes I got more of a feeling of myself than an image, but the desired effect was achieved. I got a new perspective with each "camera."

"So, somewhere inside me, I know what needs to be improved in my performance."

"Yes, and how to change it."

"Because every experience I've ever had is on videotapes on file inside me, so to speak."

"With sound and in color. And you can add music, if you like."

I imagined hearing The Talking Heads playing at my college reunion and felt how hearing them in my mind while preparing—and even giving—the speech might have affected the spirit of my presentation. Marion says she sometimes creates a character by asking herself what music that person would listen to and then hearing it in her mind while playing the person.

"What's this technique called?"

"Have you ever seen a hologram?"

"Sure, it's a three-dimensional image. It looks real, but you can walk right through it."

"Well, I call this exercise The Hologram, because it's an image you can walk in and out of and coach yourself."

I spent a little more time walking back and forth between the rocks, thinking about what we had done. The late afternoon sun was on the horizon, and the sky looked like it was brushed with red and purple watercolors.

Watching the sunset, Kumi and I talked about the exercise on the rocks. He told me a woman once came to him—a cellist from a symphony orchestra—with a debilitating bursitis in her right elbow. Her doctor gave her drugs, but nothing helped. The muscles of her arm and shoulder finally became so inflamed that an operation was recommended, and she was scared. Kumi taught her a technique for relaxation and then showed her The Hologram, which fascinated her.

For a coach she chose Yo-Yo Ma, the famous cellist, because he was not only a great musician but a very bright and articulate person. She played her cello for a while, then stopped, put the instrument down and moved over to the coaching position. Looking back at the chair she'd been sitting in, she watched and listened to herself playing the cello through the eyes of Yo-Yo Ma.

Kumi said she stood very still for some five minutes, then walked over to the performer's chair, reached out to where her right arm would be—the one that held the bow—and made a slight adjustment. Then she walked back to the coach's chair and continued watching herself play. Returning to the performer's chair, she again became herself playing the cello. She picked up her instrument and started playing with her right arm now several inches lower than it had been before, as she had just coached herself to do. Months later she contacted Kumi and said the inflammation in her elbow was gone. She had been holding her bow arm in a slightly unnatural position and when she lowered her arm a short distance the strain gradually went away and didn't return.

Kumi admitted that, aside from giving her relaxation exercises, he didn't know how to help her. But he was confident that the answer lay *somewhere inside her* if she could only find it. Getting outside herself and watching herself in the Hologram enabled her to see the flaw in her arm position. Her ability to make this physical adjustment with confidence was enhanced by the idea that she had a great cellist coaching her—she was looking at herself with the expert eye she thought Yo-Yo Ma would use.

But this wasn't the end of the story. She returned to Kumi some months later, happy about her bow arm but feeling insecure about her playing. As her arm had gradually gotten worse she had developed stage fright and that still hung on, so Kumi showed her a simple variation of the Hologram. Sitting indoors without the cello, he instructed her to establish three positions in her mind: 1) Playing the cello on stage, 2) Watching herself play the cello from a seat in the concert hall, 3) Watching *both* these selves simultaneously while sitting in the balcony.

She was very amused by the idea, especially of watching herself watch herself. He had her mentally jump around between these three positions at random until she was giggling from the confusion. When he asked her to feel her stage fright again, she said it was difficult to get the feeling back. She said later that, aside from the occasional feeling of performance nerves—which is a natural condition for any conscientious performer—her debilitating stage fright never returned. If she ever felt performance tension too strongly she would do this exercise again—what she jokingly called "the balcony scene from my life"—and it would amuse and relax her.

"Like The Hologram," Kumi explained, "this variation is a simple dissociation exercise—getting out of your body for a moment to free yourself from your own limited perspective and emotion."

"I can't believe her stage fright went away so quickly," I said. "Just from one simple exercise."

"Some cases don't go away so quickly, especially when a person's beliefs get in the way—like the belief that eliminating fear quickly isn't possible."

I glanced at Kumi and he looked away.

"But in many cases, especially where there was a specific frightening incident, the fear can be taken away as fast as it was created. Remember, it only takes a second to establish a phobia. A snake falls out of the tree in front of you, you magnify it in your mind to the size of a house and, bang, you've got a phobia! So, you do an exercise in which you shrink the snake back down to normal size, step way back so you can see it at a safe distance, laugh at the whole thing and you're back to where you were before the snake fell out of the tree."

"What about fears that have been there many years?"

"The number of years doesn't change the fear."

"But the more years you have a fear, the more embedded your beliefs about it become, right?"

"Then you work on those beliefs separately, which is much easier once the fear itself is gone."

I wasn't fully convinced, but I was getting chilly and went into the cabin and got a sweater. When I came out Kumi was looking over the valley. The light was orange on his face. I walked over to him and sat down.

"I can see the Hologram might work for things like preparing for presentations," I said, "but I'm not so sure it would help you long-term with your life."

"Long-term outcomes are made up of many short-term actions."

"But in this exercise and others you've shown me, you're implying you can almost go back and undo past mistakes."

"You can go into your past and learn specifically what you did, which can give you a new perspective on your actions."

"So you can correct them."

"Not 'correct,' alter. I don't judge behavior as right or wrong."

"You mean you can't do anything wrong?"

"I mean there are no mistakes in human behavior, only outcomes."

"So the unabomber was right in killing people?"

"No. The unabomber did the only thing he knew how to do within his very limited perspective."

I was surprised by this twist of logic and didn't know what to say. "I'll have to think about all this some more."

"I hope so. If you start agreeing with me too quickly I'll get worried."

I smiled and nodded.

"The whole point of the Hologram is that life can be much more than just looking at the world from our own individual standpoint. When someone else speaks, we often filter what is being said through our own experience and from our own vantage point. This is a natural first step for any comprehension, but it is only a beginning. To learn well we need a variety of viewpoints, because changing perspectives gives us insight into our actions.

"Small children start out seeing things only from their own perspective—that's all they're able to do. After a few years, they begin to be able to see themselves from the outside, the way a coach does. Only somewhat later are they able to step into other people's shoes and see the larger situation, taking the world view. Unfortunately, most of us don't develop this last ability nearly as far as we could. But those who truly want to understand the thoughts and feelings of others will usually make these shifts of position quite naturally."

He was silent for a long moment.

"Are you saying I don't care about the thoughts and feelings of others?" I said.

"You tell me."

I thought of Marion. "Maybe understanding is a gift that some people are just born with," I said. "A kind of psychological magic that enables them to temporarily take another person's position."

"We're all born with it. That psychological magic, as you call it, stems from being really concerned about others and paying close attention to them—what the Latins call *simpatico*. Such people seem to understand another person in a deeper way because they have, so to speak, temporarily entered that person's world. You've heard the saying about not judging someone until you've walked a mile in his shoes? Well, you don't need a mile—a few steps will do.

"Be aware, however, that there are potential dangers to entering another person's world. You can become so sympathetic to the other person's feelings that you lose track of your own. This can happen when you admire someone so much that you continually try to be just like him or her and lose your own individuality. Similarly, you can identify so deeply with another's feelings that you take on their emotions as if they were your own.

"Years ago I worked at an addiction center with a great therapist who had this kind of empathy. She entered the experiences of her patients so fully that she adopted their pain and began to have their problems. She would even get sick and develop allergies, have headaches and insomnia, just like the people she was treating. She was good at her work, because she really understood her clients, but she suffered terribly and it cost her too much. She knew how to get inside a person, but she didn't know how to get back out again."

Marion had told me that some actors play so many roles they sometimes have trouble getting back to their real selves. Kumi walked over to his porch and pointed to a heavy brass ring bolted to the outside frame of the door.

"Ever heard of a 'whiteout?' That's when the snow and wind get so intense you see only whiteness—no ground, no sky, you lose your reference points. You can get lost ten feet from your front door and freeze to death. So when I have to go out in a snowstorm I tie a rope to this ring and around myself so I can find my way back. My friend didn't use a lifeline. She entered the other person's emotional world and lost sight of her own."

"So, you're saying The Hologram offers you a lifeline."

"Yes, a way to enter another person, feel what they feel, learn what they have to give you, and then return to yourself enlightened and enriched but undamaged."

"Because you've clearly differentiated your position from theirs."

"That's right."

"A variation of this is the kind of person who wants the approval of others and continually sees things from *their* standpoint instead of from his or her own. This person is so concerned with public opinion that he might neutralize his own individuality in the desire to please everyone. Have you ever seen Arthur Miller's play, 'Death of a Salesman?'"

"I saw it on television."

"Well, the Willy Loman character is such a person. He would say, 'It's not enough to be liked—you must be *well*-liked.' Such people are convinced you can please everyone. People in the public eye, like politicians, entertainers and artists with a desire to be famous, are especially vulnerable to the seductive power of the audience position. They seek approval from the whole world."

"So, how do you get out of that position?"

"First, you must realize you're in it. The Hologram gives you the chance to learn about these positions by practicing going in and out of them. That way you will recognize more easily when you've fallen into one you don't want to be in at the moment, or are stuck in one for too long."

"So, what if I find I am stuck?"

"Step out, look at yourself, and get into another position."

"You make it sound so easy."

"It is easy, when you practice and become familiar with it. The goal of this exercise is to be continually flexible in switching positions, seeking the understanding that these alternate perspectives offer, and constantly applying what you learn to your life. Ultimately, this process is practical—it helps you get what you want. But it's more than that, it is humane, because you learn to step outside your own world and enter the worlds of others. If the unabomber had ever truly stepped into the shoes of his victims, I don't think he would have even made the bombs.

"You can create a whole new set of worlds for yourself by learning to see and hear and feel from the positions of others, a vast space in which your mind is free to soar with the grace of that bald eagle." He pointed to a large bird floating over the trees and then went inside to make supper.

Lying wide-awake in my sleeping bag that night and reviewing the day, I recalled Kumi's eyes when he was walking between rocks and explaining the various positions of the Hologram. When he was thinking to himself, I believe he was looking down to his left. And just before he spoke I think he looked straight to his right. He repeated this pattern over and over. Does that mean he was talking to himself when his eyes were down left? And then constructing the wording for the thought in order to speak it to me when he looked straight right? When I was in the different positions in the Hologram, I believe my eyes looked straight left when I was recalling my speech, and right when I was the coach, thinking of the advice I'd give myself. I got up and drew a possible diagram for auditory eye positions:

(my left)   (my right)
Recalling sound ←   → **Creating sound**
                                          (words, music)

How My Eyes Work

Here's how a finished eye scan chart might look, showing the positions for all the primary senses:

Eye Scan Chart
(my left—my right)

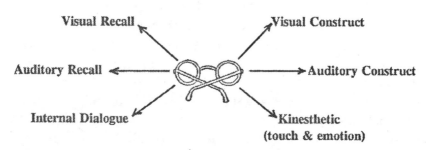

Going by this diagram, it seems our eyes actually look in the direction of the sensory organ that is processing a given thought. For example, our ears are directly right and left of our eyes, and that's the direction the eyes seem to go in when recalling and constructing sound. And the eyes themselves are up above and our mouth and hands down below—eyes up for visualizing and eyes down for internal dialogue and feeling! If anyone had ever suggested this crazy idea to me before my experience with Kumi, I'd have laughed at them. But the evidence keeps piling up.

Thinking about the people I know, each seems to have a favorite sense. Marion's is visual, Charles' is auditory, and, if Kumi is right, mine is kinesthetic. I like to "get a feel" of a situation, Marion likes to "get a picture" of it, and Charles always says, "Sounds good."

Could it be that the basis of my communication problems is that I usually try to "feel my way" through a situation? If that's true, then my emphasis on feeling might actually *preclude* my use of the visual sense! I may have failed to "see" things because I was too busy "feeling" them—as in that last conversation with Marion in Riverside Park. She was seeing a long-term goal—into the future—and I was feeling stuck in the past. Now that I think of it, her eyes were up a lot of the time and, if I'm not mistaken, mine were down, especially when I was beginning to feel uneasy.

Pondering all this, I wondered if goal-oriented thinking is automatically visual. Could the simple mechanical act of placing my eyes in the up position while thinking actually get me out of my feelings, and maybe even help me get out of my past and into the future?

As my thoughts began to fade into sleep, I recalled Marion standing at the railing in Riverside Park during our last conversation. And then I saw myself, sitting on the bench watching her, deeply involved with my own feelings. Then I felt myself walking over and taking the place of Marion, trying to feel how she must have felt during that exchange. As Marion I felt left out: this man I'd been talking to was committed only to himself, and I felt afraid.

Awake again, I talked to the shadows on the ceiling. "You're going to get free of yourself, you sonofabitch, if it's the last thing you ever do on this earth."

(My notes on the Hologram are on page 281)

4

MARIO AND TERESA IN THE BEDROOM

...BORROW ANYBODY AND GET AWAY WITH IT

"The brain records everything it sees, hears, feels, tastes and smells. Undirected, your life is a random recording. The difference between those who get what they want and those who don't is that successful people don't leave this recording process to chance. They choose their models."

The next day, Kumi and I took a walk in the mountains. Kumi said some snowcaps in the distance brought back memories of his childhood in Baffin Island.

"When I was a boy in Pangnirtung, Baffin Island, my hero was a man named Solomon Alukyuk. He was the greatest hunter in our village. He could spot a white bird at two-hundred feet in the snow just by the red slits of its eyes. Once on a hunt, he replaced a broken machine part in the motor of his snowmobile with a piece of antler he whittled from the horn of a caribou. He saved me from a polar bear when I was ten years old by jamming the base of his spear in the snow and raising the point of it at the last moment so that the bear impaled itself in mid-charge. When his mother needed surgery he directed a dog sled from Pangnirtung to Frobisher Bay through a three-day snow storm. The man is mythical at home, but he is a real man, not a myth. He's still alive at age eighty-nine. I just visited him last year. He looks healthier than you."

"That wouldn't be too hard," I said. Kumi laughed with that infectious, child-like "hee-hee" sound of his.

I followed Kumi up to a promontory that overlooked a big space with aspen and cottonwood trees surrounding a small lake. We sat down and took in the vista.

"I admired Solomon so much I identified with him very deeply," he said. "As a child I would pretend to be him, imitating his voice, his walk, acting out stories of his adventures. He became a part of me. To this day I have a piece of Solomon inside me—the part of me that comes through in a crisis. Do you have a part like that?"

"He sounds like quite a man," I said "but I don't live in the Arctic or plan to become a hunter."

"But you are a hunter. Isn't that what you're doing with me?"

"Well, in a way, I suppose."

"The first day you came to me I asked you to clarify for yourself what you wanted. You can hunt only when you know what you're hunting. Then you look for someone who has what you want so you can learn from that person how to do it."

"A model you mean."

"Yes. You need models for the important things in your career, your marriage or anything you want to do well. The more heroes you have to imitate, the more things you can learn to do."

I looked at the lime green and burnished yellow of the trees against the black mountain and blue sky. I remembered a high school art teacher saying you should never combine blue with green—just another of the stupid things I had to unlearn.

"I have this friend I really admire," I said. "His name is Mario. He's an architect. He'll only take on a project if it's good for the whole community. He was offered a big contract recently that could have made him almost a millionaire, but when he found out the construction would disrupt a whole community of Portuguese families, he turned it down. His colleagues said he was crazy, that if he didn't take the job somebody else would. His answer was simple: 'It's just not right.' And he said it so quietly."

"Well, he knows who he is."

"How do you mean?"

"He was a person before he was an architect."

A flock of birds landed noisily in the trees below.

"Another thing about Mario is his marriage. He's very devoted to his wife, Teresa, and respectful. Lets her live her own life. I have to admit I could have used some of those qualities in my marriage."

"Do you want to get married again?"

"I don't know, I need to think about that. But I have met a nice woman. She's an actor and a singer. She's the first person I've been with since my divorce a little over a year ago. I'm a little reluctant to get involved again."

The sun got hot so we headed back. When we got to the grassy plateau leading up to Kumi's cabin, he said, "C'mon, I'll race you to the cabin."

I looked at Kumi and laughed. He was a trim and vigorous man, but I couldn't see him racing over mountaintops. "Well, alright," I said tentatively.

"To the big tree," he said pointing to a tall pine about a hundred meters away.

I was amused at this sudden competitive side of Kumi. I didn't want to beat him, but I thought a little run would be good for me. "Okay."

"Ready?" he said. He counted in a high-pitched voice: "One-two-three-*go,*" and took off like a rabbit. By the time I got to the big tree he was already in the cabin putting on some water for tea. He stuck his head out the door and said, "You are in very bad condition. We have to talk about that."

I walked up to him, panting and holding my hand on my side. "God, Kumi, how can you run so fast at your age?"

"I think of myself as a particular animal."

"Which animal?"

"That's a secret."

I sat down on the porch with my tea and a piece of bread and jam and looked at the mountains. I found myself thinking about Mario and Teresa. Kumi's voice interrupted my reverie. "I want to show you something."

"No more races today," I said.

He giggled and sat down on the step next to me. "You said you like the way your friend Mario is with his wife. Would you like to be more like him when you're with your girlfriend?"

"Well, yeah, I guess so. What do you mean, *like* him?"

"Tell me how he is with his wife," he said

I thought for a moment and tried to imagine Mario and Teresa together. The image was vague at first then came in clearer. "Well, he's very responsive to her in a quiet way—he touches her and talks to her in a soft voice. He always seems to know what she needs."

"Feel for a moment what it would be like to be Mario, feeling that way for Teresa and speaking to her in that soft voice—the way you did in the Hologram when you became Jack Nicholson."

As I began to get that feeling, Kumi squeezed my right shoulder gently. I looked at him.

"Go ahead," he said. "Continue."

"And he's very patient—he never seems to take offense if she corrects him or anything like that." I felt Kumi's hand on my shoulder again. "Feeling like him, I feel really *connected* to her." Again he pressed my shoulder, and the feeling of being like Mario got even stronger.

"Stand up a moment," Kumi said.

I stood up and had a little stretch and then sat down.

"So, what's this we're doing now, Kumi?"

He pressed my shoulder as he had before, and the feeling of being like Mario came back again. I described it.

"Now replace the image of Teresa with Marion," he said. "Nod when you see her."

I took a deep breath and closed my eyes. After a moment, Marion came into view standing near me. I nodded. Kumi pressed the same place on my shoulder and I heard Marion's voice as I touched her arm and spoke softly to her. It was a tender moment. She was smiling.

With his hand pressing my shoulder we repeated this exercise several more times.

"Time out," he said, stepping off the porch. I stood up and stretched. I walked around the back of the house and looked at the horizon, rubbing my bum, which was a little numb from sitting on the hard porch. When I came back to the front of the house, Kumi reached over and squeezed his own right shoulder, the mirror action of the squeeze he'd given mine. As he did this he looked at me and raised his eyebrows with an acknowledging look. The feeling of being with Marion came back to me. We were talking softly and I had my arm around her.

I looked at Kumi.

"The feeling came back, right?" he said.

"Yeah, it did. What did you do?"

"Now you have a piece of Mario in you." he said.

"Kumi, you've got to be the weirdest guy I've ever met."

"Hee-hee," he giggled.

"What's with the shoulder?" I asked.

"A little more Pavlov—associating a memory with a touch, like the finger squeeze. We just transferred Mario's way of being with Teresa over to your way of being with Marion."

"That's nonsense."

"But you just did it."

"Yeah, but that was just in my mind. That's not really the way I am."

"You said you admired the way Mario was with Teresa."

"Yeah, but I'm not Mario."

"Would you like to be like Mario?"

"Well, yes."

"Okay, that's how to start. A fast way to do it is to tie your responses in with his. A piece of Mario is now built into your neurology—if you want it, that is."

Every time I get a handle on Kumi's thinking he comes up with something that completely surprises me. I didn't know what to think of this idea.

"Sounds like brain-washing," I said.

"Maybe your brains need a little clean-out."

I burst out laughing.

"Tell me, how's Mario in bed?"

"*Mario*! How do I know?"

"Let your imagination fly!" he said.

"Kumi, that's crazy" I said, feeling embarrassed. Suddenly I saw Mario being a passionate lover with Teresa. I felt my skin flush, as if I'd been caught doing something I shouldn't.

Kumi reached over and squeezed my shoulder and said, "Now you're with Marion, feeling like Mario."

I saw Marion and myself, rolling around naked on a bed, and then suddenly I blended with the image. Her face was inches from mine. I smelled her hair and felt her body against me. I looked at Kumi to see if he could tell what I was experiencing.

Before I could think, he said, "Squeeze your shoulder" and pressed his own shoulder to demonstrate.

Reflexively, I mirrored his action, squeezing my own right shoulder with my left hand. The feeling of being with Marion intensified and I blushed. I was having an intimate experience right in front of Kumi! I rubbed my eyes and stepped back. I was perspiring.

"Not bad, huh? Now you have something new to take back to your girlfriend."

I turned around and walked away, then walked back again and looked at Kumi. Part of me understood what was happening and the other part was completely confused.

"I don't know, Kumi," I said, as I walked around in a circle shaking my head. "I've heard you're a shaman. Is that true?"

"Me, a shaman?" he said, "Hee-hee-hee-hee!" Then he did an elegant little dance, jumped up the stairs and disappeared into the house.

Later I watched him put the finishing touches to one of his famous soups. This one was lentils with carrots, mushrooms, garlic and basil. We half-drank, half-spooned it out of large mugs while sitting on the porch looking at the mountains. I wondered about some of the things we'd done this morning and my face must have shown it because Kumi looked at me.

"You have some concerns about today's work?" he said in a quiet voice, picking up on my mood.

My feelings were mixed. I had enjoyed what we'd done, but I also felt uneasy about invading Mario's privacy. Maybe I was really concerned about my own privacy and felt Kumi's exercise had been a little invasive. "Yeah, a little," I said, nodding my head.

"Remember you said that Mario wouldn't build a new building unless he thought it was good for the whole community?"

"That's right," I said.

"Well, we have just built something new in you. It's important to make sure it's good for everybody in *your* community."

"What do you mean?"

"You have many functions going on inside you, and they need to cooperate in order to get everything done. For example, you have a professional part—that's the Computer Man, right?"

"You could call it that I guess."

"Then another part of you likes to go out with your friends—call that a Social Part—and another part that takes care of your son—a Father Part perhaps?" He looked at me raising his eyebrows and I nodded. "And so on. All of these parts must work together and each has its own needs."

"Uh-huh, yeah," I said, wondering where he was going with this.

"So you just put a new part into yourself—that's like putting up a new building in a community—you want to make sure it works for all the other parts inside you." He looked at me. "So, does any part of you object to having Mario in you?"

It was a strange question, but in fact Kumi described exactly how I felt. "Yeah, Mario is kind of lost when Teresa isn't around, and I'm more self-sufficient emotionally than that—so is Marion."

"Then just take from Mario what you need. Your Self-Sufficient Part can still take care of you, but maybe it's willing to share some of that job with Marion. Take a load off of it."

I watched a small army of ants marching toward an ant hill near my shoe, while I imagined myself acting like Mario in some ways but still being me. After a few minutes I raised my head and said, "Yes, I can do that." Kumi patted his shoulder, signaling me to reach up and squeeze my shoulder again. As I did I let out a loud sigh and realized I had been holding my breath.

"Is that better?" he asked.

"Yeah, better," I said. I felt as though a slight pressure had been taken off me.

"Respect these different parts of yourself. In fact, keep track of them. Define their functions. Whenever you do something new, check to see that everybody on your inner committee approves of it. Get a building permit," he said smiling.

"Sounds funny to put it that way, but it's true," I said.

"So what are you going to call this new Mario part?"

"Call it?"

"Yes. Give it a name and a function. What would Mario call it?"

"He'd probably call it something like 'Loving Mate?' But that doesn't exactly sound like me."

"What name would you like?"

"I'd like to be like Mario. Maybe that name's okay."

"So what does this part do for you? Say it as if you were the Loving Mate talking."

"You mean, 'I am a loving person'—like that?"

"That's it."

I shook my head. "I don't know about this, Kumi. I'm a realist, you know."

"Okay, so what does the Realist want?"

"To make sure I don't get burned again. Mario would only love somebody who really appreciates him."

"So, ask the Realist to keep an eye on the Loving Mate—to make sure it's always appreciated. Make them partners, form an alliance."

"Sounds kind of silly to me."

"So be silly." He raised his eyebrows and looked at me.

"Okay. If the Realist can be in on it, I'll do it."

I re-defined the part's function.

Loving Mate

"I am a loving person, unafraid to commit my feelings where they are appreciated."

"Good! Now notice what's going to be different now that you have this part of Mario in you."

I pictured myself with Marion feeling a little more expressive—lighter, less serious, more relaxed. I saw Marion looking at me with a new interest.

"Understand that this new part isn't carved in stone like one of Mario's buildings. You can change it if you want. Try it out for a while—two weeks, a month—and then modify it, or even remove it if you don't like it."

"What if I want to remove it but it won't go?"

"That means some part of you wants to keep it, and you need to hold another council meeting."

Before I went to sleep that night I thought about having a piece of Mario in me. What if I'd had that five years ago? Ten? I recalled the blowup we had when Andrea wanted to go back and complete her degree after Charles entered first grade. I wasn't against her getting a degree, but she was breaking the routine and I felt I was losing control. Of her? My God, what kind of monster was I? Kumi said you could have negative models too and I remembered the way my father was with my mother—the traditional paternal household. At the time that way of life just seemed natural to me. I didn't know anything different. Had I been imitating him without even knowing it? And how many other models might I be following that I'm not even aware of?

The next day I expressed some of these thoughts to Kumi.

"Modeling is a natural process," he said. "You've been doing it all your life without knowing it. You start at birth by imitating everything around you, language, attitudes, behaviors. The brain records everything it sees, hears, feels, tastes and smells; your playback of these recordings becomes your identity to others. Undirected, your life will be a jumble of random recordings. The difference between those who get what they want in life and those who don't is that successful people don't leave this recording process to chance. They *choose* their models."

"But I didn't have to choose Jack Nicholson. I didn't 'install' him—he just popped up when I needed him as a speech coach."

"Because you had already created him without knowing it. Unconscious modeling. We do it all the time—identify so deeply with someone we admire we adopt their behavior. And that's fine, as long as you make sure the behavior fits you. The techniques I'm showing you are designed to not only help you create models consciously, but to enable you to ferret out negative models that you may have adopted unconsciously. For example, have you ever noticed that many female opera singers are fat?"

"I've seen some cartoons."

"I've worked with a number of singers. Often they have their biggest meal late at night after a strenuous performance and go to bed with all that food in them. But that's only part of the reason. The main reason for many of them is that they identified at an early age with an admired diva who was overweight and then carried this image with them to adulthood, unconsciously fulfilling it in their later years. This image is supported by the belief that the bigger the body the bigger the sound it can make, which is nonsense."

"Marion will be interested in this."

"You'll be interested in it too, because that's what we're going to do on your next visit—learn a technique for dismantling outdated models."

On the flight back to New York I thought about what's changed in me since I've been working with Kumi. Originally I thought I was going to him because of stage fright, but he seemed to sense there was more to it than that. When he asked me to go away and think through what I wanted, I realized I needed more confidence in general, in my personal life and in business. I wanted to feel that

I could express myself and be taken seriously. But underneath it all there was something else, some kind of obstruction in me—somehow I was blocking myself. Now I felt that blockage beginning to break up, like a log jam where a few key logs have been dislodged, allowing the mass to begin flowing down the river.

I didn't know if the idea of "installing" parts and getting the approval of "inner committees" and conditioning my reflexes by squeezing shoulders (not to mention fingers) was right or wrong for me, but I felt a new part of myself beginning to come through, not just a person who could speak better in public, but a performer in a broader, more complete sense, as a human being. But I was still new at this, and wasn't sure if I was doing everything right. I still had a long way to go, but that was the exciting part, because I was discovering things about myself. I was learning that I don't have to feel discouraged if I screw up. I'd just been following the wrong models, or I'd had no good models to follow. So the message was, keep your eyes and ears open. The world is abundant with good examples if you look for them.

That's when I got the idea of finding a "support friend," someone who was also interested in changing and learning new things, who could interact with me as a kind of "Kumi." I needed someone to give me a little kick-start every so often, to keep me going on these exercises so I didn't slip back. Also someone to act as an objective eye, to see if I was doing it right. And I might be a "Kumi" for that person, too. Alcoholics and over-eaters do that sort of thing, after all, and it seems to work. Who would I use? Would it always have to be the same person? Maybe I could use several different people, depending on which lesson I was learning.

The first thing on my mind when I got to Manhattan was Marion. I phoned her and said I wanted to take her to dinner. But first I wanted to talk. I showed up at her apartment on West End Avenue wearing my best suit and carrying a bouquet of flowers and a bottle of champagne. I felt like a college kid on a prom date. She laughed when she saw me, standing shyly on her doorstep. I'd carefully rehearsed everything I wanted to say, but I never got a chance to say it. Before I knew it, my tie was half way off and I was stumbling out of my shoes. The champagne never got to the fridge and the flowers landed on the sofa without water.

Afterward we slept, a sleep like I haven't had in months. When we awoke, we ordered a pizza and rented a movie featuring Jack Nicholson. I was especially interested to see him now that he was my new public-speaking coach. I told her about the concept of modeling Kumi had put me through.

"He's nuts, you know. But he's got something. He talked about identifying so deeply with someone you admire that you actually absorb their behavior and do what they do."

"Well, actors and entertainers are always modeling themselves after somebody," she said. Robin Williams memorized Jonathan Winters comedy records and Richard Pryor modeled Bill Cosby. But they found their own personalities later of course."

"I was reading about Andre Agassi," I said. "When he was just a little kid he could imitate the styles of the major tennis players. He had a thing where he'd say 'Connors forehand,' 'Nastase backhand,' 'Laver volley,' and then execute the shot perfectly. He's a blend of all these great ingredients, like one of Kumi's soups."

"Is Kumi a good cook?"

"According to him he is."

"Well, whatever he did with you on this trip I like it," she said, giving me a suggestive side glance as she caught a piece of mushroom sliding off her pizza.

"There're lots of examples of imitating in music," she continued, "or 'modeling,' as you call it. Beethoven sounded just like Mozart at first, and Mozart sounded just like Haydn. And every rock group owes something to the Beatles. People always talk about originality as if it's so pure, but in art you've got to be somebody else before you can be yourself—that's just how it's done."

"Same with anything, I guess. I just never thought of it that way."

"Hillary Clinton's a good example," Marion said. "Did you know that she modeled herself after Eleanor Roosevelt? She read everything she could about her and would even hold imaginary conversations with her. When she was bombarded by critics, she would ask Eleanor what to do and she'd get an answer: 'Get out and do it, and don't make any excuses about it.' I love that."

"Kumi and I were just talking about that, having conversations with yourself." I told her about Kumi's idea of people having parts and of installing new ones when they need them.

"Well, that would be a natural part of modeling. Hillary calls them 'identities.' In college she used to 'try on' different selves. She had a part for January that she called the Dedicated Student, and a February part she dubbed the Indulgent Self, and her March part, the Social Reformer, and her April part—The Hippie. And later she became an activist, organizer and speaker, as well as a wife and mother..."

"Maybe having all these parts is what makes her so flexible," I said.

"With Clinton for a husband she'd have to be!"

"I can see who your model is," I said.

"Oh, I have lots of models. When I learn foreign accents I pretend I'm Meryl Streep. When I'm learning a song I'm Whitney Houston. When I dance I'm John Travolta."

"*John Travolta*! But he's a man."

"I don't hold that against him." She kissed me on the nose.

"How would you like to coach me in modeling? Be a kind of 'Kumi' for me. Being an actor you're really experienced at it."

"Hmm." She took a sip of her coffee and looked around the room. "Okay, we can try. Lesson number one. Who do you most admire out of all the people you've met in your life?"

"You mean anyone?"

"Yeah, but mainly related to your profession. Who would you want to be like?"

"Well...I have to think about that one."

"Okay. You know where to reach me for lesson number two. That'll be ten dollars."

"You take Visa?"

"No, but I might barter for it," she said, gazing at me with half-closed eyes, one of Marion's more powerful communications.

Later, recalling models from my earlier life, my eccentric math professor, Joseph Mueller, came to mind. He was always inventing crazy mathematical formulas to prove the impossible, just for the fun of it. His hobby was holography. If you said something couldn't be done his eyes would light up and he would say, "That's because you haven't found an equation for it."

An idea had been buzzing around in my head that seemed all but impossible, yet it continued to intrigue me. If I could make it work, it'd be the biggest development in video since live-image transmission itself. I phoned his office at the university.

"Nicholi, my friend, how are you."

"Professor Mueller, I need your help. I need a formula for sending a live holographic image on-line over the Net."

He whooped with laughter. "So far, my friend, they're not even transmitting holographic motion pictures with a receiver and antenna!"

"You mean it's impossible?"

"Ah-*ha*! Okay. I think you should talk to Gregor."

"Who's Gregor?"

"Ah! You're in for an interesting experience. I better talk to him. I'll be in touch."

(My notes on Modeling are on page 288)

5

HOW TO GIVE YOURSELF STAGE FRIGHT
(AND TAKE IT AWAY)
...*A GAME TO PLAY WITH YOUR INNER COMPUTER*

"It's too easy to get lost looking for the cause of a problem, thinking that will show you how to fix it. Many analysts' patients can give you detailed explanations of all their problems after years of therapy and still not change their behavior."

"I've made a decision," said my son, Charles. "I'm going to work in television." Charles dropped this bomb at Marion's Thanksgiving dinner. With dark hair and a somewhat dark, serious look around the eyes, which are often scanning downward like he's trying to remember where he put the car keys, he looks disturbingly like me.

"Doing what?" I asked

"The news," he said. "I want to be a news anchorman."

"Where'd this come from?" I said, looking at Marion.

"I guess it's always been there, I just never knew it."

"So how do you know it now?" I said. I felt a small lump growing in my stomach.

"I've been thinking about it, and watching some of the best. I want to be like Peter Jennings."

"But you don't know anything about it. Where would you start?"

"Journalism school. That's how it's done." He looked at me like he'd just explained the obvious.

My face felt hot. "So you just decided without talking to me about it. How do you expect to pay for it?"

"I'll work. I've applied for a scholarship."

"Oh, Jesus, you're dreaming." I reached for my wine glass too quickly and knocked it over.

"Hey, boys, time out! It's Thanksgiving," said Marion.

Later, after everyone left, I discussed it with Marion over a nightcap. Charles had always been interested in computer programming. Now he was speaking about a career I knew nothing about. The more we discussed it the more I realized this was not a pipe dream. It turned out that he had already been accepted for journalism school and was starting next semester.

"This is a big switch," I said.

"You should be happy," she said with a shrug. "He knows what he wants. He's even got a model for it."

"You mean, unlike me?"

"C'mon, Nick."

"What does he know about setting goals and modeling people? I'm just learning about it."

"You're his father. Take some credit."

"But how does he know this is *right* for him?

"He's following his instincts."

My mind did a quick review of Charles as a boy.

"Come to think of it, he always was a reporter by nature. He even had a column in his school newspaper when he was ten years-old, called Chuck's Corner. He'd profile outstanding people. He interviewed a nuclear scientist once, and a painter. At the end of his column he had a thing called, 'And remember...', where he'd finish with a memorable quote from the person. One of my favorites was: 'And remember what Benny Lieberman of New York City said: *Behind every great man is a very bored woman*.'"

Marion guffawed. "Oh, he's found his profession alright. How could you ever doubt him?"

"I just wasn't ready for this."

"So, let it go. You don't always have to be in the driver's seat, just because you're his father."

We sat quietly for a little while, a tension suspended between us, the way you feel when you know there's more to be said but aren't sure what.

"He's just so skilled at computers. I hate to see that go to waste."

"A skill is one thing, your true nature is something else. There's a big difference between what you do and what you really are."

"You mean being an actress isn't what you really are?"

"No, it's what I *do*."

"You lost me."

"I heard that Monica Seles told a young tennis player who was upset at losing a match, 'It's only a game, you know.'"

"Well, when a hundred thousand dollars is at stake it's more than a game."

"Sure, but it's not life."

"There's such a thing as reality, and sometimes you have to face it."

"Oh? Whose reality should I face?"

"Very funny."

She got up to refill our glasses.

"I don't think your real self is what you were doing at Globalcom."

"You mean computers?"

"I mean what you were *doing* with computers. You're an inventive person."

"But I was creating programs."

"Yeah, on corporate order, to suit *their* needs."

"That's still creative."

"Not really. It's like a writer writing ad copy instead of writing his novel."

"But I was supporting a family, I had a responsibility."

"I'm not criticizing you, Nick. I'm just encouraging you to be what you really are. And I think you're starting to do it."

I was beginning to get a slight headache.

Marion said, "C'mere." She got up on her knees on the sofa and kissed me. Then she started rubbing my neck.

"You okay?" she said.

"Yeah."

The drive to Kumi's cabin took much longer this time because of the snow. I wondered what I'd do if I got stuck on that godforsaken mountain road. The snow tires ground their way through the snow-covered ruts and rocks and spun a few times, giving my heart a flutter, but I got to the top alright.

I turned off the motor and sat there, spent. I got out of the jeep and stood, listening to the silence. Everything was still. Mist blanketed the ground so that Kumi's cabin looked like it was floating in space.

I trudged toward the house with my knapsack, my sneakers filled with snow that was half way to my knees. Kumi wasn't around. The door was unlocked and I entered the house, took off my parka and shoes and wet socks and fell onto the couch.

When I awoke I smelled food.

"Greetings, my friend," he said.

"Hi," I said, yawning. The room smelled of aspen logs burning in the fireplace. "You don't happen to have any liquor, do you?"

He pointed to a cabinet over the sink. I found a bottle of rye and sat with my drink, staring into the fire.

"You drink this stuff?" I asked.

"Every so often a little blast to take out the chill."

After supper I unpacked my laptop and he was fascinated. "Teach me something about computers," he said.

I turned on the computer and the screen lit up. I tapped out a few commands on the keyboard to get it started. A little line blinked in the upper left hand corner of the blue screen.

"There. Now you're ready to type a document. What would you like to say?"

"'Hello, I'm Kumi,'" he said.

"Alright, go ahead," I said, nodding at the keyboard. He looked at me and then studied the keyboard for a moment. Then he picked out the letters and smiled as they showed up on the screen.

"Now you want the computer to memorize what you've written, so you give your document a code name. What do you want to call it?"

"'Kumi!'"

"Okay, so press F7, then Y, then K-U-M-I, then Enter." After he tapped out these commands the laptop made a series of little noises. "There, now it's filed. And you can retrieve that information whenever you want it."

"Pretty good," he said.

I left him playing with the laptop as I got ready to go to bed. The gentle clicking of the keys mixed with low guttural mutterings were the last sounds I heard before nodding off to sleep.

I awoke early and looked out the window. The snow was pink and the sky was grey and crimson. The mountaintops were partly obscured by strands of clouds.

I toasted bread in the frying pan and scrambled eggs while Kumi made tea and rekindled the fireplace. After breakfast he said, "Computers are very interesting. Now I know where God got the idea for people."

"You mean people are like computers?"

"No. People have imagination and a soul, and they can create. But our brain works very much like that machine—everything we do is a series of commands in a certain order."

"How so?"

"I watched you making breakfast. First you got out the eggs and the bread, then you greased the frying pan and lit the burner, then you put bread in the pan, then the eggs, etcetera. It was all a series of steps."

"Of course. How else would you do it?"

"Exactly. And that's good, because if it all happened simultaneously you could never change your way of doing it."

"What are you talking about?"

"With a sequence of events you can change the order of doing them."

"To what purpose?"

"To get a different outcome. Come over here for a moment," he said, pointing to a straight-backed chair. I moved over and sat down, wondering what he was up to now.

"When you first came to me you said you had stage fright when speaking in public. Maybe you have control of that now because of other things we've done."

"Well, it's getting better, but I wouldn't say I'm home free. I still don't fully understand it."

"Let's assume having stage fright is like making breakfast—that it's not a single event but a series of events. So, in order to have your stage fright, what must you do first?"

"What do you mean?"

"It has to start at some point—I'm looking for the very first moment your brain says, 'I'm scared.' Maybe it happens when you see your audience, or the moment you wake up on the day of your speech. What's the thing that triggers your anxiety?"

"One time my boss said to me, 'Nick, I want you to explain the new program to the buyers on Friday.' My stomach fluttered and my knees felt weak."

"Alright. What made your stomach flutter?"

"My boss's voice."

"No, that was the trigger. Hearing his voice must have made you remember something that scared you, that made your stomach flutter and your knees feel weak. Otherwise, why would you feel scared? There has to be an unpleasant experience to remember."

"That's true. Yes, I remember now. There was this one really embarrassing moment in a talk I gave to the buyers at a promotion meeting."

"What happened?"

"Well, shortly after I started talking, someone interrupted and asked me a question I couldn't answer. After that I felt I'd lost them."

"How did you know you'd lost them? By the way they looked?"

"I really wasn't looking at them too much. I heard them whispering to each other and I felt I'd lost my credibility."

"Good! Boss speaks—that's the trigger." Kumi wrote on his note pad. "One: Nick can't answer question—hears audience members whispering to each other. Then what?"

"Then my stomach fluttered and my knees felt weak."

"Two: Nick's stomach flutters and his knees buckle."

"Felt weak…"

"What?"

"My knees didn't buckle, they felt weak. Don't make it any worse than it was."

"Okay, what next?"

"Uh, let me think. I said to myself, 'I know I'm going to screw this up.'"

"Okay, we're building up a sure-fire stage fright here. Step number three: Nick says: 'I know I'm going to screw this up.' Then what?"

"My heart began to thump and I broke out in a sweat."

"That's number four. Then what happened?"

"That's about it. Somehow I managed to make the presentation, but I was drained for days afterward."

"Step number five: Gives talk, drained for days afterward," he said, writing. "Look at the list." He handed it to me. I tried to decipher Kumi's scrawl.

Trigger: Boss asks Nick to talk.

1) Nick hears a buyer asking him a question he can't answer, and
   the other buyers whispering to each other.
2) Nick's stomach flutters and knees go weak.
3) Nick says, "I know I'm going to screw this up."
4) Nick's heart thumps and he breaks out in a sweat.
5) Nick feels drained for days after the talk.

"Yeah, that's about it," I said. "What do you mean, 'trigger?'"

"The trigger is the action that triggers the first response—it usually comes from outside yourself. In this case, the trigger is your boss asking you to give a talk—that triggers the memory of the unsuccessful talk, which in turn causes your fear."

"So you're saying a behavior is a series of actions linked together, like a chain."

"Yes, and if you replace the first link of the chain with a new link you get a new reaction. The idea is to replace the memory of those whispering audience members with a productive memory, so you feel confident instead of scared. That new step will automatically start up a new sequence."

I looked at my list of reactions. "How would you create a new link for me, so when somebody asks me to give a speech I get a new response?"

"You tell me. What's needed in your sequence to make it go the way you want it? You're the computer man. Analyze it. What sense are you not using?"

I realized there was not one visual step in the whole sequence. "I'm stuck in my feelings and talking to myself."

"Which is common with stage fright, or any fear situation. The senses can easily distort, or be blocked out of memory altogether, by a strong emotional reaction. Loss of visual recall is a typical example. People commonly report frightening experiences with sentences like, 'Everything went dark," or 'A curtain came down,' or 'My mind went blank.' So what do you need to do?"

"Insert a new step that's positive?"

"What kind?"

"Visual? Then I'd be using all three senses."

"Where?"

"Just after the trigger—the moment someone asks me to give a speech."

"Okay, first let's find the new step we're going to insert. Recall a time when you gave a successful presentation. One you were really pleased with."

"That's not so easy. Wait a minute—one time I demonstrated a new program for Charles' friends at someone's house, just an informal thing. The response was really warm and friendly. I remember all the smiling faces. They actually applauded when I was finished."

"And how did that feel?"

"Good. I felt very comfortable."

"Now get a strong image of that time in your mind. Be there, seeing those smiling faces. Make the picture panoramic and bright, with color and sound."

This image came back easily, maybe because it felt so good.

"Okay."

"And get back that warm, friendly, comfortable feeling."

"Yeah…it comes by itself."

"Now squeeze your fingers."

As I squeezed, the smiling faces became more vivid. My breathing became deeper and my whole body relaxed.

"Um-hum…"

"Now, continuing to squeeze, transfer this good feeling to a new location, where you might be giving a talk."

I imagined seeing a corporate room full of business people with smiling faces, and felt the same warm friendly atmosphere I'd felt with Charles' friends. I told Kumi what I saw and felt.

"Now, looking at this image and getting this feeling, what do you want to say about how this talk is going to go?"

"I'm going to do a really good job."

"Alright! Now, as you continue to see these new smiling faces and feel this warm, friendly atmosphere, say these words to yourself."

As I heard myself say I was going to do a really good job, I felt a surge of energy. "Yeah…okay."

"Now let's program this sequence into you," he said. "I'll be your boss speaking to you. As soon as I speak, you squeeze and see that image and say those encouraging words to yourself." Kumi walked away for a moment and then came back, suddenly speaking in a gruff voice, acting out my former boss. "Nick, I want you to explain the new program to the buyers on Friday."

I squeezed my fingers and looked up. I saw the image of smiling faces and felt that comfortable feeling I had with Charles' friends. Then I saw the corporate room with an audience of smiling business people and heard myself comment on the good job I was going to do. I nodded my head to Kumi.

"Okay, let's do it again." We rehearsed the new sequence repeatedly, with Kumi role-playing various authority figures and me squeezing my fingers and responding to a smiling audience.

"Now make your presentation," he said.

I got up and walked around the room, imagining I was addressing a group of buyers. The image and good feeling of talking to Charles' friends seemed to blend with that of the buyers. I said a few words aloud. In my mind I saw receptive faces, smiling and nodding their heads.

"How does it feel?"

"Good."

"Just 'good'?"

"It feels very good."

"C'mon, Nick..."

"What do you want from me? It feels great!"

"Thank you! I don't work for just 'good.' Take a break, shake it out. In a minute we'll test your new sequence to see if it took."

I stretched and walked over to the window. The pines were weighted with snow. The glare was so bright I had to squint. Kumi's voice interrupted my reverie. Suddenly he was imitating a bossy person with a sour look on his face walking into the room. "NICK, I WANT YOU TO EXPLAIN THE HISTORY OF THE COMPUTER THIS AFTERNOON AFTER LUNCH FOR THE LEADERS OF THE INDUSTRY. YOUR PROMOTION IS ON THE LINE."

I couldn't help smiling at Kumi's soap opera characterization as I automatically looked up and saw an audience of smiling faces. I got a warm feeling and told myself that everybody was going to be knocked out by my presentation. Then, using the kitchen area as my audience, I gave a short, energetic speech to an imaginary group of prospective buyers.

"So how was that?" Kumi asked.

"I felt myself being there, giving the speech to the buyers. I was in the image, surrounded by it, and I felt comfortable. But..."

"But what?"

"I wasn't gesturing enough...I want to be more animated."

"Okay, so if it doesn't go the way you like it the first time, you can step out of it and see another way to do it. Use your Hologram, be your own coach."

I stepped over to the fireplace, turned and imagined seeing how I looked in the kitchen when I was speaking. I altered the image and saw myself speaking animatedly. Then I stepped back into the kitchen and spoke again, moving around and gesturing freely.

"That feels better," I said.

"Good. You're experiencing your speech-giving both ways, from the outside, watching yourself speak, and the inside, feeling yourself being there—dissociated and associated."

"So what does that mean?"

"It means you're becoming versatile."

Kumi wrote on a clipboard for a few moments, then held out his arms and announced to the room: "Ladies and gentlemen, we have ourselves a new speech-giving sequence for Nicholas! Look at this," he said, handing me what he'd written.

NEW SEQUENCE:

Trigger: Authority figure speaks.

1) Nick sees Charles' friends smiling as he speaks, and he feels good.
2) Nick transfers that feeling to a corporate room, seeing smiling faces of business people and feeling good.
3) Nick says, "I'm going to do a really good job."
4) Nick speaks to the new audience and
5) Nick feels good.

"So what's the difference between the old and the new sequence?" Kumi asked.

"I use my visual sense in the new sequence—twice—and all three senses are active, and they're positive. This sequence starts with smiling faces, so that sets up a new mood. The whole thing looks brighter to me, more upbeat. But one thing bothers me."

"What?"

"Well, I feel fine doing it out here in a cabin in the woods. But what about in the real situation? We're just hoping the old reaction won't slip back in."

"Not hoping, *choosing*. That's the whole idea of resequencing. Every behavior is a series of events, each depending on the previous event in order to complete itself—like a chain, as you said. Take out that first link and the chain is broken—the sequence can't complete itself. Once you know what *triggers* that first step in your stage fright sequence—the sound of a voice, the sight of a building, the smell of a perfume—you can substitute a new step *right at that point* and give yourself a new sequence and a new outcome. It will run just as reliably as your stage fright sequence did. That's how you reprogram yourself—just like a computer.

"But be sure you identify that trigger point accurately—the exact point where you need to install the new sequence. You could put it in the wrong place. In fact, that's what stage fright is—a perfectly ordinary program, possibly even a useful one, but stuck in the wrong place. In a city parking lot at night fear might save your life. Feeling fear before going on stage, however, could jeopardize your career."

"What if I don't have a new sequence to replace the old one with?"

"That's where you use your visualizations and holograms and modeling, to help you clarify your goals and understand what you want. People hesitate in difficult situations either because they're unclear about their goals or because they have no inspiring images or models to click into."

I shook my head. "I understand the logic. But I can hardly believe the change is that simple."

"Who said it was simple? It's just clearer. Now that you know the sequence that works best for making presentations, what are you going to do?"

"Practice it." My voice was very quiet.

"Right, over and over again, until your brain gets the message that the new sequence feels good and the old one feels bad."

"Are you trying to tell me that the old reaction will just go away? I don't believe that."

"Oh, no, it's still there—you just don't have to use it."

"Huh?"

"Because your brain now has a second choice it didn't have before. As I said, the old fear response might be useful sometime, to keep you alert when you need it. We want to *add* choices, not take them away."

I thought about this for a moment.

"Well, if my brain has a choice what's to stop it from going back to the old one when I give a speech?"

"Nothing, but it's not likely."

"Why?"

"Because brains make the choice that feels best."

"What do you mean—a habit's a habit."

"Did you ever have the habit of riding a bike?"

"Yes."

"Why don't you still ride one?"

"A car's more useful to me now."

"Right. Now you have a choice of habits, and you can use the one that works best for you."

"Actually, I take the subway more than I drive when I'm in the city."

"A third choice!"

I looked down at the floor."I don't know, Kumi. I've had this fear of talking in public since I was a kid. It's so deeply embedded it's almost a reflex."

"Of course it's a reflex. What else could it have been when you had no other choice?"

I couldn't refute that argument. "I'd just like to be sure that my brain knows what you say it knows."

Kumi drew very close to me and spoke in a low, intense whisper. "Then tell it."

I sat quietly, looking at him.

He spoke in a soft, kindly voice. "You're still acting as if your reactions are things that just *happen* to you—as if by some force outside your will. I'm offering you the opportunity to *create* your response."

He paused a moment and then spoke with increasing intensity, his voice building in volume. "Make a decision right here and now, Nick: 'I'm going to respond *this* way. I'll feel *this* way. Period. It's not a throw of the dice. I'll *make* it happen.'"

His passion was almost like a force of nature.

"What d'ya say?"

My heart was beating very fast and I had trouble catching my breath. I got up, put on my coat and hat and went out on the porch. The sky was gray. An icy wind was blowing and the pines were waving like dark green sheets in the wind. Could I really make the important things in my life happen the way I want them to? What about all those years where I just let myself be blown like those trees? If I accept this self-governing idea of Kumi's I'll have to admit that I may have wasted half of my life, fitted into a slot created by someone else. But I didn't come to Kumi to think about my past. The point is what I do *now*. The idea was gradually dawning on me that, unlike those trees, I could choose my position. I plant my roots and I can dig them up and replant them. Still, the prospect of creating my own future frightened the hell out of me. I stood on the porch until my face was numb from the cold and then walked back in.

"Bit of a chill in the air out there," Kumi said, handing me a cup of hot tea. I took off my coat and stood by the fire, watching the blue part of the flame.

"Hey," Kumi said.

"What?"

"Zz-zzt!" Kumi looked at me wide-eyed, like a clown.

I chuckled and said, "Zz-zzt," sitting down in the easy chair with a big sigh. "Okay. I don't know where all this is leading, but I'll go with it."

"That's the way all great adventures begin," Kumi said.

"I don't know how great my adventure will be, but at least it'll be mine. And you won't make me sleep out in the snow tonight."

Kumi puttered around in the kitchen area for a few minutes and then sat down.

"I think one of the reasons this exercise is important for you is that you've done more than install a new sequence. You've installed a new part— The Performer. What do your other parts think about that?"

"What do they think of it?"

"Yeah, your inner community. Remember?"

"Oh, yeah. Well, this is not just about giving speeches or making business presentations. It feels like, I don't know, like performing my life."

"Good way to put it. And how will you perform your life differently now?"

"I still have to process all this, Kumi, think it through and put it in place. But I think I'll be more confident in general, especially in talking to people— in public or one-on-one. And I guess it will affect my relationship with Marion. And Charles."

"You can also go back to previous experiences and resequence the events in your imagination—see how they might have come out differently."

My mind went back to my days at Globalcom. I was beginning to understand what I'd aready suspected about why they let me go. If I'd had this kind of outgoing, communicative attitude in those earlier years, maybe Streicher would have found me to be a more desirable employee. And my marriage might have taken a different direction, too.

"There's something else I want to clear up," I said. "We never did find the cause of my stage fright."

"You had stage fright because you didn't know what to do instead."

"No, I mean the basic psychological reason—why I get scared in front of people."

"*Got* scared—using the *old* way."

"Alright...*got* scared."

"There are a hundred good reasons why to be scared when talking in public—people will judge you, criticize the way you look, laugh at your ideas, ask you questions you can't answer—the list goes on. Asking *why* you have stage fright doesn't necessarily solve the stage fright. That's why I ask *how* you have it. The point is to change it, and to do that we need to know things like '*How* do you do that?', 'How do you *know* you do that?' and 'How do you know it's *time* to do that?' In effect, I'm saying, 'Teach me how to have stage fright your way.' 'How' questions bring up images, sounds, and feelings, because you need to re-live the experience to answer the question. Then you understand specifically not only *how* you generate your stage fright, you can see clearly how to *undo* it."

"So you may never understand why the person has stage fright."

"That's right, and why would you care unless you're writing a paper for a journal? Once you get rid of your stage fright there's no need to understand what caused it."

"It might help to prevent it from happening again."

"The new sequence will prevent it from happening again. And the same sequence can be taught to others to prevent them from having it in the first place," he said. "It's too easy to get lost looking for the cause of a problem, thinking that will show you how to fix it. And it costs so much time and money. I admit we're all intrigued by the mysteries of human behavior. Seeking causes can be like a detective story, a real whodunit, and we can learn something from that. Sometimes uncovering the cause will bring about a cure, especially in serious trauma cases, like child abuse. But causes are experienced at plea-bargaining with the mind and often find their way right back into the dark alleys of the psyche. Many analysts' patients can give you detailed explanations of all their problems after years of therapy and still not change their behavior."

"You don't believe in psychoanalysis?" I said.

"Psychoanalysis is the study of personal mythology, your journey through life. It gives you metaphors but not necessarily solutions. If your goal is to change something in yourself, then do it and get on with your life. When you eliminate a problem, its cause will usually disappear by itself. You'd be surprised how quickly people forget a bad habit when they no longer have it."

"So you never ask 'Why' questions?"

"Yes, there's one 'Why' question I ask all the time: Why do many people want to *keep* their stage fright once they see it's possible to get rid of it? I think the answer is that stage fright is addictive because it has so many advantages."

"Like what?"

Kumi suddenly switched into a satiric mode and mimicked someone reciting the benefits of stage fright. "Give up my stage fright? Then I might do a great job. And if I do a great job, I'll be expected to *always* do a great job. People will give me more responsibility. I won't have my fear to motivate me. The world's changing so fast—the dollar's going down, the population's going up, jobs are becoming obsolete—*but my fear I can depend on.*"

Kumi was on a roll. He rattled off a litany of characterizations, acting out each one. "Success can be frightening," he said. "It can bring rejection: 'My friends will be jealous.' Disrupt my life: 'I'll have to change my life-style.' Invade my privacy: 'I don't want to live in a glass house.' Make me appear superior: 'Why should I be better than anybody else?' Corrupt me: 'We all know people on top lose their values.' Target me for criticism: 'If I succeed, people will try to shoot me down.'"

At the end of this tirade, Kumi dropped to his knees. "'Please, dear God, don't let me succeed. Give me a safe little nook where I can be warm and dry forever.'"

Then he got up and held out his arms and answered his own plea, speaking in a deep, theatrical voice: *"MY SON, FROM THIS DAY FORTH YOU WILL BE STRICKEN WITH S-T-A-G-E F-R-I-G-H-T"*—his voice shook on the words "stage fright"—*"AND WILL THEREBY BE PROTECTED FROM ALL RESPONSIBILITY, GROWTH, CHANGE AND SUCCESS F-O-R-E-V-E-R."*

Tears of laughter ran down my face. "Oh, Kumi," I said, wiping my eyes, "I think you missed your calling. You should be in show business."

"No way," he said.

"Why not?"

"Me get up in front of an audience and do this? I'd be scared to death!"

Snuggling into my sleeping bag and listening to the cracking of the logs in the fire, I wondered how I might use Kumi's sequencing technique in my daily life. I thought about Charles and how upset I got when he didn't do what I expected. But doesn't that show independent thinking on his part? And isn't that what I'm seeking for myself? Maybe I have more of that quality in me than I know. As Marion said, "Give yourself credit."

I got up and turned on my laptop.

NEW SEQUENCE FOR ME AND CHARLES:

Trigger: Charles expresses his will.

1) I listen and develop an image from what he's saying.
2) I recall myself at his age and feel proud that he's unafraid to stand his ground.
3) I imagine his future as a successful person.
4) I ask him how I can help.

I realized I had just updated the definition of the "father part" of me.

Father

"I see and hear the world from Charles' viewpoint and offer any advice we both find appropriate."

I wondered why I felt such a sense of relief with this new definition of fatherhood. Perhaps it was a favorable response from that "inner community" of parts Kumi talked about? Whatever it was, it felt right. And, for me, that's the test.

———————————

(My notes on Sequencing are on page 293)

6

BUTTONS AND COUNTERBUTTONS

...*LEARNING HOW TO OPERATE THE SWITCHBOARDS*

"Love is the most powerful force on earth. But, as with electricity, you must learn how to handle it so you don't hurt yourself."

"You look like something out of Star Wars," Kumi said when he saw me the next morning in my parka, snow shoes and tinted goggles.

"I feel like I'm wearing tennis rackets on my feet," I said, waddling along in the snow like a duck, lifting my feet high with each step.

We walked for a while in the bright, cold morning sun, accompanied by the rhythmic crunching of our steps. The mountains were blue and I could smell the smoke from Kumi's fireplace.

Finally Kumi spoke. "Some of these drifts can be very deep. Last year a hiker fell in one and couldn't get out. Someone heard him yelling and got him out with a rope."

"What would have happened to him?"

"He'd have frozen to death."

"Nature is cruel," I said.

"Nature didn't do anything to him. He did it to himself."

Kumi's remark called to mind something he'd said yesterday that had intrigued me. "Kumi, several times you've used the phrase 'giving yourself stage fright.' Why do you say that?"

"Because that's what we do—we frighten ourselves."

"But I'd say that a situation or a person frightens you."

"Does a person have to be present for you to be frightened?"

"No, but the threat can still be there in your mind, whether the person is present or not."

"That's exactly where it is, in your mind. And you can decide whether that threat is frightening or challenging. In either case, your response is created by you."

"But why do some people get scared when threatened and others not?"

"Because some people read an event as a threat and others don't. We do what we've learned to do."

Suddenly Kumi stood still and held up his hand. I followed his sight line and saw a large deer not fifty yards away. Kumi pointed to some trees and I saw three more. "A family," he said softly. "Those three are the mother and two young ones."

We were quiet, waiting to see what they would do. The buck raised his head and stared at us, not moving. Then the female came toward us with the two younger ones close behind her. She stopped, looked, walked closer, then closer still and stopped again. She couldn't have been more than six feet away. She turned her head slightly to the side, one eye focusing on us like the lens of a camera.

"Sorry little lady, I have no food for you," Kumi said gently.

She continued staring at us, and then turned and slowly made her way back toward the buck, the little ones following. Then they all walked into a cluster of trees and disappeared.

"My God, they're beautiful. How can anybody shoot them?"

"Where I grew up people have to hunt. You can't grow vegetables in the Arctic. The word eskimo means meat eater. They changed it to 'Inuit,' which means 'the people.'"

"Why'd you ever leave."

"School. My uncle was a representative from the Northwest Territories to the Ottawa legislature. He wanted me to have an education."

"Don't you miss it?"

"I visit occasionally. But I've always felt I had a foot in both worlds. Never entirely content. I guess that's the white man in me." He looked at me with a wry smile.

When we got back to the cabin Kumi made hot chocolate and started a fire. Holding the hot mug in my hand and staring at the flames I thought about Kumi's remark that we create our own responses. I still had some lingering doubts about his view that a person scares himself. An example came to mind.

"If someone jumps out at me from a dark alley with a knife," I said, "I think I can safely say 'He scared me.'"

"No, you can say he got a response from you."

"What's the difference?"

"A mugger simply performs an action and you decide how you're going to respond to it. Your response will vary depending on your background. If you are a black belt martial arts champion you might say, 'Ah, an opportunity to try out my new zip-zap spinneroo.' A Zen Buddhist might think, 'Everything in the world unfolds exactly as it should,' and stand calmly awaiting the outcome. If you were a mugger yourself, you might suggest the two of you go into business together.

"You respond according to your beliefs, or knowledge or experience, and these vary widely in people. And in animals. That buck today probably thought to himself, 'Those guys want my antlers over their fireplace.' The doe said, 'I wonder if those nice men have any food.' And the kids said, 'Any friend of mom's is a friend of mine.'"

I had to smile at Kumi's characterizations. I was reminded of an incident that occurred one day at Globalcom. My boss came into my office and yelled at three of us while we were having a conference. He was particularly vindictive and literally ranted. Marcia, my assistant, was deeply hurt, Allan laughed and I was bored—three totally different reactions to my boss's rage. I told Kumi this story.

"Yes, but if he had hit you all with a hammer you would all have been hurt, and each of you could rightly have said, 'He hurt me,' and that would have been true—your boss would have been responsible for causing the hurt."

"But how about automatic response to fear?"

"Fear is learned. That's why it's a questionable practice to teach babies to swim, which they do as easily as fish. They have no fear of the water. If you were careless enough to leave them alone by an unguarded pool, they could jump in and drown blissfully, not even knowing they're drowning until it's too late. In Africa, trainers in the animal reserves drive a land rover carefully over to a litter of newborn lions to teach them to be unafraid. The mother is calm, so the babies are calm, like those young deer today.

"But how about their instinctive fear of the unknown?"

"If the mother wasn't there, a natural protective mechanism would kick in when the land rover appeared. Not fear, alertness. It would wait to see what the rover would do. If the rover attacked, the lion would fight or run and then forever be afraid of land rovers. If it drove away, the animal would relax and reserve judgement."

"How do you know?"

"From people who've done it, who've made friends with wild animals. The animals are not instinctively afraid of cars or people. You have to teach them to be. But—don't get out of the rover, because then you're man-the-predator, and that the lions have *learned* to be afraid of."

I put a piece of old larch on the fire and watched the flames curl around it.

"Alright, I can see where I might be the one who creates my own thoughts and feelings in a social or professional situation," I said, "but wouldn't you say the one exception might be with people you love? They can hurt you or cause other deep emotions in you because they're so close"

"Ah, this is where it gets interesting. Let's say I agree to share my most intimate feelings with you because I trust you to honor those feelings. You become then, in effect, the co-keeper of my emotional switchboard."

"What do you mean?"

"You know where all my buttons are. You know how to push the ones that trigger good feelings in me, and you're careful not to touch the buttons that trigger bad feelings. You also help me create new buttons—new responses to my surroundings—so I can become smarter and stronger. And you allow me the same access to your controls. With access to each other's switchboards, each of us is saying in effect: I am totally open to your emotions and I open my emotions to you without reservation. In other words, we give each other the privilege of hurting or pleasing each other."

"So you're proving my point," I said.

"Not exactly," he said. "Knowing where I'm vulnerable, you might purposely or by mistake push a button that would trigger a negative feeling in me. As I said, I've given you that privilege and you have that access. The question is, do I have an alternate circuit to switch into so that I won't be hurt?"

"So, you mean you can open yourself when you want to, but you can close yourself off, too."

"Yes. People who function best under pressure have such 'counterbuttons.' Look at public figures criticized in front of thousands on television, or symphony musicians yelled at by conductors, or athletes booed for an error on the playing field. When hit at their most vulnerable point, these people are able to switch into another mode—like a computer, they can change the code on their buttons so no one can get in. This way they can maintain stability and concentrate as if nothing had happened."

"You mean they can detach."

"I think the going phrase is to 'be cool.'"

"So, these counterbuttons are a kind of circuit breaker—if your power is shut off you can immediately get it back on again."

"Yes, you can deal with the unexpected in any situation, public or private," he said. "In marriage or family it's natural to become emotionally intertwined, but each person should also maintain his or her own independent self. This is a delicate balancing act, between emotional dependency and emotional freedom, and the skill is knowing how to balance the two."

"And how do you create that balance?"

"By paying attention to your mate's needs as well as to your own. It is especially important to understand that when your mate touches one of your 'negative' buttons, which can happen frequently between two people who are continually close, he or she is not *causing* you to feel what you're feeling—you're the one who set up the responses on your own circuits and you can change those responses if you don't like them, or temporarily cut off access to the buttons."

"But how about when you're hurt because you didn't push a counterbutton in time?"

"When you understand the button system, you'll realize it's your own fault for being asleep at the panel. Also, when you understand this idea, you're less likely to take a remark personally. It does take a little practice."

"You make love sound like war."

"Love is the most powerful force on earth. But, as with electricity, you must learn how to handle it so you don't hurt yourself."

"So, you're saying one person can't really control another person, unless that person allows it," I said.

"Yes. Which is why attempts to control people don't really work. What works is helping people to respond in their own most natural and productive way."

"Using counterbuttons to change your response doesn't seem very natural."

"Your natural response the day we met was to leave and never come back. But you did come back, because you thought it would be to your advantage. Counterbuttons are the mental and emotional equivalent to your body's immune system. When something threatens your health, your body automatically protects itself. But your emotional health must be *consciously* created and maintained, and you're the caretaker."

"That's a big responsibility."

"The price we pay for free will."

Before leaving, I sat by the fireplace and logged into the laptop another new part I had acquired on this trip. Kumi and I had "installed" a new sequence of steps yesterday for making successful presentations—in effect, a new performing part. So, what would I say this part does for me? Kumi called it The Performer, but I decided to call it The Communicator, because I thought it communicated in a generic sense in my life. So, thinking about it that way I came up with a pretty clear job description:

Communicator

*"I enable you to express yourself with comfort, ease and clarity,
as a public speaker or in your personal and social life."*

Kumi said to always make sure the other parts of me approved of any new part I'd put in. I guess this was a diplomatic way of integrating a new part into my "inner community." At first I was on the fence about this inner community idea, but it was beginning to make an odd kind of sense. We have these different parts of us that perform divergent functions, and I guess they can sometimes get in each other's way. So why not set up communication lines between them, and between them and me—the one in charge of coordinating operations—and maybe defuse conflicts before they begin? (It sounded funny to speak about my parts as "them" when all these parts were really me, but it was just a way of clearly defining the division of labor.) If I could identify these parts, and clarify their job descriptions, then I'd know who they were, what they did and what they wanted. I decided to play along with this notion and see where it took me.

Kumi brought me a cup of tea and sat down in the rocker. I told him I had been thinking about the idea of inner parts.

"If these parts really exist in us," I said, "I wonder which part of me was being so negative when I first met you in August."

He smiled and nodded his head.

"It could have been any part that was frustrated because you weren't communicating with it and it couldn't do its job. 'Bad' behavior stems from positive intent—when a part wants to protect you from possible harm or disappointment and you won't let it."

"You speak about them like they're people."

"They're your Staff, carrying out assigned tasks."

"Well, I think I have a Staff member who's trying to sabotage me, always has."

"Oh? Ask that part who it is and what it wants for you," Kumi said.

"You're kidding."

"No, I'm serious."

"Will the mystery part who sabotages me please tell me who he is and why he does me so many favors?"

"If you don't take this seriously I can guarantee you won't get a response."

I sighed and looked at the ceiling.

"Nick, think for a moment. Why would any part of you want to cause you harm? You're a living thing, like a plant—your roots reach for the water and leaves reach for the sun. Everything in you cries out for life. If something in you is hurting you, take that as a message. Separate its behavior from its *intent*."

"If its intent is to help me why does it sabotage me?"

"What else can it do when it's tried every other way to get your attention?"

"That's no way to get my attention."

"On the contrary, that's why we're talking about it now."

I shook my head and looked at the floor. The larch logs crackled loudly in the fireplace.

"Alright, I'll be serious."

I took a deep breath and sat up straight.

"Will the part of me that always stands in my way please tell me what it wants?"

We sat for several moments in silence. Kumi looked at me with raised eyebrows. "Well..."

"This is totally weird. It says it wants to protect me."

"Protect you from..."

"From being hurt."

"And if you were fully protected from being hurt, what would that part still want for you?"

"To feel the way I did when I was a boy—like there was always something there, some...power." I didn't want to say "God," because I didn't know how I felt about that subject.

"And if you felt the presence of that power, what would that part still want for you?"

I felt uneasy, like we were getting too close to something I couldn't handle. I began to wonder if the part of myself I was resisting might not be the deepest part, the part I needed most.

"Kumi, this is getting a little heavy. Do you mind if we stop now?"

"There's time, Nick, plenty of time."

We sat in silence until it was time to go.

When I told Marion about counterbuttons she was ambivalent about the idea. I was surprised because she always talked about being responsible for your own feelings. She even quoted Eleanor Roosevelt about never making excuses when you're bombarded by critics, and she said she loved that idea. She was sitting on a roll-away bed with her back against the wall. I was facing her in her grandmother's rocking chair.

"It all sounds so controlled," Marion said. "How about all those beautiful Latin people who are emotionally inter-dependent and love each other passionately and 'hurt' each other all the time. Are you going to tell them to push buttons? And don't try to push this notion in Israel, or they'll laugh you all the way to the Gaza Strip."

I know Marion's a master of counterbuttons (and of my buttons) despite her arguments to the contrary. After all, that's what her profession is all about. I think she was afraid Kumi was teaching me to become even more controlled, when she's been trying to get me to loosen up.

"I think this is the actor talking now, isn't it? You want your emotions to be free to express themselves."

"On the contrary, as an actor you really have to control your emotions. That's what acting is."

"Well, so do you as a person. I've seen you do it in professional situations. You don't let people hurt you. You must be pushing something."

"I just don't take it personally."

"So how do you do that?"

She scanned the ceiling for a moment, then down at her fingernails, then up again. "I just stand back from it."

"Well, there you go, same thing."

"But that's just an instinctive reaction. I don't plan it with buttons and control panels."

"Buttons is just a metaphor to explain what people are doing when they control their feelings."

"Feelings don't always control so easily," she said.

"Why are you looking at me like that?"

"Sometimes you frazzle my brain."

"I frazzle your brain or you frazzle your brain?"

"Don't analyze me!" Her lower lip pressed upward like a bulldog's.

"Kumi's just saying it's impossible to hurt someone without physically touching them."

"Well, tell Kumi you can also hurt someone by not touching them!" With that she thrust her shoulders back so hard against the cushions that the sofa bed rolled out from under her and she disappeared behind it. Only her legs were sticking up in the air. Before I could get up to help her she recovered her balance and looked at me from behind the bed, hair in her eyes. She broke into uncontrollable laughter. I was frustrated because this gave her the last word in the argument. She knew this, and came over and sat on my lap.

"See," she said. "You made me mad, then you made me laugh."

I started to answer but she put a finger gently on my mouth.

"Nick, shut up. Just shut up."

(My notes on Counterbuttons are on page 301)

7

A NEW NOW

...DANCING WITH TIME

"People judge themselves too much. They worry either about something they've done or something they're about to do. If a dog steps on thin ice and it's paw goes into the water, it immediately recovers and goes to the next moment. It doesn't stop and think, 'Why did I do that? What's wrong with me?'"

"Nick, is that you?"

Marion saw me sitting in a chair in the middle of my living room. My body was green.

"I'm over here," I said from the dining room. She looked at me in the flesh, then back at my image in the living room. She walked over and put her hand through the image.

"It looks so real."

I had been toying with holography after speaking with Professor Mueller, but only after I did Kumi's Hologram exercise did it occur to me to incorporate the idea of three-dimensional imagery with video-conferencing.

"Can you really send such a real-looking image on the Net?" Marion said.

"I don't know. But I just met somebody who would know, and I hope he can help me."

The next day Gregor came to my apartment for lunch. He was a twenty-three year old Russian emigre, six-foot-two, about a hundred and forty pounds, round-shouldered and gaunt. Mueller said Gregory got his doctorate from M.I.T. at eighteen and that his thesis on coherent optics was already a landmark in the field. I told him my idea. His eyes narrowed and he stared through thick glasses at his untouched food.

"Binary codes, no laser."

"So you think sending live holographic images on-line by computer code is possible?"

"Transmittance of computed hologram is a linear function of the amplitude of incident light."

"Uh-huh."

He jumped up from the table, went to my computer and started keying in equations.

"So you want to work on this together? Gregor? You want your food?"

It was a bitter cold January morning when I left New York to return to Montana. Christmas with Marion's family had been a success all around. Charles and I signed a truce and he had been accepted to journalism school on a part scholarship. Marion's burly Irish father looked at me with new respect since I quietly refused to be goaded into our usual argument after he chided me about "learning voodoo Eskimo style." At first, I felt the old flash of anger and tightening of my jaw. Then suddenly I seemed to be viewing him from a distance and saw him for what he was—an inveterate skeptic about anything out of the ordinary. Then I saw myself. Look who's talking—that's why we get along!

This time Kumi met me at the airport in a jeep with an Indian friend named John Little Elk, who drove us through heavy snow to the outskirts of town. We stopped at the base of a mountain and Kumi jumped out and stood by a red snowmobile, like a waiter in a restaurant introducing me to the head table.

"What's the mystery, Kumi? Where are we going?"

He fastened my bag in a small carrier hooked on the back, grabbed the handlebar and nodded for me to get onto the back seat. "Hold on," he said and gunned the motor, circumventing a clump of bushes and spinning off into the mountains. I looked back at my bag, bouncing precariously behind me. The icy air thrashed at my face and I pulled my scarf over my mouth.

"How you doing?" he yelled, looking back at me and barely missing a large boulder. He zoomed around some trees and snow-covered mounds. I wondered how he could tell a drift from a rock since the rocks were so deeply buried in snow. A couple of times he ran one runner up on some bumpy formation and we'd tip on a sharp angle. Then we'd suddenly be upright again and then tip the other way, just missing a giant tree.

"Kumi, *slow down*!"

He bounced off a big bump that threw the snowmobile almost a foot into the air and cried out with a high-pitched "ya-hoo," like a cowboy. I fantasized that Kumi was the Angel of Death come to take me into the next world.

We drove for over an hour like this before he finally slowed down near a plateau dense with pines. We were now high in the mountains. He wove slowly between the trees for some time before coming to a clearing where he stopped and shut off the motor. I was stunned by the silence.

"Listen," he said, turning to me.

I heard distant whimpers and yiping, like a chorus of animals. "Is that wolves?" I asked.

"Dogs," he said.

We listened for a while longer, then he started the motor and drove slowly for a few minutes before rounding a bend which opened onto a huge area with dozens of kennels filled with white, grey, and rust-colored animals. A farmhouse stood about fifty meters from the dog's enclosures. Kumi drove up to the house, stopped the motor and got out.

"You hungry?" he said.

"First let me see if I can walk," I said, crawling gingerly off the snowmobile. He led me up the steps of the farmhouse, where we were greeted on the front porch by a smiling young man.

"Welcome, friend," the man said as he and Kumi embraced. An older man came out the door and Kumi introduced me to Henrik Olsen and his son Peter. I was struck by the health of the two men, faces ruddy and full of color, laughing as they showed us inside and took our coats. The smell of coffee and baking filled the room.

"Hope you like buckwheat cakes," Henrik said. He spoke with a slight lilt that came from his Scandanavian background.

Peter handed me a cup of coffee and I looked around the large wood-paneled living room. Bay windows overlooked the area with the dogs.

We sat around an old wooden table. Peter brought over a large dish of four-inch pancakes, coated with fresh maple syrup and butter. "You ever had dollar-size buckwheats?" he asked.

"How'd they get that name?" I said.

"After the old silver dollar. It used to be this big, but it shrunk." Everybody laughed.

We ate the buckwheat cakes stacked five or six high with Canadian bacon on the side. I think it was the most delicious breakfast I'd ever had. After two pots of steaming coffee and cheerful small talk, the subject turned to animals. Kumi explained to me that Henrik and Peter are professional trainers.

"We breed 'em to perform certain tasks," Peter said. "Some for dog teams, some for shows. And we have rescue dogs. C'mon, I'll show ya'"

"Remember the movie dog, Chipper?" Kumi said. "Henrik trained him."

"I never made it in the movies, but my dogs do," Henrik said laughing.

They took us on a tour of the farm. As we approached the kennels the dogs let out a chorus of whoops and yelps. "They think we might feed 'em," Peter said. "They know it's not feedin' time, but they're workin' on us 'cause we got visitors. *Quiet!*" he howled in a loud, commanding voice. I had never seen such robust-looking dogs.

Peter walked over to the first kennel which held a beautiful thick-tufted grey and white dog. He had black rings round his clear, blue eyes, like a mask. "This is Luther. He's one-quarter wolf, three-quarters husky. We're grooming him for the lead position of a dog team. He's a doer—a natural born leader. Great authority, very proud. If you could ever say a dog was an achiever, he'd be it." Luther's tail wagged so vigorously his whole spine shook.

Walking to the next kennel Peter said, "This is Hamlet," showing us a pure husky. "I thought he might be a good team dog but he's paranoid—a loner. He'll be better off working on his own—a good rescue dog."

"And here we have Kiri," he said showing us a long-legged, red-haired dog that was a combination of collie and husky. "High I.Q., very quick learner. She learns new stunts in one day. I've got a movie producer interested in her. Kiri!" he said, changing his voice tone. "How's the opera coming?" Kiri sat back, raised her head and gave out a long, melodious howl followed by a series of short howls on different pitches.

We all laughed. "You can say you heard 'er before she got famous," Peter said.

"And this is our resident schizoid. I call him Nixon. See how he turns his head and looks at you?" He was right. The other dogs had come to us, or jumped up and tried to lick our hands through the cage, but this one seemed suspicious. "Paranoid schizophrenic," Peter said.

"You're serious with these psychological terms," I said.

"You bet. Tomorrow he might be friendly and the next day he'll be like this again. He'll be better off surrounded by other dogs in the middle of a team—probably third row inside."

I was amazed at his ability to analyze and place each dog with a potential job description. "You speak about them as if they were human."

"They are, almost, except they don't think like us."

"How do they think?"

"In the moment. Everything is now, right now."

"What do you mean? Don't dogs have memories?"

"Oh, very good memories, but they don't think about them. That's why they're so good in emergencies."

"How are they in emergencies?"

"One step at a time. From here, to here to here," he said, chopping his hand in the air.

"You mean they're fearless."

"No, but they don't feel fear in advance. If they run into a bear they'll remember their last encounter with a bear and respond accordingly. But they don't anticipate meeting the bear—that's the difference."

Knowing Kumi, I had a vague feeling I was being set up for something, but I didn't know what, so I didn't say anything.

The two-hour trip from the farm to Kumi's was much saner. Instead of blazing a path as Kumi had done going up to the dog farm, we took paths and roads that were still visible despite the drifts. Kumi let me drive the snowmobile. We passed lakes, crossed frozen streams and drove through a forest of lodgepole pines, spruce and firs before finally arriving at Kumi's cabin. I made a fire while Kumi heated up some soup, which we ate out of large mugs. Then I crawled into my sleeping bag and disappeared from the world.

When I awoke it was late morning. I had slept thirteen hours.

"That's the longest sleep of my life," I told Kumi at breakfast.

"Not counting the first forty-five years," he said.

I laughed. "Okay," I said. "So what do we have on the agenda for today?"

"What did you think of the farm yesterday?"

"Beautiful creatures," I said. "And fascinating, what he said about the way dogs live in the moment. I envy them, but it's not very practical for people—at least not in the business world."

"On the contrary, it's the perfect state of mind for the business world. In everyday life it's natural to be partly in the past and future. But for high pressure situations, in business or anything else, time stops—everything is now."

I thought of Gregor and his relentless attention to the moment.

"How do you do that?" I said.

"You pay attention to each moment as it unfolds. There is only this moment, and this moment, and this moment," he said, gesturing with his hand, "a succession of moments, a series of nows, until your performance is finished."

"You mean, react like a dog?"

"In a way, yes. People judge themselves too much. They worry either about something they've done, or something they're about to do. A dog doesn't do that. If it steps on thin ice and its paw goes into the water it immediately recovers and goes to the next moment. It doesn't stop and think, 'Why did I do that? What's wrong with me?'"

I smiled at the image of one of Henrik's huskies stopping to talk to itself in the middle of an emergency.

"To a dog, a misstep is gone the moment it happens," Kumi said, "because the dog is already paying attention to the next moment. There is no 'mistake' because there is no past. And there's no fear, because there's no future. There is only now…and now…and now. Here, do it with me."

Kumi stood up and performed a kind of dance movement to demonstrate his point. He made a full step to the right, clapping his hands together as he stepped. "A new now," he said. He repeated the move and again said, "a new now."

"Do what I'm doing and say it with me—a new now…a new now…a new now," he said, moving to his right with each statement.

Together, we moved across the cabin floor like two dancers in unison, doing this odd step and saying "a new now" with each move. It became hypnotic as we repeated the action dozens of times.

Then Kumi stopped and created imaginary situations. "You're giving a speech and you say a wrong word—*a new now*," he said and moved to his right. "You have a memory slip…*a new now*…you feel a sudden fatigue…*a new now*…your concentration is flagging...*a new now*," he said, moving with each repetition of the words.

"I'm teaching you to think like a dog—or better, to *not* think the way a dog doesn't think." We repeated the "new now" exercise until it became a mantra, leaving no room for thought, focusing our attention only on the moment. I felt silly dancing around the room talking to myself, but I had to admit it gave me a good feeling—like I was continually refreshing myself.

Finally we sat down for a rest and Kumi looked at me.

"Imagine yourself doing this back in New York," he said.

I saw myself doing the exercise in my apartment. At first I felt a little self-conscious at the idea of saying "a new now" while I slid sideways across the room gesturing in the air. I imagined keeping my voice down so the neighbors wouldn't wonder about me. But I was surprised at how effective the physicality of this exercise was. I imagined myself getting up from the computer when I had a problem and saying "a new now," and moving on to the next thing I needed to do.

"And notice what will be different for you when you think this way."

I thought of some of the emergencies I'd had with computer breakdowns. One day a conferencing system went down in a Wall Street brokerage house and I got an urgent call. I handled it, but the pressure took its toll on me. I imagined now how I could have dealt with that incident. Seeing it this new way in my mind now, I think the repair might have taken place with less effort if I'd treated the whole incident like it was one big "now."

I felt hungry and looked at my wrist watch. "My God, Kumi," I said. "It's two o'clock. We've been at this for three hours."

"There, you see? You forget time. *That's* what it's like to be in the performing state," he said, punching his finger into the air.

After lunch Kumi made tea and we sat down to talk. He told me about an incident where he had done this exercise with a group of teenagers at a high school. Some parents were present and one, a fundamentalist Christian, was outraged.

"She felt this exercise was anti-Christian."

"Why?" I said.

"I guess she got the idea in her head that we were somehow disregarding the past, and leaving our present existence to go to another one—exercising a control over our lives that only God had the right to make. She wanted to sue the school."

"So what happened?"

"The principal talked to her. He was very clever. He asked her if she believed in divine grace, the idea that God forgives you if you are truly sorry for your sins. Of course she said yes. Then he said, 'Well this is an exercise in divine grace, a reminder that God forgives you and you can go forward with your life.'"

"That's good," I said. "But it's easier said than done."

"What? Forgiving, or getting on with your life?"

"Both," I said.

"Well, with this exercise you can use your God-given powers and side-step your feelings when you feel slighted."

I recalled being fired and the animosity I still felt for Streicher. "I think sometimes it's a good idea to remember when something bad has happened to you."

"Yes, if you use it as an alarm bell, to help you avoid a similar situation in the future. But to dwell on it drains your energy," he said.

He was right. I had spent countless hours being depressed and replaying confrontations with Streicher. "So how do you forget a slight and go on to the next moment?" I said.

"You don't forget it," he said. "Just file it for future reference and click on to the next document," he said, gesturing like he was tapping the buttons of a computer mouse.

"Is it really that simple. What about the emotions that go with these negative events?"

"What negative events? Your *interpretation* of events makes them negative."

"But if you feel angry or frustrated doesn't that need some kind of release?"

"That frustration is energy—*channel* it and *use* it. When I make a mistake the first thing I think is how I'm going to guarantee that I don't make the same mistake again. I place a big bright picture of what I did right up here"—he gestured up to his left—"and I say to myself, 'I'll never do that again.' Then I make an image of what I want to do instead and I put that right up here," and he gestured up to his right. "Now I'm no longer angry, because I've learned something. When I'm about to make the same mistake again, the image of the mistake will flash in my mind and trigger the image of what I want to do instead. So that mistake is now my teacher, and the lesson was created by the energy of my frustration."

I got up and stretched and looked out the window. Snow was falling in thick tufts, like little parachutes landing in the trees.

"My impression of this 'new now' exercise is that it's very good for performing, because, as you say, performing is in the now. But I'm not so sure how I'd use it in day-to-day living. I mean, what are the long-term benefits of thinking in the present?"

"As I said before, a long-term is made up of many short-terms. To get where you're going, you step on from where you are now—one now after another. Your future is an accumulation of nows."

"A staircase of moments..."

"You're becoming a poet."

That night I thought about how I could apply the "now" idea to my daily life. It struck me that when I'm with Marion I'm often thinking about my work. That means I'm not really with her. I'm somewhere in the past, or the future, and I'm not fully enjoying the moment. I wonder how that makes her feel. Stage fright probably results from either dwelling on an uncomfortable past experience or anticipating an unpleasant future one, instead of paying attention to what's happening right now. I wondered how much time I'd wasted not being in the moment and having to patch things up later because of what I'd missed.

I woke up imagining how it would be to model the behavior of an animal. At breakfast I asked Kumi about it.

"Kumi, about the dogs, we know what they're *not* doing, right? That they're not thinking in words the way we do, which allows them to live in the "now." But then what is it they *are* doing? They have to be *doing something* to make moment-to-moment living possible."

"I don't know. But I think they direct all their senses to their immediate surroundings."

"How?"

"They look at what they're seeing, they listen to what they're hearing, feel what they're feeling, smell what they're smelling, savor what they're tasting—they're aware, step by step, of each sense."

"Well, so are we."

"Not true. We scatter our senses and don't settle on any one thing until we have to. Dogs lock on to each thing as they go."

"We should be able to do that too."

"Come over here a moment," he said, moving over to the window and motioning for me to stand next to him. "We'll take each sense, one by one. Fix your eyes on something and hold them there," he said, staring out the window.

I saw a cone on the limb of a pine tree. "Okay," I said.

"Now tell yourself what you see."

"Out loud?" I said.

"To yourself."

I see the pine cone, I said to myself. "Okay."

"Now hold your eyes there and tell yourself what you hear."

I hear the wood burning in the fireplace, I thought. "Um-hum."

"And now what you feel—physically."

I feel the floor through my socks, I heard in my mind. "Mmm."

"Now go around again, keeping your eyes on the same point, but reporting to yourself another set of things you see, hear and feel. For example, I'll keep my eyes locked on that treetop, but this time I'll say to myself 'I see the mountains.'"

I followed his instructions and said to myself, *I see the snow, I hear the wind, I feel the heat of the fire on my neck.* As I continued to identify more and more things in my surroundings, I felt a stillness throughout my body, and my mind seemed to empty.

Then Kumi said, "This time around we're going to add something. Say the following: 'I see this, I hear that, I feel this and I'm...' and then describe whatever you want for an ongoing state—like 'I'm relaxing' or 'I'm paying attention' or 'I'm enjoying myself.'"

I decided I wanted to relax, so, keeping my eyes on the cone, I said to myself, *I see the clouds, I hear my breath, I feel the shirt on my skin and I'm letting go of my shoulder muscles.*

"Keep cycling around the three senses like this," he said, "including new things you see, hear and feel and repeating what you want."

I got through the cycle perhaps two or three more times and then forgot where I was in the cycle. I just stood there, not moving, looking out the window, my arms feeling as though they belonged to someone else.

I turned my head toward Kumi but he wasn't there. He was nowhere in the room and his coat was gone. I walked over and opened the door and saw him some distance from the house, chopping wood. I sat by the fire and stared. My body felt deeply relaxed, with a pleasant heaviness. The last time I felt like this was on a summer day, many years ago when I was visiting friends at a lake and was lying in the sun after a long swim.

I heard Kumi come in with wood, take off his coat and fill the kettle. He walked over and looked at me, then walked back to the sink and washed something. A few minutes later he brought tea over to the fireplace.

"Dear Marion," he said, as if thinking aloud to himself while writing a letter, "I think we've lost Nick. Where should I send the body?"

I chuckled. "When did you go outside?" I asked.

"About half an hour ago," he said.

"Wow. Today's my day to lose time."

"Good exercise, huh?"

"Yeah. I lost track of the order after a bit, I didn't know whether I was seeing next or hearing, or what."

"That's okay. The object of the exercise is to get you into a state of concentration. Sometimes one cycle through the senses will be enough. I got a card from a musician who used it just before he played a concerto with the New York Philharmonic. He simply said, 'I feel the clarinet in my hand, I hear the musicians warming up, I see the audience and this is going to be one of the best performances I've ever given.'"

"Was it?" I asked.

"He said it was his best ever. Notice he switched the order of the senses to feel-hear-see, a typical sequence for many musicians."

"But is it such a good idea to be so relaxed when you're about to perform?" I said. "I could hardly move."

"But relaxation is what you asked for, so you tuned down. The musician asked for *performance*, so he tuned himself *up*," he said, grinning at me over the pun. "You get what you ask for."

"It seems too easy," I said.

"That's because you're used to the effort of trying to shut things out in order to concentrate. With this technique you aren't fighting your surroundings, you're going along with them. You're using your brain's natural way of learning, which is easy."

"What do you mean, the brain's natural way of learning?"

"When you report to yourself three verifiable things covering all your senses, you've got your brain's full attention. Whatever you say next it will believe, and act on as if it were true."

"It really works that way?" I said.

"You just did it. People think that to concentrate you need to empty your mind. So they make a conscious attempt to not think, which is impossible, because to negate something from your mind you first have to create it, so you're constantly creating sounds and images in order to get rid of them. A self-defeating process. It's much easier to simply acknowledge everything in your surroundings. Then your brain doesn't have to pay attention to them anymore and can go on to the next thing. You become like a child, open to new ideas."

"Then you're kind of directing your mind," I said.

"Tricking it, in fact. Sending it into a loop, always coming back to what you want."

"But what keeps your brain interested in the thing you want?"

"It's not a thing, it's an action—it gives the brain something *to do*. And you keep re-directing it's attention to that action while you eliminate, one by one, anything else it might have been paying attention to."

"Eliminate it by acknowledging it."

"Yes."

"So what you want is the only thing left."

"Yes."

Another thought came to me. "Here it's quiet. But when I'm doing this in the city wouldn't loud sounds be disturbing?"

"On the contrary, all sound is welcome—jackhammers, yelling, doors slamming. They all give you something to *use*. The more sounds you can identify the more easily you can go into a state of concentration."

"So you could use this for anything," I said.

"Even for simple things, like standing in line at the bank—'I see the bank tellers, I hear people talking, I feel the paper in my hand and I'm planning my schedule for the morning.'"

"But when you get into this state of mind, how long will it hold?" I said.

"As long as you need it. A fellow in the Air Force wrote me that he had to stand at attention in ninety degree heat for an hour at a White House ceremony where the President gave a talk. He used the see-hear-feel-do sequence and said the hour went by like five minutes."

"Maybe that's the answer to television," I said. "'I see the screen, I hear the laugh track, I feel the remote in my hand and I really am being entertained.'"

"Or even simpler—'and I'm turning it off.'"

I smiled and nodded.

"The funniest use of this exercise was by a professor who was self-conscious about medical examinations," Kumi said. "One day he goes in for a prostate check-up and in walks a female doctor. She tells him to undress and says she'll be back in a minute. He's so embarrassed he thinks he's going to have to leave. And then he says to himself, 'I see the picture on the wall...I hear the air conditioner...I feel my feet on the floor...and I'm beginning to see the humor in this situation.' He runs this sequence while he's undressing and when she returns she notices he looks different. She says 'Are you okay?' This amuses him even more, and arouses her suspicion even more. He told me the exam went fine for him, but he wasn't so sure about her."

Kumi puttered around in the kitchen while I made some notes. Among other things, I noticed I was developing a new part—my creativity. Or, I should say, I felt my creative part beginning to wake up, like Gulliver after a long sleep. I'd never really identified this part or what it did for me. I decided to call it the Inventor.

Inventor

*"I stimulate your imagination and
help random thoughts coalesce into new ideas."*

Running this "new" part through Kumi's Community Check idea, I didn't seem to get any objection about its presence from my other parts. In fact, they seemed pleased to have my creative part revived. But I got a few conflicting messages—from both The Father and the Loving Mate. I think they were concerned that a re-energized creative part would steal time from my personal relationships. I found myself negotiating with them, promising to keep a balance between work and home life. (I felt like I was living in a co-op, having committee meetings and sharing responsibilities with actual people.) Could I keep such a promise? And what would happen if I didn't?

Kumi said the creative part of us is the most important part of all, because creativity is basic to life. To me, creating something of my own is the most deeply satisfying thing I can do because I know it will be there after I'm gone. I've heard that creative people—writers, composers, painters—often think about their works as their "babies."

But you don't have to be an artist to be creative. Kumi had told me about a guy who wanted to commit suicide, but decided to do one last thing before he died—build a house in the Yukon. With the help of a few natives, and using only available materials from the forest, he carved giant logs out of trees. Finding the logs too heavy to lift, he invented a kind of jack to pry one log up onto another. When the logs got too high he created a rope-and-pulley system to lift them into place. As the house took shape, villagers came by to help. Piece by piece, a magnificent two-story house came into being. The man documented the whole process with his camera. Kumi said it was the most beautiful house he'd ever seen, that you could almost smell the wood and varnish from the photographs. The man never even lived in the house. The creative part of himself was renewed, and the house had become a metaphor for living. He returned to the States and resumed his life.

Kumi came back in the cabin and stomped snow off his boots. I told him I was making notes on my new creative part. I expressed one of the fears I'd always had about my video work—creative block.

"Creative block is a breach of trust," Kumi said.

"How so?"

"A sure way to get blocked is to break appointments with your creative part—like saying you're going to carry out a project and then not doing it. Your creative self will begin to wonder if creating is really important to you."

"Sounds funny when you put it that way."

"But not so funny when it happens. When this part loses faith in you it'll start breaking appointments, too, and eventually might just stop showing up. That's when you find yourself saying, 'I'm stuck.' Creating doesn't happen in a vacuum. All your parts need to cooperate to make it work. That's why it's important to develop a good communication within your whole system, to make a nest where your creativity can feel at home."

All of a sudden my heart jumped. "What day is it today?"

"Monday," Kumi said.

"Omigod, I thought it was Sunday. I lost a day."

"When's your flight?" Kumi said.

I looked at my watch. "An hour and forty minutes. I'll never make it."

"We'll make it," Kumi said jumping up. "Get your bag." He called John on the CB radio. Fortunately he was home and agreed to meet us at the bottom of the mountain. Kumi donned his jacket and ran out the door. I threw my stuff into my knapsack, put on my boots and grabbed my parka as I heard Kumi start up the snowmobile. "Oh, no, Kumi. Not again!"

"Get in!" he ordered.

I was hardly into the back seat when he took off, thrusting us onto the winding road down the hill. Snow sprayed my face as we hit a bump and skidded sideways. The trees on our left protected us from going over the edge of a deep slope.

"No problem!" he yelled. "Hold on!" He gunned the motor and got back on the road, hitting something hard that grated on the bottom of the snowmobile. The snow was so deep you couldn't see where the ruts were. At times the runners cut deeply into the snow and we would tilt, especially on the curves.

"Kumi, take it easy!"

"Don't worry!" he yelled, scraping against a bush.

He veered off the road and headed straight for a precipice, waving his hand at me to get down. I hunkered down as far as I could as we went off the edge, flying in the air. We thumped down, spraying a geyser of snow in all directions, and zoomed down another hill. "Short cut!" he yelled, skidding over a jutting rock formation.

I was beyond speech. "Relax!" he called out, careening around an old fallen larch tree and spinning off into the woods.

I closed my eyes and tried to breathe deeply. *I see the trees, I hear the motor, I feel my bum bouncing on the seat and I'm a kid having fun at Coney Island.* I kept repeating this to myself until the town appeared and I let out a big breath.

Kumi wound down the mountainside to the road where John's jeep was waiting.

"This is where Little Elk turns into Crazy Horse. Hold on."

We piled into the jeep and John raced to the airport, dodging between incoming and outgoing airport traffic and skidding to a halt in front of the airport entrance.

"Hey, you got a minute to spare," Kumi said, pointing to a clock.

I hobbled out of the jeep, grabbed my stuff and raced inside as fast as I could, running up the escalator and down a hallway lined with gate numbers, my boots clopping on the floor. I saw my gate and yelled "I'm here! I'm here!"

"No rush, sir," the check-in clerk said, smiling amiably. "The flight's de-layed—de-icing."

I leaned my head on the counter for a full minute to catch my breath.

(My notes on A New Now and See-Hear-Feel-Do are on page 304)

8

FEDEX TO THE ARTERIES

...A FLEET OF CANOES INTO THE BLOOD STREAM

"'Uh-oh, something's wrong'. Blood yells, 'Where's my sugar?' Liver says, 'I've got nothing to metabolize.' Stomach screams, 'Give me nutrition!' The cells are starving and Brain puts in a panic call to the Liver and gets an answering service—'I can't come to the phone right now, but your health is important to us...'"

"Where do we put all this stuff?"

A gruff, bald-headed man in a leather jacket pointed to boxes of electronic equipment piled in the hallway.

"You must have the wrong apartment," I said.

He checked his clipboard. "We're looking for a Gregor Vereschenko."

"Oh, come on in."

Two men carried the boxes into my computer room. One of them handed me a receipt for $19,347.21, charged to my line of credit at Globalcom! "Have a nice day," he said.

Gregor arrived a few minutes later. When I opened the door he walked past me without speaking and disappeared into the sea of computer and optical equipment, which was already spilling out into my living room. I followed him into what was left of my office.

"Gregor, what the hell are you doing? Who told you to buy all this stuff? And you forged my signature! That line of credit's not even valid anymore."

"Constructing synthesizer for new emulsion contrast factor," he said,

"A new synthesizer! My God, Gregor!"

"Is necessary."

"Money is necessary, too. Where am I going to get it? You can't just buy things without asking me. I'll go bankrupt. And what are these greasy chicken containers all over the place. I'll have roaches in no time."

But he was lost in a tangle of wires. I took a deep breath, squeezed my fingers and said to myself, *I see the computer, I hear it humming, I feel my fingers and my breathing is slowing down...slowing down...*

I hired him, so I'd better learn to get along with him.

At night I worked with Gregor, developing thousands of lines of computer codes for the compression of video images. During the day I called everyone I knew in the computer field, including some large corporations interested in the concept of three-dimensional video-conferencing. I asked them to support our project and offered stock in our corporation. I even swallowed my pride and approached Globalcom, but they immediately said my idea was "hare-brained."

I didn't care what anybody thought. I knew what I wanted—I saw it, I heard it, I felt it and I went all out for it. The more Jack Nicholson coached me the more like him I became.

"Why should we invest in an experiment that has only a marginal chance of working?" said a vice-president of IBM. I handed him our reams of equations for computerized holography and I think he was impressed, especially because I think he didn't understand them.

"Every experiment has only a marginal chance of working. But you're not investing in an experiment, you're investing in me," I said with uncharacteristic force in my voice. I could hardly believe it was me talking. "Just look at the person standing in front of you and ask yourself, 'Do I trust this man's judgment?'"

To my astonishment, he gave us $10,000.

But deep inside I wasn't always so sure of myself. I wavered between absolute certainty and black despair over the workability of this idea. And even if it worked, would anybody really want it? Marion was losing her patience with me. Days would pass without my calling her, and one of them was her birthday.

On the way home from rehearsal she dropped by to pick up a sweater of hers I'd long since promised to return. The apartment was a mess and the kitchen was a disaster.

"I think you need another meeting with your parts, Nick," she said. "The balance between your Inventor and your Loving Mate isn't working." She said "loving mate" with a scowl.

"Marion, life is crazy right now."

"Is that a kiss-off?"

"Aw, c'mon."

"Don't touch me."

"I'm going all day on this thing, I've got bills, I've got that madman in there on the computer half the night…"

"You're running yourself into the ground," she said. "You look terrible."

"Will you stay over tonight?"

"No."

"Look, I have to stick with it, Marion."

"Well, dammit, I don't," she said slamming the door so hard even Gregor looked up.

Flight delays got me to Montana late and I was exhausted when I arrived after dark at Kumi's. We ate and went to bed early, but I had trouble falling asleep. I'd left without talking to Marion and my mind buzzed with a dozen different things. Was I getting in over my head with this holographic project? And was I really learning this stuff of Kumi's? Here I am under pressure and I'm coming apart. But Kumi's work requires diligence. Do I practice it enough? Did I think I was getting a quick fix with Kumi and then everything would be okay? Maybe Kumi was right when he said I've been asleep for the first forty-five years of my life. Am I awake now? Well, I sure as hell am—it's one-thirty in the morning! Why do I still harbor feelings against Streicher? Kumi says don't ask "Why," ask "How." Maybe it has nothing to do with him anyway. Maybe I just felt powerless. But I thought I'd licked my need to control, or is self-control just another form of control? You can't win. I watched the shadows of trees dancing on the ceiling. *I see the shadows…and…I hear the wind…and…I feel my head on the pillow…and…I'm falling asleep.* I repeated this several times to myself and started to yawn, but I wasn't falling asleep. "This isn't working, Nick," I whispered aloud. And that's the last thing

I remembered before waking at nine the next morning to the sound of a crackling fire.

The morning air was still and the fir trees white. I saw an animal disappear behind a bush. The snow under foot was coated with a layer of ice crystals that crunched with each step we took. I felt prickling in my nose when I inhaled.

"I want to show you something," Kumi said, trudging over to a clump of bushes. He reached down and dug deep in the snow, clearing a space around a small green plant. "This is a short-stemmed willow," he said. "A tough little guy. It's leaves hold nutrients and minerals and water so it can grow in any soil, even in the Arctic. Snow can cover it, animals trample it and it will just spring back up and keep growing. It can be in the ground for years before a single plant produces a seed crop. Imagine being under ice and snow at fifty below zero for two or three winters. And then you blossom!"

I stared at the plant for a long time. When I turned to look for Kumi, he had gone back to the cabin. I went over to the chopping block, split some logs and carried them inside. We sat by the fire and drank tea.

"You sure drink a lot of tea, Kumi."

"My Inuit upbringing. They drink about three gallons of tea a day up there. That's one reason they have such low cholesterol, even though they eat mainly meat. I've learned to drink green tea, though, without caffeine."

"You don't seem to get cold very easily. Is that an Eskimo thing?"

"Eskimos are born with an extra layer of fat, ready for the elements. But I've lived down here so long I've shed most of mine. But you, my friend, have more than a little bit."

"I've tried everything, but I can't seem to get rid of it."

"Eat right and exercise. It's simple."

"I know, but I have a heavy schedule and going to a health club takes time."

"Exercise at home. You should pump your heart for fifteen or twenty minutes a day—gets more oxygen to the brain, makes ideas flow, burns off frustration."

I thought about my friend Matt, a neurosurgeon who is very conscious of his health. "I know a doctor who runs up and down the stairs every morning with a thirty-pound weight on his back."

"Good doctor to know," Kumi said.

Kumi made a snack of cheese on Swedish rye crackers. "Mmm, what kind of cheese is this?" I asked.

"Champagne. Fifteen percent fat."

"Is that good?"

"Many cheeses are thirty, forty percent, and more. What kind of cheese do you eat?"

"It's orange. Packaged in slices."

"I think it's time we had a talk about nutrition."

"I hate diets. They don't work for me."

"You don't have to diet when you eat right. Overweight is a form of undernourishment—malnutrition actually."

"What do you mean?"

"When your body doesn't have the food it needs it demands more. Eat junk and you'll always be hungry. More than once someone has come to me with what he or she thought was a psychological problem that turned out to be nutritional. I'm amazed when I give workshops at universities how ignorant students are about food. One young fellow on a swim team asked me if I had any mental exercises for headaches. I asked him what he had for breakfast. 'I don't eat breakfast,' he said. His first food of the day was a baloney sandwich on white bread and a coke around noon. He had a candy bar mid-afternoon, then supper at home. His mother would make spaghetti with tomato sauce and meat—no vegetables—or hamburger steak and mashed potatoes with lots of butter. At night he went out and had Cokes and French fries, so he had no appetite in the morning.

"I told him I had a magic cure for headaches: eat a full breakfast with whole-grain bread, fruit, eggs and low-fat milk. He wasn't allergic to dairy foods. For lunch, a tuna fish or chicken sandwich with lettuce and tomato on whole grain bread, a cup of soup and a glass of milk, but no soft drink. For supper, pasta or rice but with lots of fresh—not canned—vegetables. If he wanted meat he could have fish or chicken. Snacks should be yogurt or fruit or unsalted nuts. No sweets until he got into these new eating habits. After three days of eating like this, he said to me, 'Hey, your magic method works!'"

I thought of all the Cokes and coffee I was drinking now, and I began to wonder if my fatigue could be related to my nutrition. Would I have more energy if I'd eat differently? I just assumed fatigue was normal when you're working hard. Look at Gregor—he hardly eats at all! But then he looks worse than I do. Imagine how he'll look when he's forty—if he gets to be forty.

"Why is good eating such a mystery?" Kumi said. "Schools, of all places, should have good food in their cafeterias. It's almost impossible to find decent bread on many campuses, or vegetables that haven't been cooked to death, but hamburgers and hot dogs are everywhere."

I remembered the food courts at college—a string of Burger Kings and Taco Bells. "I guess they expect people to take care of their own eating," I said.

"But few people know how. You're educated, but not about nutrition. When someone tells me they have performance nerves, I have to wonder if the real issue isn't low blood sugar."

"What is low blood sugar exactly?"

"The fancy word for it is hypoglycemia—abnormally low glucose in the blood."

"So what do you do for that? Eat sugar?"

Kumi stared at me and sighed. "Sweets are the worst thing to eat when your blood sugar is down. Do you know anything at all about how your body processes food?"

"Well," I said, venturing into the lion's den, "you eat and your stomach extracts the vitamins and the rest goes out. Right?"

Kumi smiled. "You hope the rest goes out. It depends what you put in. Some people do all their reading in the bathroom..."

"The biggest library in the house!" I said.

"Now, listen up, Nicholas—that's what the gang leader says in action movies when he wants your attention."

"We're not going to talk about nutrition, are we?" The most boring class in school was hygiene, usually taught by the world's dullest person telling you to eat "balanced meals."

"No, we're going to talk about saving the only body you're gonna get."

I decided to let him talk and get it over with.

"When you eat, your body extracts the nutrients from food and gradually feeds them to your cells for hours. The two big players in this drama are called Pancreas and Liver. Liver stores the glucose, and Pancreas signals with insulin the amount of energy Liver should trickle out, bit by bit, into your blood. Picture a fleet of canoes flowing out of the Liver, one by one all day long nourishing your body. That's a healthy person."

I smiled at the image of a fleet of canoes. "It sounds like a tactical naval operation," I said.

"Good image, because that little fleet gives you energy and defends you against disease. Now, let's say you've forgotten to eat for a while. Your blood runs low on sugar and the canoes stop flowing. Now you feel tired. The cells send a fax to the Blood—beeep-brrddddt: 'Hey, where's our energy?' Blood e-mails Stomach: 'Where's the nutrition?' And Stomach calls Brain and says, 'Hey, our blood sugar's going down, tell that guy to EAT!'"

Kumi was putting on one of his entertaining shows, gesturing wildly in the firelight.

"So, meanwhile, out on the street, you're walking along feeling this hunger and you see an ice cream shop and you think, 'Mmm, quick energy.' So you walk in and order a triple strawberry-vanilla-peppermint frazoo with chocolate topping and imitation whipped cream and a maraschino cherry on top." He held up his arms like he'd just finished a song in a night club act. "Now, this little creation is all sugar, so the minute you start eating it goes *FedEx* to the blood. Pancreas gets so excited it over-produces and shoots out a flood of insulin, and Liver over-responds and launches canoes full of energy thirteen to the dozen."

Kumi was getting excited now, walking back and forth waving his cup.

"And what a kick you feel!" he said. "You're ready to uproot trees. Superman's agent is calling you for an interview. Then, about a half hour later—uh-oh!" Kumi sank into his chair and his body sagged. "Something's wrong. You suddenly feel tired. You're getting a headache. The situation's desperate. Blood yells, 'Where's my sugar?' Liver says, 'I've got nothing to metabolize.' Stomach screams, 'Give me nutrition!' The cells are starving and Brain puts in a panic call to the Liver and gets an answering service—'I can't come to the phone right now, but your health is important to us...', because Liver is *out of business—no more canoes, ka-put.*"

I choked on a gulp of tea and stood up to clear my throat. "Message received," I said, coughing. I sat down again and looked at Kumi, shaking my head. "Kumi, you ought to videotape that explanation. It's great."

"Not bad," he said, rocking his hand back and forth equivocally.

"Is that really how blood sugar works?" I asked.

"Close," he said.

"It sounds like a madhouse."

"Well, imagine, you're about to get up in public and give a performance and your vital systems are burning out. You don't know why you feel so nervous—you think something's wrong with your *mind*. And it may be completely metabolic, at least at first. But after a couple of bad performances because of this state, your fear is legitimate."

"Well, Kumi, I'll guarantee you one thing. As long as I live I'll never have a triple strawberry-whatever frazoo."

"At least not on an empty stomach," he said. "I don't want to give the impression that I'm a saint. I like sweets, but I know enough about nutrition that I can do these things without hurting myself."

I listened to the crackling of the fire and thought about how all this applied to me.

"Is it possible to have low blood sugar without eating sweets?" I asked. "Sometimes I feel what you're describing just from working hard."

"Sometimes when you overwork you forget to eat," he said, "and your sugar will drop. You've got to keep those canoes flowing. Some people eat too little as a habit—especially women who want to stay thin—and they're tired all the time. I worked with this fashion model—I'll show you her picture. I come up to her chin and she weighs less than I do. Sneeze and you'll blow her off the mountain. She had stage fright about walking on the runway—you know, that long platform they parade on at fashion shows? She said she'd feel faint before walking out and would lose her confidence. Eventually, she developed a real fear of performing and was in therapy for two years talking about her parents and her sex life. It cost her thousands of dollars. But apparently the analyst didn't notice she was under-nourished, because they never discussed her eating habits.

"When I asked her about food she was totally ignorant about nutrition. She thought it was always healthy to eat *less*. She wouldn't eat all day before a big show, thinking that would keep her more alert. She didn't have a problem with her parents. And the only trouble with her sex life was that she was so nervous men didn't want to be with her. The poor woman was starving!"

"But you could fix that easily by having her eat good food, right?" I said.

"In her case, not so easily. She was like a refugee from a concentration camp—I had to put her on a gradual eating program to bring her back to normal."

"It can really get that bad?"

"It can get worse—caffeine binges and alcohol to keep you going. They drain your body of vitamins, exactly what you don't need when your blood sugar is down. You can get depressed, start having mood swings, turn to drugs. Drug addicts are classic hypoglycemics. All the visualizations and finger squeezes in the world won't help you when your nervous system is shot, because that's the network that operates your programming."

Kumi's mention of mood swings hit home with me, especially thinking about some of the late night sessions with Gregor. And sometimes I'd feel suddenly depressed without knowing why. Now that I thought of it, good food or exercise often brought me out of a slump. "What you're really talking about is care and repair of the human instrument, right?" I said.

"Right. Most people treat their cars better than they treat themselves."

Kumi got up to make more tea and I stood up to stretch my legs. Light snow flurries were blowing against the window.

"When you exercise and eat right you feel better. And you look good. That gives you confidence. Why do I even have to say this? Isn't it obvious?"

"'Eet eez better zu look good zan zu feel good,'" I said.

"What?" Kumi said.

"Oh, just a joke from an old TV show. Billy Crystal making fun of our preoccupation with looks."

"The mirror can be a great inspiration for trimming up," Kumi said.

"I never thought of you as vain," I said.

"If vanity will get you to exercise I'm all for it. I'm practical," Kumi said, leaning forward and raising his eyebrows. "A performer needs to be ready for *anything*. Film actors sometimes wait on a movie set all day and then suddenly have to do a two-minute scene and be alert. I once saw a hockey game that went into two-and-a-half hours of overtime. You *know* the winner of that one was the team in the best condition."

"But those are rather extreme examples, aren't they?" I said.

"Life can go into overtime for anybody," he said. "One of the biggest complaints I hear is that people don't have enough time. Some people really are overworked, but many just don't know how to budget their energy."

"I've heard it said we don't need more than four or five hours of sleep a night," I said. "That we sleep half our life away."

"Nonsense. You should get all the rest you need. Listen to your body. Sleep is a creative state—it gives your brain a chance to process what happens during your waking hours, and that's an important psychological need."

"What do you mean 'process?'"

"Your brain doesn't stop thinking when you go to sleep. That's when it puts ideas together and comes up with solutions. Haven't you ever gone to bed with a problem and woken up the next morning with the answer?"

"Yeah, sometimes."

"Artists talk all the time about getting ideas in their sleep. I can function on four or five hours sleep a night for everyday things, but I'm creative only when I've had my last dreams, which usually come in my seventh or eighth hours of sleep. My brain needs that time to work out all the details."

I put another log on the fire. "Then why do people deny themselves sleep if they need it?"

"Good question. Probably one of the reasons is the work ethic, the idea that working harder will make you more successful. Sleeping less doesn't mean you get more done, and sleeping more doesn't mean you're lazy. It's the results that count. Three hours of quality work is better than six hours of slogging. Also, you need time to relax and enjoy yourself. Fun can be as valuable as sleep, it gives your brain a chance to run and play. That's when brains come up with ideas."

"So you're saying the brain needs some private time to be creative, and it gets that time during sleep."

"And that creativity is essential to your health."

"So what happens if you don't get enough sleep?" I asked.

"Well, you've felt the effects, haven't you? You can't think straight. A classic brainwashing technique is to deprive someone of sleep. You get disoriented, lose your willpower, question your beliefs. You can create your own torture chamber by stressing yourself out so much you can't sleep, and then you go to the doctor for help. The medical solution is drugs. Nature's answer is rest. The Kumi method is to avoid the problem in the first place."

That night I dreamt I was watching myself in a movie. I was on an island in the Caribbean, surrounded by friendly little ghost-like beings, floating all around me as I walked. I had an unusually strong feeling of well-being. Suddenly a hurricane came up. I awoke from the dream to the sound of a howling wind. The front door of the cabin was open and warm air was blowing from every direction. I stepped outside and saw the pines bending with the wind. Slabs of ice were sliding off the roof and rivulets of water were flowing down the paths previously covered with snow. Water was dripping everywhere. It must have been fifty degrees. Was I still asleep and dreaming? Just yesterday I had icicles in my nose.

Kumi came in and closed the door. "Chinook," he said.

"What's that?"

"A weird weather condition. A warm wind suddenly comes up from the west. Thaws everything out. Really screws people up. They think winter's over, but don't be fooled. Two days from now it'll be freezing again. I call it 'false spring.'"

We ate breakfast and Kumi showed me his nutrition charts. I made notes on my laptop. I felt weirdly disoriented by the weather.

"That's natural," Kumi said. "You're expecting one thing and the opposite happens, so learn to go with it. A good metaphor for health."

"Marion, I need your help. You were right. I've been going at this whole thing like an ape. Please come over when you get home from rehearsal."

She'd probably check her voice mail from the theater, where they were rehearsing an off-Broadway revival of a sixties musical. She said Kumi's visualization techniques helped her memorize her part. When I told her how I put my images on a mountain top, she tried putting hers on top of skyscrapers. "I see my first act entrance on top of the World Trade Center!" she said.

When she arrived we went out for sushi, her favorite food. Normally I would have suggested a steak house, but Kumi said big chunks of beef drain energy. ("Just look at a lion panting after a kill. He can't even sleep he's so fatigued trying to digest all that protein.")

I apologized for the way I'd been acting and I asked her if she'd "Kumi" me on the subject of food, and health in general. Normally I don't think she would have accepted my apology so quickly, but it was such a switch for me to talk about health that I think I caught her by surprise. So she reluctantly agreed. Maybe she felt I was doing this for her as well as myself, which was partly true. But I could see she was keeping a kind of "wait and see" attitude. I'd have to prove I was seriously interested in getting my act together.

She had me make lists of all the things Kumi wanted me to eat and tape them to the bulletin board in the kitchen. I even had food tips taped to the mirror in the bathroom. Kumi had given me simple recipes he says "even you could learn to make." He said if I ate the right things, I could eat practically all I wanted, because good food satisfies you and you simply stop eating when your body has what it needs.

Together we joined a health club on West 74th Street, just two blocks from my Riverside Drive apartment. They had a pool and a large gym where I could jog. Marion would teach me how to play squash. "That way I'll get my revenge," she said.

I started doing calisthenics for about fifteen minutes every morning to get my body going. Marion has some good ones she learned in aerobics, more like dancing, so I put on Sting. A good waker-upper.

Kumi had given me a couple of good books on nutrition and natural healing that I began reading. At first, I didn't see any sense in studying nutrition—after all, I went to him to regain my confidence and learn how to organize my life, not take cooking lessons. But he convinced me that if you want to perform at your best in life you need to take care of the instrument you perform with—your body and brain. And while you can trick your brain, you can't fool your body where nutrition is concerned. No amount of visualizing is going to turn Doritos chips into whole grains.

I began to see that studying the effects of food on my system was an adventure in itself, like taking a trip into a whole new universe. I was amazed at how complex and interdependent our body chemistry is. For example, the B vitamins are a chain. If I take one B vitamin over a long period I will increase my need for all the B vitamins, and the increased need for those I don't take can create a B deficiency and weaken the chain. And cholesterol— if I eat too little of it my body may over-produce it! I realized good health was not just a toss of the coin, but something I can create if I take the time to learn about it. I wanted to be like that arctic willow Kumi showed me, strong and self-reliant.

It occurred to me that Gregor might be more of a human being if he ate better. He certainly knows nothing about nutrition. How could I ever get anything across to him? I'm lucky if I can get him to respond.

I noticed his eyes were always down left or straight left and right. If my analysis of the eye positions is right, he's doing a lot of internal dialogue and analyzing. What if I talked to him on his own "channels," so to speak? Get him interested in nutrition by reading him some technical stuff. He wouldn't even know I was reading because he never looks at me anyway.

"Say, Gregor, did you know that vitamin C metabolizes phenylalanine and tyrosine and converts folic acid to folinic acid?"

"Also protects thiamine, riboflavin and pantothenic acid against oxidation," he said.

"Uh...yeah, right."

It's one thing to know, and another to apply the knowledge. I was beginning to see a bit of myself in Gregor.

Thinking over this last trip to Kumi, I was reminded of his remark that I'm the sole caretaker of my body. I've been having some serious communication with my all-but-forgotten Jogger part (which I've always kind of thought of as my health part, because I had that old locker-room idea that being "in shape" meant I was healthy, which I see now isn't necessarily so). I told the Jogger I have a new view on health and wanted to renew my relationship with him. (I did this more with a feeling than dialogue, but I sometimes talked to this part, too.) With Marion's help and following Kumi's recipes and food tips, I worked out an eating and exercise plan and put the Jogger in charge of it. (K. said parts like being given responsibilities, like employees being assigned to jobs. It motivates them to have something specific to work toward.)

As I pictured myself exercising, I actually felt a kind of thrill in my stomach area. When I asked my inner committee how they felt about resuscitating my health part I heard cheering! (I better be careful who I talk to about all this parts stuff. I'm trying to build credibility as a businessman in New York and the idea of "talking to your parts" would definitely put me on the fringe list.)

Jogger

"I make sure you exercise for 20 minutes a day and eat a lowfat diet high in complex carbohydrates."

I've been thinking of making a chart of all these new parts I've been developing. First, I copied each part with its job description on a separate piece of paper and put it up on the wall. Then I moved the pages around to see where I liked them in relation to each other. Seeing the relative positions I gave them on the wall told me how I ranked them in importance, although I knew those relationships would probably change from time to time.

From these pages I made one grand chart showing all the parts on one piece of paper. This comprehensive chart went on a bulletin board over my desk, where I could review it daily and see what the parts were doing for me. This gave me a kind of boost and reminded me of the goals I was setting for myself. I decided to call this "Charting."

Chart # 1: My Parts So Far

Looking at my Chart, I recalled Kumi's remark when I told him I was a little concerned that maybe I was becoming a multiple personality. "We're all multiple personalities. The difference between the certifiable MP and you is that you know who your parts are and have an open communication with them, or are beginning to anyway. The trouble begins when you start dissociating from these parts and they begin to operate unilaterally. That begins with a part of you doing something that's not 'like you.' At the extreme, you could wake up one morning in the wrong town and wonder how you got there."

(My notes on Kumi foods are on page 309)

9

WALK-ONS

...THE LONGEST WALK OF MY LIFE

"Off-stage you are in your own private world. On stage is a public world. To perform, you have to get from the one world to the other. Between these two worlds you are nowhere—no longer where you were and not yet where you're going. I call this in-between area 'no man's land.'"

When I first mentioned the idea of having Kumi come to New York, Marion was suspicious. Her feelings about Kumi were split. Although she liked what he was doing for me, she felt he was gaining too much importance in my life. I didn't know if that meant I was becoming dependent on him or somehow growing away from her.

"What would he do here?"

"You said his stuff sounds like it might be good for actors. I thought you might want to meet him, do a little work with him."

"Why not?" she answered a little too quickly, not looking at me. We were sitting in my apartment watching the sunset over the Jersey skyline.

"Look, Marion, this is only if you feel okay with the idea."

"Maybe Charles would like to meet him, and his new girl friend."

"New girl friend?"

"A law student from Korea. Her name's Kim Sun-ee."

"You've met her?"

"Yes."

"Why haven't I?"

"You haven't been here. You're either in the mountains or in your computer dungeon."

A tugboat made its lonely sound on the Hudson.

"If you don't want him to come I'll cancel it."

"No, I want to meet him. I want to see what he's really like."

I felt a strange uneasiness going to the airport to pick up Kumi. In addition to Marion's on-the-fence feeling about Kumi, something had been bothering me all week about his visit. It had more to do with me, and every time I asked myself (my selves) what was the matter, I wouldn't let myself get close to the answer. I saw Kumi waiting for us near the security area at LaGuardia, an open space of some twenty feet was between us, but it felt like a mile. I walked toward him with apprehension.

I think Kumi sensed my feelings, but Marion was oblivious because she was paying attention to Kumi, not me. If she had any mixed feelings about meeting him you wouldn't have known it from her behavior. She'd be the perfect host in a political situation, because you'd never know what she was really feeling. They talked the whole way from the airport back to Manhattan. Kumi was extremely charming. He told Marion about a little boy he'd been playing and exchanging jokes with on the airplane.

"Have you heard the one about the lion who said to the monkey 'Who's the king of the jungle?'" Kumi said. "'Oh, you are Mr. Lion,' the monkey says. Then the lion pins down this boa constrictor with his claws and says, 'Who's the king of the jungle?' 'No question about it,' says the snake. 'You are.'"

Kumi had Marion enthralled with his child-like enthusiasm as a storyteller.

"Then he walks over to this big elephant and says, 'Hey, Jumbo, who's the king of the jungle?' And the elephant wraps his trunk around the lion, waves him around in the air and throws him into a tree.

"'Well', the lion says, 'just because you don't know the answer you don't have to get nasty about it.'" Then Kumi whooped with laughter.

My son, Charles, and his girl friend Sun-ee were also coming into town late the same day. They were driving in from the University of Michigan to join us for sessions with Kumi and would be staying in my apartment. Sun-ee was studying to be a litigator. I felt an instant kinship with her. She moved with grace and had a way of turning her head slightly to the side when she spoke. Most of her life had been in the States, but Korean mores were still deep in her blood and she was embarrassed at the idea of sharing a room with Charles in his father's house. That meant Charles got the couch.

But not everything went as planned. When we told Kumi we had arranged to go to the Inuit exhibit at the Whitney museum he shook his head.

"I don't want to see the work of a bunch of Eskimos," he said. "I know all that stuff."

Marion and I looked at each other. "This exhibition is a big deal in New York, Kumi. They've got sculptures," I said.

"I've got sculptures all around me in the mountains," he said. "What do I need to go to a museum for?"

"Well, what would you like to see while you're here?" Marion said.

His eyes saucered and he said, "I want to go to one of those big video arcades."

"Video arcade!" Marion said.

"I heard you were adventurous," Kumi said.

"But those places are so tacky."

"Venture out, meet the other half. You're an actress—get some new ideas for the stage."

We found a video palace on Times Square that was almost a half a block long. A giant fat man wore an apron with pockets full of quarters. The customers were a mix of rough-looking teenagers and street people who worked the machines with competitive desperation. The room was hot and the air smelled of body sweat and damp clothes. A cacophony of sirens, beeps and whistles assaulted the ears, like a dozen car alarms going off at once. Kumi bought a handful of quarters and went from game to game, shooting aliens, knocking off muggers, fighting wild animals and driving racing cars. Marion looked pale in the neon lighting, but the more she watched Kumi the more fascinated she became. "He's like a kid," she said.

When we left, my ears were ringing. Kumi saw the marquee of a Bruce Willis action movie. "Can we go see that?" he said. So we sat through a barrage of explosions and machine guns and cars running off cliffs and helicopters crashing in fiery heaps. Kumi was absolutely mesmerized, staring at the screen and eating popcorn.

We got to Marion's apartment past midnight, bushed except for Kumi, who wanted to sit up and watch television. He was staying at Marion's because Charles and Sun ee would be with me.

"Well, I've had it," I said. "I'll see you guys tomorrow."

When I got to my place I found that Charles and Sun-ee had arrived earlier in the evening. Charles was already asleep on the couch and the door to the guest room was closed, so I assumed Sun-ee was also asleep. I took an aspirin and went to bed.

About seven-thirty in the morning the phone rang. It was Marion.

"Kumi doesn't feel so good," she said. "Can you come over?"

I left a note telling Charles we would be at Marion's. When I got there, Kumi was in the bedroom, holding his stomach and groaning. "What's wrong, Kumi?"

"Oh, those little yellow flowers," he said faintly.

"He means the popcorn," Marion said. "He finished the bag last night."

"You ate all that popcorn?" I said, trying to see his eyes.

"Uh-huh."

"That was a family-size bag, Kumi."

"Uhhhhh."

"Look at you...and after the way you lectured me on nutrition."

"Uhhhhh."

I walked into the living room. "Didn't you give him dinner last night?"

She looked at the floor. "He wanted to snack in front of the tube. He ate some leftover pizza, a bag of potato chips, a can of sardines and a jar of pickles."

"Omigod, Marion."

"So I screwed up. I'm not perfect you know. And he's not the easiest person in the world to control."

"So now what?"

"I just offered him an Alka-Selzer and some Pepto Bismol but he said he didn't want anything," she said.

We ate breakfast in silence. I looked at my watch. "Charles and Sun-ee are due any minute. I better call and tell them not to come. There won't be any session today."

The doorbell rang and Marion let Charles and Sun-ee in. We offered them breakfast and explained what happened. I apologized. "I guess this is a big adventure for him and he just went ape," Charles said.

Suddenly Kumi appeared looking chipper and smiling. "Are you guys ready?" he said

"Kumi," I said, looking at him in surprise. "Are you okay?"

"Of course I'm okay," he said, rubbing his hands together. "Got anything good to eat? I'm starved."

"How'd you recover so quickly?" Marion asked. "Don't tell me you've got a technique for that too?" Marion said.

"It's called the ancient ritual of the water closet," Kumi said. "You go to the smallest room in the house, kneel before the magic bowl, raise your arms in an apologetic incantation to God, and then insert a finger deep into your throat."

"Okay, I think I got it," I said.

"There's a second part that's really interesting…"

"No, Kumi, that's plenty!" I said. "Say hi to Charles and Sun-ee."

He shook Charles' hand and bowed to Sun-ee. "Welcome. We're going to have fun today." He took his tea and toast into the living room and looked around for a moment. "Set up chairs like this," he said, indicating a half circle near the wall on the long side of the room. When we sat down, we were like an audience facing a stage with two wings, the dining room on our left and the hallway on our right.

"When Nick asked me to come to New York and give some lessons for him and his friends I wondered what would be the best thing to do. Then I thought, Marion's an actress, Charles is studying to be a newscaster, his friend Sun-ee…do I have your name right…?"

"Yes," Sun-ee said.

"…Sun-ee is studying to be a courtroom lawyer…criminal law…?"

"That's right."

"To protect the innocent, like me?"

Sun-ee smiled.

"So I asked myself what you all had in common and the answer was, in one way or another, you are all performers. That includes Nick, who's venturing out on his own, meeting people, raising money and so forth. To me, an entrepreneur is a performer."

"And Matt will be joining us on Saturday. He's a surgeon," I said.

"Well, a surgeon's certainly a performer," Kumi said.

"How do you define a performer?" Charles said.

"A performer is someone who performs a skill under pressure with a time limit and usually under observation," Kumi said without blinking.

"Well, that seems to cover it," Charles said.

"But in deciding what I would do with you, I wanted to present techniques that would be useful in both your work and your life. So, as you learn these techniques think about how you could use them in various contexts."

"So what are we going to do today?" Marion said.

"Watch."

Kumi walked out of the room and disappeared into the hallway. We looked at each other, wondering what was going to happen.

That uneasy feeling came back to me again. Our work in the mountains had been very intimate, and now I would be working with him in a group—and in the city. I realized I didn't want to share him. I even resented Marion's presence.

Kumi came back into the room with a sprightly gait and an engaging smile, stopped in the center of the room and said, "Good morning. My name is Kumi. I play video games and experiment with exotic food combinations. Thank you." He smiled and exited to our applause, maintaining this cheerful state until he disappeared into the dining room on our left.

He reappeared and said, "I call this a walk-on. It's what we're going to do this morning. The idea is to make your audience feel welcome and to make yourself feel that your audience is welcoming you. The mechanics are simple. Enter from over there as I did," indicating the hallway on our right, "walk out and introduce yourself, tell us what you do, say 'thank you' and exit."

We looked at each other. Charles, who was sitting at the end, said, "I guess I'm first." I began to feel uneasy, knowing my turn was coming up soon. I would be expected to perform well since I was Kumi's student.

Charles exited and a moment later came walking in. I realized I had never seen him appear in front of people in this way, and I was suddenly moved at how adult he looked. His walk was more lumbering than Kumi's and he looked straight ahead as if he were controlling himself in order to get through a difficult task. At the center of the room he turned and looked at us.

"Good morning. My name is Charles Cole. I'm a struggling student. Thank you."

We gave him a perfunctory round of applause. Looking straight ahead, he walked "off-stage" and circled back around to his chair.

Kumi nodded to Sun-ee. She floated gracefully out of her chair as if pulled by a string attached to her mid-section. She looked down shyly and walked out.

When she reappeared, she walked with perfect posture and an elegant gait, eyes partly down, stopped in the center of the room, turned and looked at each of us for a moment and said, "Hello. My name is Kim Sun-ee. I am studying law and plan to be a litigator. Thank you."

She walked off, again with grace, as if she were on a narrow path and wanted to be sure not to misstep.

When Sun-ee sat down, I got up and left the room. My heart was racing and I felt very nervous. "We're only in Marion's living room," I said to myself, but I felt I was appearing before a group of strangers. I walked out and introduced myself.

"Good morning. I'm Nicholas Cole." I felt tense but I covered it up with a joke. "I'm the host for our video-game specialist from the northwest. Thank you." I acknowledged the warm patter of applause and walked off, and then came back and sat down.

Marion said, "My turn," and got up and walked out. I knew her entrance would be good and I felt almost jealous about it. We waited for a long moment. She walked crisply to the center of the room, head high and shoulders back.

"Good morning breakfast lovers, and honored guest," she said, nodding toward Kumi. "I'm Marion, and I'm the star of the home shows in this apartment. Thank you." Charles said 'Yeay' and whistled and we applauded as she walked off into the dining room in the same manner as she had appeared, like a queen.

Kumi stood up and looked at us. "So, how did that feel?" he said.

"Like the longest walk of my life," Charles said.

We all laughed. "That's how most people feel," Kumi said. "I know a professional actor who can go through a whole evening as a character in a play, but ask him to get up and say a few words in public as *himself* and he breaks out in a sweat. The walk-on is one of the most difficult things for anybody to do. Isn't that curious? All you have to do is walk in, tell us your name and profession, and leave. So why should that be so nerve-wracking?"

"Well, everybody's watching you," Charles said.

"But haven't you ever been watched by people before?" Kumi said.

"Yeah, but this is different," Charles said. "You feel more self-conscious because you're in front of an audience. You're in the spotlight and they're going to scrutinize everything you do."

"And how you look," Marion said.

"Even here, among friends?" Kumi said.

"We're sure to be compared to each other," Marion said. "'Oh, that was good.' 'How's she going to do it? Oh, not so good.' Like that"

"You mean you're competing with each other?" Kumi said.

I felt my neck get hot. "Well, you want to do your best," I said.

"I appreciate that," Kumi said. "But the truth is, the walk-on catches most people by surprise. You may have spent a lot of time preparing your presentation, but you probably gave no thought at all to how you're going to get *to* your presentation."

"What do you mean," Charles said.

Kumi walked over to the hallway. "You are here, off-stage, waiting to go on, and in a moment you will be over there," he said, pointing to the center of the living room, "addressing an audience. These two positions represent two completely different worlds. Off-stage you are in your own private world. On stage is a public world. To perform, you have to get from the one world to the other. Between these two worlds you are nowhere—no longer where you were and not yet where you're going. I call this in-between area 'no man's land.'"

Kumi stepped to the center of the "area" and looked at us. "This innocent little walk of twenty or thirty feet between these two points can be torture for any performer who hasn't planned for it. Today we're going to learn how to make the transition between these two worlds. And we're going to learn *when* to make it. You won't be making the transition here," he said, pointing to the "on stage" area, "you will make it there," pointing to the hallway. "I want you to be completely into your performing state *before* you ever walk on."

"But first, let's comment on the walk-ons we just did."

Charles groaned.

"We're not going to criticize each other. What I'm interested in right now is the *feeling* you got from each person's walk-on. I want you to become aware of the effect your walk-on can have on an audience."

Marion spoke first. "I think Charles came across as a good-natured person, but I got the feeling he didn't really want to talk to us, that he wanted to get it over with."

"You hit it!" Charles said. "I wanted to get the hell out of there."

"And Marion?" Kumi said.

"She looked very good, very outgoing." Charles said. "But maybe a little, uh, how could I put it…?"

"Kind of professional—like a talk show host," I said.

I felt Marion look at me, but I kept looking at Kumi.

"And Sun-ee."

"Oh, she floats like a bird when she walks, so beautiful," Marion said. "I felt calm just watching her."

"Yes, she walks and speaks very nicely," I said, "but she felt to me kind of unreachable—as if she were in her own private world." Did I really mean that? Or was I sending up a smoke screen because I was afraid of the criticism I might get for my own walk-on?

Sun-ee nodded.

"And how about Nick?" Was it my imagination that Kumi looked at me with the faintest smile?

"I liked the way Nick walked out," Sun-ee said. "I thought he looked very in control. But maybe a little formal. Not completely letting go."

She said it so kindly I felt a pang of guilt. "Yeah, that's true," I said. "I felt a little stiff."

"And how did you feel in response to that?" Kumi said to Sun-ee.

"A little tense, like I should sit up straight."

"Alright," said Kumi. "Now I'd like you to play back the walk-ons in your mind with special attention to each person's eyes as they entered and exited."

We sat in silence for a long moment. I realized I had been so anticipating my own walk-on I had completely forgotten to notice people's eye movements, which have become so significant to me since creating the eye chart. I tried to quickly play back my walk-on, taking the spectator position with myself. Somehow I couldn't see my own eyes but I got a feeling about me of being someone who was alone, and not in front of an audience.

Charles spoke first. "Everybody's eyes were different. If I remember correctly, Sun-ee looked down. Marion looked at us while she walked on and spoke, and then I think she walked off smiling but not looking at us, right?"

"That's true," Kumi said. "And how about Nick and Charles?"

"They were pretty much the same," Marion said. "Eyes straight ahead and kind of down as they walked, then they looked at us when they spoke, then I think straight ahead as they exited—no, Nick's eyes were down, kind of away from us."

"What do your eyes have to do with the way you walk on?" I asked innocently, feeling like I was harboring my secret discovery about eye movements and wondering if this was the time to spring it.

"Watch me do it again," Kumi said. He walked into hallway, and then came back in, doing the same walk-on he had done before. Now that we were so conscious of the eyes, I noticed that he never took his eyes off of us. We discussed this point and all agreed.

"And what was the effect of that?" Kumi said. "How did it feel?"

"I felt you were really with us the whole time," Marion said. "I thought I did that, too, but I guess I looked away after I talked."

"Yes, and the moment you looked away you lost our full attention, because we felt we lost yours," Kumi said. "Let's all do something together. Everybody look down for a moment. And tell me what that's like for you."

My heart was racing. We all looked down for a few moments and then Marion said, "This is how I feel when I'm alone."

Charles said this was his studying state of mind, or when he was "thinking things over."

"Nick?"

I was trying to relate all this to the eye chart and his question caught me by surprise. "Um, I'm like this when I'm into the computer," I said.

Sun-ee was the exception. She said Korean people often look down during conversation, especially when guests are present.

"That's because it's considered disrespectful to look at people while talking to them, right?" Charles said.

"It isn't that it's disrespectful to look straight at someone, but rather that looking down puts you in a subservient position, like a child who listens and heeds what is being said and is thus showing respect."

"I'm sure you realize that's a cultural thing, Sun-ee," Kumi said. "It's the exact opposite in the West—especially in North America. Here you look at someone when they talk to show you're interested—even when you're not interested. Kids learn this fast. 'Look at me when I'm talking to you,' the mother will say. So the kid looks at her and mom thinks she's got his full attention." We laughed.

"I know," Sun-ee said, "but it's hard to change the habit. The American way is so direct."

"Well, today we're going to change some of our old habits," Kumi said. "Okay, now let's all look up," Kumi said. The room was silent while everyone's eyes scanned the ceiling. When I looked up I saw the mountaintop at Kumi's cabin.

"This feels very different," said Charles. "It's more outgoing, brighter."

"Oh, definitely," said Marion. "I like this position. This is where the action is for me."

"Sun-ee?" Kumi said, looking at her with a smile.

"I agree it's more outgoing. It's a little strange to do it in public, but I'll get used to it."

"For you it's just a question of making a switch from East to West at the appropriate time. In fact we all need to learn how to make that switch—eyes down for going inside, eyes up for going public."

"Alt/tab," I said.

Sun-ee smiled and nodded.

"What's that?" Kumi asked.

"A computer command for switching between documents," Sun-ee said.

"Good idea," Kumi said. "A command for shifting states. We're gon-na shif-ta to the West, *up*, and-a shif-ta to the East, *down*!" Kumi did a little dance step as he spoke the lines like a rap tune. "Everybody do it, c'mon," he said as he started pulling us out of our chairs. "And-a-shif-ta to the West, *up*, and-a shif-ta to the East, *down*!" The others danced around the space and rapped in rhythm with Kumi. I felt silly dancing around the room like a child and left the room.

When I came back they were snacking on sandwiches Marion had pre-pared. She eyed me into the kitchen.

"What's wrong, Nick?"

"I had to go to the bathroom."

"This is no time to talk, but I have to say it." She spoke softly so the others wouldn't hear. Her voice had that sound she makes when she's hold-ing back her anger. "You're still trying to control situations and you don't even know it."

"Sounds like you're trying to control the situation now. If I don't want to dance I don't have to."

"I don't care if you dance or if you walk on the ceiling, but your attitude is affecting the others. Ever since Kumi's been here you've been acting like a jerk."

I studied my sneakers. They needed washing.

"I'm just asking you to lighten up, let go a little—for yourself if not for us."

After lunch, we returned to the living room and our audience set-up. Kumi stood in front and spoke to us.

"This morning I showed you how to control your 'off' and 'on' stage self by switching your eyes back and forth between these two worlds. The eyes-up position says to an audience: 'Hello! I'm here to be with *you*.' You could say this eye position is a performance signal directing your attention outward. This outward attention changes your gait, and the new gait signals you that it's performance time. This is built-in bio-feedback.

"So now we're going to do another walk-on, and this time we will prepare the transition from our inner to our outer world *before* walking on stage. Like this."

Kumi walked into the hallway, standing so we could see him. "Let's pretend you can't see me. I'm a performer standing backstage. A short while ago I may have looked like this," he said, looking down and standing casually. "Maybe I was thinking about lunch, or where I parked the car. Mundane stuff. But now I'm about to go on stage and I look like this." He took a deep breath and looked up, straightening his body, assuming a stance of readiness. "Now I see—and sometimes I can even feel—the audience in my mind. They are expectant. They can't wait to see me. I can't wait to get out there and be with them. I'm visualizing what I'm going to be seeing when I walk on stage and how that's going to feel. I'm looking at the audience and smiling, and they're smiling at me. They like me. As I stand here visualizing all this—or getting the feeling of this image—my eyes are always up, up, up. My concentration is so focused on this vision of what I'm about to do, you could stick a pin in my arm and I wouldn't feel it. I get my cue and here I go. Now I'm going to see my actual audience and my eyes will be level with theirs."

Kumi enters at a natural gait, smiling pleasantly and looking at each of us as he goes. Then he stops in the center, scans the four of us with his eyes, and says, "Hello, you lucky people. I'm Kumi and your life is about to change. Aren't you glad you showed up here today instead of staying home to watch your favorite soap opera? On my channel you're never bored. Thank you."

I laughed and felt myself relaxing. This was the old Kumi of Montana, and I suddenly felt closer to him. We applauded as he bowed and walked off smiling, his eyes finding each of us as he went. He disappeared into the dining room, maintaining eye contact to the last moment. I couldn't take my eyes off of him.

Kumi came back into the living room and said, "That's how I want you to do it. The entrance will be in your own style, but do the preparation as I just showed you, with your eyes up *before* you ever enter. And as you walk on, you *see your audience immediately and keep looking at them every inch of the way until, finally, you're completely off-stage*. That means your eyes never go down. It's almost as if your eyes are pulling you forward, toward the public, always looking ahead, every second you're on stage, even if you have to prop them open with toothpicks. Okay, who wants to do it?"

I felt exhilarated by Kumi's energy. A sense of confidence seemed to pervade the room now that we had a specific technique for approaching the walk-on. Charles got up and walked into the hallway. We watched him as he looked up and took a deep breath. He stood in silence for a few moments and then walked out. The lumbering gait was gone and he appeared taller. He squinted his eyes slightly, conveying a sense of urgency as he looked at us while walking. He stopped in the center of the room, finding our eyes one at a time and then spoke in a commanding voice.

"Good morning. An unconfirmed report from Moscow says that the Crimea has just fallen into the Black Sea. Ukrainian officials hope this event will eliminate the problem of collecting taxes from impoverished voters. This is Charles Cole in Washington."

Maintaining this confident smile he walked off, looking at us as he went. His eyes flicked down at the last second before disappearing into the dining room.

I heard Marion whisper, "Oh," just before Charles exited. When he came back we discussed his walk-on. "It was so good right up to the last second," Marion said, "then it was as if you disconnected just before you finished."

"You're right, I did," Charles said. "I think I was congratulating myself."

"Interesting, the effect that has, isn't it?" Kumi said to us. And then to Charles, "You were very persuasive, and suddenly that feeling was gone."

"You mean I can't even look down *once*?" Charles said.

"Maybe, if it's appropriate, but you created a certain level of intensity and drama, and it was important to hold on to it," Kumi said.

Marion got up and walked into the hallway where we couldn't see her. After a moment, she walked out with a stately gait, looking at us as she went. Then she stopped and spoke. "I am going to sing for you a Brahms lullaby." She took a breath, cast her eyes down for a moment, looked up again and looked at each of us as she sang. The song took a little over a minute. Then she smiled, bowed and walked off, her eyes on Kumi as she exited.

"Well, you all saw what she did," Kumi said.

"She purposely looked down," Charles said. "She came out in this very outgoing manner, but then she wanted to change the mood, so she went inside herself. She turned us around."

"Very effective, wasn't it?" Kumi said. "And then she changed the mood again by looking at us, and she stayed that way right through to her exit. In fact, she looked at me as she left, but looking at one person in the audience can sometimes be like looking at the whole audience. How many of you noticed that her eyes did flick down for a split second just after she entered?"

"Oh, damn, I wondered if you were going to catch that," Marion said, hitting her hand on her leg.

"It was very slight," Kumi said, "but the overall effect would have been a bit stronger if your *only* downward glance had been the intended one. But that's what we're doing this exercise for. Going in and out of yourself is an unconscious process that we do all day long. We're paying *conscious* attention to it here now to control it and make us better performers."

Sun-ee got up and walked to the hallway. She re-entered with quiet dignity, walking slowly, looking at us as if we had just asked her a question. Then she stopped and spoke. "And so, ladies and gentlemen of the jury," she said, casting a slow glance at each of us, "you can punish this man for eating a jar of pickles, or you can ask yourselves if he hasn't suffered enough for his indiscretion. Thank you." She turned and walked out, looking at us half the way and then looking straight ahead to exit.

Suddenly she popped her head back in the room and, with an anxious look, said to Kumi, "You're not offended, are you?"

Kumi held up his hands like he was being arrested and said, "Your honor, I promise as long as I live I will never eat another pickle."

"I felt completely under her spell," I said. "I do think if she'd kept her eyes on us all the way to the end of her exit, that would have been more dramatic. She was riveting up until then and I didn't want that mood to change."

Sun-ee nodded.

"I agree, though I do think she won her case—no plea bargain necessary," Kumi said with a wink to Sun-ee. "Okay, Nick."

I walked out and stood in the hallway. I took my time getting ready. I visualized the group as Kumi had suggested and I saw myself going out and addressing them. I squeezed my fingers and took a deep breath and then walked into the living room. Jack Nicholson was right beside me and I felt very at ease. At the center of the room I stopped and was surprised to hear myself say, "I just want to say how much I'm enjoying being with all of you today. Thank you."

I walked off keeping my eyes on everybody and then turned at the portal of the dining room and waved goodbye, walking away backwards so I could keep my eyes on them. I bumped into the dining room table, upsetting two Javanese cups.

I had to laugh along with everyone else, but I also got a hand.

We took a break and I made tea while Marion prepared a snack. As we passed each other she touched my arm softly. We sat in the easy chairs in the living room and talked.

"You emphasized the importance of holding the audience's attention every second until you're completely off," Sun-ee said. "Why is that so important?"

"You're not there just to deliver a speech or a song or an appeal to a jury," said Kumi. "You're delivering *yourself*. As long as you are visible to your public, your performance is still going on. You may be performing words or music, but the main communication is your state of mind. If you break that state of mind at *any* point in your performance we will see and feel it. You saw the effect when Charles dropped his eyes for just a blink before leaving—the dramatic effect he had created collapsed. In other words, your state of mind is our state of mind—if you lose it, for even a split second, we lose it."

"Kumi, just for the sake of argument, what would happen if you didn't change from your inner world to the public world before entering?" I said.

"You run the risk of not connecting with your audience. I was at a dinner in a private home with some classical musicians who were about to perform a new piece of music. To my surprise, the soloist opened up a little silver box, took out some marijuana, rolled herself a cigarette and smoked it. I know jazz musicians used to smoke dope before playing, but I'd never heard of concert musicians doing that. When I asked her about it she said, 'I am of the belief that if I feel good, the audience will feel good, too.'"

We chuckled. "Well, that's one way to do it," Marion said.

"Oh yes," said Kumi. "She felt so good that her seventeen-minute performance lasted over twenty minutes, which is a huge difference in a piece of music because timing is so important. The composer was furious. Some of the audience walked out."

"She wasn't thinking about her audience at all," Sun-ee said. "She was thinking about herself."

"She should have been thinking about her future, because she's gonna lose work." Charles said.

"We're talking about communicating with the audience," Marion said, "but isn't the eyes-up idea also a way to remind *yourself* that you're about to do something special?"

"Good way of putting it," said Kumi.

"I have a friend who was in a Broadway musical," Marion said. "One night she came out to do this song and she went completely blank. The orchestra stopped and started again but she just stood there. Then she said to the audience, 'I don't know what's wrong with me. I've sung a hundred and fifty-seven performances of this musical and I just forgot the words.' Then she said, 'Oh, I remember' and sang the song. Wow, what a hand she got!"

"Sure, everybody could identify with that," Charles said.

"Right," Marion said. "If she hadn't been honest about it they would have crucified her. Instead she was a hero. But you know what she said to me afterward? 'I forgot I was going on stage.' She had sung so many performances of that musical—eight shows a week—she could hardly tell the difference between her daily life and her performing life. So I think it's a great idea to have a way to tell yourself—'Here I go, I'm about to do this really important thing and people are depending on me.'"

The words "depending on me" cut right through to me. The only way I'd ever thought of anyone depending on me was financially—it's my job to pay the bills. But the idea of people depending on me emotionally was new.

"I have a question, Kumi," Charles said. "The basic smiling walk-on you had us do, isn't that kind of the 'plastic' variety? You know, 'Here I am, the big success,' and all that stuff. Is that really the best kind of entrance always?"

"No, it depends on the audience and the occasion. In some cases, an energetic, smiling walk-on might be resented. Take for example a scientist giving a talk to colleagues, or a politician addressing the press on a serious issue. Can you imagine a minister or rabbi stepping before a congregation in a 'hale and hearty' frame of mind? They'd think he was selling shares in Heaven."

"I've seen one or two like that," I said.

"On the other hand," said Kumi, "if a priest were announcing a bingo game, a brisk walk-on and a lighter spirit might be just the thing. The rule is to be your most natural self and have a sense of the appropriate mood for the occasion."

"Well, today's talks weren't all 'hale and hearty,'" Marion said. "Charles' news report was dramatic and Sun-ee's talk to the jury was quiet."

"The idea," said Kumi, "is to communicate with your audience in the most effective way possible. When Marion looked down to set the mood for her song, she wasn't really going inside herself—or maybe she was a little bit." Kumi looked at Marion.

"I wanted to establish the mood for myself," Marion said, "but I was very aware that people were watching me and I was hoping that they would go into that mood with me."

"Yes," Kumi said, "she was sending a message about what she expected us to do. That's how she pulled us in. So, you can walk in fast or slow, be smiling or solemn, speak loud or soft, just so you do what is appropriate to connect with this particular audience. And that's easiest and most natural when you are directing yourself outward, toward others."

"I once heard an actor say you can't hide on stage," Charles said. "The way you walk, the way you sound, the way you move your hands—all these things say more than your words."

"You can use that to your advantage when you perform," Kumi said. "Think of the message you want to send. If you think, 'I want your attention, I have something important to give you,' then every unconscious gesture you make will convey that message to your audience. Remember, walk-ons are not just for the stage. They can be for something simple, like entering your workplace in the morning. Then you don't get caught off guard by some business matter simply because you were still in your casual state."

"A student could use it prior to an exam," Sun-ee said.

"But who'd be your audience?" said Charles.

"You don't have to have an audience for a walk-on," Kumi said. "The walk-on is really an exercise for switching mental states, making sure that you have the appropriate state of mind for the occasion. For an exam perhaps you imagine the exam room and how it'll look. Maybe even how you'll look in it when taking the exam."

"I could use it when I go to ask for money for my project," I said.

"I'm pretty good at walking on stage, but I still get the shakes when I have to audition," Marion said.

"Maybe your walk-on could start at home," Kumi said. "Use it as a transition state between your apartment and the audition?"

"In New York, I think it's safer to pay attention to your surroundings when you leave your apartment. You need to be alert. But when I get to where I'm going I could start the walk-on."

"How about a walk-on for the city streets?" Charles said. "Imagine the muggers, the car thieves. 'Hey, fellahs, how's it going. Leave the hubcaps, will ya?'"

"This will be very useful for me," Sun-ee said, "but I'm afraid I might forget to use it when I need it."

"I think you have to practice it until it becomes second nature," Marion said. "Same thing with new acting techniques. I need to do them over and over or I might forget them."

"I used to practice walk-ons every day," Kumi said. "I would do a walk-on rehearsal prior to every high-pressure situation. I still practice them for situations that are new to me, to get the focus."

"I think that's true for all these exercises," I said. "At first they seem strange—in fact some of them *are* strange—but after you practice them a while they can become automatic. Like visualizing. When did I start that, August? Now it's April. It's still a stretch for me, but sometimes I find myself doing it without even thinking about it."

Kumi looked at Sun-ee. "I suggest you take a few minutes every day and just repeat to yourself, 'Eyes up—eyes up—eyes up.' That may seem mechanical at first, but it will shake you out of your old pattern. In fact, we all need this, so let's do it right now." Kumi stood up and waved us to our feet. "Everybody walk around and say it over and over—'eyes up—eyes up—eyes up.'"

For the next few minutes we milled freely around the living room, repeating this command out loud and looking up. We sounded like a religious group reciting some strange prayer.

"Freeze!" cried Kumi. We all froze in position. "Recall the two walk-ons you did today. See yourself walking in the first time. Listen to the way you sounded and watch yourself exit. Then see yourself preparing for your second walk-on with the eyes-up position. Notice what's different the second time you entered and spoke. Compare the *feeling* you get from each walk-on."

We stood there in a silent freeze-frame, watching ourselves. I half-saw, half-felt my first walk-on, which looked stiff and tense. I got a clearer picture of the second one, which was relaxed and confident. My voice was also fuller the second time, and I spoke more slowly. I was impressed at how good I looked. I'd held the group's eyes to the very end. My bumping into the table seemed unimportant, even funny to me now.

"Now imagine where you will want to use this new technique in the near future," Kumi said, "and how it will affect your state of mind and your presentation. See it happening, notice how it feels. Be there for a moment and notice the response of others and the results that brings."

I imagined myself demonstrating a holographic computer video to a group of backers in this new way. First I saw myself doing an excellent job and noticed their enthusiastic response, like I was watching a movie. Then I stepped into the image and felt myself doing it as if I were actually there. The presentation felt very comfortable. I stayed in this state for a moment and then "returned" to the present, feeling confident about the presentation. Was this wishful thinking? Or a natural response to the performance I saw and felt myself giving?

We agreed to meet again at ten the next morning. Marion and Sun-ee had some shopping to do and Kumi went in to lie down. Charles and I sat down with a beer.

"How would you like to help me with my walk-ons," I said.

"Me? But wouldn't you want to ask someone like Marion? She's got the experience."

"That's why I don't want to ask her. You're in the same boat I'm in. We're both learning it, so I think we could help each other."

"Well, yeah, I'd like that."

"Do you have any suggestions? Now?"

"There's one thing." Charles stood up and put down his beer. "I get the impression you, well, like you're trying too hard sometimes. Kind of overkill. Your natural way when you're speaking is really nice—I always liked the way you told stories to me when I was a kid. What if you had that same feeling when you spoke in public, kind of relaxed and intimate."

He walked around the room demonstrating how I might look if my physical demeanor reflected the story-telling state of mind he was talking about.

"Why don't you try it. Here, I have an idea."

I stood up and he positioned me, then sat down on the floor, like a child in a classroom.

"Now talk about computers, but tell it to me as if it were a bedtime story and I am five years old."

I turned away from him quickly to hide the tears that were coming to my eyes. I grabbed a handkerchief and blew my nose, clearing my throat to mask the sudden flood of emotion that the memory of him as a child evoked.

"Okay, now…give me a minute. Do you want me to walk on?"

"Whatever."

I walked to the edge of the rug and looked down a moment. This was tricky. I'm supposed to talk technical computer stuff, like to a class at NYU, but with the feeling of telling Charles a fairy tale. I got the picture in my mind of young Charles and then a group of children who might be waiting for a good adventure story. I turned and walked toward Charles, who was my live audience, and stopped. I burst out laughing and Charles laughed.

"Wait a minute. Let me do it again."

I walked off, took a deep breath and looked up, waiting a moment. Then I turned and walked on. I stopped and looked at Charles, and then spoke as if I were saying, "Once upon a time…"

"To create a primary file for form documents, you have to know the field number for each variable item."

Charles looked entranced. "That's it! That's the idea. The words are dry as toast, but it sounds like an adventure story." He jumped up and said, "What if you said something like, 'Once upon a time there was a king who needed to create a primary file for form documents.'"

I said, "And he called together his knights and proclaimed…"

"…my daughter for the man who finds a field number for each variable item," said Charles.

We applauded ourselves and exchanged high fives.

"I think that calls for another beer," I said.

We walked to a student bar-restaurant near Columbia University and ordered two pints of draft and giant hamburgers with everything. (Sorry Kumi, just this once.) It must have been past twelve when we finally called it a night.

Sun-ee was asleep when we got back and Gregor was working in my office. I said goodnight to Charles and sat in bed with my laptop to make some notes and add a new part to my Chart:

State Maker

"I prepare your state of mind
appropriately for any event. "

I got this odd image of The Loving Mate talking to the State Maker, suggesting I use the walk-on technique not only for public performance but also to help me switch into the right state of mind for social and personal relationships. Marion has been concerned that I spend so much energy on my work I short-change my time with her, and that when I am with her I'm not fully there. Perhaps a State Maker/Loving Mate alliance will make me pay equal attention to home and work, and help get Marion and me back on track. Charting seems to make these things clearer.

On the subject of promises, Kumi has reminded me time and again to make sure I keep the promises I make to my parts. He said that breaking agreements with myself can have a demoralizing effect on parts. They can lose faith and become sluggish. That's when I become tired for no reason, or depressed or even ill. He said that's why it's important to check in with parts, take a quiet moment, look inside myself, ask for feelings. I told him that idea sounded a little hokey to me, that everyone knows germs and viruses create disease. I recalled our dialogue:

"Yes, but it's your immune system that fights off those germs and viruses. And for that it needs energy."

"But loss of energy results from stress, overwork, lack of sleep."

"You are the sum total of your parts, Nick. When they don't sleep, you don't sleep. Insomnia is unfinished business—the restlessness of a dissatisfied group of workers unsure of what they're supposed to do."

I still feel a little weird about the idea of communicating with inner parts. How do I know they're really there? How can I be sure I'm getting a message through to them, or that I'm getting their message? Kumi says I need to be open to my senses, that my body is sending me messages constantly. I remembered my challenge to him:

"How can you be so sure of that, Kumi?"

"How's the temperature in here for you?"

"A little chilly. "

"How do you know?"

"Alright, you're going to tell me I felt it. But that's not necessarily a message from some part of me. That might be just instinct. I'm talking about things like ideas and emotions."

"How do you know when you have an idea or an emotion?"

"It just comes to me."

"How?"

"How do I know? I just hear a … I don't know."

"You hear a voice, or get a feeling, or see an image."

"Alright, so…?"

"So how many messages are you missing because your head or your heart is turned off. Your brain is like a giant internet. I'm saying stay on-line, get your messages."

Question: Why have I been feeling so uneasy with Kumi in a group? Is it that I want him all to myself? That's a childish thought. C'mon, State Maker—if you're really there—help me feel better about sharing Kumi with others.

I closed the laptop and looked in on Gregor. He was sipping a giant-size coke and looking at an intriguing equation. I knew I really should get to bed. I sat down at a second console and turned on the screen.

(My notes on Walk-Ons are on page 318)

10

MEETING AMY

...CATCH A BANK ROBBER WITH YOUR VOICE

"Babies can cry for hours and not get laryngitis. That's how you call out when you're crying for your life. I'm just showing you how to revive the voice you were born with."

The next morning didn't go as planned. We were meeting at Marion's for a lesson with Kumi at ten o'clock. Charles, Sun-ee and I got there shortly before ten, and the doorman said Marion and Kumi had gone out a half-hour before. No mention about where they were going. We went upstairs and I let us in with my key. I couldn't find a note and I was puzzled because this wasn't like Marion—she's so punctual. So, I assumed they'd gone to the store for a few things. I made us a pot of tea, picking up Kumi's habits. At ten-thirty they still weren't back and I started to worry.

Then the phone rang. It was Marion speaking in an excited voice. She was calling from the bank. "You won't believe what happened. Kumi caught a bank robber! We'll be home in a minute." She hung up before I could ask any questions. Her bank was on Broadway, only two blocks away. In a few minutes I heard her key in the door and she and Kumi came bounding in.

"When I turned around you were gone," Marion said to Kumi.

"I didn't want to hurt him—just wanted to catch him. I felt sorry for him," Kumi said.

"So what happened? Tell us!" I said.

"Well, you won't believe this," she said.

"This morning I suddenly remembered that I had to cash a check before the weekend. We get to the bank and had to stand in one of these intolerably long lines. All of a sudden one of the clerks yells, 'Stop thief, stop that man!' I look around and people are pointing towards the entrance. So I run outside and see Kumi running up the block toward West End Avenue chasing this guy who's carrying a cloth bag—I suppose with money. I'm thinking 'Omigod' and I yell at Kumi, but he doesn't hear me because he's yelling 'Police! Stop that man! Police!'

"So I run after him. They turn the corner on West End and go north, and then left on a Hundred-and-Third, and all this time Kumi is yelling 'Police! Police!' in a voice that sounds like a fire siren, and people are looking out their windows. Two guys come down and start running with Kumi, and the robber jumps over the wall into the grass at Riverside Park. Kumi takes the stairs two at a time, and chases him across the baseball field toward the Hudson Parkway, yelling like a monster, when two joggers join in, so now there are five guys chasing him. The robber is starting to limp—Kumi thinks he hurt himself jumping down from the wall—but he gets to the parkway. Traffic is bumper-to-bumper and he runs out into the southbound lane! Brakes are screeching and he's dodging between cars, and they're honking, and now he can't go any further because there's the Hudson River. But he's out of juice anyway and just collapses on the ground from exhaustion. Kumi is standing on the median yelling, 'Give it up, man, there's no place to go.' Then this unmarked police car comes along and the cops see something strange is going on, get out and handcuff the guy and take him away.

"So we go back to the bank and Kumi walks up to the teller and says, 'We caught him,'—and the teller says, "I know, we heard it on the police scanner. Get back in line." Well I give that teller holy hell and go to the bank manager and tell him what happened. He says 'Oh, was he the guy?' and takes down our name and phone number. Then I called you."

I looked at Kumi. "Are you crazy? He could have had a gun."

"I knew he didn't," Kumi said.

"How did you know?" I said.

"Because he didn't use it."

I stared at Kumi, speechless. Just then the phone rang. It was the bank manager calling to talk to Kumi. Kumi listened on the phone for a minute and hung up.

"They're giving me a one-hundred dollar reward and a free lifetime checking account."

"A hundred dollars!" Marion said.

"He apologized for the amount. It's bank policy that they give a percentage of the recovered money. The robber dropped the money bag somewhere along the way, and they only recovered about a thousand."

"You should have stopped chasing him and picked up the money," Charles said.

"Maybe a free checking account means all the money you want for the rest of your life," said Sun-ee.

Kumi chuckled as he went for a drink of water and Marion said, "You wouldn't believe how loud Kumi's voice was. It was echoing off the buildings."

"That's what really got him," Kumi said, as he came back. "That I was yelling so loud. He thought he was being chased by some kind of wild demon. If he'd taken just a second to look at me he would have stopped, bopped me on the head and walked away."

"Where'd you ever get such a powerful voice, Kumi? Did you study singing?" Marion said.

"When I was a kid in the Arctic we used to call to each other. If you got lost in a white-out, your voice was all you had."

"So, how do you project your voice like that?" Marion said.

"I'll show you," Kumi said. "I was going to do some voice work with you anyway. It's very invigorating."

We laughed. Marion started to set up the chairs.

"No, I'd like you to stand up for this," said Kumi. "Voice work is physical." We all gathered in yesterday's performing space and looked expectantly at Kumi.

"The secret is to open the larynx wide—that's your voice box—and you do that by making a nasal sound, like the baa-ing of a sheep—'Ba-hah-hah-hah. Ba-hah-hah-hah-hah.' Or like the crying of a baby." Kumi screwed up his face and cried like a baby—"Waaaaaaahhh." The sound was extremely penetrating.

"You feel that strong vibration in your nose and in your forehead. Kids make this sound all the time. Remember calling to your friends on the play-

ground? Here, let's imagine we're kids and we want to call our friend 'Amy.'"
Kumi demonstrated calling, "Aaaaaaa-meeeeee."

Kumi's voice cut through the room with a sharp, hard-edged nasal sound.
"Let's all do it together," he said, and we joined in with "Aaaaaaa-meeeeeee."
We looked at each other, a little embarrassed at acting like such kids.

"Okay, now imagine Amy is further away—across the hall in the kitchen,"
Kumi said. We called "Aaaaaaa-meeeee" again, this time louder to reach our
imaginary friend two rooms away. The sound was surprisingly strong, almost like a small chorus singing. I was beginning to wonder about the neighbors.

"I don't see how this ties in with the other stuff we've been doing," I asked.

"You're tuning yourself for performance. Your voice is your most persuasive instrument," Kumi said. "Influential people get our attention the
moment they open their mouths because they know how to focus and modu-
late their voices. And when necessary, to use them with strength and power,
like at a political rally.

"Come over here," Kumi said, opening the window looking onto the
courtyard of the apartment building. "Let's imagine Amy is on top of that
building over there and we have to reach her." Kumi had us take a deep
breath and asked us to hold the syllables of Amy's name as long as possible.
So we took a collective inhale and called in a long, loud chorus,
"Aaaaaaaaaaaa—meeeeeeeeeeee."

The sound was galvanizing. We seemed to be connected by a common
vibration that shook our bodies as we filled the courtyard with sound. Kumi
was right—it was invigorating.

Suddenly we heard a voice from one of the windows, "Shut your face,
for crissake, I'm trying to sleep."

Marion covered her mouth and we ducked away from the window. "See?"
Kumi said. "He did it too," referring to the caller. "Did you hear that nasal
sound in his voice? You do it by instinct when you want to be heard."

"I think you made your point, Kumi," Marion said. "But it would be nice
if we could learn this without being evicted."

"Oh, that was just to show you how much power your voice has when
you focus it through the nasal cavities," Kumi said. "The long vowels 'eeee,'
'ayyy' and 'ahhhh' are what open up the voice box. That's where you get
your power. The second syllable of the word 'police' has the 'eeee' sound,
just like the second syllable of 'Amy.' But you can do it softly too, now that
you feel what it's like to get that vibration in your nose. Watch."

Kumi stood on his head and sang "Aaaaa-meeee" in a normal speaking volume. We all stared in amazement.

Still standing on his head, he said, "You hear how my voice sounds in this position? When you stand on your head your larynx opens automatically. Now notice my speaking voice when I stand up." When he stood up and spoke, his voice was deeper and more mellow than usual. "Now I'm getting this warmer sound with no effort, because the voice box is open."

"I'm a little confused, Kumi," Marion said. "You say the sound starts in your nose?"

"You first *hear* the sound when it vibrates in the bones of the nose, but the air starts with a contraction in your abdomen, which forces the air upwards and fills out your chest and then focuses right up here," he said, squeezing the upper part of his nose.

"Don't tell me you have to stand on your head to develop a good voice," I said.

"No," said Kumi, "that's just a quick way to experience it, because your voice box opens automatically when you're upside down. But you can do a kind of half-headstand to get the effect. Here, do it with me."

Kumi got down on his knees and placed his head upside down on the floor as if he were going to do a headstand. In this position he said, "You see, my head is upside down. Now listen to my voice." We heard again the distinct nasal sound. "It's your turn now."

"This is stupid," I said.

"Nick!" Marion burned a hole in me with her eyes.

I was afraid the others were going to laugh at Kumi, and, by association, at me. After all, I brought him to New York. But his nature was so infectious everyone was suddenly kneeling down, heads touching the floor, seats up in the air, looking through their legs. First, he asked us to call "Amy" in a normal voice, then in a soft voice, and I felt the nasal vibration throughout my head. I had to admit, when we stood up and spoke, our voices sounded noticeably fuller, more rich and resonant.

"Now that we're standing up, notice that when you lean your head and torso slightly forward, you get somewhat of the same nasal sound." We leaned forward on a slight angle and spoke again and I found my voice did indeed alter, the sound seeming to vibrate again in the upper palate and nose.

"This way you're using your voice effortlessly," Kumi said. "If you try to sing or speak loudly from your throat using your everyday conversational voice, you won't get any carrying power and you'll tire your voice. In fact you'll hurt your throat. Children's voices don't get tired on the playground because they're using them properly. Babies can cry for hours and not get laryngitis. That's how you call out when you're crying for your life. I'm just showing you how to revive the voice you were born with."

"But I don't want to sound like a crying baby," I said.

"Of course not," said Kumi. "The nasal sound is just to get the sound vibrating in the mask—the bones of your face. Then the voice broadens out by itself, using the head and chest as resonating chambers. But the nasal cavities are the leading edge of the sound."

"That's true," Marion said. "That's how opera singers project their voices. There's always this little bit of a nasal edge to a great voice. You don't notice it unless you listen for it."

"The nasal edge is like a little knife cutting its way through to let out the full strength of the sound," said Kumi.

"What would happen if you didn't have the nasal edge?" Charles asked.

"The sound would center in your throat."

"And that's bad?"

"Your voice would have no carrying power. When you'd try to speak or sing louder you'd be straining and you'd lose your voice."

Kumi demonstrated singing from the throat. When he sang softly it sounded like an amateur voice. When he sang loud from the throat it became a wheeze and he coughed. "It only takes a few minutes of that kind of singing to give yourself laryngitis," he said. "But when you do this"—he leaned forward and focused the sound in his nose and his voice came out with penetrating clarity—"you bypass the throat and send the sound straight to the head."

"Are you saying we should all be singers?" Sun-ee said.

"Not exactly," said Kumi. "For your purposes you want a strong, controlled speaking voice," said Kumi. "And the best way to achieve that is to train your voice as if you were going to be a singer. It all starts with your breathing."

Kumi knelt down on the floor with his back straight, sitting on his heels.

"Back on the floor again?" I said.

"C'mon, join me. Kneel down and let your arms dangle at your sides. Take a deep breath filling out your stomach and lower back and then your chest all the way to your neck, like you're filling your torso with water."

At first, I inhaled too quickly and only partially filled my lungs. I sneaked another quick breath to fill out my torso completely. This was the deepest breath I'd ever taken.

"Then, gently singing a long 'eeee' sound, very slowly lower your torso and head forward down to the floor, allowing the sound to last for one long exhale."

I tried the "eeee" sound but didn't feel the nasal vibration. Then, as I started bending my torso forward, I heard and felt the sound resonating in the bones around my nose. I held the exhaled sound as long as I could as I leaned forward, but I ran out of air just before getting to the floor. I would have to take a bigger breath next time.

"When you're at rest, your chest will be touching your thighs," said Kumi, "and your arms will be resting on the floor. Your hairline will be touching the floor and you will be looking between your knees at your feet."

Looking between my legs I saw Charles behind me.

"Then slowly straighten up your torso into an upright sitting position on one long, slow inhale, again filling your entire lungs with air. Then go back down again, exhaling on the 'eeee.' Let's repeat this about ten times."

We all did the exercise in unison, although Marion and Charles seemed to be able to hold the "eeee" sound longer on the exhale. We sounded like a primitive tribe doing some strange ritual. I felt a little foolish and thought the odd nasal sound I was producing would make others laugh. But nobody was paying attention to me, so I gradually forgot about it. After several repetitions of the exercise I began to feel more relaxed. I noticed as I got closer to the floor on the exhale, that my voice sounded strongly nasal and started to resonate throughout my head, feeling almost the way it does when you get water in your ears. After about ten repetitions I felt light-headed.

Then Kumi asked us to stand and walk around the room speaking in a normal voice. My limbs were extremely relaxed and my voice sounded deep and mellifluous. So did the voices of the others. The irritation I'd been feeling at doing something silly was gone. He asked us to practice speaking to an audience with this voice. We each headed off to find a private corner, I into the hallway speaking to an imaginary backer. My body had a floating feeling, like I was walking underwater. I heard my voice resonating throughout the room and found I was able to project the words effortlessly.

After a while Kumi called us back into the living room. I was deeply relaxed and didn't want the feeling to stop, so I just remained standing in the hallway, squeezing my fingers.

When I returned to the room everyone was seated and Marion was pouring juice. "Do you do this every day, Kumi?" Marion asked.

"For years I did it every day," Kumi said. "Now I do it occasionally, as a reminder when I need it."

"Was this a vocal exercise or a breathing exercise?" Sun-ee asked.

"Both. Two for the price of one," he said grinning. "I call it 'Kneel and Bow to Amy.'"

"They always say newscasters should develop good voices," said Charles, "but they don't show you how—not like this. This is great. I'm going to sound like Prometheus on the mountain."

"Did Prometheus speak from a mountain?" Marion asked.

"I don't know, but he would have if he'd studied with Kumi."

"Let's take a stretch," Kumi said. Marion went to make a phone call and Sun-ee sat down to write out some notes. I looked out the dining room window at the street twenty stories below. The cars looked like toys and the people like insects.

Kumi came up behind me and looked too.

"Once when I was a kid some people were visiting and my uncle took them on a hunt without telling me," Kumi said in a soft voice. "I came out and saw them starting off some distance away with the dogs. I could have caught up with them but I just stood there in the snow, watching them go, feeling sorry for myself. Maybe I felt more that way because he was not my real father and I wanted him to be mine."

Marion interrupted us, offering a tray of snacks. I took tuna fish on a cracker.

"So what does a person do in a case like that?" I said.

"Depends how resourceful the person is," Kumi said, walking back into the living room.

I stood there looking out the window. Sometimes I got tired and sometimes I just got tired of myself. I suddenly took a deep breath and stepped to my right. "A new now," I whispered to myself. "A new now...a new now...a new now."

Kumi called us together again in the living room. "Now that you're aware of this nasal sound, let me show you the microphone hand technique. You might be especially interested in this, Charles. This is another way to achieve the 'Amy' effect in a normal speaking voice. Make a fist and speak into it as if it were a microphone, like this." Kumi held his fist up to his mouth, speaking into the curl of his thumb and first finger. "When you press your fist against your mouth your fist captures the sound and bounces it right back to your ears. The effect is that you hear your voice amplified. It sounds almost like a megaphone—that's the nasal edge."

We all tried it, speaking first in normal voice then with the microphone hand. Sun-ee said, "I'm not getting it," and Kumi asked her to hold her fist closer to her mouth and speak a little louder until she heard the nasal edge. I too needed to speak a little louder until I heard the megaphone sound. Gradually we were commenting on how each other's voices were projecting. We sounded like a group of activists at a rally talking through megaphones.

"This is an especially good technique for rehearsing some written material you have to present. You can pretend you're reading it on the radio," Kumi said, "or into a tape recorder. And, by the way, listening to a taped playback of your voice can be very enlightening. You never sound the way you think you do. You usually find you're speaking faster and higher-pitched than you thought. Good public speakers take their time—it helps enunciation and it's relaxing for the audience."

"I think the 'Kneel and Bow to Amy' is a good exercise just by itself," said Sun-ee. "I do yoga and this breathing exercise is very similar to a yoga technique."

We sat down to have some juice and tea. Marion and I went into the kitchen for cups and glasses.

"Do you have any peanut butter?" I asked.

"No. Does Kumi know you're eating that commercial stuff?"

"He's not my father, you know."

"Sometimes you act like he is."

"What's with you?"

"I was going to ask you the same question."

Before I could answer she carried the dish of snacks out to the others.

"Breath control is basic to performing," Kumi said. "In the first place, it's healthy because it stimulates blood circulation, and your blood carries oxygen to your cells. It's also very relaxing, so it's a natural way to counter stress."

"Taking a deep breath has saved my life more than once," Marion said. "Or the life of the person I wanted to strangle."

"What are you looking at me for?" I said.

Kumi smiled at me. "I also use a deep breath as a separator—a divider for states of mind. For example, let's say you're talking business on the telephone." Kumi got up and went over to the telephone. "Now I'm in my business state of mind. 'Blah, blah, blah,' and then I hang up. Now I want to take my mind off of that conversation and maybe write a letter." Kumi took a deep breath and let out the air. "Now I'm ready to think about what I want to say." Kumi sat down and mimed writing the letter. "Then I'm finished with that and I want to be social, so…" Kumi inhaled and exhaled deeply. "Ahhh. Now I'm ready to be with my friends."

"What would happen if you didn't take the deep breath between activities?" Charles said.

"You might find yourself discussing business in a social state of mind. Or trying to be creative while your mind is still thinking about business." said Kumi. "It helps you sort different activities cleanly, one from the other."

I thought of the many times when I'd be talking to myself about one thing while I was trying to do another.

"So, Kumi, what are you saying? We should do this vocal stuff every day and we'll have more power?" I said.

"You'll have a more powerful speaking voice," Marion said.

"Bill Gates speaks softly and everybody jumps," I said.

"That's because he's a billionaire," she said. "They all want his money."

"But a voice alone doesn't make you influential," I said.

"How about Martin Luther King?" Charles said. "He didn't have any money. But when he spoke everybody paid attention. Just the sound of his voice was moving."

"A beautiful voice is like music," Marion said. "It influences you emotionally."

"And you can scare the hell out of bank robbers," said Charles.

"In fact," said Kumi, "if you ever do get into trouble, a trained voice can be used for self-defense. Criminals are superstitious. Pull a gun and they might shoot you. Yell like a banshee and they freeze."

"That's what the 'ki-yi' is in Karate," said Charles. "It disorients the opponent."

"And focuses your physical power," said Kumi.

"Is that why a powerful voice can break glass?" said Sun-ee.

"Sound breaks glass because sound is physical," said Kumi. "You think sound is just something you hear, but it's a force you actually absorb right through your skin. When you're close to live music you can *feel* the sound of the instruments and voices entering your body. Marion's right. A powerful voice bypasses the mind."

"And goes straight to the heart," Marion said.

Today I recorded a new part for my Chart:

Amy

"I project your voice with power and control."

I was surprised that I'd accept the idea of "voice lessons," but in fact I felt more confident with a controlled voice. But I got a lot of objections from other parts of me concerned about the noise Amy makes. I assured my developing inner community that the last thing in the world I wanted was to have the neighbors hear me baa-ing like a sheep. Kumi said that soft vocal work is as effective as loud, just so I achieve the open larynx nasal sound. Then when I get to an isolated spot in the country or by the ocean I can do some loud practice where no one will hear me. (I do hear singers all the time through the walls and out the windows in New York, but of course they sound slightly more beautiful than I do.)

I asked Amy if she'd like to work with any other part of me, like my Loving Mate/State Maker alliance. Suddenly I heard the word "Communicator" in my mind—just like that. Knowing I have a stronger vocal instrument makes me feel more like communicating with others.

I told Kumi that I was enjoying the idea of working with "parts," and that Charting was getting more and more interesting. But that I was a little concerned about talking to myself like this all the time. Kumi's response, as usual, gave me a whole new slant on it: "But isn't it nice to know you can have an intelligent conversation with someone you're sure is listening?"

Thinking over my behavior these past two days, I wondered if I'd been using Kumi as a father substitute. Is that the strange feeling I had when I saw him in the airport? Because I didn't want to share him? And is that what makes these New York sessions with him so uncomfortable for me? This might be a good time to step out of myself and just observe the interaction between Kumi and me. For that reason, if no other, I decided to show up for the next day's session.

(My notes on Amy are on page 323)

11

TUNING THE HUMAN INSTRUMENT
...NOTHING'S HAPPENED YET, SOMETHING'S ABOUT TO HAPPEN

"Muscles have memory. Every time you have an emotional encounter some muscle in your body reacts and the emotion you experience can lodge itself in that muscle, even disable it with chronic tension. Stretch your muscles daily and you not only dislodge the emotions associated with unpleasant memories, you can prevent stressful emotions from ever implanting themselves there."

On Friday, Marion and I took Kumi out on the town, with one proviso— "No video parlors and no bank robbers." We ate dinner at Lucia's, went to a musical and finished with a glass of wine on top of Manhattan Towers. From the 39th floor you can see the lights for miles. "New York is upside down," Kumi said. "The stars are down below."

"Maybe that's why this town's so screwed up," I said.

"It's not screwed up," Kumi said. "It's the city of trances."

"Trances?"

"Everybody's in his own trance. You're in your computer trance. Marion's in her actor's trance. Charles and Sun-ee are in their student trances. New York's got the Broadway trance, the Wall Street trance, the fashion world trance, the publishing trance—you got everything here, roaring all at once. You walk down the street and everybody's talking to themselves. You talk to them and you're interrupting their internal conversation—the urban trance. Outside New York you've got the suburban trance and beyond that the rural trance, but people in those places interact more because they're in the same trance. Here you've got thousands of different trances colliding with each other. You have permission to be anything you want."

"It's crazy," Marion said.

"No, it's life," said Kumi. "Since I've been here I've seen a guy walking down the street with a bag over his head playing a trumpet, an evangelist giving away dollar bills, a woman taking off her clothes in the middle of Broadway and a blind beggar getting into a Toyota and driving away. Yet nobody seemed to notice. They're each in their own trances. Where else but New York could you see that?"

"I never thought of it that way," said Marion.

"This is the stuff we've been talking about—performance is a trance state. New York should be called Performance City because everybody here's in that state. Walk down the street in this town and you get free lessons in self-hypnosis. And they do it in all this noise and traffic. Maybe that's why they tell actors and musicians to go to New York. Live here a couple of years and you can concentrate under any conditions."

We ended up at Marion's, sitting up and talking into the wee hours. I could see that any fears Marion may have had about Kumi being in my life had softened considerably. This made me feel a little better, because my judgment was vindicated. But I still had an edgy feeling. Even though I'm the one who invited him here, I felt he was giving away something that belonged to me when he shared himself with the group. At one point Marion asked Kumi why he never married.

"I did. My wife was killed in a car accident, but my daughter survived."

"What happened?" Marion asked.

"Drunk driver."

"Did they catch him?"

"Oh, yeah, he was in the hospital, but he walked out after a few days."

"Was your wife Inuit?"

"Finnish."

"Do you miss her?"

"I talk to her every day. She advises me. I'm grateful for knowing her as long as I did."

"I bet you wanted to kill that driver," I said.

"I never wanted to kill anybody. Maybe there was a moment there when I wanted an eye for an eye. But that feeling is destructive. I wasn't going to let him kill me too."

"How old's your daughter?"

"Thirty-two. She's an archaeologist. Working on a site in Guatemala."

"Is she a maverick too?

Kumi looked at Marion and smiled. "I spanked her once when she was a little over two years old. She didn't cry, she just looked at me, and from that look I knew I had something special on my hands."

"You could tell that early?" I said.

"I saw it the day she was born. She was just—*her.* Lying there in that crib, those little black eyes checking me out. She was unique. That's when I realized what's meant by the word 'soul.'"

"You saw it in her," I said.

"No question."

"The one thing no one can take away from you," Marion said.

"You can take it away from yourself," I said.

"Naw," Kumi said. "You can misplace it, but it's always there someplace."

I hoped Kumi was right. As time passed I became increasingly aware of a gap in me that would require more than a few exercises to fill.

"Did you ever spank her again?" Marion said.

"No, but she never crossed the street without looking both ways again either. Kids are born independent. You have to *teach* them to conform."

"Well, we have lots of teachers," Marion said.

"In that case call me an un-teacher."

The next day Matt Bernstein joined us at Marion's for another session with Kumi. Matt is an intense man of seventy-five, a former neurosurgeon who knew a thing or two about performing. His receding hairline is the only sign of his age. His stomach is flat and his penetrating glance is unswerving in its intensity. I've heard him talk about his state of mind leading up to an operation and you'd think you were listening to someone preparing for the Olympic finals. Kumi was impressed that Matt runs up and down the stairs every morning with a thirty-pound pack on his back for exercise and wanted to meet him.

"I've already heard about you," Matt said, shaking hands with Kumi.

"And I thought your kind didn't exist," said Kumi. "A doctor who thinks about health."

"But that's what doctor's do," Marion said, "take care of your health."

"No, they take care of your *illness. That's* what they usually think about," said Kumi.

Matt smiled and nodded his head. "That's right. If somebody's healthy, we're not interested."

"But why should you be? A healthy person doesn't need you," said Marion.

"But we need them," Matt said, "to show us how they do it."

Kumi asked us to clear the largest space possible in the living room, so we moved the sofa, easy chair and table and rolled up the rug. The open area was easily twenty-four by sixteen feet, adequate for six people to move freely. I'd been exercising for the past month playing racquetball with Marion and had lost eight pounds. But since Gregor and I started working late into the night I've been slacking off. I felt the need for exercise. At Kumi's instruction we were wearing loose clothing. We sat in a circle on the floor.

Kumi walked to the center of the floor and slowly started to undress. First he took off his slippers and socks, then he unzipped his fly and wiggled out of his jeans. Underneath he had on black running shorts. Next he unbuttoned his shirt, scanning us with his eyes. He was playing it for full effect and I watched the others for their reaction. Matt was staring at him intently, Charles had his mouth open and Sun-ee's head was tilted to the side like she was watching a bug on a leaf.

Suddenly, Kumi ripped off his shirt and gyrated his hips like a belly dancer. I was flabbergasted. I looked at the others to see if they were embarrassed, but nobody flinched. Kumi rolled his shoulders, first clockwise then counter-clockwise, extended his arms, curling and rotating his wrists and elbows, stretched his hands open with all the fingers spread, turned his hands at right angles to his wrists and wiggled his fingers, shook his hands so fast his fingers were a blur, walked with a dipping action to each knee while holding out his arms and rotating his wrists, one slowly, the other quickly, and making the funniest clown faces. Then he leaped in the air and pulled down an imaginary rope and leaped again, then fell on the floor, stood up again, leaped for the rope and fell again. His skin had a rosy sheen and his movements were fluid and graceful. He looked like a children's toy full of springs, performing a crazy kind of dance.

Afterwards we applauded and Kumi bowed.

"I call that The Tuning Dance. You use these moves to 'tune up' your body before performing. It's made up of six mime isolation exercises that stretch the main tension areas of your body—the shoulders, neck, pelvis, face and hands. But I've laced the moves together into a kind of dance, just to make it more interesting. The Tuning Dance is so easy you can learn it in one day.

"Before we start, I have a request. We will be communicating this morning with the body only. To emphasize that point, I'm going to ask you not to talk throughout the learning of these moves. I want you to learn them without any association to thought—just pure movement. In fact, don't even talk to yourself."

"How do you do that?" Charles asked.

"Imagine your voice is on radio or tape and you're holding a volume control—just lower the volume down to where you don't notice it." He gestured up in the air to demonstrate the point. We must have looked odd reaching up, turning dials and clicking imaginary remotes.

"One more thing before we start. Participate only in the moves that are comfortable for you, especially if you have any physical impairment or have had a recent operation. Use your good judgment about what your body should and shouldn't do."

He took us through the six moves, this time starting with slowly reaching for an imaginary rope. I guess he wanted to start us off easy. He had us stretch our arms up into the air to our absolute maximum.

"Go as high on your toes as you can" he said, reaching for the ceiling. "And continue breathing. People tend to hold their breath when they're exerting themselves. But, as you breathe deeply, you'll notice there's no strain. Breathe even deeper. When you're at the maximum stretch, reach an inch higher. You have more in reserve than you think. Feel the pull at your waistline, which should feel like steel to the touch. Look at what you're reaching for." Then we leapt into the air, catching the imaginary rope and pulling it down.

After several repetitions of stretches and leaps he said, "When I say 'change' I want you to move to another place in the room and just stand there. *Change!*"

On his command we each moved to a new location and looked at Kumi expectantly. Then he said, "Nothing's happened yet—something's about to happen."

We looked at each other for some explanation. Then he moved his shoulders up and down, forward and backward, demonstrating that shoulders have "corner positions." He had us draw imaginary squares in the air with our shoulders—as if we had a piece of chalk sticking out the side of our shoulder bone—then draw circles by moving the shoulders slowly to each corner of the square and rounding them out. As we went through these maneuvers he walked around adjusting our shoulder positions with his hands.

Gradually, I felt the tension of the past few days slipping away.

"By stretching to the corners you get the most complete shoulder stretch in all directions. Then when you rotate your shoulders you know you're getting the biggest circle possible. Over two-hundred muscles tie into the upper back and neck and we're stretching them all. Unless you've had an accident or an operation on your back or shoulder area, both of your shoulders should be able to move identically. Often people find one shoulder responding differently from the other, maybe not going up as high as the other, or as far back, or forward. That tells you you're constricted in that area and suggests you've been using that shoulder in an unnatural way—sitting too high or low at a desk, tensing up when typing, holding a musical instrument wrong, whatever. By doing these shoulder stretches daily, you become more sensitive to any flaws in your working posture.

"Another point. Unworked muscles are like unused rooms—they accumulate the junk of unwanted emotions. Every time you have an emotional encounter some muscle in your body reacts and the emotion you experience from that event can lodge itself in that muscle, even disable it with chronic tension. This is the basis of a psychosomatic disorder—a paralysis with no apparent physical cause. Stretch your muscles daily and you not only dislodge the emotions associated with unpleasant memories, you can prevent stressful emotions from ever implanting themselves there in the first place. So let's clean house. *Change!*"

We moved and he repeated, "Nothing's happened yet—something's about to happen."

What did he mean? Now I'm talking to myself and we're not supposed to do that. I "clicked" my internal dialogue down to soft with my imaginary remote.

Then he had us rotate our hips, like a belly-dancer. "Don't be self-conscious," he said. "No one's looking at you." We moved our hips to the right and left, back and front, and then marked out the corners of a square—right front corner, right rear corner, left rear corner, left front corner. He was strict about keeping our torsos straight while moving our hips.

"You're like a marionette builder testing the marionette for flexibility at the hip joints. Your upper torso should be completely still while your hips are gyrating, so imagine you have a coin on each shoulder and don't want it to fall off. You could be talking to someone over a fence and they would never know what you're doing below the waist."

That got a big laugh and I began to relax. I realized I'd been trying too hard and started doing the moves with a more natural ease, letting the muscles almost float through the movements by themselves, the way Kumi was doing.

Then he combined the two movements—alternately making corners and circles with our shoulders while we gyrated our hips. This was a mental as well as a physical stretch, performing two separate actions at the same time.

"*Change!*"

We moved to other positions and stopped.

"Breathe normally. No strain, no tension—as if nothing's happened yet. Why do I say that? I want to embed the idea that you constantly pay attention to your goal—where you're going, not where you've been—until you are completely finished. That way, if something goes wrong, you simply go on as if it never happened. The same idea applies when things go *right*. You haven't time to stop and congratulate yourself, because something else is *about* to happen. Build that idea into these moves. Say it. 'Nothing's happened yet, something's about to happen.' Say it."

We repeated this sentence (the only words he'd let us speak) together several times. A feeling of excitement began to fill the room as the idea of concentrating fully on an outcome started to take hold.

He had us stretch our hands and then shake them energetically. Our hands flailing in the air looked like frantic birds, the fingers blurring as the hands shook. Then he added the hand actions to the shoulder and hip movements, and we were now doing all three things at once. Watching the others gyrating, rolling their shoulders and shaking their hands, we looked like rubber people trying to learn to walk.

"*Change!* Nothing's happened yet...something's..."

"...About to happen," we all chimed in unison. Then he suddenly had us make clown faces, stretching our foreheads up and the cheeks down, and then foreheads down and cheeks up—like we were alternating expressions of surprise with smiles. To that action he added the rotating of each wrist at a different rate of speed while bending each knee alternately and extending it out over each foot. The face, hands and knees made three entirely separate simultaneous movements.

"I call this the 'three-part independent coordination.' *Change*."

"Nothing's happened yet...something's about to happen," we said.

"Now add one move of your own. Something unique to you. Anything at all."

For a moment we were caught by surprise, then each of us started to move in our own way. Charles did a kind of rock dance movement, Marion a high-step walk, Matt a sort of swimming motion through the air with his arms, and Sun-ee turned in circles, like a ballet dancer. I did a kind of duck walk, something I liked from my high school gym class days that had always invigorated me. After a few minutes of this Kumi had us finish in a frenzy by all leaping for an imaginary rope and falling on the floor, getting up, leaping, falling, leaping and finally falling in a heap. Then we sat up and looked at each other, pleasantly exhausted. We spontaneously applauded.

I felt completely relaxed—perhaps "released" is a better word. The excruciating tension in my neck and shoulders was almost completely gone. For the first time since Kumi's arrival I felt completely at ease with him and comfortable with the group. And I felt free of myself. I began to realize I'd been self absorbed the whole time in these past days. I found it was easy now to observe myself and Kumi, because I was no longer afraid of what I might see.

"Anybody want some water?" Marion said. "Oops, can we talk now?"

Kumi nodded and Marion went into the kitchen for a pitcher of water and some glasses. I sauntered into the kitchen and started helping her. She looked at me with an expression of mild surprise. I smiled and put my arms around her and just held her for a long moment. She made no move to resist. When we came back into the living room Charles was talking.

"Well, that wasn't too hard," he said.

"It's not supposed to be," said Kumi. "Anybody can do these moves, regardless of age."

"Where'd you get these moves, Kumi?" Charles said.

"Mimes do them to test the body's flexibility before going on stage. I like these moves because the hands, face, shoulders and hips are basic to movement and need to be loose. They're also practical. You can do them in a suit and tie or in a dress just before performing."

"Except for leaping for the rope," Marion said, pouring water.

"Well, even then, if you don't leap too high..." said Charles.

"Ruffling your clothes a bit can be a good idea," Kumi said. "Usually we practice our presentations in comfortable clothing, then find ourselves feeling a bit constricted in our dress clothes at the time of the event. The Tuning Dance tells your clothes, 'I'm wearing you, not you wearing me.'"

"Why do you call this 'The Tuning Dance'?" Matt asked.

"Because you're tuning the instrument you are going to perform with—your body. Tuning is different from exercising. Exercise is cardio-vascular, to build muscles—especially the heart muscle—with repetitions that may last up to an hour. The Tuning Dance can be as short or as long as you want it to be, and you don't even work up a sweat."

"Well, you had us working a little bit there at the end," Charles said.

"That was just to finish in a flurry," Kumi said. "But the intent of the Tuning Dance is completely different from regular exercise. First, it stretches the muscles and circulates the blood in the central areas of your body, which is both energizing and relaxing. Second, it signals the body that's it's time to perform, like the 'eyes-up' signals the brain. Of course, the mind and body interact as one instrument, so you're automatically preparing the brain when you work the muscles, and vice versa. But The Tuning Dance is aimed specifically at the physical part of the human instrument. Mimes do these moves before performing, not just to warm up, but to send themselves the message that now it's time to perform."

"Kumi, I can see the shoulders and pelvis being central to movement, but why the face and hands?" I said.

"The face and hands are very expressive. But they are also two areas that store a great deal of tension. Remember how some of you yawned when you stretched your cheeks and foreheads? That's not fatigue, that's tension being released. Your face and hands greet the public with smiles and handshakes. Our faces communicate emotion as well as express our moods, and we use our hands continually for nonverbal communication. Sun-ee is comparatively free of this facial tension because in Korean culture the face rarely expresses emotion and therefore has fewer associations with emotional events—except perhaps the most powerful ones, like grief or joy."

"Even then we're good at not showing it," Sun-ee said.

"But you've become pretty westernized," Charles said, looking at her.

"I'll develop some tension in my face so I can be more American," she said.

We laughed and Charles said, "Your hands give you away—you look too relaxed."

"But I have tension here," she said, pointing to her stomach area, "where no one can see it."

"Kumi, is the 'nothing's happened yet' idea related to 'a new now'?" I asked.

"Nick is referring to an exercise where you repeat the words 'a new now,' to remind yourself that a performance is always in the now. 'Nothing's happened yet' is to keep you focused on your goal, that you're always going forward toward an outcome. Sometimes I combine the two and say, 'Nothing's happened yet, something's about to happen—*a new now*.' Repeating those combined sentences over and over when you do The Tuning Dance is a way of pre-programming yourself to pay attention to where you're going in your performance regardless of what happens. Since the moves of The Tuning Dance are associated only with performing, building this outcome-oriented idea into The Dance will become part of your overall performing attitude."

"You mean you should ignore mistakes?" Sun-ee said.

"While performing, yes. *Afterward* it's useful to go back and replay your performance and analyze what went wrong so you can correct it for next time."

"Why did you have us change positions in the room?" Sun-ee asked.

"To change your perspective—same goal, new view."

"When do you do The Tuning Dance?" Matt asked.

"I would do it every day," said Kumi, "at any time of day that's convenient. To connect The Tuning Dance to the idea of performing you might visualize an upcoming presentation while doing it. But remember to keep the *internal* dialogue out—don't comment on what you're doing. On the day of your performance I would do the whole dance while running the performance in your mind and then perhaps portions of the dance about ten to twenty minutes before your presentation. The Dance is also very effective when you're tired and need a little energizing—better for you than coffee—and you can select any of the moves that seem most beneficial at that moment. Like the shoulder and neck movements after long hours at the computer." Kumi looked at me as he said that.

"But you need a place to do it where you won't attract attention," said Matt.

"Yeah, I'm not going to gyrate my hips in public," Marion said.

"You never know, it might open up new opportunities," I said, protecting my ribs from Marion's elbow.

"After a few days practicing these moves you will begin to feel which ones you need to concentrate on to help your body become loose," Kumi said. "You will also begin to notice how they affect your comportment. For example, the pelvic movements will have a distinct effect on your walk, the motion coming from the hips instead of the legs. It's more elegant."

"I can see uses for The Tuning Dance as an actress, especially to alleviate stress," Marion said. "A friend of mine recently did a voice-over for a documentary on television. The producer is known for giving actors a rough time. On the first take she muffed a line and the producer yelled at her, 'Can't you remember a simple sentence?' On the next take, unbelievably, she muffed the same line again. 'Where did we *find* this woman?' he said. The director assured him she would be fine and the rehearsal ended on that note. This was a Friday and the final taping was the following Monday. I was worried about how she was going to handle this when she returned after the weekend to do the final take, especially with two days to think about it.

"On Monday she looked rested and confident and she performed beautifully. 'I spent the weekend on Fire Island, swimming in the ocean and walking on the beach,' she said. 'I feel great!'"

"Your friend was lucky she happened to have an ocean nearby," Kumi said. "What if she were traveling at the time and didn't have even a swimming pool or a tennis court or health club? What would she have done? Performers often have unpredictable schedules—film actors especially—and they have to be ready for anything. They need a form of physical movement that is simple, that can be done without exercise machines, is time-efficient and do-able anywhere. The Tuning Dance is perfect for that.

"I might add, smart people don't wait until a challenge occurs and then suddenly try to get in shape for it. The true professional knows that he or she might be called upon any time to participate in what could be a career-altering opportunity and prepares *in advance* for any emergency. The Tuning Dance reminds you to tune the human instrument every day—just in case."

"I imagine The Tuning Dance could be a good picker-upper when you're pooped or under the weather," Marion said.

"I know a musician who caught a bug and had a sleepless night prior to a morning children's concert," Kumi said. "At 7:45 A.M. she took a shower, had some orange juice and toast and met her host. While she was being driven to the concert she visualized the hall she would be playing in (though she had never seen it) and saw herself doing The Tuning Dance in that space. They got to the school about a half hour before the concert. She went to the stage and did The Tuning Dance while visualizing the audience she'd be playing for. She played the concert and said it was one of her best.

"Her body and brain had associated The Tuning Dance with energy, concentration and joy, not illness or fatigue. After doing the dance her body and brain simply didn't think she could be sick, so she wasn't."

"And she knows now she can perform under almost any conditions," Marion said.

"In my experience, if you think your body is well it behaves as though it's well," Matt said. "We have a lot of examples of behavioral conditioning at the hospital, like a nurse walking into the ward and seeing a patient getting up to open the blinds and saying, 'Oh, I'll do that for you.' It's a little thing, but it sends a message: 'You shouldn't do that, you're sick.'"

"And The Tuning Dance tells you 'You're feeling great so get out there and do it.' Good for stage fright," Charles said.

"Well, how can you have stage fright when you're rotating your hands at two different speeds while making faces like a clown?" Marion said.

Afterward, Matt and I stayed a while to "Kumi" each other on some of the moves. My right shoulder felt funny when I moved it backward. He said I was raising it up in the air, instead of moving it straight back. He held my shoulder down firmly as I stretched it backward again.

"Ow."

"That hurt?"

"Kind of."

"Well, there's nothing wrong with that shoulder. You just have to give it special attention."

"Could it be from operating the mouse?"

"Yes, if you tense your shoulder while doing it. Or even from just sitting too long at the computer. Why not stand up and do some shoulder stretches every forty-five minutes?"

"I get too lost in the work."

"Set a timer."

"Is that true what Kumi said, that we have emotional memory in our muscles?"

"I don't know. But we seem to work out emotional problems when we exercise the muscles. Look at the effect of jogging and swimming."

"I guess I do feel better after I exercise."

"These mime movements are a little different from the usual exercise. It's more systematic. Gets right in there at key places—shoulders, hands, hips. Musicians put tremendous strain on their fingers. They sometimes practice four or five hours at a time—and may never stop to stretch their fingers. Same with you at the computer."

"But I exercise."

"Not at the computer you don't. Just stand up and rotate your shoulders, flick your hands a little, reach for a rope."

"Okay, doctor."

"That'll be fifty dollars."

"Hey, you're getting cheap."

"I'm retired."

"Then you don't need the money."

"So buy me a pizza."

"Deal."

I had a new part for my Chart:

Body Tuner

*"I remind you daily to tune the instrument
you communicate with."*

When I did my Community Check on this new part, The Jogger asked that the Body Tuner's job (specified muscle-stretching as a performance signal) not supplant his job (cardio-vascular exercise—pumping the heart). I was aware of the difference and promised myself not to confuse the two. It occurred to me that these two might make another good alliance.

Communicating with inner parts brought up another question: When I talk to these parts, who am "I" as opposed to "they?" Kumi said that I'm the conscious self who creates, organizes and guides my "Staff." In effect, I'm the Director of Me. He said many people don't organize themselves well and need to install a manager. He has a mediator part who goes back and forth between him and his other Staff and takes care of the many little details that don't need his attention. This allows him to stand back and give his parts some breathing room, something he says I might consider since I tend to be highly controlling. (Marion would applaud this, of course). He reminded me that when I insist on having a say in every step of every operation, my parts will tend to stop taking initiatives and become mechanical in the same way that people would. Good leadership is knowing how to guide, not control, so my parts can feel free to improvise and come up with ideas of their own. So how do I stop controlling? Kumi recommended I experiment once in a while. Let a part operate its own way and see how I like what happens.

I began to notice that I was feeling good, that The Tuning Dance had freed up my mind as well as my body. After doing it, I found I could switch to the observer position with ease. From this perspective, I saw not only that I'd been coveting Kumi, but that Marion had been worrying about me the whole time. My God, I've been trying to own him. Added to that, I thought I had to be extra good at everything we're learning because I'm his special student and I should set an example. *I'm slipping back into my old pattern again—focusing completely on myself.* What a waste of time! Solution: get the hell out of myself for a while, Nick, and see how things look to the rest of the world!

(My notes and exercises on The Tuning Dance are on page 329)

12

YOU'VE DONE EVERYTHING YOU CAN

...NOW DO YOUR HOMEWORK

"Performing well is the most natural thing in the world. It's as exciting as being a kid at your own birthday party. You can't wait, you're so excited. Communicating your message is an invigorating and inspiring experience, because you love it."

"Who'd like to make a short presentation?" said Kumi. "Nick, how about it?"

"Presentation on what?"

"Anything."

"Okay."

"So, go out and get it together and come in when you're ready. We'll just make ourselves comfortable here. Nice relaxed family setting."

Out in the hallway I rotated my shoulders and fluttered my hands to loosen up and took a deep breath. Eyes-up I saw my audience. I wanted to make Kumi proud of his student—show 'em all how it should be done.

I came in smiling and walked vigorously, looking at everyone. Kumi, Marion and Matt were sitting on the sofa, Sun-ee in the easy chair and Charles on the floor. In order to have them all in my view I had to step farther back, but then I was too far from the sofa and lost the feeling of contact.

"Heh, kind of awkward," I said.

They just looked at me with a pleasant smile, waiting.

"Um, so…" I was uneasy about standing so far away from them in order to have them all in my field of vision. I felt a flush of embarrassment at the pause and forgot what I was going to say. I wanted to tell them about holograms, but I didn't have a good way to kick it off.

"I'm going to tell you about holographic videos, which are very interesting. To create them you exploit parallelism as much as possible, both optically and electronically…"

Their faces were blank.

"Maybe I should tell you a little first about how holograms are made, in case you don't know. You get a hologram by splitting a beam of coherent light in two directions…"

Marion was squinting and Charles' mouth was open. Sun-ee looked sideways, like she was trying to remember something.

I stammered on in this fashion for five or six minutes and finished saying, "So that's the basics. Um. If any of you would like to know more about it I could show you at home."

I looked at Kumi. "What do I do now, walk out? Or crawl out?" I put my head in my hands. "God, I've never felt so uncomfortable in my life."

Everybody laughed.

Kumi stepped up and patted me on the back. "You did good. Dirty trick to call on you on the spur of the moment. How about a big hand for a good sport."

I sat down on the sofa, red-faced.

"What gets me is, I did everything right—I used all the techniques. Why should I feel nervous in Marion's living room, in front of you guys, for godsake?"

"Well, obviously you had no time to prepare your thoughts, and that's the most important prerequisite for any performance—knowing your material and how you want to present it. But aside from content, there are several basic practical things to prepare as well. You gave a simple talk in a friend's living room, which is not so simple. It's full of traps, and Nick walked innocently into most of them. I've seen experienced performers tripped up by the smallest things. For example, for any kind of presentation—large or small, audience of a thousand or friends in your living room—you need to *create your own space.*

"Seasoned performers give the impression they *own* the space in which they're performing. Often I've noticed that a skilled professional will go to the stage, or studio, or boardroom and make some physical adjustment, however small just before a presentation. Adjusting the position of a water pitcher, a microphone, a chair, can make you feel more at home. This may look like simply fixing a few details before performance, but actually they are *personalizing* the performance area for themselves—making it *theirs*.

"In Nick's case, he found himself trying to talk to five people who were spread over an awkward distance, which meant he had to adjust his physical position to his own disadvantage. This can be very disorienting."

"Tell me about it," I said.

"Well, here you are, feeling nervous and not realizing it's because of a simple thing like the physical set-up. Underneath, you feel like a dolt for not having thought of it, right?"

"Right."

"But in an informal setting like this you can ask people to move. Often it takes very little to make it right, and people even like that—they get up, talk to each other, move a chair—and you've already established some relationship with them. Also, a small message has been sent—they know you're in charge, and they like that."

"But what if you really can't change the set-up?" I said. "I've seen board rooms where the table and chairs are fixed."

"Then look over the place beforehand and decide where you want to stand or sit. Once I had a talk to give at a luncheon. The tables were all set in the shape of a square with me in the middle, so I would have had to keep turning to address everyone. I suggested I sit on the outside of the square where I could see everyone, and that worked very well. People are usually accommodating because they want you to be happy, especially if you're the guest speaker. Remember, it's your show—make yourself comfortable."

"Point number two—match the energy level of your audience. Audiences give off an energy of their own, the force of their collective concentration. You feel it when you stand in front of them. If you come out to perform and you're at sixty percent energy and your audience is at seventy percent, you'll be 'knocked back' by their power, you can feel it, and it's very difficult to recover your equilibrium.

"Or, if you come out at a high energy level and your audience is at a much lower level like we are here, you could appear formal, even overbearing."

"That's true. I primed myself for a high-power situation and I felt kind of awkward when I found everybody so relaxed. I should have known, but..."

"You hadn't thought about it. That's all. Now you're aware of it."

"So how do you match their energy?" Charles asked.

"Take a look at them," said Kumi. "Get a 'feel' of them. You need to know beforehand just how tough your audience is going to be. Generally the more sophisticated and informed about your subject, the more energy they emit. They're anticipating more. Don't take any chances. Most performances require a high level of energy, so make sure your engine is going stronger than theirs well before you make your appearance. Your energy focuses their attention and relaxes them."

"I'm so glad you said that," Marion said. "Most people don't realize that audiences are usually as nervous as you are. They need to be put at ease."

"And when you get that balance of energy between you and your audience, you feel more confident," Kumi said.

"Balance?" said Charles. "You said your energy should be higher than your audience's."

"At first, yes, to get their attention. Then you fall into a kind of rhythm with your audience—a back and forth feeling of communication as your mutual energies tend to level out. A sense of flow develops between you. That's why it's important to get a feel of your audience before you start, maybe sitting with them beforehand, or even in a similar audience elsewhere. On occasion I've sat in the empty hall where I will be talking and imagined what the audience would feel like. This also gives you a feel for your performing space."

"Okay. Point number three—what does your audience know about your subject? Nick, you know your subject of course, but you hadn't prepared it for *this* audience. How many times have you explained holography to lay people?"

"Hardly ever."

"How did you feel about the content of your presentation when you were getting ready to talk to us?"

"I felt confident, because I know the material."

"And then how'd it feel after you got out here and actually started talking?"

"Well, you heard me, I stammered."

"And why was that?"

"I was getting all these blank looks. And I was puzzled, because I felt so good when we did our second walk-on Thursday."

"On Thursday your content matched your audience—you were simply introducing yourself. Today you had a highly technical subject and a lay audience, so the two were out of synch. The best speaker can be a big success one day and 'lay an egg' the next by not adjusting the subject matter to the listener. Be sure to match it very carefully, because halfway isn't good enough—you won't communicate."

"What do I do when I'm not sure how knowledgeable they are?"

"Ask them before you start. What would they like to learn? This also gives you a personal contact with them in an informal way and creates rapport. And you feel more comfortable."

"I guess I took the whole thing for granted. It seemed so easy—a few friends in a living room."

"Underestimating the situation is the biggest trap of all. I call that 'Mark Spitz drowning in the bathtub'"

"Who's Mark Spitz?" Charles asked.

"He won seven gold medals for swimming in the 1972 Olympics," I said.

"The better you get, the more likely you are to feel over-confident," Kumi said. "Then when you screw up you wonder, 'What's the matter with me?' and your confidence gets shaky. 'But I did my visualizations, walk-ons, Amy and The Tuning Dance,' you might say. Yes, but these prepare your physical and mental state for performance. You can do all that and still be nervous if you don't know your audience and your performing space."

"My colleagues in the medical profession should hear this," Matt said. "Unfortunately, more and more of them are prescribing beta-blockers for performance nerves because they don't know what else to do. Performance medicine is a fast-growing new area for doctors these days."

"What's a beta-blocker?" said Sun-ee.

"It's a drug that blocks the flow of adrenaline to the heart. Calms you down," said Matt.

"Is it bad for you?"

"No one knows the long term effect of taking drugs."

"Why would you want to take a drug when your body can make its own drugs?" said Marion.

"Exactly," Kumi said. "Adrenaline is a natural stimulant. It conveys a message: 'We have an important event to deal with, so here's some quick energy.' A beta-blocker gives a contradictory message, 'Calm down, it's not important.' Which message should your brain believe? Which message is most appropriate to the event? Is calmness the appropriate state for an important performance? The best performers I know feel excited about performing—that's why they're performers. They feel a healthy nervousness—not fear, but *energy*. They're about to engage in a challenge that requires all of their ability and concentration, and they've been inspired by great performers that they want to imitate. And the audience is excited, too, expecting a stimulating experience. Energy and excitement are the essence of performance. A beta-blocker neutralizes that performer-audience flow of energy."

Matt nodded his head vigorously. "I know a musician who takes propranolol, a common beta-blocker known commercially as Inderal. When I asked him about the effect he said, 'My fingers move okay, but I don't seem to care as much about the performance.'"

"But that takes away the whole meaning of it," Marion said. You're out there, because you *care*."

"Who wants to spend money on a performer who doesn't care?" Charles said.

"I'll try anything before prescribing beta-blockers," Matt said. "There might be an exceptional case when it could be used, just to get a person through a one-time difficult situation. Or to teach someone who has never learned how to perform with control what it feels like to be under pressure without falling apart. But, in my opinion, continual use of a beta-blocker is not only unnecessary, in the long run it's debilitating—the effects start wearing off, but the side-effects don't."

"What side-effects?" Charles asked.

"Sleep interruption, cold feet and hands, increased blood fat, decreased levels of HDL cholesterol."

"That's the good cholesterol, right."

"Right. High-density lipoprotein. Aids cholesterol metabolism and excretion."

"Wow. Complicated," Marion said.

"Your body is the biggest pharmaceutical company on the planet," said Kumi. "You can create your own beta-blockers with relaxation techniques and stimulate endorphins with exercise."

"What are endorphins exactly?" I asked

"One of the peptide hormones that bind to opiate receptors in the brain," said Matt.

"Would you say that again?" said Charles.

"Morphine—the brain's natural drug."

"I've got morphine in my own brain and didn't know it?"

"When you say, 'I need a drug to get me through it,' what does that do to your confidence?" asked Kumi. "When you perform you need to know that you can draw on your own resources. That's how you gain confidence. When you use a drug to get through a tough experience, your body and your brain feel betrayed. They know they can supply any physical or mental state you need and you're not asking them to do it. That's demoralizing."

Kumi was excited about this point. It reflected on his basic philosophy about performing itself.

"Performing well is the most natural thing in the world. It is the typical state of the young child, where stress and tension are unknown. Remember the thrill you felt when you decided you wanted to be an actress, Marion? Charles, to be a newscaster, Sun-ee, a courtroom lawyer? It's thrilling, isn't it? You love it! It's as exciting as being a kid at your own birthday party. *You can't wait,* you're so excited. *That's* what performing is. Getting up in front of people and communicating your message is an invigorating and inspiring experience, because you love it. Don't ever forget that. Otherwise performing will become an obligation and everything connected with it will become a chore."

"How about when you realize you may not be as good as you thought you were?" I said.

"You don't need to be the best in the world," Kumi said. "You just need to be *the best you can be.* And the most natural way to do that is to prepare your body and brain and let them guide you."

We sat there quietly for a few moments. Then I said, "Okay, I want another shot at it."

"It's all yours," Kumi said.

"Alright. Charles, I'm going to ask you to sit next to Sun-ee." Charles walked over and sat on the floor next to her easy chair. Then I removed the small coffee table in front of the sofa. That damn thing had been bothering me the whole time. I didn't want anything between me and my audience. Now the set-up was right for me.

I went into the hallway, took a deep breath and visualized the entire living room. I remembered Charles' suggestion to me about delivering technical information in a story-telling mode. I entered with a casual gait, scanning each of their faces with a smile, and then spoke softly:

"Imagine this room in semi-darkness. You hear a piano playing a romantic tune. Al Pacino sits at a table with a drink, so close you can almost touch him. A woman walks over to him and takes out a gun. 'How could you do this to me?' she says and fires.

"You're watching your first holographic movie right in your own living room. Two parallel red lights beam across the room, but you don't see them. And you're not worried about how you're going to pay for the two 18-channel Acoustic-Optic Modulators and the six tiled horizontal mirrors that bring you this movie in virtual reality. You're just wondering one thing: 'How's Pacino going to get out of this one.'"

I went on to explain in simple terms, but still in a mysterious voice, how video holography works, occasionally pointing out how these techniques can help create the mood of the murder scene I was describing. My aim was to give my ten-minute talk an aura of mystery.

"Don't stop," Marion said when I finished. "I want to know more." The others chimed in and asked me to go on.

"That's all you get, folks. To be continued," I said. I winked at Charles, my secret audience from now on for giving talks.

People love to walk in New York. The sidewalks are wide and you can saunter along comfortably, talking and watching people. Walking and looking is one of the city's best entertainments. In no time at all you discover you've walked for miles. Kumi's favorite street was Broadway because, as he said, "I love to watch the crazies." It was one of those rare, clear days when you could occasionally smell the ocean.

The six of us walked from the nineties down to Verdi Square at 72nd Street and across to Central Park. I marveled at how many restaurants and cafes had popped up in this stretch along Broadway and on Columbus Avenue in recent years, replacing gated-up storefronts and garbage everywhere. People thought New York was bankrupt and going down the tubes, then it bounced back. Maybe it's the energy of its people. So many of them are newcomers with dreams, and when they get tired and leave, a new bunch of dreamers come in. For all of New York's faults, I don't know any other city that has such a constant influx of energy. In this way, New York continually erases its past and creates a new future. An Irish pub I liked at 52nd and Broadway had disappeared and become a parking lot. Then seemingly overnight the parking lot was turned into an office building! New York is truly a "Nothing's happened yet, something's about to happen" town.

We entered Central Park at Seventy-Second Street. Kumi was fascinated by all the joggers, roller-bladers, and skate-boarders. One lady was speed-walking while taking her pulse and smoking a cigarette.

"I thought Central Park was dangerous," he said. "It looks like a festival here."

A frisbee flew our way and Kumi picked it up. "Where'd this come from?" he said.

A German shepherd ran over to Kumi and looked at him expectantly, saliva drooling. Kumi threw the frisbee in the air and it ended up wobbling on the grass like a coin on a tabletop.

"I never did get the hang of those things," he said.

The dog intercepted the yellow disc and carried it to a group of teenagers. One of the boys threw it in a soaring trajectory, the shepherd racing after it and clamping it in its teeth in mid-flight.

"Magnificent!" Kumi said. "Did you see that? He just flew in the air, like it's the easiest thing in the world."

"Well, it's a dog, Kumi," I said.

"It's a *trained* dog," he said.

We sat on the grass for a while and watched the parade of people. A kid went by on a unicycle eating an ice cream cone. Matt and Sun-ee passed around peanuts they'd bought from a vendor.

"Kumi, there's one really important part of preparation you only mentioned but we didn't talk about today," Marion said, "and that's knowing your material. I know people who think they've practiced properly when they haven't. Then they get on stage and they're nervous and they think it's psychological. They don't realize that they don't really know their lines or their music."

"Or studied properly for their exam, or done research for their debate," Charles added.

"Right. Doing your homework," Kumi said.

I thought of some of the talks I had given at Globalcom about computers and equipment. Often I was going on my general knowledge and wasn't really prepared for all of the questions I might be asked. Thinking about it now, I realized that the more research I did on some new software the less nervous I was talking about it.

"You mean if you know your material really well you will automatically feel less nervous?" asked Sun ee.

"It means you will feel more competent and you can perform with greater authority," Kumi said. "Top people in their professions give painstaking attention to detail. I know a professional tennis player who flew across the country just to meet a retired tennis star because he'd heard this old-timer had an unusual way of gripping the racquet on his serve. He just *had* to know everything possible about tennis."

"That's normal for artists," Marion said. "I heard about a fifteen year-old Chinese girl at Juilliard. She was learning a very difficult piano concerto, so she memorized the recordings of this concerto played by five great pianists. She was able to imitate the playing style of each of them in exact detail. Can you imagine the confidence that girl will have? This kind of preparation takes you beyond confidence—you can be almost arrogant. That kid knows more about that concerto than her teacher or the critics."

"Yeah, but her case is a little extreme, isn't it?" I said.

"Depends how good you want to be," said Kumi.

We got up and started walking south, toward the Fifty-Ninth Street exit. A horse and buggy clopped toward us. The driver wore a black top hat and a worn waistcoat. A young couple in the open carriage leaned forward to watch the joggers.

"Are they running a marathon?" Kumi asked.

"No," said Marion, "it's just Sunday."

We crossed Fifty-Ninth Street and walked down Seventh Avenue. People sat in a sidewalk cafe with a cappuccino or a glass of wine.

"That piano student sounds like a surgeon," Matt said. "I'd rehearse an operation mentally days before performing it. Tomorrow's operation is the last thing I would see in my mind before going to sleep and I'd have every last detail in place before breakfast."

"In place how?" Kumi asked.

"I'd see it all in my mind like a movie. Driving to the hospital at 6:30 a.m., I'd visualize the best position for everything in the O.R.—the nurses, the assistant surgeon, the surgical technician, surgical instruments, the microscope, video camera, and the exact sequence of X-ray films in the view box."

"How about when something unexpected occurred?" Kumi said.

"I'd already imagined all the possible complications and the various ways for dealing with them. And I'd keep all these visualized scenarios in my mind as the operation goes on."

"Kumi, here's Carnegie Hall," Marion said. "That's one the wrecker's ball didn't get, but they sure tried. There was a hue and cry and then they renovated it instead. A victory for the good guys!" Marion thrust her fist into the air.

"How about a sandwich at Carnegie Deli?" I said.

We crossed the street and stood in a line of about twenty people waiting to get into the famous but inauspicious-looking little restaurant. Kumi looked slightly dubious.

"This is special?" he asked.

"You eat a sandwich here and you don't have to eat for a week," Marion said. "Great Nova Scotia salmon. And the waiters are real characters. It's a New York tradition."

We finally got in and found a big table in the back. Signed pictures of famous people decked the walls. The waiter came and dropped menus on the table like he was throwing out old newspapers. Charles started to ask for a beer and the waiter said gruffly, "Take it easy," and walked away. We laughed.

"Now there's confidence for you, Kumi," I said. "That guy doesn't care what anyone thinks."

"Kumi, you were talking about being ready for the unexpected," Charles said. "I'll tell you a story about a friend of mine in high school who was the fastest 800-meter runner in the state. One day he lost an important race in a regional competition. His main competitor did something very unusual in the race—he passed Brad on the third curve of the 800-meter run, the toughest point in the race for half-milers. Passing on a curve is rare enough, because you have to run out and then back in again to do it and it takes more steps. But Brad said you *never* pass on the third curve, because it's too strenuous. Well, his rival did it, caught Brad completely by surprise and won the race. After that Brad's confidence was shaky and he started wondering what else could go wrong in a race."

"It happens all the time. He thought he was prepared when he wasn't," said Kumi.

"But nobody worked out more conscientiously than Brad."

"Working hard is different from working *thoroughly*," Kumi said. "He lost the race because he closed his mind to the possibility of being passed on a curve. A good athlete should anticipate *every* eventuality."

"In fact that's what his coach said. He had Brad make a list of things that could 'go wrong' in a race—that he gets spiked or elbowed, or trips, or a competitor insults him—a whole host of things. He role-played these possibilities and imagined at least three responses to each one. He named this part of himself 'The Surprise Runner,' the part that responds to the unexpected. After that, he knew he would be in control no matter what happened, and this gave him confidence. He won the state that year."

I wondered if Brad's coach made sure The Surprise Runner had the approval of all Brad's other parts.

The waiter brought napkins and water and we ordered beers.

Marion said, "Do you have frosted glasses?"

"Hey, lady," he said, "you want frost, go to Alaska."

"Nice to know some traditions are still alive," Charles said.

"Your story about Brad reminds me of a woman I know who gave a speech at a big convention," I said. "She's on the stage of this auditorium and the event is being relayed on closed-circuit television to software managers at forty hotels in the Denver area, so she makes sure she has everything down cold—rehearses with a video camera, studies the tapes, the whole bit. So she begins her talk and all of a sudden a little boy gets out of his seat and starts running up and down the aisle, right under her nose. She watches the child, wondering when someone's going to tell him to sit down. It threw her timing off. Afterward she said, 'All I could think was, Where is that kid's mother?'"

"But how do you know when something crazy like that is going to happen," Sun-ee asked.

"You don't," said Kumi, so you prepare for anything. Be like Charles' friend and develop a 'Surprise Part' that prepares your mind for emergencies. That'd be a good exercise. Imagine how people in different performing situations might prepare for the unexpected."

The waiter returned with the beers and took our orders. Marion ordered the salmon with cream cheese on a bagel.

"With onion," the waiter said.

"I don't think I want the onion."

"You want the onion."

She looked at the waiter. "Okay, I'll have the onion."

He nodded his head like she was his student and had finally got the right answer to an important question, and walked away writing on his pad.

"Why did I feel inferior in that conversation?" Marion asked, staring into space.

"Because you weren't ready for it, right Kumi?" Matt said. We all laughed.

"Anyway, I think you can prepare all you want but you can't really know how something's going to go until you do it," I said. "You only get one shot at it!'

"Unless you take two shots at it," said Kumi.

"What do you mean?"

"Seeing Carnegie Hall reminds me of a violinist who gave his Carnegie Hall debut four weeks early—in his own living room. Doing a trial run of your presentation is normal, but this story is in a class by itself. This violinist set a mock debut date to take place in his own apartment and convinced himself this was the *real* debut. He primed everything in his life for this new date. His music practice, his social life, his family life and all his professional and personal obligations were scheduled with this mock performance in mind. He discussed with his family what he was doing so they would also cooperate in planning toward this event as if it were the real thing. As the date got closer, his practicing became more intense and he began cutting back on his social life and family time. Days before the "debut" he scaled down his practice, got extra rest and talked to no one. His family went out of town for the weekend.

"The location of this performance, as I said, was his living room. No actual people were present, because in his mind this room was now the stage of Carnegie Hall and he had an audience of twenty-seven hundred. On this debut day he rested, ate some pasta and about two hours before concert time put on his brand new tuxedo, his overcoat, got his violin and left the apartment. He went down the elevator, out onto the street, to the corner, turned around and came back to his apartment building.

"And guess what building he was entering now? He went up the elevator, got out on his floor and entered his apartment. He was now in the backstage area of Carnegie. He went to the kitchen, which was the green room, where the soloists relax before performing. He hung up his coat, took out his violin, warmed up and waited. At about seven-fifty he heard in his mind someone say, 'You're on in ten minutes.' He walked to the dining room, which was the off-stage area, and waited for his cue to go on. When he got it, he walked on stage, bowed, heard applause in his mind, played the whole first half of the program, bowed and walked off.

"After the fifteen-minute intermission, he played the second half, plus encores, and he was finished.

"Afterwards he sat back, had a beer and made an appraisal of his 'debut.' How did it go? What could he have done better? How did his energy and his concentration hold up? What does he need to practice more? Having gone through this experience, he had the luxury of giving his Carnegie Hall debut *twice*. He said that when the actual Carnegie Hall debut came a month later he felt completely ready."

"Sure, he knew what to expect because, in his mind, he'd already been there," said Marion.

"Moral of the story: never do something important for the first time," Matt said. "I can identify with that."

"He said it went beautifully, better than in his apartment. In fact, he said he was more nervous for the performance in his living room than he was in Carnegie Hall."

"Because he *believed* it and acted out the living room performance as if it were the real thing," Marion said.

Our sandwiches came and they were huge.

Sun-ee shook her head and said, "I can't eat all that."

"They have doggy bags," said Charles. "We've got food for the drive back tomorrow."

We looked at our sandwiches and made jokes about how we were going to get our mouths around them.

"This is a performance in itself," Kumi said, taking a bite of his pastrami sandwich with mustard oozing out.

"You can have 'Carnegie Hall in your living room' or 'stage fright' in your living room, like Nick did today," Charles said.

"If you're a person who insists on doing a good job, you don't differentiate between big and small occasions," Kumi said. "A performance is a performance. You have a performance-control center up in your head, run by these little guys who care only that you perform well. 'Oh-oh,' one of them says up in your brain, 'he's not ready, give him a signal.' So another one talks to you over the intercom: 'You should have prepared this better, you're going to make a fool out of yourself.' You think some evil inner judge is trying to sabotage you, so you ignore this message. 'He's not listening,' number two says. 'Okay, zap him with extra adrenaline and close his salivary glands.' They pull a few levers and you feel like a hammer just hit your heart and someone stuffed cotton in your mouth. You think something is wrong with you, but in fact you're functioning perfectly. Fear is a message from a part of you that's keenly aware of what you don't know, of a preparation you haven't made. And that part is doing its best to get you out of the situation as fast as possible—for your own good."

We hardly noticed that the waiter was standing there with our bill, listening.

"That's good, that's good," he said, nodding his head approvingly to Kumi. "You should be on TV."

We paid the bill and left Carnegie Deli. Matt said his goodbyes and caught a taxi. We walked over to Broadway and south toward Times Square, joking about getting Kumi on the Oprah Winfrey show.

"You'd have to water all this down to sound bites," Charles said. "Someone could do a documentary on Kumi, though."

"How about a workshop in the mountains. Fly us all out there," Marion said. "Compliments of PBS."

"Where is Kumi," Sun-ee said. We looked around and he was nowhere in sight.

"Did he leave with us?" I said.

"Wait here a minute. I'll check back at the Deli," Charles said, jogging over to Seventh Avenue.

"Did anybody see him when we left?"

Marion shrugged, looking around.

I saw the blinking lights of a club called The Lion's Den a few doors down. I looked at the marquee, advertising table dancing. A mild feeling of apprehension crept over me.

"Wait here a minute."

I went inside and was met by a big man in a tuxedo who looked me over and then ushered me through an inner door of phony Arabian Nights design. I entered a large space with blinking lights and thunderous music. A sit-down bar filled with men surrounded a stage in the center of the room where a nude woman was dancing with a boa constrictor. Half-clad women danced for sullen-looking men at their tables, or sat and drank with them.

In the middle of all this I saw Kumi at a table with three hostesses around him. They were laughing and one of them had her arm around Kumi. "Nick, over here," he said, waving to me. The man in the tuxedo asked if Kumi was with me and I assured him Kumi was "okay." He looked doubtful and nodded to a muscular man in a black T-shirt. I could see trouble coming and decided to get Kumi out of there. All of a sudden Kumi was up on a table top, moving his arms and undulating his hips, imitating the snake dancer. Some of the dancers laughed and cheered him on while others looked around apprehensively. The manager and his bouncer went toward him rather menacingly. One of the women tried to block the bouncer. He pushed her aside and two of her friends stepped in to defend her. Suddenly there was a fracas and everyone's attention was on this spectacle. "Leave him alone!" one of the dancers yelled, as Kumi jumped down from the table and up onto the stage. The customers whistled and cat-called as Kumi cavorted about the stage. A policeman appeared near the stage to cries of "boo" just as the music came to a crashing climax with Kumi climbing a pole and waving at the cheering audience. He slid down the pole, bowed ceremoniously and jumped off the stage. Two dancers distracted the cop while Kumi got lost in the crowd. I looked around and just saw him ducking out the door.

Marion, Charles and Sun-ee were outside waiting for us.

"What happened?" Marion said.

"You just missed the walk-on of the century, I said, hurrying us quickly along the street and into a taxi. "Whatever in the world got into you, Kumi?"

"That one with the red hair, she was really something," he said.

"So was that guy with the black shirt," I said.

"But I was good, wasn't I?"

"Oh, you were terrific!" I said.

"Aren't you supposed to have fun in those places? It looked like a morgue in there. I livened it up a little."

"You certainly did. And you almost got free room and board courtesy of New York's Finest," I said.

We got Kumi home to bed and Charles and Sun-ee went back to the apartment. Marion and I sat and talked for a minute.

"Thank God he's leaving tomorrow," I said with a sigh.

"I love him, he's so full of life."

"But he also drives me crazy."

"That's because your life is so regulated."

"You want me to chase burglars and dance with strippers?"

"I'm saying there's a lighter side to life. It's to be enjoyed."

"Well, he certainly enjoys it," I said. And suddenly I burst out laughing and couldn't stop. My eyes were watering and I tried to speak. "You should've…you should've…*seen* him," I tried to say, laughing so hard I could hardly breathe.

Marion started laughing and we were responding and adding to each other's laughter. When we finally stopped I stared at the floor and shook my head, exhausted. I got up and put on my jacket.

"Where you going?"

"I gotta get home. Gregor's coming over."

"Oh, Nick. Haven't you had enough for one day?"

"We're working on this compression thing, making images smaller for transmission."

She looked away and shook her head slightly.

"Marion?"

"Okay, so go."

I walked toward the door.

"I'm taking Kumi to the airport in the morning. Wanna come?"

"I'm busy."

"I'll call you."

"Yeah, sure..."

Before Gregor arrived I made a new part for my Chart:

Mr. Ready

"I make sure you do your research and
prepare yourself and your material thoroughly
for any important event."

Doing my Community Check, I felt a little pressure from The State Maker, who wanted assurance that Mr. Ready would not interfere with his function. I imagined them working together, helping each other make sure that I am both in a proper state of mind and fully prepared for any eventuality. I had a good feeling about that alliance. I'd give it a few weeks and then check in on it again.

In my Chart, I started drawing lines connecting those parts that seemed to relate to each other. This is what Kumi meant by coalitions, several parts bringing multiple perspectives to a task.

Here's how I look to date:

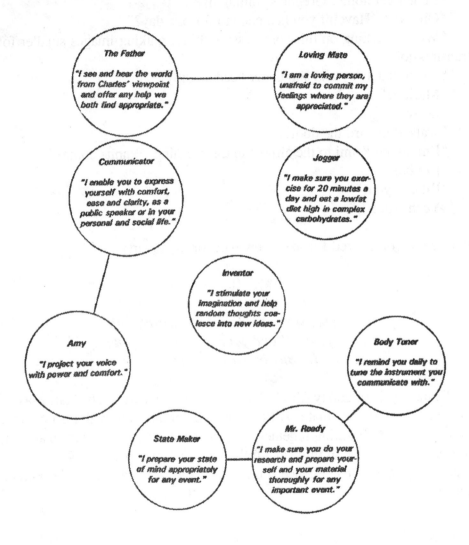

Charting was offering me many new advantages. For example, as I defined my parts and got them working in harmony, I noticed I could sometimes simply tell myself what I want and let the parts carry out my wish their own way. An example of this occurred one night after keying for hours at the computer on a difficult formula. I was about to punch my fist through the monitor when I stood up and almost yelled in exasperation, "Okay, I give up. *You* do it." I had no idea who I was talking to, I was just ranting. The next day I went back to the problem, but found myself approaching it differently. I experimented with multiple equations to prove the formula instead of using just one, and the solution suddenly seemed simple. Then I remembered my outburst the night before and wondered if I had inadvertently asked some unconscious part of myself to work out the problem for me. I remember Kumi's reponse: "So now you know that you have parts who can accomplish things on your behalf without you hovering over them all the time. You're learning to trust your unconscious."

Kumi said that maintaining a close and continual relationship with all my parts would help me break habits, because I'd be more likely to achieve the necessary across-the-board "committee agreement" for important changes. He used smoking as an example. He said smoking has many advantages: it gives the smoker a chance to take a break from work, it tastes and smells good to the smoker, stimulates the nervous system, creates a social connection for some people, is a companion when working alone, and relieves tension, to name just a few. Some part (or parts) of the person is generating smoking because it thinks it's needed. Kumi recommended talking to this part about the "benefits" of smoking and then discussing ways to satisfy these needs without smoking. He says this shows respect for the part that is generating the habit for what it mistakenly perceives to be your own good. If you just quit "on your own," ignoring the part or parts of you that make you smoke, your chances of breaking the habit would be slim. The moment you'd let down your resolve, that part would re-assert itself and tempt you with the "advantages" of smoking, and you'd fall right back into the old behavior.

Kumi speaks from experience. He said he used to smoke like a chimney, and tried many times to stop by using willpower. (And he has willpower!) Finally he started meeting with his "committee," discussing alternative ways to meet his needs without using cigarettes. These "meetings" went on for a month until he had reviewed the question of smoking with every one of his parts. He wasn't sure when his staff reached an agreement, but one day he woke up, had breakfast, walked right past his cigarettes, began his day and never smoked again. His whole self wanted the change, found alternative ways to satisfy the benefits of smoking, jointly agreed the habit was unnecessary and the desire vanished. That was over thirty years ago. He said the same kind of inner consensus needs to be achieved to end drug-use, gambling, drinking, over-eating, or any other addiction.

When I finally got to bed, I thought over all the material Kumi had packed into these past few days. When I asked him how he expected us to absorb it all in one weekend he said, "Who said anything about one weekend? It's like your Charting—you work on it for the rest of your life."

(My notes on Preparation are on page 342)

13

MEMORIES IN SPACE

...WHEN YOU SEE THE CABOOSE, YOU KNOW YOU'RE FINISHED

"Doers keep the image of an important upcoming event right in front of their eyes, sometimes for weeks or months, so they are constantly inspired and energized by it. In effect, they are continually rehearsing the event by always seeing it in the present."

On the way to the airport I told Kumi my theory about eye positions and the senses and showed him my eye scan chart. He looked at it for a moment and nodded.

"Congratulations, you got it," he said. "You can add that eyes straight ahead and defocused generally indicates visualization. And some people are reversed, particularly left-handers if they're true leftys, because many of them are actually neurologically 'wired' right-handed. All this really gets interesting with the exceptions, where people seem to see or hear in the 'wrong' place—like you when you visualize Marion down to your right, where your feelings are. True love, I'd say."

My mouth fell open and I looked at him.

"Keep your eyes on the road, these drivers are crazy here," he said.

"You knew this all the time. You're the sneakiest thing on two feet."

"Hee-hee-hee. I wanted you to discover it for yourself. I certainly led you enough, saying 'feel' when I looked down right, and, 'The way I *used* to see things' and gesturing up to the left. You did good. I'm proud of myself."

When I got back to my apartment I found a message on my voice mail from an organizer for the International Computer Conference.

"We have a slot open for our annual conference. Would you be free to make a presentation?" he asked. "This would be for a video-conference session in the third week of August."

I called him right away. "How did you get my name?"

"Heard on the drum that you're up to something interesting. We'd like to see an outline of the kind of presentation you'd make. We'd need to approve it, of course. How soon could you show me something?"

"That's a big deal," Marion said.

"Yeah, people from all over the world."

"What does Gregor say? Would you be ready by then?"

"He just shrugged his shoulders. You know him."

For the next two weeks Marion prepared for a film audition while I worked on a proposal for my research project, holographic movies sent between two computers. So far, this was a concept from "Star Wars."

We played squash several days a week and I worked out religiously every morning. I had lost six more pounds. Marion said it was not only because of the exercise but that I was eating much better. I added The Tuning Dance to my daily regimen, which Marion and I sometimes did together. She had a natural talent for the movements Kumi had shown us and was a good coach for me. Now I have two surrogate "Kumis" for that one, Marion and Matt. As I did the moves for The Tuning Dance I thought of how I would present my proposal at the computer conference. I got to the point where every time I did the hand exercises I heard my voice explaining my ideas—not how I would do it, which was secret, but what I would do with holographic conferencing. Withholding the "how" part was easy, of course, since I still didn't know how I'd do it. I felt in my gut that we'd figure it out. But by August? I know Kumi said to turn off the internal dialogue, but this was different. The moves are supposed to be a performance signal and they were helping me create sentences that sounded like I knew what I was talking about. I figured I could get away with that.

One night Gregor showed up for one of our all-night vigils with equipment to build a special image compression mechanism. I argued that it cost too much and wasn't necessary.

"No problem," he said, punching in commands on the Pentium. My business bank account appeared on the blue screen showing a new deposit of $9000.

"Where'd I get that money?"

"From IBM," he said. He clicked in a series of codes and an IBM special service account showed up on the screen showing a debit of $9000. Gregor was hacking!

"Omigod, omigod."

"Will never discover. Using encryption algorithm from old Soviet file."

"You're using KGB codes to steal money from the bank! Jesus, Gregor, the NSA spy satellites are going to pick that up. The FBI'll be at my door!"

I sat down and breathed as deeply as I could. When I gained control I spoke very slowly.

"Now, Gregor, listen to me. *Look at me!* Put that money back immediately. NOW."

I watched in fascination as he restored the accounts to normal.

"Gregor, if you ever do that again big men in raincoats will come to the door and take you away—*forever*. Like in old Soviet Union, remember? Work camp, torture, and no computers ever again."

He looked at me with bloodshot eyes. Amazing. I think I got through. I walked into the other room and made circles with my shoulders. Then I reached my arms as high as I could, stretching to touch the upper edge of the door frame. I repeated the stretches until my breathing was normal and then returned to Gregor to work through the night.

I looked forward to showing Marion Montana. After the New York sessions we decided we'd like to do some work with Kumi together in the mountains. I had come to love the place and couldn't wait to see it in the spring. We landed in Kalispell around one-thirty and rented a jeep for the trek up the mountains to Kumi's place. The smell of pine and the blanket of blue-green trees across the mountain landscape seemed to wash away the gray New York winter. I even enjoyed the rutted road as we bounced and bumped our way up the mountain. When we got to Kumi's cabin I looked at Marion to see her reaction to the view. She sucked in her breath and said "Ohhh...." very softly. I felt proud, as if I were giving her something I had created.

We sat in the jeep for a few moments looking at the mountains and listening to the silence. A breeze was stirring the long needles of the ponderosa pines. Cumulus clouds moved slowly through a blue sky, casting dark shadows on the valley. Marion got out of the car, walked over to the edge of the mountain and sang, "Aaaaaaaaaa-meeeeeeeee" loud and long over the valley.

"Oh! I sound like an opera singer!"

"Cooooooo-miiiiiiing," Kumi called. I saw him standing on the roof of his house.

"What are you doing up there?" I asked.

"Fixing a leak," he said. He edged his way down the side of the roof and jumped to the ground, rolling over and onto his feet. Marion went over and gave him a hug.

"Kumi, you could break your neck," I said.

"Don't worry. She doesn't hug *that* hard," he said.

I smelled soup as we entered the cabin. Kumi had also made bread. We brought it out on the porch and sat down.

"Kumi, it's so beautiful," Marion said.

"I arranged to have nature cleaned up for your visit. It can be pretty messy around here when the snow and ice thaws."

Marion and I took a short walk after lunch. She was commenting on the view but I hardly heard her.

"Nick, where are you?"

"Huh? Oh, I don't know. I'm in New York."

"Well, be here."

"Gregor has the key to the apartment. I hope he doesn't destroy it."

"Forget Gregor for one weekend."

"I wish I could. This is the first time I've ever ventured out on my own, and I think I've bitten off too big a piece. To send an image on-line uses 50,000 bits of information per second. To send a holographic image on-line takes at least twenty-four *million* bits of information. Add to that a live image…oh, my God, it's impossible! What's the matter with me? It'll never work!" Suddenly I could hardly breathe. I bent over and held my stomach, groaning.

"Nick! Sit down."

She guided me to a rock. I sat on it and put my head between my legs. I felt her hands and head on my back. The knot in my stomach subsided a little.

"The whole computer world's gonna be there. If I screw this up, I'll make a monumental ass of myself."

"Nick, listen to me. Set a deadline for yourself. By what date will you know if you can do it?"

"I don't know. They have to have advance notice for a cancellation. Middle of July, latest."

"Then do your best until July fifteenth. If you can't get it done by then, you'll get it done later. What's a few months, or a year? The main thing is to do it, right?"

"I'll be laughed at for cancelling. A lot of people out there want me to fail. I'll be nothing." Suddenly my breath came up short again and I felt my heart pounding.

"Oh Nick, you're talking about your image in their eyes. Computers is not what you are, it's what you *do*. We talked about this before."

"Yeah, I know."

"Remember what Kumi said about his daughter? He could see her basic self was formed the day she was born. She had a soul. That's who you *are*. A reputation's not you. It's only other people's impression of you."

"That's important too."

"Sure it is, but people are fickle. They forget what you've done. They only want to know what you're *doing*. The one thing that's constant through all that is you. You always have that basic self, regardless, and that's all that really matters in the long run. Because when you turn out the lights at night, it's *you* you have to live with."

"I'm sorry, Marion. I guess I'm tired."

"You're exhausted."

"I'm acting like a child."

"No, you're acting like a tired old adult." She walked in a circle, studying the ground. "I have an idea. You asked me to 'Kumi' you for modeling, right? How about using Kumi for a model?"

"Kumi. That'd be a big job."

"No, I mean just a part of him—his playfulness."

"How do you model playfulness?"

"Be playful. I just read about Buckminster Fuller. You know, he invented the geodesic dome and a lot of other stuff. Toward the end of his career, he was giving this lecture at Harvard and they asked him what's the secret to being creative. So he jumps up in the air three times, flapping his arms like a bird and says, 'Act like a kid! Act like a kid! Act like a kid!'"

I smiled and exhaled heavily, nodding my head.

"What d'ya say? Sometime on this trip we'll learn from Kumi how to laugh and play. And you'll add that to your chart."

My interest in the search for my elusive soul was increasing by the day. Maybe returning to the feeling of being a kid was the answer.

"Okay, deal."

She frowned at me in a parody of my seriousness, and started flapping her arms and making little jumping motions, like Buckminster Fuller.

I shook my head.

"C'mon."

Her mood was infectious and we started jumping into each other. In a few moments we were giggling and flapping our arms and bumping in to each other. We continued like that all the way back to the cabin. Inside, we unpacked and rolled out our sleeping bags for a nap. I didn't even get completely inside it before falling asleep. When we awoke, Kumi had tea for us. We drank it on the porch.

"So how are Charles and Sun-ee?"

"Charles did very well on his finals. He studied by propping his books up high on a table so he'd be 'eyes up' while reading."

"That reminds me of something I want to show you." He went into the house and came out with a magic marker and paper.

"How good are you at spelling."

"Not bad," Marion said.

"Not good," I said.

"Let's say you want to memorize the spelling of a word, like 'connoisseur.' Do you know how to spell it?

"That's a tricky one, Kumi," Marion said.

He wrote it out on a piece of paper and showed it to us, holding it for a moment in front of his chest. Then he took it away.

"Now spell it for me," he said.

"Hey, you took it away too fast," Marion said.

"Nick?"

"I didn't quite get it."

"Okay, now watch." He wrote it down again but this time divided the word into three parts, piled on top of each other:

con

noisse

ur

Then he held it up *over* his head, but for only a second and took it away. "Now spell it."

"That looks wrong, the syllables don't break that way," I said.

"That's the idea, makes it more memorable," Kumi said. "You pronounce the false syllables out loud as three separate words—'con,' 'noisse' and 'ur'— and that gives you an auditory memory of it too."

He was right. I saw an image of the kumi-ized syllables in my mind and spoke them out loud separately. Then I spelled the whole thing out as a word.

"Good. Now spell it backwards."

"Backwards!"

"Just see it in your mind up here in the air and spell it backwards."

I looked up and saw a faint image of the three syllables and recited the letters backwards. I was surprised how easy it was.

"You see? When you divide the word up into separate sounds, whether they're real syllables or not, you can remember them more easily. In fact, if the word break-up is syllabically incorrect it's even easier to remember because it looks weird. But if my way of breaking up the word bothers you, then divide it by syllables—whatever's easier for you to remember."

"But you also held it *up* the second time," I said, "so our eyes automatically signaled the visual part of our brain by looking up to read it."

"And down the first time, where poor spellers usually search in vain for the image because they're trying to sound it out," he said.

"Ah-hah."

"The tricky thing about this word is the middle part—'noisse' is like 'noise,' but with two s's, which actually makes it easier to remember. You notice little things like that when the word is broken up into parts, and you never forget them."

"But what if you have a mass of material you need to memorize, like a speech?" I said.

He motioned for us to follow him to a flat grassy area. "Most speeches can be divided into logical sections, like Introduction, Theme, Development, Summary and Conclusion. Now imagine visualizing those five sections spread out in front of you in giant colored blocks like this." He gestured with both hands outlining sections on the ground in front of us. "Your Introduction might be green, your Theme blue, Development purple, your Summary red and Conclusion yellow."

GREEN—Introduction   BLUE—Theme   PURPLE—Development

RED—Summary   YELLOW—Conclusion

(Your Position)

"Placing these five sections in specific spots around you and giving them each a color helps imprint them on your mind. Now you have the shape and content of your presentation displayed clearly in front of you. And you could add sound to each one. Your intro is green, so you might hear the sound of leaves in that area. Your theme is blue, so you might associate that with the sound of blue water. Your development is purple—so what sounds purple to you?"

"Aretha Franklin singing in purple lighting," Marion said.

"And for the last two, red could be a fire alarm and yellow could be canaries," I said.

> GREEN—Introduction (leaves rustling in the wind)
> BLUE—Theme (sound of water)
> PURPLE—Development (music)
> RED—Review (fire alarm)
> YELLOW—Conclusion (canaries singing)

"Now you have your presentation in two of your senses for easy recall—visual and auditory. To make it even stronger you could step into each section as you rehearse your speech, so that you get a *feel* of the five sections."

Kumi stood in the first block. "Here I think of making a catchy introduction, maybe a funny story." He moved to the next block. "Here I review the words I want to use to clearly state the central point of my talk." Stepping into the third block he said, "And here I think of all the variations on the theme, the sub-ideas that relate to it and will make the point stronger." Moving to the fourth and fifth blocks, he said, "Then I do a recap here, reviewing what I want the listener to remember, and then deliver an anecdote that sums up the whole thing.

"Now you have your speech blocked out spatially in pictures, sound and physical feeling right in front of you—a multi-sensory panorama of your speech. If you want to add information as you work on your speech, you simply place it in the appropriate block. You might get an idea for your Introduction, so you see that block, say 'green leaves' and hear them rustling in the wind. Or you want to add a point to your Conclusion and step into that block and hear canaries and see the color yellow.

"A hear/see/feel association provides a *triple-channel learning* of your material, which makes it easier to recall under the pressure of performance. I call this 'memories in space.'"

"Do the blocks have to be on the ground?" Marion asked. "Let's say your audience is those trees over there," pointing to a cluster of lodgepole pines about thirty feet in front of us. "Couldn't you have these blocks right up there in your audience, so to speak, so you don't have to look down?"

"Sure," Kumi said, "but if the blocks are up in the air you won't be able to step into the spaces to get a feel of them."

Marion walked over to the pines and touched them one by one. "I'm feeling them."

"But aren't the trees supposed to be your audience," I said.

"Oh, Nick," she said, "don't be so literal."

Marion and I used the triple-channel system to organize a presentation and blocked out the sections in front of us. Marion thought of memorizing a song this way, which worked well because music is made up of shapes and designs which lend themselves to being blocked out visually. I made a list of computer codes that Gregor and I were piling up fast and had to be categorized. I started with the color red to get me off to a roaring start. I wondered if Gregor sees colors when he does it. I know he always looks up when he recites codes from memory.

Afterward we went inside to prepare supper.

"You know, I already had a method something like this but had completely forgotten it," Marion said. "When I got the part of Becky Thatcher in 'Tom Sawyer' in seventh grade, I was daunted at all the lines I had to memorize. I told my father I was afraid I would forget them when I got up in front of the audience. So he came up with the idea of using the freight trains that used to run through our town. Often we had to wait a long time at the crossing for them to pass, so my dad suggested I memorize my part by associating the different sections of the play with the cars of a train. The opening scene was the engine, and the next scene the coal car, and then came the oil car, and the cattle car, and so forth, scene after scene. In my mind I soon saw key words or sentences printed on the side of the cars! When I saw the caboose I knew I was at the end."

"He understood the idea intuitively," Kumi said.

"I had an easy time memorizing the play and I never had a memory slip."

"You can use real objects, like the cars of a train, or open space the way we did. They are all variations of the same process. I know an amazing woman who shops by using a mental image of a grid with twenty-one squares, one for each meal of the week. Suppers are in a horizontal row on top, lunches in the middle, breakfasts at the bottom. So she had seven vertical supper-lunch-breakfast columns. She also has this open space at the bottom that runs the length of the whole chart. Here she pictures the groceries that correspond with the three meals for each day. Lunch and breakfast are pretty simple because they're similar every day. But the suppers are always different. So right under the Monday column she'll see maybe coffee, bread, eggs, jam, cold meats and lettuce—that would take care of breakfast and lunch—then she sees chicken, potatoes and vegetables for supper. Her eyes scan the entire week, seeing the finished meals in their respective columns and the supplies in the space running along below it."

"Was she an executive at AT&T?" I asked.

"She was a homemaker."

"Wow. Well, I'll take anything that works. Maybe I could use an idea like that for dates and names and phone numbers. It's funny—associating an idea with an image or sound complicates it in one way, but makes it easier to remember in another. I can still see this one code in my mind on that bush out there."

"Isn't that the bush the animals like to pee on?" Marion said.

"No, they like those lodgepoles, right Kumi?"

As the sun went down it started to get chilly. I put kindling and logs into the fireplace.

"You can also use space for planning and time management," Kumi said. He walked over to the fireplace holding a knife and a celery stick. "You can set up your days visually out in front of you. Let's say you have an important day coming up."

"I do," I said, thinking of the proposal I needed to present to the conference heads.

"Alright, now it's important to mark that day in your mind in a special way, so you can plan and be ready for it. First tell me how you normally think of the days of the week."

I had never thought about how I do that, but now that Kumi mentioned it I saw Monday right in front of me, Tuesday immediately behind it, Wednesday behind that, and so on, like a row of file cards. I described what I saw.

"Now see the important day. Where's that?"

"It's two weeks away, so that puts it about over there by the door," I said pointing.

"Okay. Now move that day right up in front of your face."

"You mean like we did in the Here Image exercise in my first lesson?"

"Yes, but keep it *outside* yourself where you can watch it."

I looked down my mental row of file cards going over a period of two weeks. When I saw the meeting day I "pulled it out" of the file and moved it visually from its location by the door to about two feet in front of me. I saw myself in the picture talking to the conference organizer. I heard him asking questions. My heart started to beat faster. "Okay, it's right in front of me."

"How does it feel?"

"Like it's about to happen," I said

"Yeah, I'm doing it too," Marion said, "and it's really, uh, well, *real*."

"You've heard the saying 'Keeping an idea at the forefront of your mind?' This is exactly what it means. The closer an idea is to you in physical position the more important it becomes. Doers keep the image of an important upcoming event right in front of their eyes, sometimes for weeks or months, so they are constantly inspired and energized by it. In effect, they are continually rehearsing the event by always seeing it in the present."

"A person like that must be really nice company," Marion said, looking at me.

"Listen, you do it too, lady," I said. "Especially when you have an opening night on the horizon."

"Well, that's how people get things done," Kumi said. "Some people scatter their file cards and then can't find them when they want them. That's how people get confused in their planning—they literally lose sight of what they have to do."

"I've been doing that lately," I said. "Especially working with Gregor."

"When you get the picture right in front of you, intensify it by making it big and bright, in color, and give it sound and movement. Liven it up. Adjust the picture until it feels right."

I enlarged the image of my meeting day and felt myself almost entering it as an event. I found myself automatically beginning to present my idea and I began to get ideas for how to word it.

"This is like a mix of the Hologram and visualizing," I said.

"Yes, but here we're adding *time*. Moving the present and the future around in space to positions that help you plan better. Right now you're moving the future into the present."

"But what do I do when I want to stop thinking about it?" Marion asked.

"Put it back in its normal day-of-the-week file card position."

I moved the image back across the room to its original position by the door. Now it was two weeks away again. It got smaller and smaller as it went, and as it disappeared the feeling of its importance diminished.

"I seldom write down important dates, because I see them on my imaginary file cards," Kumi said. "They're in their positions in the month but raised up a couple of inches from the other cards so I can see them. These important date cards are like a row of steps that I see very easily and can attach notes to. When I came back from New York I looked up and mentally saw you and Marion standing on a card about thirty feet away, each foot representing a day of the month. As each week passed, you got closer and closer. Yesterday you were just a card away and I knew I better fix the roof."

"How about months, Kumi?" I asked. "Do you do think of them the same way?"

"I think its good to keep the months in a different pattern from days, so you don't confuse them with each other."

"I see the whole year in a circle all around me," Marion said, "like a hula hoop that slants slightly downward toward summer."

"Where are you standing in the hoop?" I asked.

"Wherever I can see best what I want to look at. The hoop slants upward toward December, and the low point is June. And the months are in colors. If I imagine clock numbers on the hula hoop, Christmas is at twelve o'clock and it's red. January is white at one o'clock, June is yellow at six o'clock and October is orange at ten o'clock. I can see Easter in green at four o'clock and Thanksgiving in purple at eleven o'clock. This makes it easy to jump around in time and still know where everything is."

"I never knew you did that," I said.

"Well, you don't know everything about me."

"Do you place events on that circle?" Kumi asked.

"Oh, yeah, I see our theatre group on tour in September, just after Labor Day at nine o'clock on the circle."

I watched in amazement as Marion created the year in the space around her. But now that I thought of it, people gesture like this all the time. They say "Next October…" and they point to somewhere in space.

"Have you always done it that way?" I said to Marion.

"I didn't even know I was doing it until we started talking about it. It's just…there."

"Well, that's what we're doing here—taking natural unconscious processes and making them conscious, so you can use them in new ways. Some people don't know how to plan. Placing time in space makes it easy for them. This is where your eye chart comes in, Nick. You store and access memory by placing your eyes in the see, hear or feel positions to signal those parts of your brain."

"But I'm still not sure it always works like that," I said.

"How about when you spelled connoisseur backwards? And you saw Marion when she described her time circle." He looked at her. "Marion, where was Christmas again on that circle?"

Her eyes flashed upward, followed by her finger pointing to twelve o'clock as she said, "Up there."

"You see? Her eyes gave you the answer before she even opened her mouth, or gestured. She accessed the visual part of her brain, got the info, then spoke. She may not realize she's visualizing, but you do."

"So the eyes can tell you what a person is thinking," Marion said.

"No, not *what* they're thinking—*how* they're thinking. Remember your stage fright sequence, Nick? When you were omitting all visual steps? I saw you were not visualizing, just by watching your eyes. When you learn how to read the eyes you make a quantum leap as a communicator—you can literally see which sense a person is not using and help them fill it in, so they can better understand your way of thinking. When you first came to me your eyes were always in the down position. I knew before we ever started working that you needed to fill in the visual in your approach to life. Your reasoning was lopsided. You even leaned sideways, because you were so deep in your feelings, always looking down right."

"That's true," Marion said.

"I spoke to you in imagery and led your eyes upward with my gestures to awaken the visual area of your brain."

"And if a person were out of touch with his feelings, would that mean his eyes would never go down to the right?" I asked.

"No, it means his eyes wouldn't *stay* down right, because he doesn't want to dwell there."

"That doesn't make sense. When I came to you last fall I felt miserable. So why would I want to dwell on my emotions?"

"You didn't *want* to dwell on them, you just didn't know how to get *out* of them, so you indulged your feelings. There's a certain perverse pleasure in feeling sorry for yourself."

"Reading the eyes seems almost like undressing somebody mentally," Marion said.

"No more than reading smiles or frowns," Kumi said. "The eyes are just another external indication of what's going on inside. And deep down I think most people know that. That's why they avert their eyes when they don't want others to know what they're thinking or feeling."

"So the real idea behind triple-channel learning is to get a person to use all the senses," Marion said.

"Precisely."

"And when you see a person's eyes going up, down and sideways…"

"…a full scan," I said.

"Yeah, a full scan, you know they're considering a question from every angle," she said.

"Yes," said Kumi.

"Even if they're not speaking."

"Absolutely."

"So, if I were teaching somebody and I saw they've got a clear image of something but maybe not a feel of it, what would I do?" Marion asked.

"You might say to the person, 'How would it *feel* if…' and lead their eyes down to their right with a hand gesture," Kumi said. "The more you talk in feelings, the more the person needs to feel to understand what you're saying."

"So she'd be leading the person into his or her feelings, so to speak," I said

"Right."

"I told you this guy was a sneak," I said to Marion. "Can you imagine being on a date with him? A woman wouldn't have a chance."

"Unless the woman knew this stuff too," Marion said.

Suddenly Marion jumped up and stood in the middle of the room. "Ladies, and gentlemen, welcome to our TV special, SECRETS OF THE EYES, where you can witness a woman in distress making an earth-shattering decision.

(eyes up to her left: Vr)
"Is Nick really the man for me?"

(eyes up to her right: Vc)
"Maybe somebody a little bit taller - dark eyes, sexy smile."

(eyes down to her left: Ai)
"But then I ask myself, Are looks everything?"

(eyes straight to her left: Ar)
"I can hear mom now: 'How much money does he make?'"

(eyes straight to her right: Ac)
*"On the other hand, my shrink will
probably ask if he's well-adjusted."*

(eyes down to her right: K)
*"Hmm. How do I feel about
all this?"*

(eyes scan all positions and finish
straight ahead)
"Maybe I'll just keep looking."

Marion spoke aloud for our entertainment benefit, so we'd know what she was seeing, hearing and feeling in each of the eye positions. Normally she won't talk to herself when practicing the eye positions unless she's using an auditory sense. She winked and gave me big hug and Kumi applauded her performance.

"But one thing I do know, Kumi—in my next life I want *you* to be my boyfriend."

"Oh no, I'm spoken for in the next life. I can *seeeeeeeee* that life way over there," and he slowly moved his pointed finger toward the open doorway, out to the mountain spires ringed with moonlit clouds.

While Marion rolled out the sleeping bags I logged the new part I'd acquired on this visit:

Learner

*"I remind you to use all your senses when thinking through an issue,
especially when learning something new."*

The Inventor, State Maker and Mr. Ready all welcomed the Learner, on the proviso that he wouldn't operate unilaterally. I suggested the four of them would make a powerful coalition and immediately got a warm feeling in my torso—which I took to be a Yes.

Kumi said the linguistics of Charting are very important, and that I should take a very close look at the wording I use to define each part's job. If I were that part, would I know what to do by reading my job description? If I didn't, I'd waste time and energy going off on tangents. (The corporate world is full of employees who are confused about where their job starts and ends, and the results can cost a company valuable time and money.) Granted, jobs can expand and change, especially when you encourage initiative. But jobs should also have borders. Clear definitions inspire action. Without targeted challenges, people (or parts) can get restless, exceed their boundaries and create resentments in other parts. At the extreme, they'll rebel or even go on strike. Kumi said if I find I'm continually arguing with myself, I'll know my parts are disorganized and I'm heading for a showdown, if not a breakdown. When all of a person's parts argue uncontrollably at once, that's the essence of insanity.

That night I had my dream again. It's a slow motion movie where these spirit-like creatures are floating around me. I should be afraid of them, but they're not threatening. I don't understand it and that bothers me.

(My notes on Spatial Memory are on page 349)

14

THEN I STOOD ON MY HEAD

...FINDING A SYMPATHY PARTNER

*"Your head is simply surprised at this new activity.
'You've always stood on your feet,' it says, 'so why are
you suddenly standing on me?'"*

When I awoke, Kumi was making breakfast. I ambled over to the large window and saw Marion outside feeding the chipmunks. Mist was dissolving in the sunbeams that sliced through the pines, rays of light you could almost climb. In the sunlight Marion's hair was the same reddish color as the animals' fur.

After breakfast we did the dishes and walked among the pines. We needed sweaters, but Kumi said the sun would soon burn off the chill. I recalled the first time Kumi and I took this walk last fall. Now the trees had a fresh summer smell and the ground had a new layer of needles. Marion reached down and picked up a cone, smelled it and gave it to me. We walked to a clearing and sat down on the ledge, looking at a lake in the far distance.

"There's my friend," Kumi said, pointing to a bald eagle. Its head and neck, pure white against the dark body, looked like a hood as it floated below us like a hang glider.

"Its nest is in that tamarack tree." Kumi pointed to a magnificent cone-bearing hardwood tree with needle-like leaves.

Kumi climbed off the rock and looked at Marion. Suddenly they both broke into a sprint, giggling and looking back at me, like kids making a challenge. I ran after them, passed Marion, got neck and neck with Kumi, then passed him. When I got to the cabin I jumped up the steps, into the cabin, grabbed the tea pot and came back to the door. Kumi was standing by the tree looking at me, breathing deeply with his hands on his hips and Marion was just finishing in a walk. I tried not to flaunt my newly-earned physical condition on Kumi, but I couldn't help but remember our race last fall and how he chided me about being out of shape.

"Herb or regular?" I said.

Kumi nodded. "Not bad, for a city boy."

"I won't take all the credit. I was thinking of a certain animal."

"What animal?"

"I'm not telling."

Kumi removed some exercise mats from a storage space over the door. We carried them outside to the clearing where he had shown me the Hologram months earlier. He laid out the mats to cover an area about fourteen feet square. We sat on the perimeter and he took off his shirt.

"I'm glad you're in such good shape, Nick. You'll be ready for this."

Then he did a diving somersault toward Marion that sent her scrambling out of the way. I could see he was purposely surprising her, like a playful cat. Then he stood on his head. In that position, he stretched and twisted his body like a snake and shook his legs in the air, then, in one graceful move, came down out of the headstand and arched into a backbend with his head touching the mat. He sprang out of the backbend into a forward somersault and onto one foot, standing in a crouch, absolutely still, as if he were stalking an animal.

He sprang forward, then to the left, then to the right, in a series of dance-like steps as if he were dodging an attacker, then fell back into a backward somersault, rolling up onto one shoulder, arms braced on the floor. Keeping his legs in the air, he moved slowly from one shoulder to the other while bicycling his legs. Then he fell to the floor and rolled back and forth like a rolling pin, and then into a series of forward and backward somersaults.

He looked like an animal playing with something he could never quite get a firm hold of. Marion's outcries and laughter accompanied the thumps and slaps of his body on the mats. He ended up in a headstand, legs extended straight up into the air. After keeping absolutely still for a few moments in this position, he curled his legs down into his torso in very slow motion and lowered his body to the mat. Then he sat up and looked at us, almost as if nothing had happened.

"That's called The Cat."

Marion clapped her hands and said "Kumi, that's wonderful! You looked like a kid."

"I am," he said.

"Do you really expect us to do that?" I said.

"Nick is a tottering old man," Kumi said. "Today we're going to make him young."

"Did you put him up to this?" I said.

Marion stood up, ignoring my question. "I'm ready."

"First, I'm assuming neither of you has any neck or back problems. Okay. The Cat may look complicated and difficult, like you have to be an acrobat or a gymnast to do it. But when you break it down, you see it is really a series of moves of the kind anyone can do at almost any age. Notice there are no back flips, or standing on your hands or other gymnastic tricks requiring a young and agile body."

"C'mon, Kumi, some of those moves are pretty demanding," I said.

"True, but they're mainly stretching and balancing and don't require strength."

"Well, they sure require something."

"Concentration mainly. Some of the moves are ancient, like the headstand which is part of yoga, and the single shoulder stand, which comes from traditional Chinese theater. The back bend is basic to dance movement and the somersault is every child's backyard game. First, I'm going to show you how to do these moves one at a time, then you'll string them together. But since there are two of you, I'm going to have you mirror each other as you do them. This way you each have a sympathy partner."

"Sympathy partner?" Marion said.

"Yeah. Someone who accompanies you through the moves, kind of an unspoken guardian."

"Hmm. Like having somebody 'Kumi' you."

"There are two kinds of headstand—the Hatha yoga and the three-point. We'll learn the three-point first. I call it three-point because your head and arms form a tripod that holds you up quite easily, with your arms sharing some of the weight."

We started by standing back-to-back. I felt very insecure and was sure I wasn't going to be able to do this. I was going along with it mainly because of

Marion. I'd promised her I'd learn to play, and The Cat, with all its tumbling and falling, had that kind of spirit. Kumi had us get down on our hands and knees and look at each other through our legs. Seeing Marion upside-down through the space between my feet was so unusual we both giggled and felt like kids. We said "Hi" to each other.

"Position your head on the mat at a point midway between the hairline and the center of your head and place your palms flat, forming a triangle with the head. The key to a good headstand is to have a solid, wide triangle. Now, lift up your seats and 'walk your legs' forward toward your head, while keeping eye contact with each other."

Seeing the triangle formed by Marion's head and two hands helped me adjust my own triangle so that it formed a tripod broad enough to support my body.

"When you walk your body toward your tripod, you come to a point where you can't go forward any more and your legs simply go up."

Here we go, I thought. With our eyes locked on each other, Marion and I seemed to be helping each other do it. I found I wasn't thinking about myself, but rather about her. We seemed to be giving each other nonverbal feedback. Mirroring the action helped us do it. My head hurt a little when I shifted my weight onto the tripod, and I felt slightly precarious when my legs went up into the air. I put my legs back down again.

"The pressure on your head takes a little getting used to. Your head is simply surprised at this new activity. 'You've always stood on your feet,' it says, 'so why are you suddenly standing on me?'"

"So what do you suggest?" I asked, from my upside-down position.

"Tell your head, 'Hey, you're getting a new view of the world. Relax and enjoy it.'"

I shifted my weight onto my tripod again and was suddenly balancing. I felt a little shaky, but I was on my head!

"Good. You don't have to raise your legs in the air at first when you're on your tripod, just fold them into your seat. Many first-timers want to stretch their legs vertically in the air immediately to prove to themselves they're in a headstand. Then the weight of their legs throws them off balance and they fall. But you've accomplished the headstand when your legs are off the ground and your weight is balanced upside-down. You can always straighten your legs later, when you feel secure and balanced."

I raised my legs straight up in the air and fell over.

"Thanks for demonstrating my point, Nick," Kumi said.

"You're welcome."

He then led us through the other moves of The Cat. In the back bend we knelt down and reached over backwards, seeing each other upside-down, then touching hands. Our arms formed a bridge between us. This backwards stretch was much easier for Marion than for me. My thighs needed a little time to get used to the stretch.

We rolled backwards over one shoulder while holding hands, which I was amazed we were able to do together on the first try. The "Roll-over" and the "Stalk" and the somersaults we did as a game, separately rolling and falling in helter-skelter patterns, trying to surprise each other.

The hardest to learn was the shoulder stand, where you balance on one shoulder with your legs in the air and brace yourself up with your arms. We kept rolling out of it. I got frustrated and complained that we just weren't doing it right.

"Don't criticize yourself. Just have fun with the position and let the technique come later." So we groaned and chuckled and kept rolling into each other and didn't care if we ended up in a proper shoulder stand.

After about an hour we had gone through all the moves. Then we put them all together as a kind of game, improvising them in any order we wished. The Cat finishes with you just lying there, giving your body a rest. We both ended up on our backs looking at the tops of the ponderosa pines against the sky with the occasional clouds drifting by. I felt totally spent and just let my body sink into the mat.

I realized we had actually learned The Cat—not perfectly, but we understood it, had the experience of it. All we had to do now was practice it until we had control over the individual moves. Kumi reminded us that developing a high level of skill is not the goal, because The Cat has many meanings. So far, we had learned to direct our attention outward, toward something or someone else, and also how to recapture the spirit of play. In more ways than one, we were also learning to "turn our world upside down."

"Those not used to the somersault can find it a little scary at first," Kumi said. "Not because it's difficult or dangerous, but because for a moment you are neither upright nor upside-down—you are somewhere in between. That split second between worlds represents an implied loss of control, of not knowing where you are. Deep down the fear is, 'I'm entering into something unknown and don't know how I'll come out of it.'"

"So how can people overcome that?" Marion asked.

"Just do it. Having a sympathy partner helps. Once you break the ice, you've got it forever."

We carried the mats back inside. Kumi made tea, which we drank on the porch. I had that workout feeling—my whole body tingled. I breathed deeper and the mountain air smelled even sweeter.

Marion asked Kumi where he'd learned The Cat.

"From a group of Polish actors. They did a kind of theater where they'd tell one story with words and another with their bodies. So they devised movements that made up a vocabulary of nonverbal communication, and that became The Cat. They got their inspiration from watching cats play. When you can tumble and roll like a cat, you're ready for any kind of spontaneous movement. When you prepare for performance by doing The Cat, no audience can scare you. It's your complete physical performance signal."

"I think it would also be great for helping you focus mentally," Marion said.

"It's an automatic concentration exercise," Kumi said. "Since you must concentrate to learn how to stand on your head, the act of standing on your head automatically kicks in your concentration. And, as I demonstrated in New York, your voice gets stronger and deeper because you open the larynx with all the upside-down movements. You also learn how to move with more confidence, more naturalness."

"And how to communicate with your body," Marion said.

"The more freely you're able to move, the more natural you will be on stage, or in anything you do. Sometimes you'll even surprise yourself. I taught The Cat to a young man who had political ambitions. Physically he was rather awkward but he was very determined. He practiced The Cat religiously and, little by little, developed a great sense of physical confidence in public.

"A big opportunity came his way when he was asked to speak at an important election rally. But on the big day he was told he would have to speak while the stage was being reset for the next event. How could he get the audience's attention in the middle of such commotion? He'd already missed sleep from campaigning and was feeling drowsy, losing his concentration. So before his speech he went into a back room and did a partial Cat. That is, he took off his suit jacket and shoes, loosened his tie, stood on his head and did one, slow back bend. Since he knew The Cat so well, this little bit was enough to bring back the complete feeling of doing the whole Cat. It focused his attention. Then he stood up and did the shoulder and hand movements from The Tuning Dance, washed his face and got dressed. He said he felt refreshed and was in a performance state of mind.

"He went to the stage area and saw the stage hands moving chairs and tables. The hall was full. He had about seven minutes to speak, which was the time allocated to the big new stage set. When he got his cue he did something very unusual. He walked on stage, stopped in front of the microphone and *turned his back to the audience*, watching the stage hands for a moment. Then he turned to the audience and talked. The audience got quiet immediately and he said he felt very comfortable, even cracking a couple of jokes about the noisy activity behind him, which got him warm laughter.

"Afterward, he asked himself why he had spontaneously turned his back to the audience. The audience's attention was on the stage hands. By looking at the stage hands he gave the impression he was in charge of them and the audience's attention transferred to him.

"'That was a brilliant thing to do,' he said, 'but *I* didn't do it—my *body* did.' From doing The Cat, his body had learned to respond instinctively under pressure, all by itself."

"That sounds almost like a sixth sense," Marion said.

"The vestibular sense. It's not a separate sense, really. It integrates all the senses. The vestibular organ is an apparatus in your inner ear that accounts for your sense of balance, space and distance. All your senses focus through it."

"Can you say more about that?" I said.

"Well, for instance, when you walk through a doorway you don't use your eyes alone. Something has to signal your limbs to walk in the direction the eyes are looking and correct your movements step by step as you go, to maintain your equilibrium through the doorway. If your vestibular organ is out of whack you can't do it. You can test that by spinning around ten times and then walking through the doorway. You'll probably bump into the door jamb, not because you can't see it, but because the liquid in your inner ear is disturbed and the vestibular organ can't coordinate your reflexes.

"When you do movements that challenge your sense of balance—like headstands and somersaults—you sharpen your brain-limb coordination. You learn how to judge distance and use space without having to pay conscious attention to it."

"The stuff we did yesterday—placing memories and time in space—would that be vestibular?"

"Interesting thought. I think as you develop your vestibular apparatus through balancing exercises, your visual and auditory judgment of space and distance will improve," Kumi said.

"Musicians talk about balancing sound and projecting tone," Marion said. "That's also space and distance, isn't it? And actors talk about throwing their voice."

"Throwing your voice or throwing a ball is the same thing. You need to know how *far* to throw it, and that's a distance judgment. How far away is your audience? And if you're an actor or musician performing with a partner you have to balance the sound between yourselves, as well as between yourself and your listeners. Maybe you're playing in a small hall today and in a large hall tomorrow. That requires the constant adjusting of spatial judgment. It's all vestibular.

"Really good public speakers know just how far to throw their voices to give the feeling they're talking directly to you. The counter-example would be the drunk who speaks too loudly to someone standing only a few feet away. Alcohol short-circuits the muscle-eye coordination so you can't judge distance accurately. The more keenly you develop your vestibular response through physical balancing movements, the more accurately you can target listeners with your voice. Developing accuracy in your vocal projection, combined with control of physical movement, can make you a very persuasive person."

"Carrying this whole idea of the vestibular system a little further," Marion said, "I wonder if a better physical balance could help you achieve better psychological or spiritual balance."

"I think you could say that physical balance makes you more aware of the value of balance in your life," Kumi said. "You're more likely to recognize the meaning of the Balinese checkered cloth."

"What's that?" I asked.

"The Balinese wrap a black and white checkered-cloth around their spiritual icons as a reminder of the polarity of life—good and evil, happiness and sadness, good fortune and bad. They know there are two sides to everything so they tend not to judge human behavior, just balance it."

"John F. Kennedy said something like that," Marion added. "There's no justice in life, only balance."

"The Balinese learn that metaphor from childhood. Even their dances require a great deal of physical balance—like standing on one foot. The men learn the women's dances and the women learn the men's, to further their balance. Maybe we could learn from the Balinese and develop what you might call a physical/spiritual vestibular system that would put us in balance with ourselves and the world. So, yes, to answer your question, I think finding balance in your body helps you seek balance in your life and to recognize it when you see it. That may be the biggest lesson of The Cat."

Marion helped Kumi make one of his historic soups while I added a new part to my Chart:

Balancer

"I balance work with play.
I alert you when any part is jeopardizing the community balance."

I asked the Balancer to help me maintain equilibrium between individual parts. Also to help complex coalitions—like that of Mr. Ready, State Maker, Inventor and Learner—maintain a dynamic balance within themselves and between their group and the community. The Balancer would be good to help parts grow and take on new functions, and also help them integrate as they changed.

The subject of change reminded me that Kumi said an important function of Charting was to update my parts' job descriptions from time to time. A part operating on old information can cause trouble. He told about a woman who fell in love with a man but found she was unwilling to be intimate with him. Questioned about this at length, she recalled an incident that occurred when she was fifteen. She was "crazy about a boy" who fell for her best friend and it "broke her heart." She said, "I vowed right then I'd never trust a man again."

Kumi warns about making imperative commands like that—especially in a deeply emotional state—some part of you is likely to take your outcry as an assignment and carry it out with single-minded determination until told otherwise. In one angry moment as a teenager this woman had built in an iron-clad protection against men. Unfortunately, that part was unable to distinguish between those who were trustworthy and those who were not. She had completely forgotten this vow which now seemed childish to her. Kumi had her "go inside herself," identify that part and have a heart-to-heart talk with it, telling it she was older now and could make sound judgments about men. With Kumi's guidance she carried out this exercise and her attitude toward her boyfriend changed. It took a while to adjust her behavior to the new attitude but gradually the idea of intimacy with him became less threatening. Later, when she said she was glad to be rid of that part, Kumi reminded her of what a good job it had done for her all these years and suggested she promote it to Personal And Business Affairs Advisor in charge of matters of trust, which she did. Today she is a bank manager, happily married and has three children.

I wondered if Marion had put Kumi up to doing The Cat because of our discussion on the previous day about playing and acting like a kid again. The whole spirit of The Cat was playful, but two things made it feel especially like being a kid: rolling on the ground (or floor when I do it back in New York), and bare feet (I remember the effect of that also when doing the Tuning Dance). I never go barefoot, except to swim. And I do get a kind of free, youthful feeling at the pool or the beach, or even when wearing sandals in the summer.

Perhaps there is a connection between unencumbered feet and a feeling of freedom and creativity. Marion met the famous Hungarian poet, George Faludy, on a bitter cold day in January. He was wearing no hat on his wild bush of gray hair and no socks. When she asked him how he could go barefoot in sub-zero weather, he said he once met Albert Einstein who told him, "Never cut your hair and never wear socks." Einstein went on to say that socks were unhealthy for your feet (though he never said why). Going barefoot in winter is a little extreme for me, but I thought it might not be a bad idea to prepare for high-pressure situations barefoot to get back the freewheeling confidence and uninhibited spirit of play that's so natural to children.

(My notes and exercises on The Cat are on page 356)

15

SILENT PERFORMING

...BUT IT WON'T GO THAT WELL WHEN I SING IT

"Mother Teresa looked at starving children and saw them healthy. Then she asked, 'What would have to happen to make this dream a reality?' She didn't know the answer to that question, so she speculated: 'What if we did this? What if we did that?' These questions open up new possibilities. This is how we create change."

After lunch we followed Kumi's custom of having a siesta. The idea of resting in the middle of the day used to disturb me. I got the feeling I was slacking off, that nighttime was for resting and the day was for work. Admittedly, I would droop in the afternoon and drink coffee to get me over the hump. But how do you sleep a short time? And if you do, how do you not feel woozy from the nap?

So Kumi taught me the key-drop sleep. You sit in an easy chair with your arms hanging over the arm rests, holding your keys firmly in one hand. Take a couple of deep breaths, sit back and enjoy relaxing with your eyes closed. When you reach the first phase of sleep the keys will fall to the floor and wake you up. And that's it—you get up and go about your day.

Since adopting this little "time-out" in my day I've rarely felt tired in the afternoon. Sometimes I'll even stretch out and take a good nap. Not only do I get energy from it, but I feel like I'm starting a new day after my rest, refreshed and energetic.

After we rested Kumi made tea. We carried our cups outside and sat on a spruce log watching the mountains change colors. The sea of fir trees in the distance turned from green to black to green again under the moving clouds. A bull moose was barely visible amidst a cluster of jack pines.

"You see it?" I said softly to Marion.

"What? Where?" she said.

"There." I pointed.

"Ohhh…" she said softly.

We sat like that in absolute silence for I don't know how long. I guessed it was about four-thirty when Kumi finally spoke.

"The power of silence."

"You can almost hear it," Marion said.

"I listen to it every day," said Kumi. He cleared his throat and spoke in a subdued tone. "One day I was asked at the last minute to read an hypnotic induction script of mine to a group of psychiatrists at a conference in Phoenix. I had spoken to the group in the morning about hypnotic techniques. Someone there knew I had done inductions with audiences and asked if I would demonstrate group hypnosis after lunch. I had one of my scripts with me and agreed. I hadn't read it publicly for a long time and it had many markings for subtle changes of voice tone, volume and pacing. I wanted to practice reading it during lunch hour in the ballroom where we were meeting, to get a feel of the space and practice projecting my voice in it. But a meeting was being held there, so the space was not available.

"So I went to my hotel room and read the script to an imaginary audience silently. I read it exactly as I would normally read it, with full energy, normal breathing, moving my mouth and enunciating the words, but without sound. I looked out the window so I wouldn't be talking to the wall.

"The effect was illuminating. Not hearing my own voice freed me to concentrate on my timing, phrasing, volume and gestures and I felt more control over my delivery. Reading silently also built up a strong energy, because I was now feeling how it would be to read the script in that ballroom. I was itching to add the sound.

"The reading went beautifully, perhaps the best I'd ever given. The words flowed out of my mouth with ease and I was able to pay attention to all the nuances of my delivery."

"But weren't you still a little unsure of how your voice would sound in the ballroom?" Marion said.

"I think the vocal sound takes care of itself if you feel control in your body. Normally, you are so preoccupied with the content of your talk and the sound of your voice that you have little objectivity about other aspects of your performance. For example, you may be gesturing too much or too little, or not pacing your talk well, but you don't notice it because you are preoccupied with speaking—the technical matters involved with pronunciation and vocal production."

"Yes. Actors have that problem, too," Marion said.

"And if you're reading from a script, you have the task of reading perfectly—you don't want to muff the words—so you're preoccupied with that. But this silent reading—the dissociating of sound from the physical production of it—made me aware of everything I needed to do to deliver the material exactly as I wanted to. Afterwards, adding sound was easy.

"Since then I've used this technique many times, and I've taught it to teachers, public speakers, mediators, business people, singers, musicians, announcers, anyone who wants to get a firm grasp on their performance before giving it."

"Another advantage is that you can practice without attracting attention or disturbing others," Marion said.

"And when you get free of your voice this way you find yourself using it in new ways. You can surprise yourself. Would you like to try it?"

"I would," said Marion. "I wonder how it would work for singing."

Marion stood up and brushed herself off, shifted from leg to leg and looked out over the valley. Kumi stood beside her and told her to sing something silently, something she knew well. She adjusted herself for a moment and then moved her mouth like she was singing.

"No, no," said Kumi. "You are just mouthing the words. I want you to really make all the actions of singing—the breathing, the articulation, the projection of sound—as if your vocal cords were being fully activated. In other words, sing fully and completely but just leave out the sound. You need to use strong energy. Look at the mountaintop there and project it."

Marion nodded and did it again. This time she looked like she was singing. You could see the muscles in her neck flexing and she took big breaths and gestured with her hands. The whole scene looked like a video with the sound off.

"That's it," Kumi said. "How'd that feel?"

"Interesting. It feels different. It's easier, but, uh…"

"Anything you want to change?"

Marion squinted her eyes for a moment and then sang silently again. This time she looked different, but I couldn't tell how.

"I just realized I've been breathing in the wrong place in this song. I always try to sing the second phrase all in one breath and it just doesn't work. This is more natural." She looked at Kumi, then back at the mountain, like she was still considering the change.

"When you're ready, sing it with sound."

"Right now? Out here in the open?"

"You see anybody you'll be disturbing?" Kumi said gesturing out over the expanse.

"Serenade the moose," I said.

She took a deep breath, got back her concentration and started singing. I've heard Marion sing many times and I know she doesn't consider herself a professional singer. For her, singing has always been a way to develop her voice and make her a better actress. But I was surprised at the sound that came out of her now. I'm not a musician, but every note was very solid, like she was hitting it squarely and holding on to it.

"Oh," she said. "That feels *good.*"

"Do you have any music that gives you problems?" Kumi said.

"I have lots of stuff that gives me problems," she said laughing out loud.

"Well, pick something—a real challenge."

"This one song has a high C in it, and it's just impossible to get it soft."

"Do it silently and see how it feels."

She sang a passage silently and stopped. "I need to take a bigger breath," she said. She shifted her feet, inhaled and sang silently again. This time she moved her hands differently. She looked more in control.

"That was better, wasn't it?" Kumi said.

"Yes, it uh…yes it was."

"Are you doing that high note?"

"Yes."

"Do it again."

She repeated the passage this time with an even bigger breath and I was impressed at how strong she looked.

"How'd it go?" Kumi said.

"Very well."

"Now add the sound."

"But it won't go that well when I sing it," she said.

"But you just sang it."

"Yeah, but not *really*. There was no sound."

"You mean you didn't hear it?"

"Well, yeah, *I* heard it."

"And did you feel it in your body?"

"Yeah."

"Then you did it."

She looked slightly confused and nodded her head.

She turned to face the mountaintop, planted her feet squarely on the ground, took a deep breath and sang. We listened as she started with a rather deep voice and then made this sudden jump to a very high note—that must have been the high C—and then came back down. You don't have to be an expert to know when a singer hits a bull's eye on a hard note, and she hit that one perfectly.

When she stopped singing she just stood there, staring at the mountain. Then she turned to Kumi and said in a soft voice, "I've never done that before. It could have been softer, but I did it." And then she looked back at the mountain. She seemed to be in a kind of trance, so Kumi and I left her alone and sauntered back toward the cabin.

I watched the afternoon sun fading in the valley. "What did she do that made that possible?" I said.

"It's no secret. She stopped worrying about the sound and concentrated instead on what her body needed to do to *produce* the sound, to get that high note."

"So, she can really do it."

"She did it. You heard her. She sent her voice to that mountaintop."

"That's the mountaintop that has my nose on it," I said. "Now her voice is up there, too."

Later, when I looked for Marion she was sitting on a rock. I started to walk toward her when Kumi caught my arm. "No, leave her alone," he whispered.

"She's making supper," I said.

He waved me toward the house. "How about you make supper?"

"Me?"

"An overwhelming concept?"

"Well, she said she was going to do it."

"Is that how you do things—she goes to the kitchen to make dinner, no matter what?"

I picked up a pine branch and examined the needles.

"This is a special moment for her," Kumi said. "You're not jealous that she's accomplishing something, are you?"

"C'mon, Kumi."

"You know one of the big problems a woman performer has in a serious relationship? When she wants something for herself she asks, 'Am I being selfish?' Especially if her wish conflicts at all with what her man wants. She feels she's supposed to be the nurturer."

"That's not true anymore."

"Yes, it's still there, even for the woman who's financially independent, because everything in our society from children's toys to pay scales reinforces it."

"But Marion's the exception, she's an artist."

"She's still a woman."

I went into the house and poured myself a glass of wine. Then I started cutting vegetables. I remembered that "anything omelette" idea and figured I could make that. It was getting dark when I heard Marion and Kumi coming toward the house.

"You're making supper! Great," Marion said. "I'd love a glass of wine."

"Good! Make the vestibular a little tipsy," I said.

I poured her a glass, then toasted her. "To a great high C."

"Thanks, partner."

I looked at Kumi, who turned away and put some logs on the fire. We had dinner by the fire, drinking wine and watching logs burn bright. Kumi drank green tea.

"You sounded good out there today, Marion," I said. "I mean really good."

"I did, didn't I? I just pretended I was a real singer. I thought 'What if I were someone who sang high Cs all the time.'"

"That puts a nice spin on it," Kumi said. "'What if' I were a great singer? How would I do this?'"

"We have an acting exercise called 'what if,'" Marion said. "I might say to myself, 'What if you were my father, how would I talk to you?' It's amazing how that can alter your responses, how it can change you. You can use it off-stage as well."

"Well...on stage, yes," I said. "That's a kind of pretend-world. But you don't change things in real life by just saying, 'What if it were this way?'"

"On the contrary," said Kumi, "most accomplishments in life start exactly that way—by imagining them. 'What if I could fly?' 'But you don't have wings.' 'What if I built a machine with wings?' 'It'd never get off the ground.' 'What if I put an engine in it that made it go so fast the air would lift the wings off the ground?' 'It'd never work.' 'What if it did?'

"Have you ever wondered why some people have confidence and others not? It depends on what you believe about yourself. When you suspend your beliefs even for a moment by saying 'What if *this* were true instead of *that*?' you have an alternative, a choice, a chance to re-design yourself."

"Just knowing I have a choice is liberating," Marion said.

"That doesn't alter the reality of it though," I said.

"But it can change the way you *feel* about it," Marion said.

"Wouldn't you agree that the way you feel about something is what makes it real for you?" asked Kumi. "The three of us may have three different reactions to the same thing. Our reactions reflect our beliefs about that thing. Three different realities."

"I see that. But then there is the *real* reality," I said, feeling a little frustrated.

Kumi and Marion laughed. "Oh, yes, we've been through this before." Marion got out of her chair and raised her arms, "Will the Real Reality please stand up and identify yourself. Nick is looking for you."

Kumi joined her. "I offer a reward to anyone with information leading to the capture of the Real Reality."

I had to smile. "Okay, okay, okay."

"Have a little more of this reality-altering Cabernet, Nick," Marion said. "I know what you're saying," I said. "I just get tired of seeing so many people today walking around in dreamland, talking to inner guardians or looking to aliens from outer space to solve their problems. New age nonsense."

"Careful, Nick," Kumi said. "Some of the stuff we've been doing comes dangerously close to 'new age nonsense'—talking to your parts, for example."

"But that's different. You're pragmatic, you want results. That's why I keep coming back to you. But let's not go overboard. Dreaming is one thing, facing problems is another."

"Well, just because you say 'What if' doesn't mean you're not facing your problems," Marion said. "On the contrary, 'What ifs' can help you see ways to improve situations."

"What we're talking about is re-interpreting your surroundings," Kumi said, "not ignoring them and just wishing they'd go away. Mother Teresa looked at starving children and saw them healthy. Then she asked, 'What would have to happen to make this dream a reality?' She didn't know the answer to that question, so she speculated: 'What if we did this? What if we did that?' These questions open up new possibilities. This is how we create change."

"'To me, 'What if-ing' is very natural," Marion said. "Isn't that how we decide what we want to be? Children's games are all 'what ifs,' or 'as ifs.' I'll be Wonder Woman, you be Batman. You be the bad guy."

"Why do you look at me when you say that?" I said.

Marion leaned over and kissed me. "At the moment, Nick, you are looking kind of like a Scrooge."

"So just say 'Nick looks like Mel Gibson,' and you'll be happy," I said.

"How did you decide on your profession?" Kumi said, looking at me.

"I was fascinated with technology. I imagined all the things I could do with it."

They looked at each other and said, "Ahhhhhhh" in unison.

I was quiet for a moment. "Okay, score one for the dreamers."

"Nick, you know I don't mean people should just walk around dreaming," Marion said. "There's more to it than that. I just read this book about the creative strategies of outstanding people. And it said creative people have three parts: the dreamer, the realist and the critic. First you're the dreamer and you just let your mind free to come up with ideas. Then you become the realist and say, 'How much time and money would this take?' Then you stand back from it and ask, 'What's missing?'—that's the critic. If necessary you go back to the dreaming board. They say truly creative people have all three of these parts in them, otherwise the dream won't work."

"I agree with that," I said. "As long as you fantasize on a specific goal and carry it out, I think it's a very good idea. In fact, I know a manager who holds creative strategy meetings where he'll say, 'Everybody speak your mind freely—

no idea's too crazy—and we won't comment on them until all the ideas are on the table. Then we'll see which ones might work.'"

"No-fault dreaming," Kumi said.

"That's right," I said. "In one of these brain-storming sessions the goal was how to increase production without increasing costs. The ideas started flying and one of the guys said, 'How about we build a plant on the moon?' Nobody laughed because that was the rules of the game. When they appraised the ideas at the end one of the guys said, 'Your remark about going to the moon gives me an idea. What if we set up a plant in Jersey?' For sixty years this company had been exclusively in New York. He outlined the tax advantages and someone else brought up other benefits and they went with the idea. Given the company's conservative history they might never have thought of going out-of-state if it hadn't been for the fantasy atmosphere that manager created."

"All that matters to me is what works," Kumi said. "And I learn what works by observing how people get things done. And not just famous people. I might ask anybody, 'At what are you a genius?' You'd be surprised at the amazing abilities people have. A friend of mine knows a woman who can find four-leaf clovers in a field."

Marion laughed. "What a crazy thing."

"Yes, and you might say 'Who cares?' But he asked her 'How do you do that?' and she said, 'Oh, it's easy. I just delete everything in the field that's not a four-leaf clover!'"

"How in the world does she do that?"

"Exactly," said Kumi. "She's pretending there are only four-leaf clovers in the field. She creates an alternate reality and believes it. And she finds the clovers. Imagine how you could apply an ability like that."

"She should give workshops," Marion said.

"She's a gardener at an old people's home," Kumi said.

We were quiet for a moment. Then Kumi said, "I could fantasize that I'm full of energy right now, but the True Reality is that my muscles want me to take them to bed."

Marion yawned. "Me too."

"And me," I said. "See, all three of us are tired. There is an absolute reality. And I'm glad you guys finally concede the argument."

"Not concede, postpone," Marion said, stretching.

"Well, since the discussion has been going on for several thousand years, I think it'll hold until tomorrow," Kumi said.

Kumi's bedroom was the only other room in the cabin, but it afforded him privacy and we could sit up for a while without bothering him. Before turning in I defined a new part from this afternoon's work.

Realist/Critic

"I work out the details to make sure
your fantasies are possible,
and I question how they fit your targeted goal."

This was actually an old part, but I was updating it. Previously it had poo-pooed ideas before they got off the ground. Now I wanted it to work in conjunction with the Inventor, to help provide the practical under-pinning necessary to make dreams into realities. I think the Balancer was nervous at first that this "dreamer-realist-critic" triumvirate might take over his job, but I assured him he was still the balancer between all the parts.

Kumi said Charting explained those disturbing voices we sometimes hear in our heads, the ones that criticize us or judge us. He said people usually consider these voices the enemy and try to shut them off, but he said I should listen to them and follow their advice. The Realist/Critic, for example, is there to help me. He said that usually the reason an inner voice has criticized me in a caustic or frightening manner is because I'd been ignoring a message it feels I urgently needed to hear, and it had to scare me to get my attention. When it was satisfied that I've paid attention it would be quiet. He said I should be grateful to have a part that knows my needs, can advise and protect me, and that performs this service for me twenty-four hours a day—free! He said if I didn't have such an inner judge, he'd ask me to install one. So he said the next time I hear a critical voice inside me, ask what it wants and listen carefully to it's message, and then *thank* it for its advice.

But parts sometimes have to be taught *when* it's appropriate to speak up. I held a meeting with my parts and informed them that I welcome their input, but would they kindly refrain from giving advice in the middle of an important meeting or presentation when I need a clear mind for the task at hand. Afterward I'd be free to listen. Or better yet, tell me before-hand!

I closed the fireplace screens so no sparks would fly out while we slept. Marion came in from the porch and we rolled out our sleeping bags and crawled in. Half-awake, we exchanged "what ifs" about performing, about life, about life on the moon…

I slept solidly for several hours and then awoke. Something was bothering me, but I couldn't put my finger on it. It was more a feeling trying to work its way into a thought. I knew it was one of those things that would clarify itself for me when the time was right, so I tried to put it out of my mind. But the feeling came back to me as I lay there, like someone talking to me, trying to tell me something.

(My notes on Silent Performing are on page 372)

16

A POCKETFUL OF M&Ms

...YOU HAVE TO BE READY FOR ANYTHING

"I felt his hot breath on my hair and his saliva slather my neck. Suddenly he pawed at my jeans and ripped out the seat. I felt a burning scratch on my seat and thigh, followed by a warm wetness on my leg, which I knew was my own blood."

I awoke late to the smell of buckwheat pancakes. Kumi was cooking and Marion was on a mat standing on her head.

"I see something moving, Kumi. I think it's alive," Marion said, making fun of me as I blinked at the room. "C'mon and join me, Nick. It's a good waker-upper."

"Let me get used to the upright position first," I said. "I was up late last night." I walked over and looked in the frying pan. "Mmm. Looks good." Kumi was engrossed in flipping pancakes without breaking them. I padded over to the door and stepped out on the porch. A breeze was stirring the pines and the sky was pale gray. A squirrel was looking for something to eat. He came toward the house, twitching his nose.

"Don't look at me, fellah, you're on your own. It's spring. Go find some berries or something." I went back inside, got a piece of bread and walked back out. "Here, that's all you get."

The squirrel watched me while he chipped away at the bread. I wondered what it was like to be a little animal out in the wilderness, looking for food while watching out for coyotes and wolves, or whatever they watch out for. He looked at me like he was saying, "I have to trust you, I'm hungry." Soon another came hopping out of nowhere.

I went back inside and got a few peanuts. "That's it! Restaurant closed," I said as I scattered them on the ground. Then a whole bunch of them appeared, searching the ground. "You guys got beepers? Jeez."

Marion called me in for breakfast.

"They got your number, Nick," Kumi said. "Once you start, it never ends."

Pancakes were the kind of comfort food I needed. The past two days had been intense and I was looking forward to a slow and quiet day. We were leaving the next day and Marion wanted to see some of the terrain. Kumi had a favorite lookout point a short hike up the mountain that he had promised to show us. "It's time for you to see it," he said somewhat cryptically.

"You aren't having your period, are you?" Kumi said to Marion.

Marion put down her fork. "No, why?"

"We don't want to attract any unwanted guests."

"Like what?" she said.

"Anything big and furry."

We cleaned up and washed the dishes. I looked outside to see if my squirrel friends wanted our leftovers, but they were gone. Pragmatic little critters—when the food stops they vanish. Kumi directed us to fill canteens with water, wrap sandwiches in airtight bags and put them into in plastic containers. He gave us each a little bell to wear around our waist.

"Is that in case I get lost?" Marion said.

"That too," Kumi said.

"What do you mean 'too'?"

"There are a lot of things living out there. You want to let them know you're coming. Don't worry, the ones to be most afraid of are also afraid of you."

I could see Kumi didn't want to alarm Marion about mountain lions, wolves or bears. He had told me the likelihood of encountering a dangerous animal was slim, especially if you made noise on the trail. He said there are two kinds of bears up here, black bears and grizzlies. I had seen a black bear once at quite a distance, but he didn't seem at all interested in me. I guess they go their way and let you go yours, as long as you don't threaten them or attract them with food.

We went up a winding mountain trail from Kumi's cabin. A breeze was blowing at our back, which Kumi liked because our scent went ahead of us to announce our presence to animals. Every direction we looked was a picture post card view. On one side, rock formations; on another, a slope of pines; then a valley and behind us a panorama of mountaintops as far as you could see. Our bells tinkled as we walked. We had to keep an eye out for rocks underfoot, not to stumble. Occasionally we stopped to drink water or look at some point of interest. We were all talked out from the recent intense days and just kept quiet.

After about an hour-and-a-half we arrived at Kumi's lookout point. Kumi and I sat down, leaning against some rocks that formed natural backrests, while Marion inspected a cluster of flowers that grew out of the rock a short distance away. The sun had worked its way through the pallid sky and was moving across the immense valley far below. In the distance, a river snaked through a band of trees and a dark blue lake shimmered. On the far horizon were dark mountain peaks.

But the big feature was the sky, bright in the distance under a giant purple-black circular cloud formation that completely covered the valley for a span of some fifty miles. This enormous inverted reflection of the curve of the earth seemed to unite the elements of nature in one spiritual dome. I felt a deep sense of peace combined with a vague unrest—that feeling from last night coming back. Kumi leaned over to me and spoke almost in a whisper.

"The sky holds it all together, doesn't it? That's for your next visit."

Marion joined us and we opened our sandwiches in our own private mountain restaurant. We looked over the landscape, and listened to the wind as the sun gradually warmed us. Kumi held up one hand and squeezed his thumb and forefinger together, smiling at me, and I did the same back. He was right—take it with you *when* you can.

We sat there until it got too hot, and then headed back. The wind had changed direction and was blowing in from the valley, across our path. Kumi hummed as we walked. It was like a different trip walking down, because we were facing the mountains that had been behind us. Kumi let me lead the way with Marion in the middle. The path curved downward between large rocks and opened onto a thick growth of tamaracks. About fifty feet in front of me in the shadows of the trees something moved. A loud crack of twigs stopped us. Before I knew it, Kumi was in front of me, holding up his hand. Onto the path ambled a huge brownish bear with a hump on its back, grunting softly. My instinct was to climb a tree. I pointed to one of the pines with a questioning gesture and Kumi spoke very softly, "No."

Very slowly he said to us, "Lie down in a fetal position, cover your head and don't move," as he pushed down on Marion's and my shoulders. "Watch me." He curled up on the ground with his knees up to his chest and placed his hands behind his head, his arms protecting the sides of his face. With Marion in the middle we were curled up like suspects arrested by the police.

In this position I could see only the stones on the ground and the purplish-red flower of a thistle across the path with a large bumblebee on it. I listened to the bear walk slowly toward us through the shrubs, judging its distance by the crunch of it's footsteps. Kumi was closest to it. The crunching stopped about where Kumi was lying and then moved toward Marion. I thought I heard her whimper slightly, but I wasn't sure. Then it moved toward me. Surely it heard my blood pounding in my throat.

I felt his hot breath on my hair and his saliva slather my neck. Suddenly he pawed at my jeans and ripped out the seat. I felt a burning scratch on my seat and thigh, followed by a warm wetness on my leg, which I knew was my own blood. I tightened the grip on my head and squeezed my knees together.

Then silence. I heard the bear in the shrubs, then further away. He was walking away! I couldn't believe it. I waited until I could no longer hear him and then slowly opened my eyes. Kumi came over to me, examining my backside. Marion said, "Is he gone?"

"Did you have something in your pocket?" Kumi asked. I sat up and looked. Kumi leaned over and picked up a torn M&M box. "This?" he said, holding it up.

"Oh, no. I can't believe I did that," I said.

"You had M&Ms in your pocket?" Marion said.

Kumi washed me off with water from a canteen and said, "We better get you back and put something on those scratches. Fortunately, they're not too deep."

We quick-marched down the path, with me holding up what was left of my jeans. We hummed and whistled as we walked, to let everything in the forest know we were coming, just in case. When we arrived at the cabin, Kumi got the rye whiskey and a first-aid kit. He poured some alcohol over my left buttock and thigh.

"Gimme a swig of that," I said. I drank and handed it to Marion who gulped down a mouthful. Then Kumi put a yellow antibiotic salve on my scratches and taped on a bandage loosely.

"He tore the pocket right out," Kumi said.

"But why didn't he hear us with our bells and everything," Marion asked.

"The wind was blowing in the wrong direction. He didn't smell us either. We surprised him."

"Oh, God," said Marion, "I can't believe you had *candy* in your pocket." I shrugged.

"It's not funny." She hit me hard, several times on the shoulders and chest.

"Hey, take it easy."

Suddenly she put her arms around my torso and squeezed so hard I lost my breath for a second. I felt her tears on my neck.

Kumi made tea. Marion and I had ours with a shot of whiskey. We sat inside drinking, looking out the large window at the changing light in the sky.

Marion shook her head. "You make all these preparations and then something totally unpredictable happens, like the wind changing, and all bets are off. How can you plan for that?"

"You can't," Kumi said. "Just be ready for anything."

"But there's no way to be ready for something like that."

"You're alive, aren't you?"

"Well, yes, because you knew what to do."

"That's the point. To know what to do. If one thing doesn't work, you can do something else. That's why I've been teaching you so many different techniques. You never know what you'll need, so have more than one arrow in your quiver."

"Well, at least we don't have animals attacking us in New York City," Marion said.

"Oh?" I said. "The corporate world is full of them, ready to tear you apart. And you have that snake of a reviewer at your favorite newspaper. The mountains are friendly by comparison."

We sat in silence for a while. The rye helped relax Marion and me, but we still didn't feel normal. Marion's cheeks were pink, but she was staring at the floor, lost in thought. Kumi sensed our unease and stood up, putting his tea cup on the table.

"Come here, the two of you. Lie down on your backs," he said, gesturing as he sat down on the floor. "Form a triangle—each of us has our head on somebody's stomach."

We obliged like children. The back of Marion's head rested on my mid-section, Kumi's on Marion's stomach and my head was on his stomach.

"Are you guys ready?" Kumi asked

"For what?" Marion said.

"*Ha!*" Kumi said loudly.

Kumi's belly muscles jumped and my head bounced with them.

"Nick. Say 'Ha!' real loud."

"*Ha!*"

Marion's head bounced on my stomach. I chuckled slightly at the feeling of her head bouncing like a ball.

"Now you, Marion."

"*Ha!*" she said, and then giggled as Kumi's head bounced on her stomach.

"Now twice each," he said. "*Ha-ha!*"

My head bounced a couple of times and I started to chuckle involuntarily. As my stomach shook from my chuckling, it bounced Marion's head and she started to giggle, which bounced Kumi's head and he started to laugh, which in turn bounced my head. I tried to say "ha-ha," but the more I tried the harder I laughed. Marion's laughter made me laugh more, and Kumi laughed in that high-pitched sound he made when he was energetic. Our laughter grew, peaked, subsided and then started up again.

"The sight of you holding up your pants on the trail today with your bum sticking out…" Marion started to say, but laughed again and couldn't speak. We all exploded in laughter, occasionally trying to speak but it was impossible. My head was bouncing and Marion's head was bouncing on me and we couldn't stop. We laughed so loud the whole forest must have heard us.

When we finally subsided we just lay there, spent, with a few occasional dying giggles, enjoying the warm comfort of each other's bodies. I groaned from the pleasurable pain I felt in my ribs and stomach muscles. The feeling was intoxicating. Every limb felt leaden, like after a hot bath with epsom salts.

"Ohhhhh," Marion sighed. "I just want to stay like this forever."

The incident with the bear seemed a little farther away, and a picture of today's vast sky came back into my mind. A feeling came over me that I haven't had since I was a kid saying my prayers. I remembered my childhood faith in a higher power which protected me in those years, and how that feeling gradually eroded over time and I stopped going to church. I even remembered the day I walked in the house and told my parents I wasn't going to church anymore. My father asked me why and I said, "There's too big a difference between what they say and what they do." My older brother had stopped going the year before and I felt mature in my action, like I was growing up and no longer needed to believe in Santa Claus. The picture of God as a man in white robes with a long beard was distasteful to me. I associated that image with the commercialism and hypocrisy of the church. Reason and logic took the place of faith in a higher power and I felt strong enough to take care of myself.

That feeling of power lasted through my college years and well into the beginnings of my career. I knew I was good at what I did and felt I didn't have to depend on anybody or anything. Then it all began to fall apart when I lost Andrea and my job. My reason and logic were insufficient to get me through that, so I looked to Kumi for answers. But I realized that was a stopgap measure, a bridge to get me over the hump. I was hiding a need that was so basic I didn't see it—the spirituality that had guided me in my earliest years, the feeling of being a part of something greater than myself.

I'm not in charge of the universe, I'm not even in complete control of myself. The sky on that mountain today seemed to reach to the end of time and it enveloped me along with everything else. I wanted to regain that universal feeling I had when I was a child. I felt it strongly now, lying on the floor with Marion and Kumi. But I was afraid my hold on it was tenuous. At that moment the ants under Kumi's front porch probably had a better understanding of this truth than I did. What could I do to make sure I'd still have this thought tomorrow?

Kumi raised his head up off of Marion's stomach, and looked at me, squeezing his fingers. His eyes were as black as I've ever seen them. Then he winked.

On the flight back to New York I added yet another part to my Charting collection:

Joker

*"I see the humor in every situation.
I help you laugh at yourself."*

I think I actually heard laughter and applause from the rest of myself with the addition (I should say revival) of my sense of humor. It seemed all my parts wanted to work with the Joker, especially The Tuner and Mr. Ready. The Jogger said, "Thank you! He's vital to our health." But I also heard a collective warning, to remember to call on The Joker, especially when things are looking dark. Kumi said the time we most need humor in our lives is often the time we are least inclined to use it.

After almost a year's experience with Charting I had a deeper insight into Kumi's notion of positive intent. I'd begun to realize that I had no "bad" parts in me, only parts that behaved badly when I communicated with them poorly or prevented them from carrying out their jobs. In fact, I no longer believed in "good" or "bad" people. A behavior may be good or bad, but, somewhere underneath, the *intent* is always positive. When Streicher fired me he did what he perceived to be necessary for the financial survival of Globalcom. He may have done it in a lousy way, but I think that just reflects his limitations as a person. He did it in the only way he knew how. I began to see that the idea of positive intent extended even to terrible acts, too, like murder. A woman might kill to save her baby when attacked, for instance. The nice boy next door, who never hurt a butterfly, might become a brutal killer on the battlefield to "defend my country." The natural response of any system—a person, a family, a community or a state—is to survive, and usually at any cost.

I now felt that the difference between someone who kills without blinking an eye and someone who would kill only as a last alternative depended on the existence of a strongly developed "inner community" that balanced intent with behavior. If this were true, then there were no good or bad people—only complete or incomplete, balanced or unbalanced, developed or limited.

Marion disagreed. She believes evil exists as a force of nature. She cited Adolph Hitler, and was horrified when I told her I thought Hitler's intent was positive. We argued about it in the cab from the airport.

"How can you use the word positive in any connection with that monster!"

"His *acts* were those of a monster. But he truly believed killing Jews would save the Aryan race."

"So, you're justifying his actions because you think his heart was in the right place?"

"Not justifying, explaining. I'm not sure he had a heart, but I need to know how any human being could perpetrate such horrific acts. What went wrong? If we understood, maybe we could prevent it."

"He was nuts, that's what was wrong."

"That doesn't explain it. He was a highly successful leader, very well-organized. But he had no checks and balances in himself, no conscience or compassion. He was missing those parts, or had somehow lost contact with them. To him, Jews were a virus and he was the anti-virus. He was doing exactly what our immune system does."

"Immune systems don't kill people."

"You might kill me if you thought I really *was* a threat to your life."

Marion whooped with laughter. "Oh, Nick, you've just explained some of those infuriating moments. What got you so fired up about all this anyway?"

"I've been thinking about a lot of things. All my life I've wondered, if God exists, how could he condone crime and poverty and suffering? Why create a world like that? But then, I've always defined life in terms of good and bad. I'm beginning to believe God doesn't think that way. The creator of life would make life out of life. What we call death would be just a natural part of that recycling process. Maybe we're a kind of mini version of God. When we cut down a forest to build a hospital, how would we ever explain that to a squirrel or a woodpecker? I think we're neither good guys nor bad guys. Only guys."

"And gals, buster."

"Ow! That hurt."

When we got to Marion's, the taxi driver quickly turned off the meter. He thought I hadn't read it and tried to over-charge. When I caught him at it he said, "Sorry, pal, no offense, just tryin' ta support my fam'ly." To which Marion burst out laughing.

The next few weeks in New York were an important time for both Marion and me. I got my holograph proposal together and made an appointment with the conference people. Marion had an audition for a big-budget movie and was preparing herself for that. We met for squash regularly and ate our meals together. I was getting more and more used to grains and fresh vegetables and began to crave them. Whenever we had the chance, we did The Cat on the rug in her living room. We made small talk when we were together, because our minds were on our work and we had little energy for anything else. We were like commandos getting ready to make a raid.

By coincidence, her audition and my meeting were on the same day, hers in the morning, mine in the afternoon.

"So, how'd it go?" I asked over lunch.

"Really well," Marion said. "I got this great idea about how to use my sides."

"Your sides?"

"Sides, you know, the script they give you for film auditions. Two letter-size sheets reduced and printed on one piece of paper. You have only twenty minutes to look at it, so you have to hold this script in your hand while you're auditioning—unless you memorize it, which is unlikely. When you read, the camera takes a close-up of your head and shoulders while another actor stands behind the camera reading the other part. You respond to him, but you're looking down at this damn paper, which looks terrible on camera. The director is watching the whole thing on a monitor.

"Well, Kumi's always talking about looking up, so I brought a clipboard, clipped the sides on it and held it up beside the camera where the lens wouldn't catch it. That way I could look up at the clipboard, but on camera I'd appear to be looking at the person I'm talking to. So I felt very confident and did a really good job. Am I a genius or am I just brilliant?"

"So what happened?"

"They gave me a call-back."

In my meeting with the conference people I was introduced to the program director by his assistant, the one who had called me. Also present was someone they introduced as "an expert on the most advanced forms of computer technology." When we sat down the Director asked me a few questions about myself. Then he paused for a moment and closed his file folder.

"Tell me, Mr. Cole, why should we give you a forum at this conference?" The others watched me for an answer.

The question surprised me. It was my impression I had already been offered a spot. But then it struck me, why would they allow me to present without knowing me. The assistant might have jumped the gun when talking to me, showing off his importance.

That kind of "justify yourself" question has always made me feel insecure, probably because I'm overly self-critical and never totally satisfied with my own work. But now I saw his challenge to me as an opportunity to make my pitch. I looked out the window at the skyscrapers and imagined they were the mountains. I reminded myself that I had just been head to head with a grizzly bear, so I could stand up to these people. I felt a tremendous surge of strength through the middle of my body.

"There are signs that people are developing a strange kind of fatigue with the Internet," I said. "Oh, they're having fun communicating with the world through chat rooms, commercial interest clubs and meeting outstanding people in their professions. But I want to see real-looking people when I talk to them. And the two-dimensional flat images we use today are not enough. I want a three-dimensional image."

"Impossible," said the computer man. "Too expensive, totally impractical."

"Expensive, yes. Impossible, maybe. But then, so was every technical advance at some point in history."

"This is theoretical, Mr. Cole. You could make your point by giving us a demonstration."

"I can't demonstrate it fully yet. Only bits and pieces. But we're making progress."

"What will you have by August?" the director said.

"I don't know."

"Then why should we give you a spot?"

"My backers believe in me. My goal has been clearly defined."

They were quiet a moment and then the program director spoke.

"Your idea is intriguing, Mr. Cole. We wouldn't be meeting here today if it weren't. We checked you out. But you've yet to prove your ideas or yourself—what kind of *mettle* you have. Tell me why I should put my trust in Nicholas Cole?"

I looked at him with a soft smile and said, "I can't think of a reason in the world."

He looked surprised.

My eyes were fixed on his in unbroken attention. "That kind of decision goes beyond judgment," I said. "To pure animal instinct—the only thing you can ever really trust."

I saw a slight crinkle around his eyes. He nodded his head and said, "We'll be in touch."

Two days later the director called and asked me to send him an outline of my presentation "as soon as possible," which I sent immediately by courier. We faxed details back and forth for two days about the equipment I would need from organizers of the conference and what I'd provide myself. Finally the date was confirmed, Saturday, August 27th, at 9 a.m. I had forty-five minutes. The audience would be just under a thousand people.

The moment I got the news I felt a flash through my body and heard my heart thud against my chest. It wasn't fear exactly, but enormous excitement. Hearing the exact time and date made it so real. In my mind I was already there. I pictured the conference hall, what it would look like and how it would feel to be there.

I called Marion and we met at the Russian Tea Room, where we toasted our successes with champagne.

"Well, we faced our demons and survived," I said.

"And you didn't lose your pants this time."

"I ate my M&Ms before I got there. Tell me, how do I get used to you being out of town for four weeks with this play?"

"Think of it as one long creative day. Meanwhile you've always got Gregor."

"Not my type. I like 'em red-haired and feisty."

"Well, I'll be back in time for your presentation and we'll celebrate."

"If it goes well."

"Shame on you, Nick! Not 'if'—*when* it goes well."

She was right. Shades of the old pessimism still hanging on. But it was fading and I had a feeling it would never again control me. Meanwhile, Gregor and I were working around the clock to perfect the equipment. We got an on-line transmission of a live holographic image for ten seconds and Gregor got so excited he drank a whole coke in one long gulp. That's how I know he's feeling emotion. His brilliance awed me. Once we had a power outage while the power supply regulator was disconnected and lost almost two dozen newly constructed formulas which he restored completely from memory. One of his tricks in the supermarket was to add up all the groceries in his head as he'd go and then correct the clerk if the total was even one penny off. One of my big tricks is getting him to the supermarket in the first place!

Working late every night we began to get on each other's nerves. One moment we'd be making progress and the next we'd argue over some trivial detail. One night we almost came to blows over the setting of the image compression unit.

"Eighty-percent image clarity," he said.

"Sixty-percent is enough," I said. "If we go higher we're going to lose speed in the transfer."

"Speed of transfer second importance." He reached for the dial and keyed in an equation.

"A clear picture's no good if it doesn't travel fast enough, Gregor."

"Can get eighty-percent with fast transfer," he said.

"Not by August you can't."

"I build new unit," he said staring at the screen.

"Gregor, we have a deadline."

"Experiment comes first."

"No! The *presentation* comes first."

"Eighty-percent."

"Sixty-percent."

"*Eighty!*"

"*Sixty!*"

It was like trying to talk to a child. My head hurt and my heart was pounding. I was afraid I was going to hit him. I stormed out of the room and into the kitchen. I opened the fridge and looked in. "What am I going to do with him?" I muttered to myself. I closed the fridge door and looked out the window at the orange New York night sky, always illuminated by city lights. Suddenly I saw an image of myself looking back at me. I was smiling. In fact I was laughing. Some part of me actually saw humor in this situation. I felt Marion's head bouncing on my stomach and heard her giggles and Kumi's high pitched "hee-hee."

I took a very deep breath. Maybe I should thank Gregor, I thought—no one gives me more of an opportunity to practice what I learn from Kumi. I recalled the two big experiences I had on this last trip to Montana—the sky and the bear. The bear was a surprise to me in more ways than one. Mainly, when I came face to face with it, I was not as afraid as I thought I would be. I knew I might be killed, yet I felt a deep connection to the animal. I had no desire to kill it—only to get away from it if possible. I don't think I would've hurt it, even if I could. I had entered its territory and it was responding naturally, without malice. I actually thought, "If this is the way I have to go, then so be it." As it happens, I only lost the seat of my pants. That's another thing to laugh at in my next laughing circle—a bear that likes M&Ms!

Thoughts of bonding with nature seemed foolish to me in one sense, yet in another they made perfect sense. They all relate to my other big experience—the sky. I wanted that sky, I wanted it with me. It meant something to me that I couldn't define, but I think Kumi understood that—the way he looked at me and somehow implied that I was now "ready" for something. As usual, he seemed to psych out what was on my mind, what I needed. I needed to connect all of the things I'd been learning, the skills and the exercises with Kumi. I needed to somehow align all this with my life in a larger sense, to organize it into a common purpose, the way that sky united the mountains and trees and rivers. The word "God" still bothered me from my early experiences in church, yet if I were to describe the feeling I got from that sky over the valley I would say it was a spiritual message, saying it's time to return to my childhood instincts—and this time get it right.

I wondered if all this had anything to do with my "friendly ghosts" dream, which I'd had yet again. I don't put much stock in the meaning of dreams, but this has got to be more than coincidence. I'm not going to ask Kumi about it. I think it's about time for me to start working out some things for myself.

(My notes on The Laughing Trance are on page 377)

17

THE SIX PLATEAUS OF LIFE
...FLOWING WITH THE SPIRITUAL RIVER

"Jack steals the golden egg from the giant's castle and then returns to steal the goose that lays the golden eggs. Now the giant is waiting for him with a vengeance, yet this kid puts his life on the line and goes back up to get the harp. Why?"

On my next flight to the mountains I wondered what Kumi had in mind for me this time. His remark that I was now "ready" for something kept coming to mind. What did he mean? My thoughts floated back to our last time together, doing the laughing exercise, remembering how he looked at me when I was thinking about the spiritual yearning in my life. He seems to have a sixth sense about my needs and I feel we are about to do something significant. As usual, though, I haven't a clue what it could be. He did ask me to come alone this time, which works fine since Marion is working on location for several weeks.

Now that I think of it, I have no need to worry. I have made great strides in my work with Kumi. Look at all the skills I've learned: to visualize, to store good feelings and retrieve them at will; to detach myself and see situations from various viewpoints; to model others, to change habits by understanding the sequences of behavior that created them. I've learned self-hypnosis and have improved my health through good eating and physical training. I know how to walk on stage, how to use my voice, how to plan time and improve my memory. I've also learned many attitudes related to these teachings—like the idea that nobody can scare me, only I can scare myself. I can even stand on my head—kind of.

Of course, I can't say I'm an expert at all this yet, but I'm getting the idea. I've already applied many of these skills, and I find I can teach them to others because they're simple. Best of all I can share them with Marion. Without a doubt these techniques have improved our relationship. In fact, I'm no longer anxious about getting into another "emotional commitment." Marion is first and foremost my friend. I see our way of relating as something we create together, not something that is in the hands of circumstances, or society, or my job, or some other outside force.

With Marion, as in everything else, I now realize I'm responsible for my behavior, my thoughts and my feelings. I create them, no one else. And I can let go of them at will, as she can let go of hers. There are no givens in the way humans relate. Well, maybe there's one—that if you aren't loved you become sick. And I think I've learned that, too.

Summing it all up, I think I've done pretty well. But I need to somehow put all these pieces together—my life with Marion, my work, my values as a person, not to speak of my identity and my mission in life. I feel there is a force in nature that is eternal, like a celestial power station I can plug into, and that somehow connects everything I learn and powers it. I had that connection once and I lost it. Now I want it back. I realize I need faith as well as reason to create a meaningful life. Kumi picked this up. I remember that look he gave me, saying, "Now it's time," before we went to the lookout point with the awesome sky. That sky symbolized to me the unity in all elements of nature—ourselves included.

The drive to Kumi's temporarily shook all these thoughts out of my mind, because the road was worse than ever. My stomach bounced and my scarred bum banged on the springs of the seat while the jeep groaned its way around ruts and crevices. Kumi had told me that he fills in the holes with dirt and gravel every year after the run-off, but he obviously hadn't gotten around to it yet. These everyday practical things aren't his strong suit.

At the top I finally had the chance to stop and admire the green that pervaded everything. The pines were in their glory and the early July air was warm. The mountain across the way was lavender and the sky had a yellow tinge. Kumi came out of the cabin and waved. Inside he gave me a hug and the traditional bowl of soup. On the floor was a rolled-up tent and a two sleeping bags next to backpacks and two paddles by the door.

"What's all that stuff?" I asked, looking at the gear.

"I thought we'd take a little trip, go up north, do some camping."

"To enjoy the company of bears?"

"Not unless you bring the candy store."

"What are the paddles for?"

"Canoeing."

"I've only done it a couple of times across a lake, that sort of thing."

"You'll be alright."

"When do you plan to leave?"

"As soon as you finish your soup."

I unpacked and Kumi told me what I would need for the trip. He had all the necessary equipment and food. I just needed to pack my sleeping bag and clothes, two of everything, "in case you get wet." We piled everything into the jeep and Kumi negotiated our way down the bumpy obstacle course to the main highway and headed north.

"Where are we going?" I asked.

"I'll tell you after we get there. You'll appreciate it more that way."

I had the luxurious feeling that I could sit back and let life carry me for a while, let everything go. We left the main highway after about an hour and drove through dense pine forests, mountain passes, across rivers and around lakes, each sight more mysterious and beautiful than the last. Kumi drove sanely and in silence, occasionally pointing out something of interest. We were in no hurry and he seemed to enjoy the surroundings as much as I did. The mountains got more rugged, the drop-offs by the road steeper, the terrain wilder. Then we entered a forest of large, dark, old-growth pines, with only occasional beams of sunlight cutting between the pillars. I imagined for a moment I was in a fairy tale, lost in one of those big forests along with Little Red Riding Hood and Hansel and Gretel.

We drove for an hour without seeing another car, our speed slowing as the road snaked around giant trees. At one point Kumi stopped and pointed.

"What?"

"Look. Side of the road."

Just off the road I saw a very large animal with a magnificent crown of branching antlers. He looked like a horse with driftwood growing out of his head. "Is that a deer?"

"Elk."

The animal sauntered peacefully out on the road and looked at us.

"Hello, Mr. Elk," I muttered. "We've come to visit your home, with your permission."

He looked away, like a customs official deciding whether to let us pass, then gave an almost imperceptible nod and moved on, crossing the road and disappearing into the trees.

"I wish I didn't have to start the car again. I feel like I'm invading their territory," Kumi said.

He turned on the motor and drove at half speed for a while, arriving at a curve that wound its way down to a lake. Standing by the water's edge was John Little Elk, who had given us that wild ride to the airport in the jeep last January. Next to him was a van with a canoe on top. Kumi stopped and got out.

"Hey, brother," he said and they embraced. I got out and stretched and greeted John. "You aren't related to the elk we just saw on the road, are you?"

"Ah, you met The Chief," he said.

"Is that what you call him?"

"Oh yeah, he's in charge around here. He'll keep an eye on ya."

We untied the canoe and placed it in the water. The plan was for John to meet us in the jeep at a point that Kumi and I would reach by canoe in three days.

We loaded the canoe with our gear. Kumi handed me a life jacket and showed me the proper way to step into the canoe without tipping it, using the paddle as a brace across the gunwales—he called them "gunnels"—and leaning on it for balance so the boat wouldn't rock as I settled my weight. I sat in the back and smelled the water. A loon called from across the lake. The gentle buoyancy of the canoe with the sound of the clear water lapping against it was trance-inducing.

New York was a million miles away. *I never want to leave here*, I thought. *I'm going to lose myself in the wilds.*

John gave us a push-off and we glided out on the lake. Kumi guided the canoe from the bow and instructed me in some of the fine points of canoeing, for "when we hit some of the rapids." I learned that both people steer but the front person aims the canoe and the rear person corrects the direction and keeps the stern in line.

"Rapids? But this is a lake, isn't it?" I asked.

"Yes, but there are narrows connecting one lake to the next. The water will move a little in those places."

My heart fluttered. "What do you mean 'move a little'?"

"I mean 'move a little.'"

We paddled quietly along, in no hurry to get anywhere. At one point I saw The Chief on the shore watching us, and I hoped we were being protected.

My watch was in my pocket. I had decided not to use it and let time be defined by the changing light. As the sky turned red over the mountains in the west, Kumi pointed towards the shoreline. We pulled over, docked the canoe and set our gear on a rock. It was a small peninsula with water on three sides. We set up our tent facing the middle of the lake and made a fire.

"How about a swim?" Kumi said.

"Isn't it a little cold?"

"C'mon, I'll show you how to enjoy it."

As we undressed I felt a cool breeze from the woods. Kumi waved me towards the water's edge.

"First put your hands and feet in the water and submerge your wrists for a minute. Then look at the lake and say to yourself, 'I see the water, I hear the birds, I feel the water on my feet and my body is getting warmer.' Keep the See-Hear-Feel-Do going as you enter the water and even as you're swimming. And then say 'Don't...*get too warm...now.*'"

I looked at the water, which was so clear I could count the yellow and amber stones and the minnows swimming over them. The shore was a bit stony but not uncomfortable. There wasn't a soul in sight. I repeated the See-Hear-Feel-Do sequence several times as I entered the water. I felt the cold sting my skin but found to my surprise I didn't really care. I was just an animal going into the water. A few moments later I was swimming and my body wasn't cold. I moved vigorously, of course, keeping my circulation going. We splashed and carried on for a few minutes, then got out and dried ourselves and dressed by the fire.

Kumi took a bottle of brandy out of his bag. I took a swig and it went through my body like a flame.

"This is it, Kumi. I wanna die here."

We ate stew while watching the changing colors of the mountains and their reflection in the water as the sun set. Our simple food tasted like the Chef's Special at the Four Seasons.

"Remember the story of Jack and the Beanstalk?" Kumi asked.

"Yeah."

"Why do you suppose Jack went back for the harp?"

"The harp?"

"The magic harp. First, he steals the golden egg from the giant's castle and then returns to steal the goose that lays the golden eggs. This time he barely escapes from the giant, who is waiting for him with a vengeance. Yet this kid—who's completely safe at home and could buy a dozen harps with his gold—puts his life on the line to go back up and get the harp. Why?"

"Don't they do everything three times in fairy tales?"

Kumi sighed and looked at me, waiting.

"I don't know. Maybe he liked music?"

"Would you sacrifice your life to hear some music?"

"For David Bowie, maybe" I quipped. "Okay, so the harp represents something."

"Like what?"

The story from my childhood was coming back to me and I remembered being intrigued with the description of a harp that played beautiful music all by itself.

"It's the mystery of the harp, he's gotta figure it out," I said.

"Why?"

"I thought you never asked 'why.'"

"This is the exception."

"Well, a harp that plays itself is a miracle."

"But he's got all the gold he wants."

"Yes, but gold can't produce miracles. What am I saying? In my business it would produce a lot of miracles!"

"Material ones."

"Right."

"But does this harp have only material value?"

"No. It's more like a mystical thing, spiritual even."

"Is that worth sacrificing your life for?"

I looked at Kumi. "Well, sure. You have to believe in something. The harp could give his life a higher meaning."

Kumi started unrolling the sleeping bags and I poured myself another cup of hot cocoa.

"So why'd you ask about that?" I said.

"No reason."

We cleaned up the area and put our garbage in a large plastic bag and our food in another. Then we hung both up high on a line between two trees a distance from the tent. Kumi explained this is how "sensible people" keep bears away from the tent at night.

It was dark when we zipped up our sleeping bags. I lay there listening to the delicate sounds of the forest. I heard an owl, the occasional cracking of a branch, the patter of little twigs or pieces of pine cone hitting and rolling off the tent. In my mind I saw a beanstalk.

We awoke at dawn to the sweet cacophony of birds. I crawled out of the tent and looked at the lake, a sheet of pink glass. Chipmunks were scurrying around the branches as I scouted for firewood. Kumi aired out the sleeping bags and took down the tent while I made a fire. Neither of us talked as we ate oatmeal and fruit with milk made from powder. We boiled water for tea. As I drank it I thought that six months ago I could never have started my day without coffee.

"No outhouses around here, I guess."

Kumi handed me toilet paper and a small trowel. "Use this to dig a hole. Just hold on to the branch of a tree, but make sure it's not rotted," he said giggling.

I walked off into the woods and looked for a likely place, choosing some soft dirt near an aspen tree. As I situated myself, a chipmunk came down the trunk and stared at me. "What are you looking at?" I said. "Go find your own spot."

Awkward as this first-time experience was, I felt a strange sense of well-being. When I covered up the hole and looked at the area I could hardly tell I'd been there, yet a part of me had become part of the forest. When I got back to our site I mentioned this feeling to Kumi.

"It's nature's cycle, giving something back," he said.

The sun was still behind the mountains at this early hour, but the lake shimmered with reflected color as we put the canoe into the water and pushed off. We glided in silence, hearing only the quiet dip of our paddles in the water and the forlorn call of a loon. I watched the changing colors on the trees and water and saw an occasional animal or fish. I enjoyed dipping my paddle into the water almost soundlessly and watching the way the droplets would fall off the paddle and stay on the surface of the water for a moment. Around midday we pulled up to a shoreline, made a sandwich, lay on the bank and rested. Later we moved on.

"There's a small narrow around the bend up here where the water will be a little faster," said Kumi. As we turned the bend I saw a stream of mild fast water. "Just keep the back of the canoe in the middle of the rapid."

He aimed us toward the middle of the flow, which curved to the right. I ruddered with the paddle on my left to keep us in the center of the stream. It was easy and Kumi turned to me and said, "Good, that's the idea." Soon we hit another small rapid and I ruddered this time on the right to make us go left. I was exhilarated by the faster water accelerating our speed, like a kid canoeing for the first time.

Our next camp was by a small waterfall. We portaged the canoe over a strip of land around the falls and set up camp on the other side of it. Then Kumi gave me a quick lesson in fly fishing. The soft whine of the reel and the graceful float of the fly in the air were mesmerizing. I didn't care if I caught anything, just casting was satisfying. But we caught almost a dozen trout in less than an hour. He showed me how to reel in the fish by raising the pole, then lowering it and reeling in, then raising again, so the fish wouldn't snag the line on a rock. While I built a fire and oiled the pan, Kumi cleaned and fileted our fish in minutes with the sharpest knife I'd ever seen.

A weasel came out of nowhere and looked at us, very still.

"Hey, little fellah, you eat fish?"

He looked at us with innocent, beseeching eyes. I threw him a piece. We ate and listened to the waterfall, and our new dinner companion helped with clean-up.

"Nothing goes to waste out here," Kumi said.

We slept early and soundly. At dawn we were on the water, moving deeper into the forest. We were getting further away from civilization. I was reminded of those adventure stories where the hero hunts for some lost soul in the wilderness. I pretended I was searching for someone and wondering where he would be. I was looking alright, but the difference between me and those storybook heroes is that they usually knew what they were looking for.

The water narrowed and picked up speed, giving us almost twice the distance with each stroke. We went through two more rapids, each a little faster than the previous. I handled them quite well, although we did scrape a rock on the second one when I misjudged the speed of the water. Afterward Kumi showed me a few tricks for balancing the canoe in faster water to avoid rocks.

"Is it my imagination or are these rapids getting more rapid?" I asked.

We camped that evening in a kind of lagoon. We fished again for our supper and ate while watching the water. I enjoyed not shaving and got used to my feet and pants being wet.

"Kumi, where are we going exactly?"

"A nice place down the river."

"I thought you said this was a lake."

"Actually, it's a river, but it looks like a lake at first because it's so calm and wide. Here it acts like a river. I like the transition."

"What's the name of it?"

"It's called Ghost River."

"Why?"

"You'll see in the morning."

When we awoke everything was shrouded in mist. We ate and got on the water with little talking. We could see only a few feet ahead, so we paddled slowly, letting the current carry us. As the river narrowed, I saw thick trees with craggy branches like arms reaching out over the water through the mist. I felt like I was passing through a portal into some long-lost domain. Gradually the mist rose and sunlight sifted down through the woods. The river curved and sped up.

"Heads up," Kumi said.

Suddenly we were in white water rapids, the fastest we'd seen so far. I slipped down off the wooden seat onto my knees and pressed them to the sides of the canoe for balance, as Kumi had shown me.

"Go to the right of that rock," Kumi ordered. I paddled on the left along with Kumi and then let the current take us to the right. "Go left," he said.

I stabbed the paddle in the water on my left and levered the paddle against the gunnel, turning the canoe left. Water splashed into the canoe, but we made the turning. Then the river straightened out and got quieter.

"Not bad," he said.

"Hey, Robinson Crusoe back here," I said.

Kumi smiled back at me. We steered for a while, barely paddling as the river began to move faster. I heard loud water up ahead, like a waterfall. Kumi angled us to the side of the river into a backwater just short of the white water.

"We get out here."

He stepped out and we pulled the canoe up on shore. I asked him if we were camping so soon, and he said we would leave the canoe and carry our gear to the bottom of the rapids. I could see why as we forged a path beside the turbulent river, which sloped downhill over a distance of some fifty yards, around rock formations and fir trees. At the bottom was a lake surrounded by pine-covered mountains.

We propped our gear against a big rock and watched the foaming river as it rushed between rocks and emptied into the lake.

"Here we are," Kumi said, looking around.

"It's beautiful. But where are we?"

"We're there," he said, surveying the area with his eyes.

A typical Kumi statement—I just let it go.

We opened the cooler and sat down to eat. The sun had burned off the mist and the sky was clear. I could smell the water and feel an occasional fine spray on my face from the rapids.

"Shouldn't we go back up and get the canoe?"

"I want to do something else first."

Kumi stood and looked up at the rugged area we'd just walked down. "Look up there," he said, pointing up the river bank on our side. "What do you see?"

I looked up along the river and noticed a series of natural rises formed by rocks and tree roots. We had walked around these tiny "plateaus" coming down so I hadn't really seen them. They might be described as crudely shaped steps going up the bank. You could climb them and sit on them. The top one was a grassy area with a large tree. We were standing on the flat area at the bottom. I described to Kumi what I saw.

"I'm going to ask you to climb each of those levels, one by one."

"That looks easy."

"On each level I'm going to ask you a question, each dealing with a different aspect of your life."

"Um-hmm."

"The bottom here is the first level, the one you're on."

Kumi stepped away from me about ten feet and instructed me to look up-river in the direction of the terraces.

"Let's say this space you're standing in now represents your *environment*, which is wherever you live your life. I want you to see, hear and feel in your environment around you—where you work, eat and sleep, socialize, all the places that are important to you. Millions of people live in New York, but each has an individual environment within that city. I want you to recall now in detail your own personal environment."

I didn't much like the idea of being in a noisy and polluted city when I was in the middle of this beautiful natural setting, but I knew Kumi must have a good reason for it, so I went along with him.

"Should I talk?"

"That's up to you, but I want you to feel the experience, not just report it. Be there, not here."

It took me a few moments to start thinking about New York. After a few false tries, I suddenly felt myself standing in the hallway looking at my office. The window was dirty and I'd forgotten to water the philodendron Marion had given me for my birthday.

"Okay, I'm there," I said.

"Move around, take it all in," Kumi said.

In a quick succession of scenes, I felt myself walking on West End Avenue to Marion's, and to the health club, over to Riverside park and onto 72nd Street toward Broadway. There're a few restaurants I like, and I go to a place called Barney's occasionally for a beer.

As I reviewed my city surroundings I realized I had a rather limited world, but it's the one I live in.

"And then there's you and Montana," I said. "The mountains, the trees and animals. That's a part of my environment, too, right? Does that count?"

"Yes, absolutely."

I reviewed the feeling of going back and forth between New York City and the Rockies, making both environments very real parts of my life. I had a better feeling about New York now than I did a year ago. That wall of city buildings used to oppress me, but now I seemed to carry some of Montana inside me wherever I go.

When I had absorbed the pleasure of that feeling I was ready to move on and I nodded.

"Now climb up here," he said, pointing to a stone ledge. "This will be the second, what we'll call the *activities* level. Imagine yourself doing your daily activities—work, play, all the things you do."

I stepped up on a big flat rock that was warmed by the sun and stood there. Kumi moved up with me but stood off to the side. I felt myself going through the activities that make up my life—sitting at the computer, working with Gregor, raising money for our project, going to the movies with Marion, watching TV, studying with Kumi and practicing "homework" from his lessons. The feeling was trance-like, because although my body was here I felt myself moving through these actions and seeing everything around me as if I were actually in New York. I even flexed my knees while imagining playing racquetball with Marion at the club.

"Okay," I said.

"Now go to the third level and review your *capabilities*. What do you know that enables you to do what you do?"

I thought about the new software I'd created for on-line video-conferencing, and the holographic concept I'm presenting at the International Convention next month—if I can get it together in time.

"I'm a fast learner," I said, as I thought about all the stuff Kumi had taught me. "And I work at it, maybe not as much as I should, but... I'm adaptable and can adjust to change—though sometimes it takes me a little time, but I'm learning. I lost a position in the corporate world and now I'm making it on my own."

I recalled being with Charles—I actually heard his voice—and how I was becoming a pretty good father. At least I care, and I try.

"I'm patient and have a sense of humor, if you can call those abilities—maybe those are more like characteristics."

I had the feeling there were a few things I was forgetting. When Kumi saw me frowning, he said I could always remember a few more later.

"When you're ready, step up to the next level."

I grabbed a big tree root and hoisted myself up a few feet to a small knoll.

"This is the fourth level, which represents your *values*."

"You mean my beliefs?"

"Beliefs about yourself may affect your values, but this level defines why you do what you do. What impels you to make decisions about work, activities, environment. Your basic values as a human being."

I thought about how my values had changed, or I should say developed, since working with Kumi. I value technology, because I believe that information is the most important asset a person can acquire, and computer technology delivers information. But now I was thinking about how information helps us live a better life.

"I think I help educate people in my own way, enable them to gain useful knowledge." I hesitated to say that what I do makes the world a better place to live in, but that's the way I felt.

"Then there's family, Marion and Charles. Without them my life would be, I don't know...have a big gap in it." I felt the presence of Marion and Charles and how my respect for myself has grown because of them. "They keep me from becoming a computer myself."

I looked at Kumi and he raised his eyebrows. "Ready to go on?"

I stepped up onto a big knot of roots and found a flat ground between them.

"This is level five   your *identity*. Who are you?"

"Who am I? Whoa, that's a tough one. Didn't I just define that?"

"No. You told me what's important to you and why you do it. Now I want to know who you are."

"But I said I'm a computer specialist."

"That's what you *do*, not what you *are*. There's a big difference between a human doing and a human being."

"Have you been talking to Marion? That's her line."

"Good. That means you've had time to think about it."

"Well, I'm a combination of these different selves, all the parts I've been identifying that make up the whole."

"That's true, but who runs the whole operation—the fundamental self who's been inside you from day one? In other words, who are you even when you aren't doing anything?"

I thought about that for a few minutes. "I don't know. I'm, uh...does anybody know that?"

"Let me make it easier for you. If you were to compare yourself to something—a tree, an animal, the sun, anything at all—what would you say your inner nature most resembles? For example, one person told me he thought of himself as a lighthouse, helping ships find their way in a storm. Another said she was like a caterpillar that became a butterfly. That sort of thing."

"Well, I'm a technician, a creative technician. I put information together in new ways and send it worldwide."

"And what's that like? Make an analogy or a metaphor."

"Uhh..."

"Don't struggle for a definition, just think of the most natural thing."

"I'm like a...like a bird carrying messages, sending signals, performing miraculous feats in cyberspace."

I thought of a large bird that had recently made a nest in a deep niche by the window ledge of the apartment just below me in New York. I admire it every day, and I keep meaning to knock on the door of the people downstairs and ask what kind of bird it is. I described it to Kumi.

"It's about the size of a crow and it has a dark head, a white throat, its back is a kind of blue-ish gray, and its breast is sort of pale with streaks of dark brown. But its wingspan is enormous, at least three or four feet."

Kumi smiled. "You're describing a peregrine falcon."

"A falcon! In *Manhattan*?"

"Sure, that's where they're flourishing these days, in the cities. They're an endangered species. They usually live on ledges of high cliffs, so sky-scrapers are perfect for them."

I shook my head. "Those poor birds must really be endangered if they go to New York City for safety."

Then I thought that I'm like that bird. I'm a survivor. Maybe that's the way to survive today: make your first flight on your own instead of with a large organization. I'm an entrepreneur by nature and I had been denying it. I was in a world of penguins, all acting identical, walking around with their suits on. I just fell into the corporate world because it was easy and paid well, but it wasn't me.

I chuckled. "I'm like a falcon. A peregrine falcon."

"And they do perform spectacular stunts in space, dives and somersaults, especially in mating season."

"Marion will be pleased to hear that. I'll go flying into the bedroom and leap onto the bed."

Kumi laughed. "Now those are all the things a falcon does. But underlying all that, what is the being of a falcon?"

"How would I know?"

"Guess, hallucinate. You don't have to put it into words. You've watched your bird, now be a falcon."

I tried flapping my arms like a bird and then stopped.

"I feel silly."

"Kids do this all the time, Nick. Be a kid again."

I took a deep breath, straightened my back and stared straight ahead of me and up. My breathing slowed almost to a halt and gradually my arms started to rise, almost by themselves, until they were hovering over the river like wings. I must have looked like an evangelist blessing his congregation. I felt a sudden rush of energy up the center of my body.

"I'm a falcon," I called out over the roar of the river. "I fly between mountains and skyscrapers!" My body felt light, a sensation of tremendous freedom. I was looking down at the earth as I scaled cliffs. All thought had left me. I felt ageless.

Kumi let me stand there like that for a long while Then he whispered over the sound of the river, "Whenever you're ready..."

Slowly, I climbed up onto the top level, a grassy ledge and stood by a giant red cedar that must have been two hundred feet high and six feet in diameter

"I think you know what this level is. It's what you were thinking about on your last visit. I'm sure it's been on your mind ever since."

I had to re-focus my mind to recall my last visit. Then I remembered the walk to Kumi's lookout point and the way the sky embraced the valley and the mountains, and my desire to have a deeper meaning to my life. I looked at Kumi, but he just waited for me.

"I think..." My tongue felt like it was asleep. I didn't really want to talk. "I think this has something to do with, uh...remember this winter when I talked about...um, that part that...sabotages me? And you said it was...trying to protect me?"

Kumi was silent for a moment. When he spoke his voice sounded distant:

"*It* said it was trying to protect you. Remember?"

"Yeah, uh-huh, right."

"And you didn't want to talk about it."

"Yeah. Well, that feeling—like some kind of...power. I can't describe it."

"What's it feel like?"

I had a flash memory of being a child in church. "It's kind of a good feeling, but uh..." My heart was thumping in my throat.

"Let go, there's nobody around."

I felt light-headed. I wanted to get off this level. At the same time I felt solidly grounded and my torso began to sway.

"...like this tree." I touched the giant cedar for security. The river got louder. I felt as though a metal band were tightening around my head. All the pain of the recent years seemed to swell in my body with an excruciating pressure. I began to shake uncontrollably and tears streamed down my face. I heard an unbearable ringing in my ears. Suddenly I was on top of the cedar and could see clearly for miles. The ringing resonated in my body. I was like a giant bell, swaying in the wind for an endless time. Then I floated back down through space as if in a dream. All sense of self had vanished. I had become part of the tree, the ground, the water, the whole universe. All my experiences of this past year with Kumi, with Marion and Charles, with my work, were coming together, and I felt the touch of something deeper, like that all-encompassing power I'd felt as a child that lived inside me and connected me to everything. *It was still there.*

"Nothing dies," I said in a hoarse whisper, again and again and again.

Gradually I re-awakened to the sound of the river. My breathing was deep and slow, my shirt wet with perspiration, my arms and legs leaden—a feeling of deep calm. I don't know how long I stood there, my soft focus taking in the entire panorama in a haze.

"Take your time," Kumi said. "Let this feeling continue to fill every cell of your body…squeeze your fingers, zz-zzt!" He paused. "When you're ready, step down to the Identity level. Take the feeling of the cedar with you."

After a short while I stepped down.

"Now, while continuing to enjoy that feeling, let the feeling of being the falcon come back to you."

My arms went up again, like wings, but this time not as high. Just enough to get back the feeling. My gaze on the horizon was uninterrupted.

"Now carry the feeling of being both the cedar and the falcon down onto the values level. This is where you believe in educating people through technology, and the importance of family."

As I stepped onto this level I saw Charles and Marion looking at me. I felt deeply connected to them. I realized how dissociated from them I had often felt, even when physically close to them. This thought was disturbing, yet also satisfying because now I was becoming aware of how I can be more connected. I felt a deep serenity throughout my body, which seemed to connect to the timeline of my life and extend over the coming years.

I began to review my capabilities through this feeling and automatically moved down to the next level, still carrying with me the feeling of the cedar and the falcon. I felt unlimited in my capabilities. For a moment I wasn't sure what level I was on because everything seemed to be overlapping and blending inside me into one united whole.

Kumi pointed to the flat rock and I stepped down to the activity level of my life. I felt myself going through my day, doing what I do, but now these activities were imbued with the feeling of the tree and the bird, my values and confidence in my abilities. The activities I had always done now felt more solid, more flowing, somehow bigger.

I jumped down to the bottom level and Kumi reminded me I was now in my environment. Here I was, walking down the street in New York, feeling like a peregrine falcon! I'd have to be careful not to raise my arms and start talking to myself. But that's how I felt. I wanted to tell the whole world what I'd discovered, although I'd never be able to define it in words. I felt so vibrant and at the same time deeply contented and calm.

"Notice what's going to be different back home as a result of what you've discovered here today," Kumi said.

I went through a typical New York day. Everything looked big and bright, the image panoramic. I wasn't tired. I was even-tempered. I'd been heading in this direction for some time now, but with today's experience I'd taken a quantum leap. It was as if all the exercises Kumi had done with me this year were suddenly coalescing and relating to each other. I felt myself going through my life with the understanding that I didn't have to feel competitive, just do my best. Not everything I did had to produce a monumental result. I knew deeply that things happen in their own time and I would still be the same basic person no matter what happened.

I stepped out of the environment space and sat down. Kumi placed a bottle of water in front of me and walked away. I drank half of it and looked at the river pouring into the lake, a small rainbow forming in the mist of the spill. I knew something momentous had happened in me which would affect everything I would do from now on. And I felt more deeply than ever the feeling of a community of parts in me with whom I shared the responsibility for my—our—life. And that this life was part of a network of lives throughout the world, somehow affecting each other. I continued to bask in this feeling, not moving, just listening to the water and watching the colors change.

Time didn't pass, it just stood there, like it was a thousand years ago.

Finally, I stood up and stretched. Kumi walked over and patted my shoulder. His eyes sparkled at me and smile lines crinkled at the corners. I put my arms around him. He was shorter than I, but it felt like I was hugging a giant.

"Thank you," I said. I wiped my eyes and sat down again.

"You're beginning to put it all together. It's all there, it just needs to clarify and categorize. A lifetime project, but you're off to a good start."

"Sounds a little clinical after something so...rich."

"Good to be clinical sometimes. It's useful to understand how you got to where you are, see how everything fits. You're an individual, but you have categories and they need to be clearly sorted and defined. Any problem you encounter in life can be understood as a confusion between one or more of those levels." He looked at them as he spoke.

I really didn't want an explanation to that right then, and Kumi seemed to know it.

"You'll figure it out for yourself. For now, just enjoy the feeling," he said.

After a while Kumi spoke again. "Did you notice the river as you were going up and down the levels?"

"Why? Did I alter it?"

Kumi smiled. "C'mon I'll show you."

We walked up the river to a point where we could take in all the levels I'd climbed. Kumi pointed to the water and I saw that, roughly corresponding with each level, was a rush of white water, either curling around a rock or tumbling into a cross-current or bubbling at a backwash. From the little bit of experience I had canoeing in the comparatively mild rapids we had done, I imagined how one might traverse this demanding stretch of some fifty yards. Of course, you'd have to be an expert, but I had an idea how an expert would probably do it. We continued up to the canoe.

"Sometimes dramatizing an event gives you a deeper understanding of it. It's easy to idealize your life levels, especially the spiritual level. We tend to separate the spiritual and make it special, a thing by itself."

"But the spiritual is special."

"Yes, sometimes too special. We isolate it. We expect it to be peaceful and quiet and don't want to disturb it. We meditate on it, and then when the going gets rough we sometimes panic and leave it behind. It should be part of life, not separate from it. You know what happened to you when you ignored it. It banged so hard on your drum for attention you thought it was trying to hurt you."

"I see it a little differently now."

"But it took you a while to accept the idea that there's a spiritual under-pinning to everything. You accepted the exercises I showed you because they're practical and quickly re-direct your behavior. But that's only the surface. Those changes won't last unless you build them on something deeper—a foundation, a base, that's with you always, regardless of your mood or your circumstances. That basic power generates you and sustains you through the pressures of life. The cedar and the falcon are the things you need to hold on to at the times when you're most likely to let go of them, when you're scared or insecure."

The sound of the river accompanied Kumi's words. I had a slight feeling of uneasiness. I looked at the rapids again from this perspective at the top of the river, how they curled here and eddied there, some places black and smooth as silk and others turbulent with white water.

"What do you mean by dramatizing an event?" I said.

He handed me my life jacket. "Put it on."

He started pushing the canoe into the quiet water and I found myself helping him.

"Get in."

"Kumi, this is crazy." He held the canoe as I stepped in the back, then got in himself.

"Get down on your knees."

"To pray?"

"Get back that feeling you had at the cedar tree."

He paddled slowly toward the fast water and lined up the canoe to enter the rapids.

"We're not really going to *do* this!"

"Pay attention."

We back-paddled for a moment as he spoke.

"Look at the quiet water down there," he said, nodding toward the lake at the end of the rapids where we had just been sitting. The river sloped downward on a fifteen to twenty foot vertical over a distance of about a hundred-and-fifty feet. "That's where we're going to be in a minute. Knowing that, you can pay attention to where you are *now*. See that clump of large rocks up ahead. We'll go to the right of it. After that, follow the natural flow of the river. Ready?"

I felt an icicle of adrenalin hit my heart, like when I met the bear, a moment so irreversible I had no time to think, only act. Kumi paddled and I steered us toward the entry point. My attention was riveted on that first group of rocks with the violently swirling water. Suddenly, the rapids pulled us in and we plunged forward in water that roared like a jet engine. It felt like one of those moments in a dream when you're falling. Kumi chopped at the water, left then right, aiming the bow dead center into the tongue of the rapid. I thrust my paddle in the water on my right and ruddered. The river split in two at the clump of rocks. Kumi switched the paddle to his left and stabbed the water to thrust us to the right. I did the same and the canoe veered right and I saw the shadow of the rocks out of the corner of my eye as we passed them. The canoe bounced on the water and threw us slightly sideways. We dipped and swerved around a large rock and hit a bubbling backwater that lifted us up and slapped us down with a clump. *"Left!"* Kumi yelled as we squeezed between two swirling eddies of white water. *"Right!"* and we careened around a large tree root that jutted out into the river.

From here on I reacted on instinct, switching the paddle from left to right, pressing my knees hard against the walls of the canoe, sometimes holding the paddle in the air for balance. The noise was thunderous. The river soaked my face and shirt and the canoe sloshed with water. What happened next took seconds but seemed to go in slow motion. I saw the current was about to make a sharp left turn through a gateway between two boulders about forty feet in front of us. I temporarily froze at the sight of it. Kumi yelled *"Left! Left! Left!"* Suddenly the canoe fish-tailed— the back of the canoe had become the front. I was going backwards, directly toward the boulder on the right of the gateway! I turned myself around to face the direction the canoe was going. Now Kumi was in the rear and I was in the bow, aiming straight for the rock. I stabbed the paddle into the water on the right side, thrashing violently again and again to aim us left. The canoe turned and slid between the boulders like a fish. To my utter surprise, the water was suddenly calm. We were coasting into the quiet water on the lake.

I stood up and thrust my paddle in the air with both arms.

"We did it! We did it!"

Kumi yelled "Sit down!" but too late. I felt the sting of cold water and heard the "whump" of the canoe just missing my head as it overturned. I saw its shadow from under water through a flurry of bubbles. Back on the surface I looked around for Kumi, who was swimming toward the canoe. We looked at each other and laughed.

"What happened?" I said.

"We dumped."

The canoe was upside-down and our paddles were floating nearby. We retrieved the paddles and swam with one arm, pulling the canoe over to the shore and up on land.

"Sorry, Kumi," I said.

"You did good."

We took off our wet clothes and put them on a rock and dried ourselves in the sun. I took out the brandy and saluted Kumi with a swig. We ate sandwiches and drank fruit juice. The sun baked our skin. I walked up the river to look at the "gateway" where the water turned and rushed through the boulders. "My God," I thought. "I was just in that."

Kumi walked over to me. "That was some stunt you did there when the canoe turned backwards and you just grabbed the bow position. You kept us from going into the boulder."

"Yeah, and after that heroic deed I tip us over."

"You celebrated too soon. You know the saying—'It's not over till it's over.'"

Kumi said it was time to go. I took one last look at the river and the levels I'd climbed, resting my eyes on the red cedar on top. We packed up, put the canoe in the water and moved on to meet John Little Elk.

Driving from the airport to Manhattan I realized that the big challenge of this last lesson with Kumi was, as he had said, how to hold onto that spiritual feeling amidst the noise and chaos of city life. That's why he had me do those last crazy rapids—to show that it's possible to have peace of mind under duress, to feel supported by it when I feel threatened.

I was coming home with two new parts—gigantic ones. They were not really new, just being taken out of mothballs and given a new definition, like so many other parts of me:

The Falcon

"I'm your identity. I float between all parts
to remind them of the deeper nature
out of which you come."

The Cedar

"I connect you to all creation through all of time
—to the eternal."

I felt a mild glow throughout my body as I re-connected with my spiritual part—The Cedar—even here, stuck in traffic behind a big oil truck and smelling the stink of exhaust. I'd been resisting this part of me for so long that I got a huge sigh of satisfaction from all my parts when I finally accepted it. But I understood my spirituality on new terms now, without the dogmatism and self-righteousness that had come with my religious indoctrination. All my parts had seemed to shift position at once when I finally let go and accepted this feeling, which was probably why I almost fainted on that sixth level.

My Thoughts on My "finished" Chart:

*Since doing the Alignment it's clear to me that **The Falcon** and **The Cedar**—my identity and spiritual self—are the core of me, and that all my parts are connected to and nourished by them. This "finished" chart shows also the coalitions that have formed between the parts that work together as teams. Of course, any part is free to work with any other part as needed, and new coalitions will undoubtedly form as time goes on. **The Joker**, for instance, is in constant demand throughout my system—he may even have to develop some assistants to keep a healthy touch of lightheartedness in all the new developing areas of my life.*

Although I probably have many more parts than I've defined here, this grouping constitutes my central staff, the ones who run the basic operations of my life. I hold meetings with them, give them assignments and ask their advice. Kumi says they will change and develop, and that their needs might not be the same a year from now—or twenty. That parts of me will always be seeking further development, or experimenting with an idea and might temporarily be in conflict with other parts. The trick is to closely monitor these developments, be aware of my parts' needs, open to their ideas and sympathetic to their complaints. The satisfaction is in this mutual awareness and working together, not in trying to reach some perfect, unchanging, dead finality.

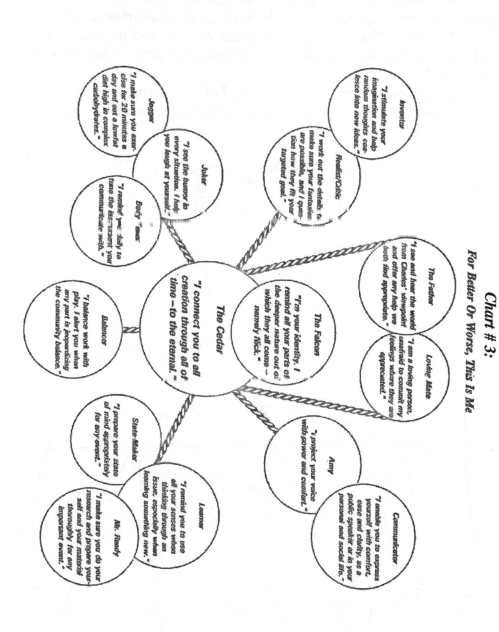

Chart # 3:
For Better Or Worse, This Is Me

I had a revelation after doing Kumi's "life levels alignment" by the river. I now understood those ghost-like figures in my dream. My parts are like spirits who are with me wherever I go. After all, we speak of being in "high spirits," or "low spirits," or of spirits that buck us up or make us "lose spirit." And Kumi has always said to communicate with all our parts so they don't get "dispirited."

So here is how my Chart might look if I showed my parts as spirits, and where I seem to feel them when I imagine them floating around me:

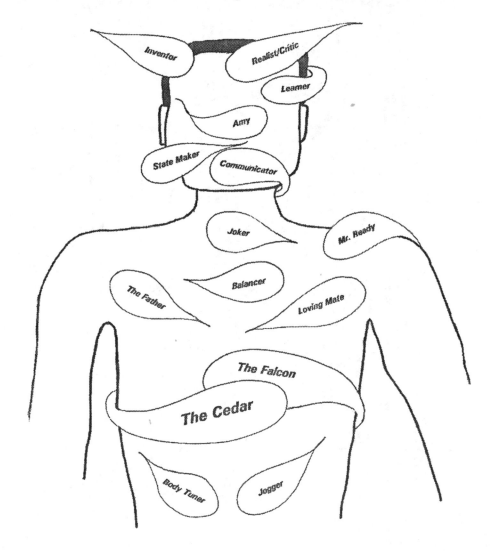

Marion looked at the notion of Charting as if her life were a play and she were the head of her own production company. Her parts are the writers, actors, designers and stage crew, and she coordinates, making sure it all runs smoothly. When new workers are needed she adds them on, and when a job becomes outdated she upgrades the part doing that job, giving it a new useful task. She says the more she communicates with everyone in her inner production company, the more smoothly the show runs. The more she utilizes her parts' resources, the more inventive they become and their feeling of domain increases. She says, "My aim with the production of my life is to have the longest and most successful run possible."

Thinking about Marion, I realized something else about Charting: not only am I a whole system of selves who need to learn how to cooperate and work together, but Marion is also a whole system of her own selves who must do the same. A marriage, then, is more than just a coupling of two people, it's like a merger of two corporations! (Or two production companies.) All the parts from both sides need to find ways to cooperate. No wonder marriage can get so complicated. And then you have a child or two and that's another couple of systems running around the house. And the family system is part of a community system, which is part of a state system, and a federal system and a world system—and then what, the universe?

Pondering the complexity of life and the seemingly uncontrollable events I see on the evening news, I started to get the impression that life was a hopeless mess. On the other hand, considering that this tremendous diversity of systems is operating everywhere at once—with individuals, businesses, governments—I was impressed that life on this planet worked as well as it did. It was part of a miracle!

Imagine if we could get all the systems in the world to do a super multi-leveled alignment. Impossible of course, and maybe we wouldn't want to. But it might not be a bad idea to at least require young couples to do an alignment exercise before they get married. It would give them some idea of what they're getting into.

Amidst this vast and complex array of world systems, I seem so insignificant. But in another way I'm not, because a single human system might be a microcosm of all systems everywhere. If I could understand how to make just one system work—my own—then maybe I could better understand how to fit into other systems, on all levels. Which reminded me of a stranger who did me a favor one day. When I offered him money he shook his head and said, "Do the same for somebody else—it'll go around the world."

(My notes on the Life Levels Alignment are on page 383)

18

THE PERFECT PERFORMANCE

...*YOU DID EVERYTHING RIGHT, NOW KEEP DOING IT*

"I stepped into the circle and felt a chill go up my back. My body straightened almost like I'd had an electric shock and my eyes focused on the far distance. My breathing slowed down. I felt confident but I wanted to challenge it, make it even stronger."

I see myself walking up the steps and across the stage of the big hall at the International Computer Convention. I feel good and look comfortable. I face the audience with a confident smile, wait a moment and say, "Good morning, my name is Nicholas Cole."

Our connection with Missoula comes on screen live and I see the Montana mountains in 3-D. The audience is stunned, history is being made: the first holographic picture is coming live over the Net.

After my presentation people congratulate me and a reporter from Internet World takes my picture. Investors beg for a piece of the action and I tell them to call my secretary.

Well, that's how the Dreamer in me saw it. Now it was time for the Realist to step in and work out the details to make it happen.

Gregor slept in my computer room, hardly eating. We had achieved a detente and found a good work-rhythm, talking only when necessary. We slept in three-hour shifts and were on-line daily with Allan in Missoula, experimenting with video settings. Our first smooth on-line three-dimensional live picture was Allan eating a peanut butter sandwich. It so inspired Gregor that he's been eating peanut butter ever since.

I attended a medical conference at a convention center as Matt's guest, observing how speakers communicated with the audience and took questions from the hall. Many of the speeches were dull. Some used slides and overhead projections, which helped, but you could see their main qualification was medical knowledge, not giving a lively presentation. The most interesting speaker challenged the medical community's "arrogant indifference to alternative medicine." His statistics from heart and cancer associations about the success of herbal remedies and "hands-on" healing were impressive, but his attitude and voice tone reeked of arrogance and condescension as he referred to "outdated medical training" and "head-in-the-sand" attitudes of doctors. He didn't show respect for their experience and didn't speak to them on their level. He might have had a good case factually, but he blew it by his attitude.

During lunch hour I went up on stage and checked out the microphones. A security guard stopped me. I told him I was Dr. Cole and was giving a talk that afternoon on liver disorders, so he let me toy with the mike—speaking into it from various positions on the stage.

Then he told me he'd been having liver troubles and asked my advice. I told him to cut back on alcohol and stop smoking (his fingers had nicotine stains). He nodded his head, saying that's what his doctor had told him.

I got an empty feeling in my stomach standing on stage in this enormous auditorium. It wasn't quite as I had imagined it. Matt, sitting in the last row of the hall, looked about the size of my thumbnail. When I spoke I heard a disturbing echo. Matt told me to back away from the mike, and that I should speak more slowly because my words were running together by the time they got to him.

Matt asked me, "If you were to sum up in one word how you want the audience to perceive you, what would it be?"

"Solid, dependable." I said.

"Which?"

"Both."

On the big day we got to the convention center at 6:30 a.m. The engineer was waiting for us. Charles had rented a truck to carry the equipment Gregor and I needed for the holographic presentation—a powerful video projector, all the laser-related equipment (Gregor had finished the complex beam splitter only four hours earlier!), my computer, and the feed cables. The whole thing cost me a bundle. I even had to pay Marion a fee because of Equity and Screen Actor's Guild, but it was all deductible now that I was self-unemployed.

First I set up the link with Missoula to make sure we had an open line. I had asked for an early morning slot so the feed from Missoula would not be disrupted by heavy afternoon Internet traffic. Then I tested the speed of my Missoula hook-up by sending out electronic "pings," measuring the time it takes for the signal to go to Missoula and back, similar to sonar.

Our troubles began almost immediately. We had found the perfect position for the projector in the aisle behind the audience. The positions of all other equipment had to correspond with the projector. A guard watched us lay the last cable and then pointed to the projector, "You can't set that thing up here, it blocks the side exits."

"But there's plenty of room to get to the exits," I said.

"Talk to the fire marshall."

So we re-set the projector, which meant we had to disconnect everything, re-set it all and re-open the line. To position the screen we needed light on stage, but we couldn't turn the lights on ourselves because we weren't in the electrician's union. The engineer said, "The electrician doesn't arrive till eight."

Now I was getting upset. I was hungry, a warm sweat was coating my back, and I still didn't know where to put the beam splitters. I wanted everything to be perfect, just as I'd rehearsed it. Then I remembered Kumi's words: "Be ready for anything."

"C'mon," I said to Marion. "Let's go have a bite to eat." We exited on 34th St. and walked over to a health food restaurant on Ninth Avenue. We sat by the window with fruit and yogurt and watched all the people passing by who didn't seem to care that I was about to make the most important presentation of my life.

"Look at her," I said, pointing out a young woman in a business suit, with a briefcase and a tense, knitted brow. "She's an editor having second thoughts about a new book she's accepted for publication."

"No," Marion said. "She's going to meet her lover and she's trying to figure out how to tell him it's the last time. There's your editor." She nodded her head toward a pale, middle-aged man who looked like he had an upset stomach.

"No. He imports surgical instruments and just got a visit from a customs investigator saying pure cocaine was found in one of his shipments."

Fantasizing about other people's lives took my mind off my own. My troubles might be trivial compared to what some of these people were facing.

"We better get back, Nick."

"First, a toast," I said. I handed her an M&M and held another one between my thumb and forefinger in a kind of salute.

She did the same and said, "To your New York debut."

Back in the hall Gregor greeted me with a dour look. "The line's down."

"What does that mean?" Marion said.

"The communication link is overwhelmed. Overloaded with data flowing back and forth. We've lost our connection to Missoula."

"So, what do we do?" she said.

"We wait. The computer is on automatic re-dial."

I caught myself grinding my teeth. I took a deep breath and squeezed my fingers. Do something, I told myself. I checked the rest of the equipment. Everything was positioned and working. Marion went to the ladies room to put on her stage make-up and I found a quiet corner in the outer lobby behind a big rhododendron plant where I stretched my shoulders and hands while imagining myself speaking my opening words. That helped calm me physically, but I still had trouble concentrating.

I saw a row of phones and imagined I was talking with Kumi.

"I'm really up against it. I wish I had that feeling I had in the rapids."

"Nick, you don't need me. You know what to do. Make up something new if you have to."

I took a piece of string out of my pocket and formed a circle with it on the floor, about a yard in diameter.

"I'm inside that circle maneuvering the canoe around those rocks," I whispered. *"I didn't think I could do it, but I did. And when I step into that circle I'll get back that feeling and nothing can take it away."*

I stepped into the circle and felt a chill go up my back. My body straightened almost like I'd had an electric shock and my eyes focused on the far distance. My breathing slowed down. I felt confident but I wanted to challenge it, make it even stronger.

A man entered my peripheral vision.

"Tell me I'm going to screw up," I said.

The man stopped and looked at me, puzzled. My eyes were still fixed on infinity.

"What?"

"Tell me I'm gonna screw up."

"You're gonna screw up." He sipped his coffee.

I felt a slight pang of fear—a remnant of the old feeling that I might not be good enough—and my eyes lowered slightly. I stepped out of the circle, got back the feeling of paddling in the rapids and stepped back in the circle again.

"Say it again."

"You're gonna screw up."

My feet were planted solidly on the floor and my arms hung naturally at my sides. I was perfectly balanced and felt tremendously energized, yet relaxed. This was my Circle of Excellence. In my mind, I knew I could encircle myself in it anywhere I want and get back this strong, resourceful feeling.

"Thank you," I said.

"No problem," he said, and walked on, shaking his head.

People were filing into the hall. The murmur of their conversation sounded like water. I entered the back of the hall and walked over to the projector. Gregor was spooning peanut butter out of a jar while reading *Scientific American.*

"Oh, line's up," he said.

Voices filled the hall. The sound called to mind the rush of white water.

"Ladies and gentlemen, we'd like to start..."

The audience got quiet.

"...we have with us today a new face..."

I walked along the side aisle toward the front of the hall.

"...with some new ideas. I'll let him tell you about it. Mr. Nicholas Cole of FalconNet Communications."

I walked up the steps and across the stage. My body was balanced and I looked at my audience with a comfortable smile. My demeanor was commanding attention and I felt at home, almost as if I were in my own living room. At the microphone I scanned the landscape of faces and waited until everyone was absolutely quiet. Suddenly, I felt my circle around me, then it begin to expand, to encompass the stage, then the front row and the whole audience, even the walls of the room. I felt as though everyone present were in the Circle with me. A tremendous surge of energy moved up through the middle of my body, which I focused into an evenly modulated and urgent-sounding voice.

"Talk. Talk. Talk. That's what we do on the Internet."

Looking at all those people from the high stage was like looking out over a valley of trees. For a fraction of a second I felt a nervous flutter in my stomach, then it was gone.

"But we live in a visual culture. How many more surveys do we need to convince us that two-thirds of human communication is nonverbal?"

I heard words coming out of my mouth, out of my body, resonating in my chest, and I felt the energy of the thousand-plus people in the hall. I was riding on the crest of my own voice. Then I came to the central action.

"We're truly satisfied only when we can *see* the person we're talking to, because it's the *images* we remember. The words I'm speaking to you now will be forgotten by lunchtime, but the image you're about to see will stay with you forever."

I signaled for the lights to go down in the hall and a screen lit up on stage. A video of a woman in a red dress appeared on the screen, walking toward us, first as a speck in the distance, then closer and closer to life size. It was Marion. Then Marion herself suddenly appeared live on stage in front of the screen as the screen dimmed. The effect was as if she had just walked right off of the screen. She stood there in all her glory before the audience, smiling, looking radiant in red.

"And now, live from our on-line connection with Missoula, Montana, land of rivers and mountains, of the bald eagle and the grizzly bear..." Marion's amplified voice filled the room. A beautiful holographic image of the Montana mountains appeared on stage. A hawk glided smoothly over a cluster of aspens and a gasp went through the hall—the life-like three-dimensional hawk appeared to be flying across the stage. They had never seen holographic pictures projected with such clarity and brightness. *And it was being presented as a live feed*. The buzz of whispers grew into applause.

"Welcome to Montana. The first three-dimensional image ever to be sent live on-line," Marion said to a sea of applause.

Suddenly the image of Kumi appeared on stage! A reporter from a local Missoula radio station was interviewing him.

"I'm talking to an Indian medicine man named Kumi who lives a mysterious life here in the mountains of Montana." Kumi's face was stoic. "Mr. Kumi, is it true you helped Mr. Cole find the answer to his invention by combining old-world knowledge with modern computer technology?"

"Mr. Cole had his revelation during an ancient Indian ritual where you burn the bark of a black cottonwood tree and fan the flames with a feather of the great horned owl."

I saw Marion suppress a smile while Kumi carried on.

"And there you have it—modern technology meets ancient wisdom in the computer age."

After the presentation, many shook my hand with unreserved enthusiasm. A distinguished looking business executive with silver hair gave me his card and asked me to call his secretary. The manager of a new computer company talked about joining forces to develop my process further. A video company producer called my project "impractical," and a computer engineer said it would cost too much. But the majority of the people who came to me were full of compliments.

Even my ex-boss, Streicher, was there.

"Congratulations, Nick. Interesting presentation. Maybe you'd like to come back and work with us."

"Probably not," I said.

"Look, I understand you might feel a little bitter."

"No, not at all. In fact, I should thank you for freeing me from the corporate grind. If it ever becomes useful to include Globalcom in my project I'll contact you."

As soon as we got home we broke out a bottle of champagne and I called Allan in Missoula. Kumi was there and got on the phone.

"Kumi, I could kill you. Did you and Allan dream up that story?"

"Good publicity. Adds mystery to you."

"Thank God it's over."

"Over! You just had a big success. The really big challenge is just beginning. You know, C. G. Jung tells a story about one of his patients who complains one day that he failed at a big task. Jung breaks out a bottle of champagne and says, 'Good. This offers us an opportunity to learn something.' Then later the same guy has a big success and Jung shakes his head and says, 'We'll struggle through this somehow.'"

"Oh, Kumi...for the moment, I just want to relax and forget about the world."
"Good idea. Then we can really get to work."

(My notes on the Circle of Excellence are on page 395)

Notes & Exercises

My personal logbook from
my lessons with Kumi

Lesson 1

VISUALIZING

"Creating an image is only the beginning. I still have to work hard to achieve the thing I'm visualizing—but the image can be the inspiration that gets me started and keeps me going."

Separating Past And Future

K. starts each visualization exercise with a very deep inhale and exhale. He calls this a "separator." It creates a psychological division between past and future, a signal to myself that I'm ending one activity and about to start another.

The Visual Stance

To facilitate visualizing, K. recommends what he calls the visual stance:

1) **Stand or sit erect, back straight (if sitting use a hard chair)**
2) **Take a deep breath and let it out**
3) **Breathe shallow, high in the chest**
4) **Focus the eyes on or above (never below) the horizon.**
5) **Construct or recall an inspiring image.**

✓ *If indoors, looking out a window will probably help me make images, because I can use the window to frame the picture.*

Exercises

Self-Modeling Image

1) K. wants me to see myself the way I look when I'm really prepared to enter any high pressure situation: I know from the look on my face, my skin color, my breathing, the set of my jaw and my shoulders, that this will be a great performance. (This is a stretch for me, because I've never given a great performance. But I'll find something.)

2) If I'm entering a room, see myself greeting and being greeted by the people present; if I'm on stage, see myself bowing comfortably and listen to the audience reaction; if I'm on TV or camera, see myself on the set with bright lights and cameras moving around me. (All of this is new to me, but K. says it's easier if I can just imagine it's a movie about someone else with me as the actor.)

✓ *K. says an athlete entering a sports arena would watch and listen to the reaction of the other players and the crowd; a teenager might see himself or herself asking a classmate out for a date; a management consultant might be greeting executives; a teacher holding the attention of a troublesome class; a comedian producing uproarious laughter. Why do I keep seeing my ex-boss, Streicher, criticizing me? Maybe I'm just flushing out memories—cleaning the pipes.*

3) Imagine I'm holding a super TV converter and adjust this mental image any way I like until it's just right. The idea is to give the image maximum intensity. Experiment with these contrasts:

— **from dark to bright**
— **from small to large**
— **further away to closer**
— **black & white/color**
— **from still to moving, fast-forward/fast-reverse**
— **slow motion (forward and reverse)**
— **sharp focus/soft focus**

— tunnel vision to panorama

— anything else to intensify the image and make me feel more confident

(I surrounded my image with bright lights, like it was a Broadway marquee.)

✓ *K. says to notice how each adjustment I make alters my feeling about the picture. This is like playing with images on a computer screen—only I'm the computer. People respond differently to various changes in the quality of their mental images. Some like the picture brighter, some darker, some closer, some further away, etc.*

I'm accomplishing three things here:

- **I'm learning which adjustments to the picture inspire me, and which leave me cold.**
- **I'm programming myself for future performances.**
- **I can reprogram past events by changing my perspective on them, like adding more of the surroundings to an unpleasant memory to see it a different way.**

4) Now move the picture toward me, closer and closer, and feel its intensity as it enters me. K. suggests I experiment transporting the image into me in a variety of ways to see which ones give me the strongest rush:

— straight in fast

— straight in slowly

— start slowly then speed in very fast

— start fast, slow down and enter slowly

— curve and come in from left or right

— circle around me repeatedly, from slow to fast to slow, and then enter

— from the back and push me forward

✓ *Repeat moving this image into myself a number of times, using any other variations of speed and direction that make the feeling of entry of the image into me most intense.*

5) K. says to see myself looking back at me—the visualizer—and smiling as I'm being congratulated after the successful performance, and then to move this image into myself in the way that feels most intense. K. says this "smile-back" tends to warm up the dissociated feeling of the exercise. *(The first time I tried this, my image stuck its tongue out at me. At least I'm getting a response.)*

Hero Image

K. says that great performers associate themselves in their mind's eye with someone great, so he gave me this "hero" exercise.

1) Make a picture of my hero, the person I most admire who is doing what I'd like to do. *(Since I'm preparing a speech I'll use my favorite actor, Jack Nicholson.).* Adjust brightness, size, color, etc., for maximum intensity, as before.

2) Next to that picture of my hero, place a second picture—that of myself in my best performance state of mind. See my hero and myself look at each other and nod. *("Hi, Jack." "Hi, Nick." Pretty good.)*

3) Move both images toward each other slowly and watch as they merge into one picture, so that I can see them both at once, as if they were transparent.

4) Allow the two to blend together into a single image.

5) Move this blended image into me any way that gives me a rush.

Animal Image

K. says aligning my personal image with birds and animals also gives me power. He recommends I should blend my image with the energy of an animal I like.

1) Picture my favorite animal or bird, or the one that best represents the nature of the presentation I'm about to give. How would I like to perform? With the smoothness of a dolphin? The playfulness of a monkey? The power of a panther? The grace of an eagle? Adjust color, brightness, size, etc., for highest intensity.

2) Beside that picture see myself in my best performance state.

3) Slowly blend both pictures into one composite as before.

4) Move the composite picture into me so that I feel a rush.

✓ *I used a lion the first time through on this one. Old macho stuff coming through, I guess—thinking about some of the people I'd like to tear apart.*

Add Donald Duck

I put a spin on this exercise and blended the image of my former boss, Streicher, with Donald Duck. Now in my mind when I hear Streicher speak the voice is Donald's. There's an image that worked!

Watch The Actor

Marion does something similar. When somebody irritates her she imagines the person being an actor playing that person. Then she can enjoy the good job "the actor" is doing, which completely changes her response to the person.

Selective Visualizing

K. pointed out that people visualize in different ways. For example, I'm very good at making images of numbers and equations, because I'm not emotionally involved with them. But I have trouble visualizing people, especially when I try to recall emotionally charged memories. I also find it difficult to visualize myself. K. calls this "selective visualization," like selective hearing, where you pay attention to what interests you and ignore all else. *(Marion says she sometimes talks to me and I don't hear a word she's said.)* K. said I will develop across-the-board visualization skills with practice. And he repeatedly emphasized the need for practice. He said the senses are like our muscles, we develop the ones we exercise.

Visualizing By Overlap

K. says a good way to vitalize a less developed sense is to overlap it from a more highly developed sense. By touching my nose I was more easily able to visualize it—overlapping my senses from the tactile, which is a strong sense for me, to the visual. I tried touching an imaginary object—Tarby, the black cocker spaniel I had when I was a kid. Not only did a partial image of Tarby come immediately to mind but I smelled his fur and heard him barking. A person

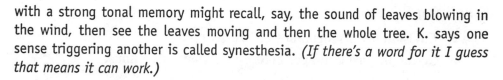

with a strong tonal memory might recall, say, the sound of leaves blowing in the wind, then see the leaves moving and then the whole tree. K. says one sense triggering another is called synesthesia. *(If there's a word for it I guess that means it can work.)*

Signaling The Brain

K. pointed out that my internal images are signals that tell my brain what I want. Examples:

- **To create my own business, see myself with people who could help make it happen.**
- **To reduce stress, make relaxing images, like the time I snorkled in Florida and watched iridescent fish swimming in the coral reef.**
- **For better relationships, picture myself with the kind of person I like most.**

✓ *In fact, that's how I met Marion. I kept imagining this lively, energetic, optimistic type of woman, and then one day I saw Marion across the room at a party and went right over and talked to her. Maybe seeing in my mind the kind of woman I wanted brought out qualities in me that I didn't usually express—like curiosity or a sense of humor—and these qualities in turn attracted her.*

Visualizing Is Basic To Imitating

K. suggests that I should keep an eye open for people I admire and then imagine myself performing the way they do. Is there a teacher I'd like to emulate? See myself addressing a group in his or her way. Do I want to improve my golf game? *(Tiger Woods looks so cool when he plays. I'd like to just step into his image and swing the club.)* Do I want to lose weight? Notice someone who looks the way I want to look, see myself at that weight and flash that image before every meal. *(What I really need is a model of someone smart at handling money!)*

Benefits

After each lesson K. wants me to list the benefits he says I'm getting from my lessons with him. He probably regards this list as an inspiration to learn his techniques, but I also think of it as a way of checking as time goes on to see if these things really work.

Visualizing Helps Me:

- ❖ Envision my performance before giving it.
- ❖ Create inspiring images before interviews, auditions, speeches, business meetings.
- ❖ Program myself for success by reviewing past successes and seeing them in my future.
- ❖ See new ways of making presentations.
- ❖ Model myself after my heroes by imagining myself performing like them.
- ❖ Remember names and phone numbers.
- ❖ Spell more accurately by seeing the words in my mind.
- ❖ See various possibilities in any situation.
- ❖ Be more objective in emotional situations by visualizing instead of indulging my feelings.

Afterthoughts

So what's the equation here? Think about what I want and I somehow attract it to myself? Sounds a little too easy. But then K. does say that creating an image is only the beginning, that I still have to work hard to achieve the thing I'm visualizing. He says the image is the inspiration that gets me started and keeps me going.

Lesson 2

THE FINGER SQUEEZE

"A performer needs to be prepared for anything—a last-minute change of schedule, a technical mal-function, upsetting personal news—and knowing you have a resource that can help you perform in spite of adversity is reassuring."

Squeezing The Fingers: A Message To My Brain

K. wants me to sit in a quiet and comfortable place where I won't be disturbed. *(Finding that in New York would be an accomplishment in itself.)* Take a deep breath, sit back and recall, one by one, a series of inspiring experiences. When I see, hear and feel each memory at its most powerful, squeeze together two or three fingers of each hand. Pressing the nail of my thumb into the fleshy pads of a finger will give me a kind of gentle shock, sending the message to my brain that I want to remember this moment. That's what he calls the "Zzt!"

K. has a favorite sequence of events he uses when teaching someone to "program" good feelings for the first time.

1) Think of an animal or child I particularly enjoy. See, hear, feel and smell its presence. Squeeze the fingers.

2) Recall a favorite nature spot. Place myself there and feel the temperature, notice the colors and shadings of the surroundings, listen to the sounds, smell the air. When I feel I'm fully there, squeeze the fingers.

3) Recall something I did that I'm satisfied with—that I created with my own hands, or planned and carried out, or an idea I came up with, or a performance I gave—that delighted me because I did it so well. Squeeze the fingers.

4) Recall other memories that are inspiring, exciting, moving, humorous, or in some way make me feel good. Each inspiring thought I remember or construct will "stack" on the others and create an ever stronger signal.

✓ *I promised him I'd practice it, so I will. But I still have my doubts that this can work as simply as he seems to think it will. It did work for the woman on the airplane, but who knows how long it'll stick? But, as K. said, if I don't believe it then I won't let it work. So part of the deal is to give it a chance. I'll try believing it for at least a few weeks, then we'll see.*

Resource Memory Bank

The whole point of the "Zzt-Squeeze" technique is to associate enriching experiences with a self-administered touch so I can retrieve those good feelings at will. K. says that programming inspiring memories every day helps me build what he calls a resource memory bank. *(I'll think of my fingers as a kind of bank card for making quick withdrawals and giving myself big emotional bonuses!)*

Zz-zzt!

K. says saying "Zz-zzt" adds an auditory signal to the touch and will help me recall the memory. Some people like to say "Zz-zzt" while programming the memory. Others find it interrupts a quiet state of repose and prefer to add the verbal signal later, after the memory has been associated with the touch. K. points out that once I've taught the "Zzt-Squeeze" to someone else, all I have to do is say "Zz-zzt" (on the telephone, for example), or simply hold up my thumb and forefinger to get the other person to smile and recall good memories.

Pacing And Timing

K. wants me to use an emotional "separator"—take a deep breath before each finger squeeze—to clear my brain. *(I think sometimes that would take more than a deep breath.)* When "programming" a memory, pause after each finger squeeze to give each memory a few moments to sink in.

No One Is The Wiser

He says I can also touch my arm, or hand or knee, whatever is convenient, but he warns that the location of the touch should be so natural that it is inconspicuous and easy to access. This way I can use it in business meetings or interviews or whenever I want to feel at ease and no one will be the wiser. He said some people like to touch a knuckle or wrist bone of one hand with a finger of the other hand. But, he says, this action occupies both hands, so he prefers touching the fingers of one hand to each other. *(I remember seeing statues of Buddha with one finger touching another. I wonder if that's what he was doing.)*

Taping The Message

K. suggests I can use my audio tape of his voice to guide me through the squeeze-the-fingers exercise because his speaking is timed to my responses, my pace of learning. For someone else the timing might be off. He explained that when he was teaching me the steps of the finger squeeze he was constantly adjusting his pace to mine, watching my face carefully for subtle changes in skin color and muscle tension, or a nod of my head that indicated whether I was ready to go on or needed more time. He also spoke in rhythm with my breathing to help create a rapport between us that facilitated learning. He said commercial relaxation and hypnosis tapes are, of necessity, timed to a kind of universal pace—one size doesn't really fit all—and are therefore only partially effective. He says in most cases it's better for people to make their my own tape, with a pace and voice tone they like. Or have a friend with a nice, warm voice record it for them. *(Marion would do a really nice job on that.)* But they would need a proper script. I could write down the words from K.'s session with me, if Matt or Charles or Marion want to use it. Then they could add in some of the thoughts they'd like to hear.

Recall Inspiring Events Daily

The Zzt-Squeeze reminds me to keep alive the best experiences of my life so that these memories continue to inspire me. *(In my case, to start having them inspire me, since I seem to have forgotten most of them.)* Somehow K. got me to promise that I'd sequester myself for a short while each day— phone off ringer—and relive the inspiring moments of my life while squeezing the fingers. He says I'll be surprised how many rich memories I have stored in my brain. *(That'll require a real F.B.I. search.)* He reminded me to use my visualization techniques to intensify the memories with brightness, closeness, largeness, color, etc. (see my notes on visualization), and when the good feeling of a memory is at its most intense, squeeze the fingers. The idea is to make it a daily exercise, so I continue to develop an ever more powerful and indelible resource *signal* that will be literally "at my finger tips."

When To Squeeze The Fingers

Some people like to squeeze the fingers to put themselves at ease a few moments before an important public appearance. K. says it's also useful just before auditions, interviews, speeches or exams, or any potentially stressful situation. He mentioned one entertainer who uses the squeeze before reading his press reviews, and claims that since he started doing so he's more objective about the comments on his work and doesn't get so nervous waiting for the reviews to come in. *(Marion could use that one.)* Also, when feeling a little low, or tired, squeezing the fingers for a few moments while taking some nice, deep breaths can be rejuvenating.

"Squeezing The Fingers Worked"

K. told me a story about a woman in a two-day workshop he gave for teachers. On the first day he taught the finger squeeze. The second day he noticed the woman was missing and his host showed him a note from her: "My father died last night. Tell Kumi squeezing the fingers worked." He hastened to point out that the squeeze did not necessarily allay the grief of this woman— nor should it have, since grieving is a normal and healthy response to loss— but that it enabled her to maintain emotional stability in the face of hardship. His point is, a performer needs to be prepared for anything—a last-minute change of schedule, a technical malfunction, upsetting personal news—and knowing you have a resource that can help you perform in spite of adversity is reassuring. *(I sure could have used something like that in some of those brutal meetings at Globalcom, especially when the cutbacks began.)*

Remembering To Use It

K. points out that there are countless circumstances in which squeezing the fingers can be helpful, but I need to *remember* to use it. All too often he has seen a person learn a useful technique and then forget to apply it when most needed. He calls that "leaving it in the room where you learned it." What will remind me to use it at the time I need it most? Will it be the sight of a certain person? A particular place? A time of day? A challenging circumstance? That's why he emphasizes taking the time to imagine when and where this resource might be useful to me—at work, at home, at play, with personal relationships—and to program anticipated responses in advance.

✓ *The Zzt-Squeeze is something I might use when talking to my son, Charles, since I seem to erupt so easily with him. I guess I still feel guilty about the divorce, knowing the way he believes two people should stick it out regardless.*

Pre-program Future Responses

K. taught the finger squeeze to a middle manager, a woman who complained about condescending attitudes from male executives—an offhand remark, a glance, a change of voice tone, an interruption. After she established the finger squeeze, she role-played dozens of possible encounters in her office dealing with remarks like, "We need a man to do that job," "A girl like you can go far in this business," "Why don't we talk about that over a drink?" With each of these remarks she squeezed her fingers and felt calm, maintaining her professionalism and emotional balance.

K. said she reported two noticeable benefits from this pre-programming of her response. Now when men expressed superior or sexist attitudes toward her she, 1) *remembered* to squeeze the fingers, because she had reminded herself in advance to use it when she needed it, and 2) she felt more detached ("No big deal") and could respond to the situation objectively.

Think Of Ways To Use It

K. asked me to think of ways people in various professions might use the squeeze-the-fingers technique to relax and feel comfortable under pressure:

— **A public speaker with a heckler.**
— **A musician with a dictatorial orchestra conductor.**
— **A teacher with a pompous administrator.**
— **A salesperson with a difficult customer.**
— **A politician with a hostile interviewer.**
— **A person going for an important job interview.**
— **A student taking an exam.**

Storing Feelings

K. says the Zzt-Squeeze will help me store inspiring feelings to help me feel confident in difficult situations. At first, this idea sounded like *Star Trek*, but then I thought of Marion who does this sort of thing all the time as an actor. She calls it "memorizing emotions," like joy or sadness, that she can use on stage when she needs them. One time we were at a party and someone upset her. I suggested we leave and she whispered to me, "No, I want to stay. I can use this."

The Zzt-Squeeze Helps Me:

❖ **Program inspiring memories and retrieve them when I need them.**
❖ **Capture happy moments and "take them with me."**
❖ **Maintain my composure when challenged, criticized or insulted.**
❖ **Regain equilibrium when I lose it.**
❖ **Deal with surprise events, accidents or bad news.**
❖ **Meditate.**
❖ **Relax.**

A Kind Of Prayer

I wonder if squeezing the fingers is the same kind of reminder as putting the hands together in prayer.

Lesson 3

THE HOLOGRAM

"The image comes to mind of Woody Allen in 'Play it again, Sam,' using Humphrey Bogart to coach him on dating women. He carried Bogart inside him as an idol, so why not use him for advice, even converse with him?"

Exercise

Switching Positions

K. showed me how to coach myself by switching between the roles of the Performer, the Coach and the Audience to give me a three-way experience as a presenter. I start by labeling three pieces of paper and placing them on the floor in a triangle about 10' on a side to mark out the positions.

Performer: I step into this position and rehearse my performance or other special upcoming situation.

Coach: I think of the person I would most like to have coach me for this event. I see him or her standing at the **Coach** position, and take a little time to visualize this person in some detail. Then I step out of the **Performer** position into the **Coach** position and become this coach, and watch and listen to myself performing. As the **Coach**, I tell or demonstrate to the **Performer** what changes I'd like to see and hear, even walking over and making physical adjustments to the **Performer's** posture or movements with my hands as needed. When satisfied, I step back into the **Performer** position again, applying this new advice. I shift between **Performer** and **Coach** as needed until I'm satisfied with my performance. (As the Coach, I am objective about every aspect of my presentation: content and style—quality of the material, mood I am conveying—and technical aspects of my delivery.)

Audience: Step into the **Audience** position and become the **Audience** watching and listening to the **Performer**. Tell or show the **Performer** what I'd like to see and hear him or her do differently. When finished advising as **Audience**, step back into the **Performer** position again and apply the **Audience** feedback.

✔ *As an audience member, I feel completely removed from the concerns of the **Performer** and the **Coach**. Here I'm interested not in technical matters of the presentation, but rather in the impact it has on me. Is it interesting? How could it better hold my attention? From this position, I can even laugh at me. That's a first!*

Move between **Performer**, **Coach** and **Audience** until I'm satisfied with my performance from all three positions.

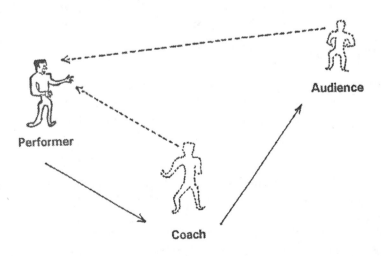

HOLOGRAM

✓ *Switching back and forth like this can be a little disorienting at first, particularly if it's done too fast. It's best if I take the time to act it out fully, really pretending to be the other person—getting the feeling in my body—to make it work well.*

Everyone's An Actor

K.'s Hologram is a kind of split-personality exercise, because I divide myself into three parts. K. suggests that a good way to do this is to imagine I'm an actor playing all three characters, switching back and forth between these roles freely. It's like having two other people helping me prepare my presentation: an expert, who can serve as a model, and an astute but disinterested viewer who can comment on the effect of my performance.

Child-Like Fantasy

I would never have believed that I could actually coach myself for a presentation. But imagining I was Jack Nicholson made all the difference. *(Maybe it's just a child-like fantasy, but I love pretending I'm him. After all, isn't that what we all do as kids when we play dress-up? Children typically put pictures of their heroes on the wall and talk to them, even ask their advice.)*

Use The Best

K. says I can imagine any coach I wish, living or dead, whether I've met them or not, and I can have as many coaches as I want. As this expert coach I can see my performance from the standpoint of his or her particular kind of excellence, imagining how this highly accomplished person would view my performance, and what criteria s/he would apply. K. suggests I pretend this outstanding individual is a friend of mine, to put myself more at ease. *(Could I really imagine Pete Sampras or Steve Martin being a friend of mine? Well, why not? I'm only pretending. Which is also what bothers me slightly about this exercise. Can pretending something make it true?)*

"Play It Again, Sam"

The image comes to mind of Woody Allen in "Play it again, Sam," using Humphrey Bogart to coach him on dating women. He carried Bogart inside him as an idol, so why not use him for advice, even converse with him? In the movie,

Allen didn't use the audience position—that would be us, the viewers. But, come to think of it, he made the film, so he had to be the audience, too.

The Dispassionate Audience Member

The value of taking the **Audience** role is that audiences are detached from the concerns of the professional. In this position I don't care about the "meaning" or the "consequence" of my performance, so I'm free to simply say how I'm responding to the performance.

Triple Position: A Variation On The Hologram

K. also likes to use three different positions to gain new understanding in personal, family or business situations. For this he slightly re-defines the function of each position:

Self: Experiencing events from my point of view.

Other: Experiencing events from someone's else's point of view.

Observer: Experiencing events from a neutral, objective point of view—just an observer reporting the facts.

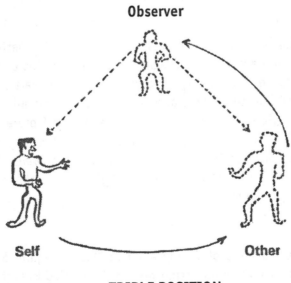

TRIPLE POSITION

In this exercise, I step into the position of the **Other** to understand the world from that person's point of view. Then I become the **Observer**, and see myself and any situation I might be in as if looking at a total stranger.

Stepping into the position of the **Other** would be a good way to get out of my feelings, and to experience what Marion or Charles is feeling, seeing or hearing when we discuss issues. The value of the **Observer** position is to be able to witness such exchanges with no feeling at all, just reporting who did and said what and when, and how people responded to each other—like taking dictation, or making a video and playing it back.

If I find I'm carrying emotional baggage when I step into the position of the **Other**, I can step into the **Observer** position and cooly view the situation between my **Self** and the **Other**. Then I can be more objective when I go to the position of the **Other**.

✓ *How often have I heard someone say, "You didn't hear what I said," or "You're contradicting yourself" when discussions get heated. The ability to detach and become the emotionally uninvolved **Observer** when the marmalade hits the fan might help me stay cool under pressure and think more clearly, instead of blowing my stack.*

Objectivity In The Heat Of Battle

K. says that good negotiators are fascinating to watch, because they will switch positions in the heat of battle and gain objectivity in complex situations. Resourceful business leaders are also an example of switching positions in the midst of the action, conducting board meetings with an understanding of divergent viewpoints. K. points out that a really good salesperson is not someone who just makes fast sales, but rather a person who sees things from the *buyer's* standpoint. Such a person looks to the future, creates a sense of trust, and develops customers through the references of satisfied clients. *(My problem is that I keep looking at the past, like someone driving a car while looking in the rear-view mirror.)*

Taking The Position Of The Examiner

When preparing for oral exams, interviews or auditions, K. recommends I take the position of the examiner. It helps to have been an interviewer, jury member or employer in order to see myself from their perspective and thereby better understand what they're looking for. Learning any new skill—a musical instrument, badminton, a new computer program—will be easier when I have my own internal teacher to work with between lessons. Any time I'm about to step into a challenging personal or professional situation K. says I should ask myself, "Which position would best help me to understand what I need to know?" *(Reviewing my last talk with Marion it was obvious to me that I had never left the* **Self** *position.)*

Reviewing Personal History

K. says that recalling the physical and emotional feelings of past experiences improves my sense-memory for events and is a way to avoid repeating mistakes (or "unproductive behavior," to use K.'s words). I reviewed some former experiences, seeing what I could learn from them by describing what I saw, heard and felt from the position of others. I recalled my early teenage years, my attempts to make the track team, my first girfriend, arguments with my parents about my career. In some cases, I already had a new understanding of previous situations. Time helps me gain a new perspective naturally as years go by and I become a new person, looking back at myself living through those events. But switching back and forth between different positions can enable me to gain this objectivity right now, the equivalent of placing myself years into my own future and looking back as if the present had happened a long time ago. *(K. astonished me with the remark that he plans fifty years in advance. When I expressed disbelief he said, "Japanese business people plan 200 years ahead!" But, he said, planning ahead doesn't mean I will automatically do everything right. I still need to adjust my plans as I encounter the unexpected.)*

Choosing Friends And Lovers

K. says people who are flexible enough to step into others' shoes tend to be more balanced in their judgments. They can hear, see and feel situations from outside as well as inside themselves and avoid getting stuck in just one way of perceiving things. Highly visual people are a good example. When something goes wrong in a relationship, they usually don't need someone to say, "If you could just see yourself you wouldn't act that way." They can play back a personal encounter as if it were a scene in a movie, notice what could be improved in their behavior and revise it. K. points out that such flexibility would help me choose friends and lovers who are appropriate for me, because

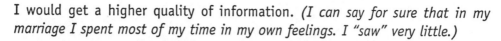

I would get a higher quality of information. *(I can say for sure that in my marriage I spent most of my time in my own feelings. I "saw" very little.)*

The Hologram (and it's variations) Helps Me:

- ❖ **Coach myself by creating imaginary mentors.**
- ❖ **Role-play behaviors and watch myself doing them.**
- ❖ **Identify with and understand the feelings of others.**
- ❖ **Detach from my feelings by standing outside of myself.**
- ❖ **See and hear myself from the position of others.**
- ❖ **Maintain objectivity in discussion and negotiation.**
- ❖ **Discover multiple solutions to any situation.**
- ❖ **Tap into my own resources for solutions.**

Warning

K. says that switching positions too much can dissociate a person emotionally. *(That would be my former wife, Andrea.)* While such dissociating offers the benefit of objectivity, it runs the danger of becoming automatic and can produce involuntary emotional detachment, even sexual unresponsiveness. *(Also Andrea— although I think I may have contributed to that, too.)* So, he says that after switching positions to get new information it's important to make sure I "come back home" to myself. The secret is to be aware of what I'm doing with my senses so I don't go out of balance. This is one of the benefits of taking different positions when used properly: I can learn how to *consciously* feel and hear and visualize interpersonal relationships in order to improve them. But I want to make sure I don't lose myself (or my friends) in the process.

Lesson 4

MODELING

"When I take on a characteristic from another person and add it to myself, I introduce this 'new part' to my inner community and make sure the whole group approves of having it there."

Installing A New Part

K. says that modeling someone's behavior is like taking a characteristic or trait or talent of another person and putting it inside me. Sometimes this just happens automatically when I admire someone, but he says I can also do it deliberately. He calls this "installing" a new part. He offered me a seven-step process.

Modeling Exercise

1) Identify a behavior, attitude or skill that I want.

2) Choose someone who's achieved it.

3) Pretend to be that person, role-playing situations as if I were him or her. (This means I must have access to, or find information about, the person.)

4) Check for negative feelings about having part of this person in me.

5) Set a trial period for acclimating this new part to my life.

6) Imagine how my future will be different, professionally and personally, as a result of having this new part in me.

7) Seal it in my memory with a touch, a sound or an image.

✓ *What uncanny timing. Just when Marion is about to give up on me for not having a plan for my life, K. shows me how to set goals by modeling others.*

Why Model?

K. says everyone learns by modeling. Whether we're learning to ride a bicycle, play a sport or establish a business, we imitate someone who's successful at it. We even learn how to kiss by imitating movie actors! Much of this modeling is unconscious, as when we learn how to talk by imitating our parents, and much of it is haphazard instead of carefully selective. K. wants me to learn how to model *consciously* so I can create and achieve my goals. That's why he emphasizes two things that are primary for succeeding in any aspect of life:

1) Decide what I want.

2) Find a model for it.

Choosing A Model

K. says models may be famous or unknown, ancient or modern, legendary or real. I might model a great world figure or the person who sells newspapers on the corner, depending on the characteristics I want to acquire. The main thing is that I believe in my model and that he or she inspires me. That person has achieved in some way what I want and is a symbol of the goal I've set for myself.

✓ *Question: How do I know I'm choosing the model I need? What if I "install" someone who's wrong for me? Answer: Check out steps four and five above.*

Role-Play My Model

K. says good modelers allow themselves to be psychologically subsumed by their models, identifying so deeply with them that they might even wear their kind of clothes, imitate their voices, ape their movements and gestures. This imitative behavior can make me feel almost as if I were that person, and therefore automatically take on the belief that I am succeeding.

✓ *I remember in college doing something like this with a classmate named Hugh Fraser. Hugh was a cross-country runner. I didn't care about being an athlete, but I envied his healthy look—the economy of his movements, the sheen of his skin—and wanted that kind of health for myself. So I started jogging around the campus whenever I could, wearing sweats and sneakers and pretending I was Hugh. K. would probably define that as "installing a health part." If that is one of my parts, it's sure been dormant for many years.*

Beware Of Negative Characteristics

K. warns that such "deep identification" modeling should be selective. The danger is that I might admire a person so much that I adopt their bad habits along with their desirable traits. My model may have a great talent or ability, but may also have a destructive lifestyle or attitude. For example, some aspiring athletes may get the mistaken impression that they need steroids to be great. Marion said many creative artists have the idea that to be true to their art they must be poor. Others believe that to be successful in politics they must double deal. *(From what I've seen, that one may be true!)* Often young people get the impression that certain negative characteristics "come with the territory," and automatically build them into their modeling process. K.'s point is to adopt only those characteristics that I want and need from my heroes and leave out the rest.

My Inner Community

K. thinks of me as a group. He says I have these separate parts of me that carry out the functions of my life—like a work part, a family part, a social part, a creative part, and so on. He says modeling a new characteristic or behavior is like adding a new person to my group. He suggests therefore that when I model someone—when I take on a characteristic from someone else and add it to myself—that I introduce this "new person" to my inner community of selves and make sure the whole group approves of having it there. He wants to be sure that no part of this inner community feels this new part is going to compete with or take away anyone's job. A new Performing Part can be especially demanding and other parts may have to make major readjustments to accommodate it. K.

wants my whole self—all the parts—to say "Yes" to this new part and adopt it with a spirit of full cooperation, even though this may take considerable negotiating with myself (selves) in some cases. *(This sounds a lot like adding a new program to a computer. The new program often interferes with the function of other programs unless I make the proper adjustments.)*

I think K.'s point is to respect the functioning of our entire system by integrating new parts into ourselves with care and respect, instead of just "slamming them in" and expecting them to get along. He says this "council meeting" approach makes for a successful installation of new behaviors.

✓ *Now that I think of it, I never integrated that Jogger Part into me years ago, never made it a part of my overall lifestyle. So when I started to work for Globalcom, exercise gradually faded out of the picture. Maybe that's the nagging little voice I hear when I see my puffy, pale body in the mirror—the Jogger feeling betrayed.*

Trial Period

K. recommends I set a trial period of several weeks to see how a new model works with my whole system, the same way an organization might try out a new employee. After this period I can make any necessary adjustments, or, if it doesn't work, remove it. This way K. says I'm not "stuck" with a part if I (or my group) find I don't want it. Trying out new models can also be a way of helping me define my goals, because I will see how various models work for me, what sacrifices may be required and whether I'm willing to change my lifestyle in that way to accommodate a new behavior.

Getting My Brain's Attention

K. emphasizes the importance of making a strong sensory association with the installation of a new part. To do this, he gently squeezed my shoulder and then had me squeeze my own shoulder the way he had done it (simply an alternate to the finger squeeze). This touch is a way of telling my brain, "Feel *that*? That means I want *this*."

Triple-Channel Learning

K. likes to triple associate any new installation with a touch, an image and a sound. The finger squeeze with the "Zz-zzt!" makes two—feeling and sound.

By holding his fingers up in the air and making a face when he squeezes his fingers K. adds a visual element when he wants me to remember something I've learned. The combination of all three senses is particularly strong. Any way I can most strongly communicate a new idea to myself—by a touch, a picture, a sound, or any combination of the three—is the way that's best for me. If I can have all three all the better. He calls that "triple-channel learning."

Making It Work

Modeling may be the link I need between seeing the future and planning the many tiny details that can make that future a reality. I've been asking myself how I can visualize what I want and know that I'm not kidding myself, being over-ambitious or unrealistic. So I need to ask myself:

- **How specifically did my model(s) achieve what I want to achieve?**
- **How can I make their method(s) work for me?**
- **How much time should I allot to make it work?**

The Model Offers Me:

- ❖ **Proof that my dream is achievable.**
- ❖ **A proven method for achieving it.**
- ❖ **Inspiration to keep me going for it.**

Modeling Helps Me:

- ❖ **Utilize skills, attitudes and behaviors of others.**
- ❖ **Recognize the qualities and resources I need.**
- ❖ **Test new behaviors to see if they fit me.**
- ❖ **Learn by example.**

Afterthoughts

In some ways this whole idea of inner parts is odd, but then again it seems quite natural. How often I've said, "A part of me wants to go to the movies tonight," but another part says, "I have work to do." Or, "I want that whole bar of chocolate," while another part says, "Remember our agreement." But does this mean we really have separate parts within us? How does K. know that? How could anybody? Maybe it's just a metaphor, to give us a handle on how we function. For the moment, I'll go along with it and see where it takes me.

Lesson 5

SEQUENCING

"My mind blocked out the visual memory of my talk to the buyers, which K. said is common when emotions become powerful. So a good idea for me was to install a positive visual step, to re-route the sequence into a new solution-oriented outcome."

Breaking Habits

K. says all behavior has a pattern. To change a behavior, change the pattern. Sequencing is a precision method for identifying the steps in a pattern. Here is K.'s point-by-point method for building new sequences—creating new habits and leaving old ones behind.

Sequencing Exercise

1) Note an undesirable behavior that's habitual.
2) Identify the trigger that initiates the step-by-step sequence of the habit.
3) List the steps of the undesirable sequence.
4) Create a new sequence I prefer.

5) Embed the new sequence in memory with a "Zzt-Squeeze."

6) Role-play the action that triggers the unwanted sequence, and

7) Insert the new sequence immediately following the trigger using the "Zzt-squeeze."

8) Repeat the installation until my brain learns it.

9) Test the new sequence by initiating the trigger and noting if the new sequence has replaced the old. If not, re-embed the new sequence.

10) Imagine what will be different in my behavior now that I have this new sequence.

Here is my old sequence:

Stage Fright Sequence

Trigger: Authority figure asks me to give a talk.

1) I hear a buyer asking me a question I can't answer, and the other buyers whispering to each other.

2) My stomach flutters and my knees go weak.

3) I say, "I know I'm going to screw this up."

4) My heart thumps and I break out in a sweat.

5) I give the talk and I'm drained for days afterward.

Here is the sequence I prefer:

New Sequence

Trigger: Authority figure asks me to give a talk.

1) I see Charles' friends smiling as I speak, and I feel good.

2) I transfer that feeling to a corporate room, seeing smiling faces of business people and feeling good.

3) I say, "I'm going to do a really good job."

4) I speak aloud to this imaginary new audience and —

5) I feel very comfortable.

Coding Sequences

Something is missing for me as I look at these sequences. I think the computer man in me wants a set of symbols to codify these steps, make them even more specific. How about a code for the primary sense associated with each step?

V = Visual

A = Auditory

K = Kinesthetic

✓ *I'm using the word "kinesthetic" to indicate the feeling sense, both physical and emotional, even though kinesthetic actually refers to a sensation of motion. Since both emotion and touch suggest a feeling of motion, it makes sense to me.*

Time, Place And Mood

I could also add subscripts to tell myself if a particular action is:

a) past or future (time)

b) outside or inside myself (location)

c) positive or negative (my emotional response)

The coding might look like this:

r = Recalled (past)

c = Constructed (future)

e = Outside myself (external)

i = Inside myself (internal)

+ = Pleasant picture, sound or feeling

- = Unpleasant picture, sound or feeling

This coding relates nicely to the eye chart. Now I can see a sequence two ways: as a written formula, and in terms of eye positions. Here's how the eye scan chart would look if I were watching someone else's eyes:

Eye Scan Chart For Typical Right-Handers
(This person is facing me)

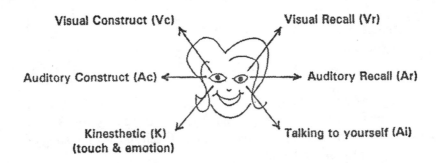

✓ *I've noticed that some people are right-left reversed, or show other exceptions to this eye scan chart generalization. By paying attention, I can quickly figure out how each person's eye positions correspond to their senses.*

Coding Stage Fright

Trigger: **Auditory external (Ae)**: Boss asks me to talk.

1) **Auditory internal negative (Ar-)**
   I hear a buyer asking me a question I can't answer, and the other buyers whispering to each other.

2) **Kinesthetic negative (K-):**
   My stomach flutters and my knees go weak.

3) **Auditory internal negative (Ai-):**
   I say, "I know I'm going to screw this up."

4) **Kinesthetic negative (K-):**
   My heart thumps and I break out into a sweat.

5) **Auditory construct external / Kinesthetic negative (Ace/K-):**
   I give the talk and I'm drained for days afterward.

Coded summary of sensory steps for stage fright sequence:
$$Ae: \longrightarrow (Ar\text{-}) \longrightarrow (K\text{-}) \longrightarrow (Ai\text{-}) \longrightarrow (K\text{-}) \longrightarrow (Ace/K\text{-})$$

"Nick, I want you to make a presentation to the buyers in fifteen minutes."

(Notice the omission of visual steps)

Fear Distorts The Senses

K. said that, in traumatic situations, a disproportionate attention to events may occur in each sense, so that our memory of what we see, hear or feel can be distorted, or even blocked out completely. In my case, my mind blocked out the visual memory of my talk to the buyers, which K. said is common when emotions become powerful. So a good idea for me was to install a positive visual step, to re-route the sequence into a new solution-oriented outcome. Seeing my "fear sequence" in abbreviated form like this makes all this much clearer. I can quickly see from the coding alone that all the steps have minuses: the only steps I was conscious of were negative words and feelings. This sequence is literally a formula for failure—a very effective one!

Coding The New Sequence

Trigger: **Auditory external (Ae):** Boss asks me to talk.

1) **Visual recall positive (Vr+):**
   I see Charles' friends smiling as I speak, and I feel good.
2) **Visual construct (Vc+):**
   I transfer that feeling to a corporate room, seeing smiling faces of business people and feeling good.

3) **Auditory construct positive (Ac+):**
I say, "I'm going to do a really good job."

4) **Auditory construct external (Ace)**
I speak aloud to this imaginary new audience and —

5) **Kinesthetic positive (K+):**
I feel very comfortable.

Coded summary of steps for new sequence:

Ae: —> (Vr+) —> (Vc+) —> (Ac+) —> (Ace) —> (K+)

"Nick, I want you to make a presentation to the buyers in fifteen minutes."

(All three senses are consciously active, starting with the visual.)

✔ *There's a glitch in my notation: a picture or sound has to have a feeling accompany it in order for me to know if it's pleasant or not. So what do I notate for, say, a pleasant picture? V+ or V/K+? Or should I make them separate steps? I think I'll just wing it for the moment, and use whatever helps me remember each step more easily.*

Success Uses All Three Senses

This new sequence is a success sequence. Two visual steps have been added, all three senses are used, and all three have plus signs—a powerful strategy for eliminating stage fright. It's amazing to me that, outside of creating computer programs, I had been using so little of my visual sense. K. seems to be saying the same thing I'm discovering by watching people's eye movements—that most of us have a favorite sense, one that we rely on and have a lot of practice with, and for me that seems to be the kinesthetic. I like to feel my way first. Some people are highly developed visually but undeveloped kinesthetically and have to work at utilizing feelings. Others rely primarily on the auditory sense.

Sequencing And The Eyes

Sequencing underscores the point that a key factor in my stage fright has been the lack of conscious internal imagery. I look *down* most of the time: I talk to myself and go into my feelings and therefore don't *see* the situation I'm in. More evidence that omitting the visual in my thinking has been a root cause of many of my problems, personal and professional.

Several Minutes A Day

Question: How can I make sure I'm using all my senses in any situation? Marion had a great idea for that: why not practice the eye positions for several minutes a day to notice what each position does for me? She's already been playing with the idea, because she says it gives her insights into how to play different characters as an actor. She suggested I pick any situation I want to understand better and think about it while holding my eyes in each of the basic eye positions. This way I get a triple-channel understanding on any issue.

✓ *Practicing eye positions might also help me make new sequences, especially if I get good enough at noticing my own eye movements as they happen. That would give me another way to identify the sense I'm using for each step in a sequence.*

Blueprinting Habits

Using coded scripts to abbreviate these steps helps me see at a glance exactly what kind of step needs to be inserted (or omitted) to make a sequence work. I can go over all my old habits and see from the coding alone where they are strong or weak. A code is like a blueprint for a habit. But Marion was turned off by the idea of coding sequences:

"Too complicated."
"But with coding you can see at a glance what sense you're using—or not using."

"It looks like one of your mathematical equations. The idea is to simplify ideas, not complicate them."

"What could be simpler than this? Look, a behavior is a series of actions. First you do this, then that, then something else, and you're done."

"That part's alright. But when you add all these little letters and plus and minus signs it's like you're making a person into a machine."

"But the brain does work like a machine."

"How do you know how the brain works? And how many people have you tried this with?"

"I'm sure Kumi's done it with a lot of people. Besides, it's logical."

She made an exaggeratedly serious face and said, "Oh, logical, of course, then it must be right."

Maybe I am too analytical. I'd like to think I'm a little more spontaneous and human than the machines I program every day. *(Is that the creative part of me speaking? Or maybe even some long-lost spiritual part?)* But we all program ourselves. That's what habits are, mechanical operations that help us live our daily lives. Driving a car, brushing our teeth, dressing ourselves—we don't have to think about those things because they're completely automatic. But we had to practice to learn how to do them, and only then did they become unconscious. If they didn't become unconscious, our minds would be cluttered with the mundane and we'd never get anything done. *(I guess Marion's real fear is that I'm becoming a mad scientist, programming myself and the world—the dreaded age of mind control.)*

Sequencing Helps Me:

- ❖ Identify and analyze patterns in human behavior.
- ❖ Find the precise point in a pattern where a new step is needed to change it.
- ❖ Recognize outdated patterns in myself and create useful new ones.
- ❖ Understand the steps needed to learn a new skill or behavior.
- ❖ Train others with greater precision.
- ❖ Realize that I can change any behavior I can clearly define.

Window To The Soul

The eyes may be the window to the soul, but they're also the channel to the brain. Maybe by learning how to use all three channels—or how to re-direct them as I wish—I can learn how to take full advantage of what my brain has to offer.

Lesson 6

COUNTERBUTTONS

"We choose to give loved ones access to the secrets of our hearts, and we can interrupt this access any time we wish. We still hold control over our emotions."

Freedom To Respond

K. says I create my own thoughts and emotions, that no one can scare me or make me happy—I scare myself and make myself happy. Although others can cause a *physical* response in me (by touching me), they cannot cause an *emotional* one. Someone may criticize or compliment me, smile or yell at me, but I'm completely free to decide how to respond. People can't grab my emotions the way they can grab my arm, unless I *allow* them to—a privilege I can withdraw any time.

Granting Access To Emotional Switchboards

But he admits that when we love someone we let them into our hearts and allow them to help create our emotions. He calls this granting access to the buttons and counterbuttons on our emotional switchboards. In fact, we like our feelings to be controlled at times by those we love. Opening our emotions to another is a true sharing of ourselves. And we trust that person will exercise that emotional control for our own good and for our pleasure. That's what love is—ultimate trust, and K. admits trust makes us vulnerable. But he is quick to remind me that we *choose* to give loved ones access to the secrets of our hearts, and we can *interrupt* his access any time we wish. We still hold control over our emotions.

Exercise

Counterbuttons

K. showed me a quick way to detach from my feelings when someone "hurts" me.

1) Imagine someone close criticizing or insulting me.
2) Make a small sound, like "Hmm," and shift my physical position, all in one action.
3) Consider the *intent* behind the person's remark.
4) Note what's *useable* in the remark.

This exercise is another form of dissociation, like those I learned from K. in the Hologram. The difference is, this one is auditory/spatial (I make a *sound* and *position shift*), whereas in the Hologram it's spatial/visual (I *move* to the position of the **Other** and *look* back at myself).

The effect in both cases is the same: to create an instant separation between myself and the source of the remark or action. Now that I think of it, I have seen people do this sort of thing when irritated or impatient. They will say, "That's it!" or "Basta!" or "I've had it!" and usually motion in some way with their hands. This is an overt action, of course, but the same thing can be done *inside* ourselves, where we "click off" or "stand back," as Marion puts it, without any overt sign. This is what top people do in tense situations when they need to re-orient themselves under fire. Anyone in the public eye must be able to "click off" and "click on" at will without showing it.

Invisible Movement

In both the Hologram and the counterbutton dissociation, the physical action can be so small it is almost imperceptible. K. says to practice it big to

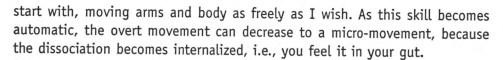

start with, moving arms and body as freely as I wish. As this skill becomes automatic, the overt movement can decrease to a micro-movement, because the dissociation becomes internalized, i.e., you feel it in your gut.

That Audience Scares Me

I've often said, "That audience scares me," but, as much as I hate to admit it, I see now that's impossible. I've been scaring myself and K.'s Sequencing and Counterbuttons techniques show me specifically how I've been doing that and how I can change it.

I Hurt Me

The idea that I've been causing my own suffering is a revelation to me. It's also disturbing, because that means I'm responsible for my feelings. I found it convenient to blame my boss, or Charles, or my former wife when I felt hurt, but it's becoming clearer to me now that, as much as I don't like to admit it, I may be the one who's been hurting me. That doesn't mean others are always innocent of unpleasant behavior, just that I didn't know how to handle it. Nor did I try to understand it, being so preoccupied with my own feelings.

Counterbuttons Help Me:

- ❖ **Realize that I am responsible for my own thoughts and emotions.**
- ❖ **Understand and learn how to deal with my vulnerability in personal relationships.**
- ❖ **Protect myself against unwanted influence.**
- ❖ **Remain cool under stress.**
- ❖ **Avoid becoming a victim.**

Knowing What To Program Myself For

Whether we're talking emotional control panels or behavioral sequences, I think K.'s point is to be aware of these programs and how they drive us. Are they beneficial? Did we install them ourselves or passively allow others to install them for us? *(He says successful people choose their models, so that means they must do their own programming.)* But once we get these "programs" in place we don't have to think about them. We can just go ahead and enjoy our lives. It all comes back to the Big Question: What do I want? Then I'll know what to program myself for.

Lesson 7

IN THE MOMENT

"When the brain hears three verifiable facts in succession (what I'm seeing, hearing and feeling) it tends to readily accept the fourth—what I want —and act on it."

Exercise

A New Now

1) Hold my palms together in front of my waist.
2) Step to my right, simultaneously moving my right hand to my right, then bring my left foot and hand to meet my right foot and hand.
3) When I draw my hands together say, "A new now."
4) Keep repeating the action, stepping to the right and repeating the words. As I move to the right feel myself moving into the future.
5) Imagine myself doing this exercise minutes before my next performance and notice how it makes me feel.

Isolating Present From Past And Future

The New Now exercise is intended to help me maintain a performing state of mind by isolating the present from the past and future. When I plan, I'm in the future. When I recall, I'm in the past. But in order to pay full attention when I perform (or create) I must be in the present. K. says inadvertent sliding into the past or future while performing is likely to lead to performance anxiety.

"That Was A Stupid Thing To Say"

K. says the New Now can also help me move freely from one event to another, carrying me on to the next moment. For example, I could use it to clear my head after an irritating conversation, a frustrating business meeting, a disappointing piece of news, flagging concentration, a mistake in a conversation or a presentation.

I recall a clever friend of mine using a kind of New Now to escape an embarrassing moment in a business meeting. Three of us were standing at a flip chart and he misstated a simple statistic. We both looked at him and he laughed, stepped to the side, looked back and pointed to where he had just been standing, and said, "That was a stupid thing to say."

We laughed and immediately forgot his clumsy remark. He had changed his position and was no longer the "stupid person" who had made the remark. He was now a new person commenting on it.

Future On My Right, Past On My Left

With the New Now exercise K. is validating my eye scan chart in yet another way—that the future is on our right and the past on our left. (Though some people are reversed.) I say this because K. stepped to his right to create a new now, and placed the memory of a past event up to his left for quick recall. Judging from the eye positions and the corresponding physical gestures I've been observing so far, human beings generally plan and set goals in the area on the right side of their bodies and fine-tune their planning by recalling past experiences on their left. So, if I were watching a good planner—like Marion—thinking through an issue, I would see her looking up alternately left and right and gesturing left and right with both hands. In fact, that is what she does when she's working something out.

Exercise

See-Hear-Feel-Do

Report to myself what I see, hear and feel in my immediate surroundings—in any sensory order I prefer—and then follow that string of reports with a statement of my desired state of mind or body, i.e., relaxation, physical readiness, courage, whatever. Let's say I had an important interview coming up. Doing the exercise at home, a typical drill might go like this:

1) **I see the window**
2) **I hear the traffic**
3) **I feel my shoes**
4) **And I'm ready for the interview**

(Note: These reports can be made aloud or spoken silently to myself.)

Attend To My Surroundings

K. says the See-Hear-Feel-Do concentration exercise is an extension of the "new now" concept. It centers my attention on the present time and place, because I am attending to my surroundings and reporting on them. This exercise is a form of meditation or self-hypnosis, because it creates a state of highly focused attention. He says I can easily plant suggestions in my mind in this state because when the brain hears three verifiable facts in succession—what I'm seeing, hearing and feeling—it tends to readily accept the fourth—what I want—and act on it.

What Do I Want?

Start by deciding what it is I want to achieve—either immediately or long-term—and then define the action, or series of actions, that would be best to achieve it. That will be the "Do" step. *(When K. taught me this exercise I used relaxation as my goal, and the letting go of my shoulder muscles as the action step to accomplish it.)* The See-Hear-Feel-Do technique can be used to create any state of mind and can serve any purpose.

Present Tense

K. says the "Do" step should always be in the present tense: "I'm *ready* for the interview," and "I'm *listening* to the questions," not "I *will* be ready," or

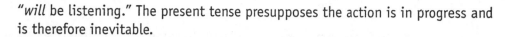

"will be listening." The present tense presupposes the action is in progress and is therefore inevitable.

Use My Imagination

If I run out of things to see, hear and feel in my surroundings, I can use images, sounds and feelings from my imagination. So I can be in my living room but be seeing and hearing the ocean and feeling the wind on my face. But start by identifying the physical things in the immediate vicinity.

Don't Editorialize

K. says to be like a reporter and don't interpret what I see, hear and feel. For example: say "I see the window" (not the big window); "I hear the traffic" (not the noisy traffic); "I feel my shoes" (not my new shoes). The "feel" step should be a report of physical feelings only, not emotions, because emotions can divert my attention from the exercise.

Exercise

Breathing With The Words

K. says it helps the process if I time my breathing with my sentences and add the word "and" as follows:

I start with a big inhale, then exhale as I speak.

1) **(Exhaling) I see the window...(inhale)...and**
2) **(Exhaling) I hear the traffic...(inhale)...and**
3) **(Exhaling) I feel my shoes...(inhale)...and**
4) **(Exhaling) I'm ready for the interview...**

Find Your Own Pattern

K. adds that this breathing pattern may not be ideal for everyone, and that each person should breathe in the rhythm that is most natural for them. In any case, always start the exercise with a deep breath, which acts as a separator, "clearing the slate" of all previous thought and getting my mind ready for something new. He says timing my internal dialogue to my breathing pattern produces a rhythm conducive to auto-suggestion.

Repeat Or Vary

K. suggests that each time I come to the "do" sentence it can be either an exact repetition or a variation. For example, first cycle: "I'm ready for the interview." Second cycle: "I'm listening to the questions." Third cycle: "I'm concentrating only on what's relevant." Etc.

Dropping Internal Dialogue

K. points out that once I become practiced at the See-Hear-Feel-Do technique I may prefer to simply see, hear and feel my surroundings directly, without reporting what I experience in words. But, he says, verbalizing the See-Hear-Feel-Do sentences can act as a kind of guide or mantra which helps me enter the concentration state. If I do stop the reporting, make sure I continue identifying my surroundings in all three senses, keeping the same sensory sequence throughout.

Taste And Smell

I asked K. why smell and taste were not included in this cycle of the senses. He said they are not necessary to gain the state-altering objective of the exercise, but to add them if I wish. He made an interesting point: as important as the gustatory and olfactory senses are, they are rarely the basis of major decisions for human beings. When choosing a restaurant it's really important to recall flavors and aromas, otherwise I won't remember a good from bad restaurant. But when deciding on a career I am influenced by images, internal dialogue and feelings.

The New Now Idea Helps Me:

❖ **Live in the moment.**
❖ **Change moods quickly.**
❖ **Quiet internal dialogue.**
❖ **Invigorate myself and refresh my mental outlook.**
❖ **Re-focus my thinking when interrupted.**
❖ **Keep my mind actively engaged.**

Lesson 8

KUMI FOOD

"Yogurt was described by one nutritionist as 'a vitamin B producing factory.' It's a wonderful protein and has all of the essential amino acids except one—cystine. A few unsalted, dry roasted peanuts can make up for that."

KUMI'S KICK-START BREAKFAST

Fresh fruit juice, whole grain bread with a low-fat natural cheese, herb tea (preferably green tea), no sugar, and a glass of light milk (1% or skim). Add a poached or soft-boiled egg once or twice a week.

I think K. designed this breakfast for me because he knows I'm used to eggs and he didn't want to shock me by too extreme a change. This breakfast cuts most of the fat, and uses dairy products and grains in place of meat for protein. When I told him I've heard cheese is fattening he told me about the many low-fat cheeses being made these days. Some taste like cardboard, but some are surprisingly good—you just have to look for them in a cheese shop. Fortunately I'm not allergic to dairy products.

KUMI'S MORNING SPEEDO

Any mixture of non-fat, whole grain cereal (muesli, grape nuts, wheat all bran cereal, no-fat granola, wheat germ) with fresh fruit and skim milk or yogurt. Read labels of cereal boxes (if that's how I buy it) to avoid a load of refined sugar or chemicals.

✓ *K. recommends I have the Kick-Start and Speedo on alternate mornings, to cut down the fat from cheese and eggs.*

KUMI'S MOUNTAIN SPECIAL

Spread low-fat ricotta cheese on whole-grain bread. Add some sliced cucumber or tomato with a sprinkling of scallions or herbs. Top with a slice of low-fat cheese and give the whole thing a quick melt-down in the toaster oven. If I'm starved I put a poached egg on top. K. does eggs by heating a bit of water in a teflon frying pan. Then he cracks the egg and puts a lid on while it cooks for a few minutes. It becomes the perfect poached egg. Usually he finishes his breakfast with fruit—whole fruit, not juice.

Can I Live Without My Fix?

When I told K. I didn't think I could live without coffee (K. calls it my "fix") he said caffeine drains iron and vitamin B from my system before it can be properly absorbed, especially when drunk with food. He wants me to drink tea, preferably herbal tea or green tea. He told me to give up caffeine for two weeks and if I'm at death's door at the end of that time I can revert to coffee—but only one cup a day. When I said I needed something to wake me up in the morning he suggested I exercise.

✓ *I still miss my coffee, but K. says every time I think about coffee—or bacon, or butter or ice cream—I should flash an image in my mind of the trim and vigorous self I want to be.*

Vitamins Lost In Corn Flakes

K.'s breakfast has everything—fruit, vegetables, grains and cheese—balanced and high in protein. When I complained that his breakfasts had no corn flakes, he said most of the vitamins are lost in the refining process of making corn flakes. The same goes for most other commercial breakfast cereals. Corn flakes has only 2.3 grams of protein per cup, whereas granola has 11.5 grams and wheat germ 32.9 grams per cup. K. says the lower the protein content the lower the essential amino acids needed to synthesize the protein in my body. So not only are most of the vitamins washed out by refinement, the little bit of protein I do get in corn flakes may not be retained. *(When I argued that corn flakes still taste good, he said that was because I was addicted to sugar which they provide in abundance.)*

Hypoglycemia (Low Blood Sugar)

Put simply, low blood sugar is a loss of energy, often sudden, K. says. I can get low blood sugar from going too long between meals, drinking too much caffeine or alcohol, smoking or eating a big blast of refined sugar, as in choco late, soft drinks or ice cream, especially on an empty stomach. I feel the dizziness, stress, irritability, depression, anxiety, nervousness, aggressiveness, loss of temper, insomnia or fatigue from low blood sugar when the glucose supply in my blood is depleted.

Here's how it works: insulin from my pancreas signals the liver to secrete glucose which the insulin converts to energy. Excess sugar intake over-stimulates the pancreas, which supplies the blood with an excess of insulin, which hyper-signals the liver to secrete its stores of glucose. In short, the liver blows its wad. This gives me a rush of excess energy and then leaves me tired.

Solution: keep the blood sugar supply even all day with a steady, balanced supply of protein and carbohydrates. Ideally, I would eat five or six times a day to avoid a sudden drop of blood sugar: three regular meals (moderate portions) and two or three snacks (see K.'s snacks on p. 315.)

Excessive Salt

K. warned me that excessive salt interferes with my body's ability to absorb and utilize protein, and may cause the loss of potassium, which is important for a healthy nervous system, stable blood pressure and regular heart rhythm. Excessive salt causes fluid to be retained in the tissues which can lead to high blood pressure and contribute to congestive heart failure, some forms of kidney disease and premenstrual syndrome. Since so many canned and processed foods are high in salt, K. says the best way to reduce excessive sodium intake is to prepare your own food and go light on the salt shaker.

✓ *Note: K. is not exactly a vestal virgin when it comes to using salt on food, and sugar too, but his use is moderate. Mainly, he depends on herbs to season his food.*

Learn Nutrition For Self-Defense

K. says that educating myself about food is a necessary self-defense. Food manufacturers today are not in business to make me healthy, he says. They want to make money. I told him I thought that was an exaggeration, that there are laws to protect us, and he pointed out that lobbies may get around those protections. He said that at congressional hearings in Washington, scientists presented evidence showing the results of feeding the so-called "enriched" commercial white bread to rats. The bread was so low in the necessary nutrients that, after a few days, the rats tried to eat their own feces because that at least had traces of vitamin B produced naturally by their bodies. When the president of one of the major food companies was questioned about this he said, "Man does not live by bread alone."

KUMI QUICK PICK-UP LUNCH

Plain yogurt with fresh fruit and raisins. Bananas, mangos, oranges, strawberries, blueberries, peaches, nectarines, grapes, kiwi and pineapple taste great in plain yogurt. Add a little honey or raisins if I need it sweeter. A sprinkle of low fat cereal can top it off. *(Yogurt was described by one nutritionist as "a vitamin B producing factory." It's a wonderful protein and has all of the essential amino acids except one—cystine. A few unsalted, dry roasted peanuts can make up for that.)*

Seductive Suppers

K. says that great dinners can be thrown together quickly if I keep a stash of fresh ingredients in the fridge: potatoes, carrots, peppers, onions, zuchini, broccoli, tomatoes, eggplant, mushrooms, lettuce, cucumber or whatever vegetables I like. (Or live close to a green grocer and have that be my fridge). With rice, pasta and grains in the house, those vegetables can quickly be made into pasta dishes, soups, Chinese stir-fry, risotto, or I can have just plain vegetables with chicken or other meat. It's "having nothing in the fridge" that often makes me order in pizza or grab some fast food on the way home.

In the protein department, K. says to always have cans of tuna, salmon, sardines and crab meat. Things like feta cheese, chicken breast, fish fillets and tofu I can buy fresh or keep in the freezer. K. told me to eat beans, but they blow me up like a balloon. His solution: soak the beans overnight in cold water with a tablespoon of baking soda. *(This is getting a little complicated for me—I'm not a great cook—but Marion's going to show me how to do it. She says we'll cook up a large portion of these non-gassy beans and store them in small bags in the freezer. Then I can just dump them in a pot with rice.)*

K. says little things—like herbs and spices, fresh garlic and ginger, sun-dried tomatoes, olives, pepperoni and nuts—add taste, and they can be kept for a long time.

Here's what K. told me I can do with all those things.

THE "ANYTHING" PASTA

I had a roommate in college who used to make an "anything omelette," because almost everything works with eggs. The same goes for pasta and rice, because they can be served with any steamed vegetables, herbs and a little meat. A can of tomatoes is great here. Use the juice for steaming, and thicken the sauce at the end with a teaspoon of whole wheat flour. Top with fresh-grated cheese, like Romano. *(I sound like a cook book.)*

KUMI STIR-FRY

First, I start cooking the sticky Asian white rice, because it takes about 25 minutes. (I can use brown rice if I prefer, but that will take 45 minutes.) Cut the chicken breast into small pieces and soak for 15 minutes in a mixture of soy sauce and wine with a dash of sugar, then stir-fry it in peanut oil for about 3 minutes in a wok and set it aside. Chop vegetables into bite-size (broccoli, mushrooms, carrots, etc.) and stir-fry in the wok. Then add the chicken with chopped garlic and ginger, and a sauce made from my own mix of hoisin, plum, bean and chili sauce. *(Buy this stuff in Chinatown to get the authentic taste.)*

SALADS

With all the vegetables I now keep in the fridge I can always make great salads. I happen to like Greek salad with cucumber, onions, olives, bell peppers, tomatoes and feta cheese, but anything goes—tuna, avocados, nuts or grated cheese. A slice of whole-grain bread goes well with salads. *(Here is K.'s standard salad dressing: 1/3 balsamic vinegar, 2/3 virgin olive oil, a crushed clove of garlic, 1/3 teaspoon each of sugar and salt, dash of Tabasco—a little goes a long way.)*

Make My Own Milk

I've almost kicked the coffee habit, but I'm still battling the skim milk. It tastes so watery. K. mixes his skim milk powder with spring water and adds a third more milk than it says on the bag. It does taste good. But he said I need to search for a tasty brand of skim milk powder.

Vitamins: Listen To My Body

K. recommends taking vitamins but says I have to find for myself what my needs are. When I asked him how I can tell, he said, "Listen to your body and follow your instincts."

BASIC VITAMINS FOR THE DAY

K. takes 1000 milligrams of vitamin C four times a day, 400 milligrams of vitamin E twice a day, and one multi-vitamin/mineral pill daily. He also takes omega-3 supplements (flax oil) for the fatty acids essential to the cells, and 60 mg of coenzyme Q10, which aids circulation, stimulates the immune system and increases tissue oxygenation. *(Not that K. needs all that—he's more energetic than I am.)* For many, vitamin C can only be absorbed in small portions, so I take 500 milligrams of C five or six times a day. That feels right. *(The only problem is remembering to keep taking it, so I put a bunch of tablets in a dish in the morning and pop them throughout the day.)*

I've noticed that K. eats frequently but in small portions. Here are some of his recommended snacks.

KUMI SNACKS

- A banana or other fruit with a glass of skim milk will raise blood sugar levels very fast. The potassium in bananas is good for the nerves.

- Low-fat ricotta cheese (instead of butter) on whole grain bread with jam tastes almost like cake and makes a substantial snack.

- Peanut butter on whole-grain bread is a great (though fattening) snack. Commercial peanut butters have additives, including oils, sugar and salt. Health food stores will grind fresh nuts into the real thing for me, and they have other nut butters for those who can't eat peanuts.

- Whole-grain crackers are tasty with low-fat cheese. If I drink a glass of skim milk, my energy stays high for a longer time than it does after eating meat or drinking coffee. (Soy milk works for those who are allergic.)

- Trail mix (mixed nuts and raisins) is an excellent, if high-calorie, snack. Kumi likes a handful of peanuts, dry roasted and without salt, because of the high protein. (Good if you're not allergic.)

KUMI FOOD TIPS

- K. says mayonnaise still tastes like mayonnaise if I mix in 2/3 low-fat yogurt, but it will have much less fat.

- Equal parts of ketchup and wine vinegar with a dash of chili sauce and sugar make a quick spicy sweet and sour sauce, served hot or cold.

- Thinly sliced onions and mushrooms add a great taste (and bulk) to scrambled eggs, and reduce the need for salt.

- 1/3 beans and 2/3 rice combined are a time-honored protein substitute for meat.

- Fresh garlic and onions cut cholesterol. *(But they also might lose me some of my friends, so take a breath mint.)*

- Ice milk, gelato and frozen yogurt come in many flavors, and contain only 0% to 3% fat. Look for natural fruit flavorings.

- Commercial yogurts with flavoring are often not yogurt, but milk products with gelatin. Real yogurt is simply milk and lactobacillus—nothing else—and should be eaten within a week of purchase.

- Yogurt and fresh fruit juice make a great milk shake. Put yogurt in the blender with a banana and wheat germ for a fast breakfast.

- Say "No MSG" when ordering food in Chinese restaurants. Monosodium glutamate is a flavor enhancer that gives many people headaches. Besides, with tasty Chinese cooking, who needs it?

- Don't believe what I hear about the "safety" of tap water. Buy spring water and drink lots of it. (But check my source, because the U.S. has no safety standards for bottled water). Often a craving for coffee is really a need for fluids, and a big glass of water can be a real pick-up. Also, water helps flush out toxins.

- K. says vegetables should be lightly cooked or steamed to maintain their nutrition. Rinse vegetables but don't soak them, because the vitamins in some vegetables are water-soluble.

- In place of salt when cooking, I can use fresh garlic, herbs and spices, like parsley, basil, bay leaf, oregano, curry and chili peppers.

• Consider meats an extra—as do the Chinese, whose food is mainly vegetables. Chinese people love to eat a lot, but how many fat Chinese do you see? Most meat has little taste and absolutely no fiber.

• Invest in a large wooden cutting board and a couple of great knives—no need for fancy machines.

• K. says I may think I'm too busy or too tired to cook, but that's just because I haven't planned in advance. Now I'll stock up on all these basic ingredients and supplies.

Good Nutrition Helps Me:

❖ Feel energetic and avoid fatigue.

❖ Improve metabolism and aid digestion.

❖ Develop a balanced appetite.

❖ Maintain an appropriate weight.

❖ Avoid illness and fight off disease.

❖ Think more clearly and work more efficiently.

❖ Be more attractive physically.

❖ Enjoy a feeling of physical well-being.

❖ Remain youthful in body and spirit.

❖ Live longer and enjoy life more.

❖ Reduce medical bills and insurance premiums.

❖ Enjoy physical activities.

Afterthoughts

I notice when I ask people what they like to eat they often look down to their right. Smells seem to also get the same eye reaction. If the olfactory and gustatory senses share similar neural pathways as the kinesthetic, that might explain why eating is such a problem for so many people—emotions and food on similar sensory circuits!

Lesson 9

EYES UP

"A good walk-on sends a message: 'This is a person to pay attention to.'"

The Walk-On: A State Of Mind

Today K. showed us how to walk "on stage," which means how to enter any high pressure situation. He said the walk-on is a state of mind that we prepare long before we enter. K. recommends we rehearse these steps for an imaginary audience (or a few friends) at home:

Exercise

Eyes On The Audience

1) Stand "off-stage," take a deep breath, straighten my back, look up.

2) Visualize my performance space and my audience.

3) See myself walking on and looking at my audience.

4) Walk on, keeping my eyes on my audience from the moment I enter and never look at the floor.

5) When my performance is finished, walk off looking always at my audience.

Entrance And Exit

The eyes-up rule is primarily for the entrance and exit, and any other time in my presentation that is comfortable and natural. Once a performance begins, my eyes will of course move to whatever positions are necessary to carry out the performance successfully—like reading a speech or playing an instrument. Or in social and business situations, going into and out of whatever personal states of mind are necessary to express my point.

No Man's Land

K. warned us that the walk-on is such a simple physical act that it is usually taken for granted and rarely practiced. But the walk-on is not simple. K. defines two distinctly different physical and psychological positions for the performer: "off-stage" and "on stage." He says many performers overlook the simple point that they must get from the one position to the other in order to perform. He says the short trip to their point of delivery can sometimes be more unnerving than the presentation itself, because they're in transit, not yet speaking or singing or playing. Yet they are already before the audience. K. calls this in-between area "no man's land."

Leave My Private World

K. says the walk-on idea could apply to things like making a proposal to your boss (especially if it'll cost money), or dealing with important personal or family or psychological issues. In fact, when I saw K. in the airport I felt a kind of no man's land between us and I didn't know how to cross it. Fortunately, Marion's presence covered it up. *(Maybe the next time I have to confront Gregor about something outrageous I should do a kind of mental walk-on to make sure I'm in an externally focused state. I wonder if that's what Marion does with me sometimes to keep her brain from imploding.)*

Create A Bridge

The walk-on is a bridge from my non-performance state (casual, relaxed) to my performance state (high energy, high concentration). K. says the secret to building this bridge comfortably is to think of it as part of the performance, and to rehearse it as I would rehearse the performance itself. This means the performance actually begins *before* I walk on stage.

Walk-Ons Tell Who I Am

A good walk-on sends a message to others about who I am. It says, "This is a person to pay attention to." The impression I create in that brief moment walking on stage—or walking into a meeting—can have as strong an effect as my presentation itself.

Be Aware Of The Occasion

K. points out, however, that a smiling, energetic entrance may not be appropriate for all presentations or situations. For instance, if I were giving a eulogy, looking down would be appropriate because the occasion is solemn and calls for a sense of inwardness. Eyes down would naturally reflect my inward feeling (as we learned in this session with K.). Awareness of the nature of the occasion is crucial, because three different situations might call for three different kinds of entrances.

Non Public Performance

The idea of the walk-on applies also to non-public performance. A surgeon, for instance, an air traffic controller or a police person. Their performance is not "on stage," but they have a high-pressure task to perform that requires a high level of concentration within a designated time frame. While they may not have to "walk on" in front of an audience, they nevertheless have to change their mind-set from their casual everyday state to their high pressure performance state. And they must do this well before entering their place of performance. Therefore, their "walk-on" preparation is basically the same as that of any public performer.

Game Face

The walk-on technique could help me with office politics, putting on my "game face" well in advance when relating to the corporate world. Seeing the front door of a building, or the elevator when I enter, could be the trigger to remind me to get ready (*eyes up!*). This skill would also have been useful at Globalcom when I was late for work and hadn't had my coffee yet. I well remember being overwhelmed at times by walking into the office in my "casual state" (*a euphemism for half asleep*) and being caught off guard by a remark or even a glance that put me off for the day, especially from my boss, Striecher. I don't depend on coffee now anyway, so I can use my eyes instead

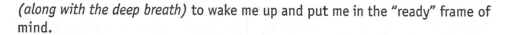

(along with the deep breath) to wake me up and put me in the "ready" frame of mind.

Walk-Ons And The Eyes

When K. had us look up and then down for a few minutes each, we found that looking down correlates to an inward or private state of mind, and looking upward helps direct our attention outward toward others. *(I could hardly contain my excitement when I saw how these states of mind fit with the eye positions on my eye scan chart.)* Since K. says the visual state is optimal for making the transition from "off-stage" to "on stage," he obviously equates the visual with the walk-on state. But he is quick to add that once I am into my presentation I don't have to continually look at the audience. After I've connected with the audience, my eyes might go in any direction depending on the feeling or idea I want to convey.

Switching Mental States

This eyes-up-eyes-down exercise also made it strikingly clear to me that eyes-down switches on emotion and internal dialogue. I have already established that my old habit was to look down when about to address people in public—which tells me I was talking to myself or feeling emotion, the exact wrong state of mind prior to a public appearance. Being locked in my own internal world like that, when I'd look up and suddenly see the audience in front of me my brain would say, in effect, "What are you doing out here in front of all these people?" The "eyes-up" is a exercise I can practice to help me avoid that surprise.

My Eyes Affect My Gait

In discussion we all agreed that this visual state also affects our stance, voice tone, gestures and gait. Therefore, the eyes-up position prepares me not only mentally but physically for my walk-on, giving me a look of alertness and readiness.

Hypnosis Or Magic?

K. recommended we also use the "eyes-up" technique to pre-visualize future performance. He's had me plant ideas in the future several times before, asking me to make the images big and bright to increase their intensity. For me, this "future-planting" of an idea has a powerful effect. When the actual time of the pre-visualized event comes my reflexes kick in automatically, enacting the event I had visualized. *(I'm thinking especially of the Mario-Teresa modeling exercise, which brought surprising results the next time I saw Marion!)* It's like a post-hypnotic suggestion. Is this hypnosis? Or just plain magic?

The Walk-on Helps Me:

- ❖ Stand up in front of people with confidence.
- ❖ Command people's attention non-verbally.
- ❖ Establish rapport quickly with any group or audience.
- ❖ Feel comfortable in the spotlight.
- ❖ Switch my state of mind from private to public.
- ❖ Understand how my eye positions can affect my mental state.

Lesson 10

AMY

"Nowhere is my state of mind—my intent—more evident than in the sound of my voice. The more nuance of expression I have the more persuasive I will be."

Exercise

Calling Amy

1) Stand in an open space where I feel free to project my voice (hard
    to find).

2) Call the name "Amy," drawing out the first and second syllables for five seconds each, like this: "Aaaaaaaa-meeeeeeeee," like I'm calling a child outdoors.

3) **Aim for the sharp nasal sound, not the soft, smooth sound that comes with my normal speaking voice. I'll feel it vibrate in my nose and palate.** (*And try not to be embarrassed at the harshness of the sound.*)

4) **Call "Amy" at varying distances, including softly.**

Nasal Focus

Despite my reluctance, I struggled through the meeting with "Amy." And I learned to my surprise that when I practice the mechanics of vocal work as if I were a singer, my voice feels good and gets people's attention. It also gives me more volume with less effort when I need it. (*Maybe it'll help me to control Gregor.*) The idea is to "focus" the sound through the nasal cavity.

Threading The Needle

K. showed us a trick for focusing the nasal sound: I should hold the thumb and first finger of one hand in front of my eyes and direct my voice between my fingers as if I were threading a needle with the sound. Vary the distance between my fingers until the opening is very slight. Imagine the sharpness of the nasal sound increasing as I bring my fingers closer together.

Stay Out Of The Throat

K. warned me to continue the "eeee," "aaaa," or "ahhh" sound only as long as I feel the sound vibrating in my upper palate, nose and forehead. If for even a second I feel any pressure whatsoever on my throat, stop immediately, re-focus the sound through the bones of the face and resume. I'll know when my voice has "fallen back" into my throat because I'll feel like coughing, a sure sign I've lost the nasal focus.

Working With A Partner

Working with a partner is helpful for feedback. My partner will hear when my vowel sound is coming out with a crystal clarity, and can cue me the moment I've lost the nasal focus. (*I'm lucky to have Marion help me with this since she's a singer. Though she's still mad at me for the way I was acting up during these vocal lessons.*) Note that while I will hear my own voice, my primary self-monitoring is the *feeling of the vibration the sound makes in the bones of my face.* When this vibration is strong I know I am focusing correctly.

Exercise

Kneel And Bow to Amy

1) Kneel on the floor and sit on my heels, with my back straight and my arms hanging to my sides (*I feel like I'm some kind of monk kneeling to pray when I do this.*)

2) Slowly, take a very deep breath, feeling the air as though it were water filling out my lower back and stomach and moving up into my chest. (*K. says this long breath might take 8-10 seconds. I'll feel like my entire torso is being blown up like a balloon.*)

3) Exhale while making a long nasal "eeee" sound (as in "easy") and slowly lower my torso to the floor, rationing my lung supply forthe full exhale—about 10 seconds (to an observer it will look likeI'm bowing to an icon). The downward motion of my torso will end with my hairline touching the floor and my chest resting on my thighs. At repose, I'll be seeing my feet between my knees.

4) Slowly raise my torso back up to a sitting position, inhaling on a 10-count, filling my entire torso with air as before.

5) Repeat this exhale-inhale action using the long vowel "aaaa" (as in "Amy") on the exhale.

6) Then exhale on the combined "Aaaaaa-meeeee," taking at least ten seconds to sing the word "Amy."
(*I found the syllable "ahhhh", as in "am" is also a good larynx opener.*)

✓ *K. says this exercise is extremely relaxing because of the deep breathing. It's a good way to get my mind as well as my voice ready for a presentation. I think the more I do it the less self-conscious I'll feel about it.*

Cry Like A Baby, Baa Like A Sheep

K. says to practice baa-ing like a sheep and crying like a baby. (*Good luck with the neighbors on this one.*) These sounds automatically create the long "a" and "e" and "ah" sounds that open the nasal cavities. These "nasal" sounds create a powerful vibration in my head which gives my voice its greatest power with the least effort. Marion says this vocal sound is really a kind of controlled yell. *(But that I should never let a singer hear me say that.)* I'll know I have it right when I feel the resonance in the bones of my face and forehead (not in my throat). Practicing this kind of vocal production eliminates "smoky" or "foggy" voice tone.

Breathing As A Separator

K. points out that a deep breath can help me change my state of mind—to "clear the slate" for my next activity. For example, I might be working with Gregor and then meet Marion for lunch and then have an appointment to raise money for our project. So I take a deep breath at the end of each of these activities as a separator, to avoid having the state of mind of one activity carry over into another. *(I've seen K. do this and I know he's talking about a really deep breath, the kind that makes you want to close your eyes and stretch.)*

K. says a deep breath helps blank out internal dialogue (good when I'm about to make a presentation). And he says it'll also help me gain control over my emotions under stress. *(Taking a deep breath to control anger is common wisdom, but that idea never worked for me. Maybe I just never breathed deeply enough, or breathed enough times. K. says I might need two or three deep breaths for particularly stressful occasions.)*

Answering The Phone

I should use this separator breath before answering the phone. How often have I let someone into my private space when I've been relaxing and resented the intrusion because I didn't want to think about the outside world at that moment. Or been in my work state of mind and didn't pay proper attention to the content of the phone call, and inadvertently agreed to something I really didn't want to do. So if I'm going to answer the phone I should make sure I completely leave what I'm doing—mentally as well as physically—and a good, deep breath my be the fastest way to do that.

Exercise

The Microphone Hand

K. gave us this exercise for preparing to read from a script in public. *(Good for me, because I sound stiff when I have to read from a printed page.)*

1) Make a fist and press it against my lips, speaking into the curl of the first finger and thumb as if it were a microphone. I'll hear my voice amplified to myself. *(The increased volume is due to the sound being captured by my hand and deflected back to my own ears instead of going out into the room. Continue speaking until I achieve the nasal sound.)*

2) Test my voice with and without my "microphone" hand until I achieve the megaphone-like nasal sound.

3) Read aloud from a book using my microphone hand, projecting my voice to the entire room.

4) After a suitable period of time, take my hand away from my mouth and continue speaking, maintaining the nasal tone of the microphone voice with the same volume and projection I had with the hand.

Born With A Megaphone

K. says nature endowed us with a powerful megaphone in our throats to call out our needs to the world. A baby can cry all night and never get tired. Marion says opera singers use the baby's vocal technique so they can get through a four-hour opera without fatigue while singing at the top of their lungs. We think of the voice as ephemeral because it produces sound using air, but sound is *physical* and *the voice is a physical instrument. (If I'd known that before I would have beat the hell out of my boss, Streicher, with it.)*

A Note On Attitude

K. notes that some people avoid vocal exercises because they are embarrassed by some of the "odd" sounds they hear coming out of themselves. *(I can certainly identify with that.)* He says the simple answer is to work where no one will hear me. Also, soft vocal work is as effective as loud, K. says. Even more so sometimes because I'll be using less effort and can be more conscious of sound production, breath control and muscular relaxation. But K. added that some people are vain about the sound of their voice and are reluctant to distort it in any way, whether someone is listening or not. He suggests we will learn better if we approach these exercises like children, and not be self-conscious about the "funny" sounds we might be making. He says everybody feels uncomfortable at first when baa-ing like a sheep or crying like a baby, or even just making the nasal "e" and "a" sounds in "Amy." But he says usually when people see the benefits they achieve—improved vocal tone, increased volume and projection, and the confidence that comes with the knowledge that they have such a powerful instrument at their disposal—they shed their self-consciousness and make vocal work a part of their physical exercise.

The Persuasive Voice

K. emphasizes that nowhere is my state of mind—my intent—more evident than in the sound of my voice. The more "tuned" my voice is through proper vocal work, the more nuance of expression I will have when speaking, and the more persuasive I will be. Influential people use their voices like musical instruments—and sometimes like swords—persuading as much by subtle shadings of vocal tonality as by their words. And numerous studies point out that voice tone, gesture and comportment account for the largest percentage of the message (usually two-to-one) in any person-to-person communication.

✓ *But we don't need statistics to prove that. K. scared the hell out of a bank robber just by using the power of his voice. The poor guy probably thought K. was a linebacker for the New York Giants, simply by the power with which he projected his voice across Riverside Park.*

Vocal Work Helps Me:

❖ Project my voice with comfort and ease.

❖ Communicate more persuasively.

❖ Speak and sing with greater richness and range of voice tone.

❖ Feel more confident about public speaking.

❖ Influence more effectively on the telephone.

❖ Command attention in meetings.

❖ Avoid vocal fatigue.

❖ Energize my body.

Lesson 11

THE TUNING DANCE

"If I do the Tuning Dance in the space where I will be making my presentation, I establish there the fun atmosphere of being 'at home' with friends. K. says this makes me feel I own the performing space."

Performance Signal

K. taught us a set of mime isolation movements today designed to release tension in the muscles and tendons and prepare the body to perform freely and naturally. Since these moves are psychologically associated with the idea of performance they are a signal to my brain that now it's time to perform.

Exercises

Six Moves Of The Tuning Dance
I. SHOULDERS

K. says the upper back is a mass of muscles that connect to the neck, making the upper back and shoulder area particularly vulnerable to stiffness and tension. These stretches circulate the blood in that area and increase flexibility. It's like getting a massage.

1) Up and Down: Stand erect before a mirror and raise the right shoulder (RS) as high as it will go, aiming for the ear, then drop it as far as it will go. Repeat this up-down pumping action ten or more times. *(Note: K. says don't lower the ear to the shoulder.)* Repeat with the left shoulder (LS).

2) Forward and Backward: Hold the torso still, stretch the RS straight forward as far as possible, then straight back behind me as far as possible, then back to neutral (N). *(Note: it helps at first to hold one hand on my breast plate to keep the torso from shifting. Check this in front of a mirror. The idea is to isolate the shoulder movement from the torso. Repeat with LS.)*

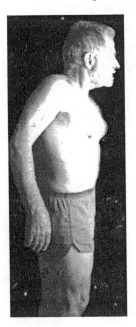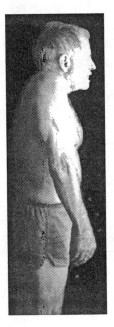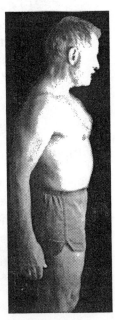

3) Forward and Backward in Upper Position: Raise the RS as high as possible, hold the position a moment, then stretch it as far forward as possible, then straight behind, and continue going back and forth. Repeat with LS.

(Note: K. wants us to keep the line of movement straight, avoiding curving downward in the far forward and far rear positions.)

4) Up and Down in Forward and Rear Positions: Stretch the RS straight forward as far as possible, hold the position a moment, then go straight up and down as far as possible in this forward position, then back to N. Then stretch the RS as far behind me as possible, hold this position a moment, and go straight up and down as far as possible in this rear position, then back to N. Repeat with LS.

5) Draw Squares and Circles: The positions above outline the corners of a square: lower forward, upper forward, upper rear, and lower rear and back to neutral. To form a mental image of these corners, K. suggests I imagine I have a piece of chalk sticking out from the side of one shoulder and draw a **square** on a blackboard next to my body. First draw it clockwise, then counter-clockwise with each shoulder. Now draw a **circle** clockwise with one shoulder—going fully to each corner before rounding it out—then counter-clockwise, and repeat with the other shoulder.

Isolate The Shoulders

These moves are intended to isolate the shoulders. Pretend I'm a marionette maker checking the shoulder joints for flexibility, making sure the shoulders are moving separately from the neck and torso. K. insists that the torso remain still, almost as if in a vise.

Shoulders Should Be Equal

Watch for differences in the response of each shoulder. One may be more flexible than the other. This suggests that the less flexible shoulder is either undeveloped or is being used the wrong way. The object is to get both shoulders moving with equal freedom. K. says this way I'll find the most natural and comfortable position for my shoulders. (I found my right shoulder was more tense and less flexible than my left. Thinking about it, my right hand is the one that operates the mouse on the computer, and I've been holding my right arm up because the telephone is in the way. So, rearrange my desk.) Also, these shoulder movements can eliminate kinks and fix long-standing neck and upper back problems, helping correct bad posture.

II. PELVIS

Center Of Balance

K. told us the pelvis is the center of physical balance and the point from which all body movement is generated. In the martial arts you focus your attention on the opponent's navel to predict his next movement. So the ability to control the pelvis gives me smooth and relaxed control of the whole body, enhancing confidence and adding grace. *(I found my hip movements were a little inhibited. But watching K. inspires me to loosen up and gyrate my mid-section a little bit. Marion liked it when I did that!)*

> 1) **Left and Right:** Stand erect in front of a mirror, with a very slight bend in the knees to allow for freedom of motion. Move my hips to the far left, and then to the far right, and continue alternating back and forth. *(To make sure my torso does not move with the hips, imagine I'm balancing coins on my shoulders.)*
>
> 2) **Back and Forth:** Stick out my seat straight back. *(K. demonstrated the comic way Groucho Marx walked while holding a cigar. For our purposes, though, he says Groucho's knees were bent too deeply, placing undue strain on the thighs.)* Then press my pelvis all the way forward, as if I were holding a dime in my navel. Then move back and forth—stretching the seat back and forward—making sure the coins don't fall off my shoulders.
>
> 3) **Make a Square:** Holding my seat in the rear position, move it as far to the left as it will go, and hold it. This is the left rear corner. Now move it straight forward to the left front corner, now straight across to the right front corner, and then to the right rear corner. I outline this square with my hips, then do the same counter-clockwise.
>
> 4) **Rotate in Circles:** Move the hips in a circular motion, going first to each corner to assure the circle is the widest stretch possible. Make these circles both clockwise and counter-clockwise.

Fluid Movement

As these pelvic movements become more natural, K. says I'll gain better balance and an overall economy and fluidity of movement. Walking, as well as dancing, will become more natural—I might even *want* to dance. Also, pelvic movement is the fastest way to stimulate blood circulation, so it's an excellent method of quelling pre-performance "chills."

III. HAND STRETCHES

Hands Hold Tension

The hands hold a surprising amount of tension. With our hands we greet, touch, comfort, caress and in countless other ways express our emotions. K. points out that the hands are of special importance to musicians and athletes, as well as to public speakers who use them expressively, so it is essential to exercise them thoroughly before performance. *(When I think of all the people I've touched in my lifetime—some wisely, some not so wisely—I can only wonder at all the emotion stored there.)*

Breathe And Let Go Of My Jaw

K. reminded us repeatedly to breathe deeply while doing handwork. Also, let go of my jaw and tongue, and avoid tensing my shoulders. The idea is to isolate the hands, working them only while the rest of my body is in repose.

1) **Prisoner And Jailer:** Stand erect and let my arms hang down in front of me, palms outward. Fold the fingers of each hand into the palm and press the thumbs across the fingernails, holding the fingers firmly in place.

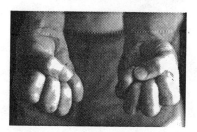 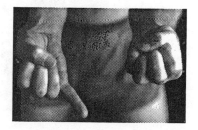

Then, one by one, allow my fingers to "escape," by pressing vigorously against the thumbs, starting with the little finger, then the ring finger, middle finger and first finger, until all my fingers have sprung out from under the thumbs.

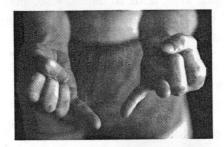 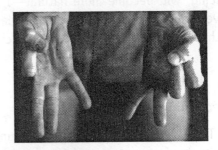

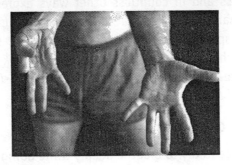

2) The Fan: Then, open my hands, palms up and arch the palms as much as possible while spreading the fingers as widely as possible. K. says I'll know I'm stretching the palms to the extreme when I "feel heat" in the palm of my hand.

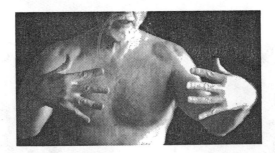

3) The Shelf: Let my arms hang down, elbows locked, fingers of each hand folded into the palm, and raise the backs of my hands up to form right angles to my wrists. Looking down, I'll see each hand as a small shelf. *(K. wants me to be able to balance a toy car on the back of each hand.)* In this position, curl my fingertips under until they touch the pads at the front of my palms. Keeping the fingers curled, raise them one by one above the level of the back of the hand, breathing deeply. Continue this until the backs of the hands feel somewhat numb. *(I'm not harming myself, but I will feel considerable pressure at the wrists and in the tendons of the back of the hand.)*

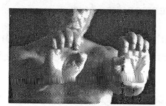
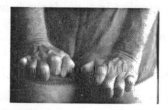

4) The Flutter: Flutter my hands in the air as if I'm flicking water off the fingertips. When I get used to this action, I should be able to flick the fingers with such speed that I hear the fingers flapping like the wings of a bird and see them in a blur (breathe deeply). As I continue to flick the fingers, hold my arms straight out to the sides, straight in front, and over my head. These positions are good for blood circulation in the arms and improve my control of the hand movements.

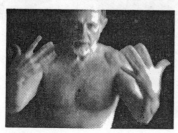
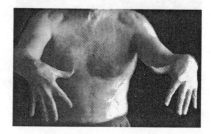

IV. CLOWN FACE

Facial Tension

K. emphasized that in North America impressions are usually created visually. The face is the first thing we see and is therefore a great source of self-consciousness for many. Relaxing the face is vital for complete physical comfort and readiness, especially for those who sing, speak publicly or make business presentations. Marion said relaxed facial muscles are essential for singers, because intonation is most easily controlled by feeling the vibrations in the forehead and cheeks, not by listening (because you can't really hear yourself accurately). So singing in tune depends on a tension-free face.

l) **Forehead:** Stand erect and stretch my brow alternately as high and as and low as possible. Continue this action until my forehead feels numb. *(K. says not to worry—my forehead won't break.)*

2) **Cheeks:** Raise and lower the cheeks as high and low as possible. When the cheeks are up, I'm making an extreme smile; when the cheeks are in the down position, my whole lower face is pulled down so that my upper lip is stretched tightly over my teeth and my mouth is wide open. This exercise serves to isolate the facial muscles. Repeat until my cheeks are numb.

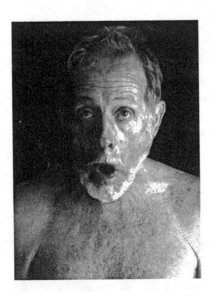 

3) Clown Face: Simultaneously stretch my brow up and my cheeks down. *(This makes me look surprised.)* Then reverse the action: lower my brow as far as possible while raising my cheeks high. *(This makes an extreme smile).* My cheeks and brow should almost touch, partly obscuring my vision. These exercises together give the clown effect. Repeat until my face feels numb.

V. REACH AND SPRING

l) The Reach: Stand as high as possible on my tip toes, reach one arm up into the air as high as possible (breathe freely). When my hand has reached the highest possible point, I stretch it yet one more inch. *(K. says there's always a little more stretch in reserve.)* Let go of my jaw and tongue and breathe normally during this stretch. Now do the same with the other arm. Alternate arms and repeat. *(Note: K. advises standing flat-footed if I have a problem with my feet.)*

2) The Spring: Look upward at an imaginary rope, then bend my knees and spring gracefully upward (leaping up from the tip-toes, not jumping), reaching for the rope with one hand. Then dip my knees again and spring into the air reaching with the other hand. Repeat several times.

3) **Enjoy Relaxing:** K. added a nice touch to this exercise. He had us spring and reach while noticing how it feels to "enjoy relaxing on the way up." Then spring and reach again, and notice "relaxing on the way down." Then spring and reach and create the illusion that I actually "stop at the top for a moment" before coming down.

Free Of My Clothes

K. points out that dress clothing can sometimes make us feel self-conscious or uncomfortable. Reaching and springing into the air, even though it might slightly rumple a tux or elegant dress, tells the brain "I want to feel as physically free in my dress clothing as I do in jeans."

VI. 3-PART INDEPENDENT COORDINATION

Concentration

These movements help me learn to pay attention to several things at once (Marion calls it physical counterpoint). It is therefore an excellent concentration exercise before performing.

Action # 1—The Dip: Spread my legs two feet apart, feet parallel. Bend down partially on my right knee, with the knee going straight out over the foot. Straighten up again and bend down on my left knee in the same way. Then alternate bending each knee.

Action # 2—Rotating Hands at Two Speeds: Standing erect, hold arms out straight to the sides. Make a fist with the right hand, and rotate the hand slowly. *(K. says, "Tell the hand to continue on its own.")* Then make a blade with the left hand, and rotate this hand rapidly. Both wrists are rotating at different speeds. Now switch right and left hand actions so that the slow and fast rotations are reversed.

Action # 3—Clown Face: "Open" and "close" the face continually. This is the extreme "surprise" and extreme "smile" expressions from #3 in the **Face** exercises.

Now do all three actions simultaneously.

Design My Own Dance

The Tuning Dance is an improvisation combining all six isolation movements. The moves may be done in any sequence. The only "rule" is that the movements themselves should be done correctly, meaning to stretch the muscles fully.

K. suggests first doing each movement separately and then combining them into an interesting dance of my own making.

Add Something Of My Own

K. recommends I add at least one move of my own to the Tuning Dance to make it truly mine—something that I can perform in dress clothing. *(He mentioned one person who didn't like the moves of the Tuning Dance and wanted to make a whole set of his own. K. agreed as long as his moves were stretches that got to all the vital spots holding tension.)*

Associate The Dance With Performance

K. reminds us that The Tuning Dance is to be associated with performance and nothing else. As I do the moves, visualize the surroundings where I will be making my presentation and hear the voices of people who might be present. *(But without talking to myself.)*

When To Do It

The Tuning Dance should be done before I run through my presentation at home, before I rehearse on site, and shortly before I perform. K. says many people use it to relieve unwanted tension just prior to an exam, interview or audition. It should be done before a walk-on, in conjunction with the "eyes-up" signal. Any time in the day I might do parts of it —shoulder isolations for a few moments, or hand stretches—whatever I feel I need. During rehearsal breaks the performer might use any of the stretches to stimulate tired muscles and to help stay alert during unpredictable delays.

The best timing will be to finish the whole set l0-l5 minutes before my performance. Any earlier could make me ready too soon, and too close to a performance could be distracting. Each person needs to find his or her own ideal timing. Even after having done the whole set, I may feel I want to flutter my hands a bit, or roll my hips just shortly before my presentation—a last little nonverbal communication to myself that says, "Here I go!"

Bare Feet

A nice touch, if circumstances allow, is to do The Tuning Dance in bare feet, which tends to make me feel like a kid again. A professional speaker who studied with K. said he liked to do the Dance without shoes in a space near where he'll be speaking, about fifteen minutes before performing. He'd say to himself, "I wonder what that audience would think if they could see me now!" This put a smile on his face and suddenly his "important presentation" became light and enjoyable.

Claiming Ownership Of The Space

If possible, do The Dance in the space where I will be making my presentation. Since I learned these moves in a fun atmosphere with friends, that feeling of being "at home" tends to transfer to any space where I do it in the future. K. says this makes me feel I own the performing space. If I learned The Dance with a partner, the spirit of this partner will go with me—and the feeling of well-being associated with the space will also stay with me. If I'm unable to get into the performing space, K. recommends doing the moves somewhere nearby—even in a hotel across the street or down the block—while visualizing the performing space I'll be in. This helps the feelings associated with these movements transfer to the performance space.

Performance Signals Are Not Exercise

K. stresses that The Tuning Dance is not a substitute for exercise. These moves are essentially stretches and do not require extended muscle exertion and rapid deep breathing that characterize jogging, swimming, tennis or other strenuous cardio-vascular exercise. Therefore, he advises that on top of developing a physical signal system for performance like The Tuning Dance, I do some kind of heart-pumping, lung-stretching exercise for a minimum of l5-20 minutes a day to tone muscle and stimulate metabolism.

"Nothing's Happened Yet..."

K. told me the best performers maintain concentration by focusing on their goal. Mistakes don't disturb them while performing because they are only concerned with where they are going—the next now—not where they've been. Thinking "Nothing's happened yet, something's about to happen" as I practice the moves of The Tuning Dance is Kumi's way of planting this goal into my very body.

(K. says this is internal dialogue, but it's directing my attention on the performance—an affirmation of intent.)

Note: Any kind of physical workout will put me in a "kinesthetic mode," which tends to quiet my internal dialogue. However, only moves and stretches associated solely with the performance state—like The Tuning Dance—can act as a signal to the brain that now is the time to perform. And that's K.'s prime purpose for The Dance.

The Body Stores Emotional Memory

K. told us that our bodies hold not only physical tension but also store emotional memory. *(I recall when he taught me the Zzt-Squeeze how he asked me to find the location in my body of a happy memory, and I noticed to my surprise it was in my upper chest. I never thought about how many undesirable emotions I might have stored in various locations of my body.)* He claims that working the body systematically—especially the shoulders, pelvis, hands and face—not only tones the muscles, but can dislodge negative feelings. When I asked him if there was any scientific proof of this he said, "Unscientific research from all over the world going all the way back to the Greeks substantiates this idea." *(I can say from my own experience that the very first go at K.'s Tuning Dance had the effect of releasing my own pent-up and unexplained feelings of anxiety toward him.)*

The Tuning Dance Helps Me:

- ❖ Signal my brain that it's time to perform.
- ❖ Carry myself with agility and grace.
- ❖ Communicate more spontaneously with my body.
- ❖ Increase circulation to my limbs, joints and fingers.
- ❖ Increase coordination and sharpen motor reflexes.
- ❖ Stimulate my metabolism.
- ❖ Wake up when I feel drowsy.
- ❖ Control performance nerves by channeling excess adrenaline.
- ❖ Reduce internal dialogue.
- ❖ Dance more freely.

Lesson 12

DOING MY HOMEWORK

"K. says I may think I'm ready for an important situation when I'm not. But some part of me will usually be aware and whisper a warning, and this can turn my mind into a battleground."

Performance Traps

K. made us aware today of the traps awaiting a performer and how to avoid them.

1) CREATE MY OWN SPACE

K. says that making a physical adjustment to my performing space gives me the feeling I created the space myself. This, combined with doing the Tuning Dance where I'm performing, gives me a strong feeling of domain—the place becomes mine. When I achieve this kind of comfort, others sense it and my authority is established before I even begin to perform. K. says I will carry myself with the authority of an animal in its natural habitat. *(Charles said that animals mark the perimeter of their territory by urinating on it. I said I thought K.'s techniques were more socially acceptable ways for performers to accomplish the same thing!)*

Marion and I discussed how various kinds of presenters might prepare their space before performance:

Myself Speaking In Public: Check to see if the microphone is to my liking. Familiarize myself with the lock mechanism on the microphone so I can adjust its height or detach it to make it portable if I want to. Speak a few sentences to check the volume. *(Technicians are usually willing to help if I give them enough time.)* If there is a lectern I don't like, have it replaced or removed. If I'm using a lectern or other prop, place it exactly where I want it. If anyone else uses the space before me, make sure the position of equipment I use has been marked with tape, to get it back in the exact position I want. Stand silently for a short while looking at the hall and the empty seats and get a feel of what it will be like to speak to this audience. In fact, *touch* everything I'm going to use—a table, flip chart, overhead projector, so that I have a *tactile* familiarity with everything in the environment relevant to me.

Concert Pianist: Go on stage and make sure the piano and piano seat are exactly where you want them to be. Check the seat for height. Even if the piano is in the right position, move it a tiny bit this way or that to get the feeling that you placed it exactly where *you* want it. Look the stage over thoroughly to see what's there: do you want anything removed? Do you need something extra? Play a little on the piano. Walk around the stage, sit on the edge of the stage and talk aloud to the empty seats for a moment. Do any physical or mental exercises you wish in this space.

Teacher/Lecturer: Walk into the empty classroom and introduce yourself to the imaginary class. Practice speaking silently from different positions to see which angles you like for different kinds of delivery. Stand in silence and "feel" the presence of the imaginary students. Write your name on the white board. Do whatever else you wish to make the room yours.

Lawyer: Find an empty courtroom and get a "feel" of the entire space, including the public seating area. Sit at your table, walk the distance to the witness box, speak to an imaginary witness silently or aloud, sit in the witness box. Sit in the jury chairs to get each juror's perspective on you. Speak to the judge, sit in the judge's chair and project your voice to the whole room. Move around in front of the jury box and speak to the empty chairs aloud or silently.

Athlete: Dressed for the competition (whether it's game day or not), enter the court, field, stadium or other area where the game or contest will take place. Take a moment to look all around and acquaint yourself with the entire space; stand in the middle of the playing area and visualize key moves, and run through several of them in slow motion; if you're on a basketball court, throw some free throws with an imaginary ball; if you're a gymnast, perform a few moves, or imagine the feeling of your body going through the moves if the necessary equipment is unavailable; if you're a swimmer and have access to an olympic pool, jump in the water and play they way you did when you first discovered the joy of swimming. Whatever your sport, do anything necessary to make the environment feel familiar and comfortable.

In the Boardroom: Go to the room in which you will be making a presentation and walk around the space to get a feel of it. Check out the overhead or slide projector, the position of the screen and of flip charts. If necessary, call the maintenance person to adjust the lighting, room temperature or air conditioning to your liking. If there is a large conference table, stand at different points around the table speaking silently (or aloud if you're alone) to get the "feel" of the room and to hear how your voice will sound from each position. Imagine possible criticisms of your presentation and improvise and rehearse appropriate responses, respecting the critic's positive intent and maintaining a good-humored state. Notice the favorable response of the imagined members present.

Place It In My Future

Imagine an upcoming presentation and see myself preparing my performance area. Watch myself take over the space and make it my own, down to the smallest detail. Apply the same idea to the room at home where I practice my presentation. Scan the space, and if any object is disturbing me, move it or cover it.

2) THE ENERGY OF MY AUDIENCE

K. said audiences have a special energy and I can feel it when I step out in front of them. He warns that my energy level must be higher than theirs in order to maintain my own equilibrium and to command their attention. He also cautions that I scale my energy level so I don't "overshoot" an audience by having too high an energy for the occasion. *(The way I did in my holography presentation in Marion's living room.)* Experienced presenters charge up their energy with visualizations, affirmations and physical work-outs. K. says an interchange of energy takes place between you and your audience—you can actually use the audience's energy to re-charge yourself as you go. This is a reminder to use some of the energy-giving techniques he taught us and to practice them until they become second nature.

3) MATCH CONTENT WITH MY LISTENER

K. says good communicators are very sensitive to the various response levels of audiences. I might make a successful presentation today and think I can do it the exact same way tomorrow. But have I considered possible differences in the background and experience of my listeners? K. notes that even professionals slip up on this point. Examples of this might be a symphony orchestra playing a composition that is too long at a children's concert; a lecturer using technical jargon with lay people *(the way I did in my presentation at Marion's)*; a comedian telling "in" jokes about city life to rural people.

Alternatives To Drugs

K. and Matt said I don't need drugs or sedatives to get me through a performance. My body produces all the chemicals I need, even a morphine-like substance, which I can activate with exercise or relaxation techniques or the Zzt-Squeeze, which always produces in me a deep feeling of well-being.

✓ *Question: What if I didn't know these alternatives to drugs? I'm learning all these techniques that eliminate the need for drugs, but schools and the medical profession don't yet train people in these methods. Too bad.*

Do My Homework

K. says I may think I'm ready for an important situation when I'm not. But some part of me usually is aware and will whisper a warning. This conflict between my unrealistic conscious assessment (thinking I'm ready) and my unconscious awareness of unpreparedness (knowing I'm not) can turn my mind into a battleground and cause serious performance anxiety. No amount of visualizations or finger squeezes or Holograms or Tuning Dances can help me perform well if I don't know my speech or haven't studied for my exam. The strongest confidence comes from doing my homework. Experienced professionals are constantly developing and rehearsing their material, and they prepare *painstakingly* before making a presentation.

To underscore this idea, K. suggests I imagine how different people might prepare for a performance:

A student going into an exam: Do you know everything the exam will cover? Have you planned your time adequately to study for it? Have you budgeted your energy to be alert? Have you asked others about this teacher's strategy for testing? Have you gone the extra mile and done some extra reading to give yourself an edge?

A consultant giving a workshop: Do you know the needs of the group to whom you will be presenting? Are you aware of the values, beliefs and presuppositions that underpin this group's view of the world? Do you have backup exercises in case the ones you plan don't work? How will you deal with possible resistance to your ideas?

Requesting money from an organization that wants to cut funding: Have you researched the organization you're speaking to in order to speak their language? Have you studied their usual reasons for rejecting requests and developed and rehearsed appropriate answers? Have you studied the strategies of successful fund-raisers? Have you practiced your delivery with colleagues who can play devil's advocate?

A public figure being interviewed: Do you know the interviewer's style so you can anticipate possible questions and answers? Have you thought of what you will say in case the questions are irrelevant? How will you deal with a surprise question? How will you respond if the interviewer gets aggressive or makes fun of you?

A commencement speaker: What do you know about this school? Who has addressed this audience successfully and what did they say? How many good commencement addresses have you studied? What makes them effective?

A panelist: Have you researched the subject and know what you want to say? Will you write down your brief statement or speak extemporaneously? What if others speak longer than expected and you're asked to cut your remarks short? How will you deal with an argumentative panel member or chairperson?

An actor auditioning for the role of Hamlet: How much have you read about this role? About Shakespeare? How many live performances of Hamlet have you seen? How many videotapes or movies of great Hamlet performances have you studied? How many actors have you talked to who have successfully performed the role?

Fear Is A Friend

K. says that some nervousness is natural and healthy before a performance, a sign that you're ready and your adrenaline is running. But debilitating fear is often a sure sign that you are ill-prepared for something important, and then you have good reason to be scared. K. suggests I look at fear as a friend, warning me that I'm in trouble, and need more time to prepare. Listen to it, and ask it what I need to know. The idea is to ask this question well enough in advance to be able to do something about it, and not wait until the day of a big performance.

Never Do Something Important For The First Time

K. gave an example of truly dedicated performance preparation—a violinist who gave his Carnegie Hall recital in his living room, living through the exact circumstances of the upcoming recital and preparing for it for weeks, as if it were the real performance. K. made the point before: if you believe something strongly enough your brain won't differentiate between the belief and the reality. This man created the opportunity to experience what his brain believed to be the real thing, so he knew what the real experience would be like before he did it. He had two shots at doing his debut for the first time.

Waiting For The Bell

K. says when you're prepared to this degree for a performance—when you've replicated the kinesthetics of a future event—you're like a thoroughbred seconds before a race, waiting for the bell to go off, because your body is already experiencing the event before you actually do it. The more demanding and sophisticated your audience, the more excited you feel. You know you will perform well, because you've already done it. This is the kind of self-assurance you see in highly accomplished people—but they *earned* it with hard work.

Good Preparation Helps Me:

❖ **Feel confident for exams, interviews, talks, meetings and public events.**

❖ Research my material from every standpoint.

❖ Adjust my energy level to that of my audience.

❖ Personalize and prepare my performing space.

❖ Pre-perform an event so I know how it's going to feel.

❖ Ask: "Have I done my best to be ready?"

Lesson 13

SPATIAL LEARNING

"A good way to work on a creative project is to think of it as taking place in a single 'creative day,' even though this 'day' may span months in calendar time."

The Brain Likes Building Blocks

K. says the brain likes to link small pieces of information together to make one big picture. He says any performance—a speech, a concert, a demonstration, an athletic game—can be divided into smaller blocks to make it easier to learn and to remember. K. worked with the players of a professional football team who had to memorize some three hundred plays—one hundred basic ones with about two hundred variations—and color-coding these plays spatially helped the players recall them quickly.

Here's how K. said I could divide complex information into logical sub-parts when planning a presentation:

Exercise in Spatial Memory

1) Facing my imaginary audience, see a large transparent screen between them and me (or above their heads) on which I can place images.

2) Divide my presentation into sections. (*K. likes Introduction-Theme-Development-Summary-Conclusion, but suggested I subdivide my information in any way that is best for me, or right for the content.*)

3) Place these blocks of information on my screen in their order of appearance. Up-to-down like a list, or left-to-right, in a circle or any other way that helps me recall their order.

4) Give each block a color. (Visual)

5) Give each block a sound. (Auditory)

6) Give each block a feeling. (Kinesthetic)

7) As I add new information to my presentation, I can place it into the appropriate block and rehearse each block in all three senses.

✓ *I still find that sometimes when I set out to visualize something I end up feeling it. But I think that's okay too, as long as I learn what I want to learn. I am visualizing more and more clearly as time goes on.*

Linking Ideas To Image And Sound

Marion and I thought up ways of linking ideas to mental images and sounds that might be useful for people in various professions:

● A salesperson might keep track of products and their prices in her mind with color-coded lists. "Hot" products might be listed in red, new product lines in green.

● A decorator designing more than one interior at a time might mentally sort house interiors on the right, apartment interiors on the left and offices in the middle.

● A person budgeting money might imagine holiday planning and home expenses on separate screens with different colors.

● A student might place her studies in front of her and her social life behind her while preparing for an exam, and then reverse the two when she wants to have fun.

- A football player memorizing plays might arrange them by category—*blocking plays:* (red) lower visual plane; running plays: (green) middle plane; *passing plays:* (blue) upper plane.

- A musician could do ear-training by imagining a large keyboard on the floor and stepping onto each giant note as he sings it. Larger intervals would require a small jump, giving him a "feel" of the distance between each pitch.

Time In Space

K. says we naturally sort time spatially. Most people place future events on their right and past events on their left (some left-handers may be reversed), with the far past behind us. Others will have a front/back timeline, with past events behind them and the future in front. *(Watching people's eye movements will often show us exactly where in space they've stored a memory and in which sense.)* We tend to see future events in front of us, either close or far depending on their importance. The closer an event appears in our internal imagery, the more connected to it we feel.

A Good Use For Procrastination

K. taught us that good planners visualize upcoming events close in front of their eyes, which makes the events seem more real. When I had my panic attack on the walk with Marion, the mental image of faces at the computer conference was gigantic and I felt them almost pressing up against me. So I decided to use K.'s technique in reverse. I moved the image of the computer conference as far away from me as I could until it was a tiny dot in the distance. And it worked! I didn't think about it again until I got on the plane for New York. Maybe this is what is meant by "putting something off"—I had discovered a good use for procrastination!

Marion and I reviewed different ways we might sort upcoming events on a spatial plane:

Fast Forward My Day

I might view a single day as a video with a succession of events moving from left to right. Fast-forward and fast-reverse the video to any point where I need to fill in details. Or the events can be placed vertically, like on a computer screen, so I can "scroll" up and down to see what I want to see.

Filing Memory

I already see short-term events on terraced file cards, moving upward as they go further into the future. K. likes to "pull up" important cards a little bit, so that important successive events can be clearly seen, one behind the other. *(I wonder if I could file feelings this way, too.)*

The Year Is A Circle

Marion sees the year as a circle, like a clock lying on its side, with December at twelve o'clock. Trying this for myself, I like to place important upcoming events on the circle like pieces on a Monopoly Board—big and in color—so I can see the big events of the year at a glance. I like to give the four seasons a change of color to enhance the spatial effect and section off the year more clearly. It's nice to see winter colors (white, gray) changing into spring (green) and then summer (yellow) and fall (orange) as my eye scans the yearly circle. If I have a holiday planned, I can more easily plan for it by looking at its position on the circle. Money planning can also be facilitated by seeing income on the yearly circle *(especially for free-lancers like me)*. I can budget in advance for "dry" periods and plan my buying or investments for higher income periods.

Vertical Faxes, Horizontal People

See events of the week or month in a horizontal or vertical line, or a combination of both. Listings—like phone calls, faxes, mailings, e-mails—lend themselves to vertical alignments. People, places, shopping, repairs and appointments might be horizontal. *(But there is no rule, so use whatever works best for me.)*

See Events In Front Of Your Eyes

For an important upcoming event I should use a combination of yearly, monthly and daily planning. I could place it in front of my eyes daily to review details, then see it again in the future position to place it in context with other events. As my performance day draws closer, the space between the present and future images will gradually close, allowing me to time my energy and get ready, physically and emotionally. K. says this is one way good planners manage to be at their best exactly when they need to be.

Time Is One Large Space

K. sees time not as a line with a beginning and an end, but rather as a large space within which we move. To him, clocks are an artificial measurement of time. He says children know this instinctively and have to be forced to measure time, otherwise they create their own time. *(I know some adults like that, too.)* Pets often learn to sleep and eat on a schedule to accommodate the habits of their masters. K. uses clocks and calendars only to keep track of time when traveling and meeting with others. Otherwise, like children and animals, he works at his own natural pace whenever possible. He says that's when his brain feels most free to run and play. But he hastens to point out that, to be creative, a brain must be directed and needs its own special kind of schedule.

The Creative Day

For example, K. says a good way to work on a creative project is to think of it as taking place in a single "day." As I plan the start of my project, see my completion date, both on the calendar and spatially on my personal timeline. This interval—this space—from start to finish of my project, defines one giant "creative day," even though that "day" may span months in calendar time. Thinking of it this way, I tend not to let other events or obligations interrupt until I'm finished, because I'm always in the same day. Such tenaciousness to a creative assignment—normal for artists, scientists and other thinkers, but also possible for anyone who chooses to enter this creative state—is an example of a special use of *time*. It represents the stopping of measured time as we think of it, and entering a space free of clocks and calendars.

"You're Not All There"

Of course I must also attend to mundane matters, like keeping appointments and paying bills, but I can usually attend to these without consciously interrupting the Creative Day. Such unflagging maintenance of the creative state accounts for the "absent-mindedness" or dream state often attributed to creative people, and may explain why we think of such people as impractical. K. says they are in fact eminently practical in relation to their project, maintaining a single-minded concentration on a goal to the apparent exclusion of all else. When I'm working on a video project, friends and colleagues sometimes get the impression that I'm "not all there," which in fact I'm not.

And K. warns that an extended Creative Day is impractical—even cruel—to my loved ones, because such single-minded dedication to work can create an emotional detachment. That may be why we usually think of creative artists as being a bad bet for marriage. *(Maybe also computer scientists?)*

Exit And Re-Entry

So he said I need to find a way to "step out" of my Day to be with loved ones and "step back in" again to continue my work. *(This is another application of K.'s lifeline idea: he ties a rope around his waist and secures it to a brass ring on the cabin porch when going out into a whiteout, so he can find his way back. He wants me to be able to reorient myself when I make mental and emotional crossovers.)* I was reminded of Charles' quote that behind every great man was a bored woman. I'm not a great man, but Andrea certainly became a very bored woman. When I took on a project, Andrea and Charles must have thought I'd been abducted by aliens—which, in effect, I had been. So the idea is to find my own way to exit and re-enter the Creative Day so that I can still be a human being and have a family life.

Teeter-Totter

K. admitted that not everyone may be temperamentally suited for the Creative Day state of mind. But he said single-minded attention to outcome is the way people accomplish astonishing tasks. I thought of Gregor whose whole life seems to be one long Creative Day. He accomplishes great things, but his life's a mess. This concerned me because I didn't want that. I brought up this point with K.

"*I understand the value of the Creative Day concept, Kumi, but whatever happened to the idea of moderation?*"

"*Too boring. The fun's in the extremes.*"

"*But you've emphasized the importance of balance. How can you have balance and still go to extremes? Especially if you're two people with equally demanding worlds, like Marion and me. How can you have two Creative Days in one household?*"

"*Remember the teeter-totter? I go to my extreme, you go to your extreme, and we meet in the middle. There are reasons why some games never go out of style.*"

Spatial Learning Helps Me:

❖ Organize my learning in manageable segments.

❖ Plan and memorize speeches more easily.

❖ Create a mental filing system.

❖ Set up a mental calendar of events.

❖ Organize projects and schedule time using a mental timeline.

❖ Utilize all my senses when planning presentations.

Lesson 14

THE CAT

"Standing on my tip-toes and crouching, I stalk my imaginary prey slowly, then rapidly, then standing still with one foot poised in midair, always aware of stepping soundlessly..."

A Metaphor For Performance

The Cat is K.'s favorite performance signal. The movements resemble a cat at play—tumbling, rolling, stalking and stretching with abandon. K. says The Cat is a metaphor for performing because it is in itself a performance. But he doesn't want me to think of it as something I have to perfect. Rather I should enjoy it. I must say, rolling around on the floor makes me feel free—like I did when I was a kid playing with my friends in the yard. He gives a warning however: these moves are physically demanding and I should check with a doctor before trying them out if I have any neck or back problems. But since I started exercising again I've had no trouble with my back.

The moves, which should be learned separately and then strung together in free improvisation, are as follows:

Headstands

Shoulder stands

Back bends

Somersaults

Shoulder rolls

Leg crawls

Roll overs

Stalking

The wake-up

Sympathy Partner

To learn these moves I need an open space, a padded floor and, ideally, a "sympathy partner," though I can do it alone. The Cat has a sense of adventure to it, and having a sympathy partner gives me someone to share the experience with. Marion does The Cat with me and offers an objective eye, coaching me in the details to make sure I'm doing everything the way I think I am. If I'm working alone I can imagine Marion, to increase the feeling of play and to direct my attention away from myself.

The Moves

Headstand (three-point)

K. calls this the three-point headstand because my weight is on both hands as well as on my head, forming a tripod. The secret to learning this headstand is that my head and hands form a triangle, not a straight line.

Warning before I start: K. says the headstand can be dangerous for an overweight person who is muscularly undeveloped. So proceed with caution. (Fortunately, I've lost weight and have gotten myself back in shape, so I think I'll be okay.)

1) Make sure I'm surrounded by open space. Get down on all fours and place my forehead on the carpet or mat. The recommended place for the head to touch the carpet is the point midway between the hairline and the center of the head.

2) Place my hands palms-down and at right angles to myself, fingers splayed. Check that my head and hands are placed so that they make a tripod.

3) Holding the head firmly in position (don't let it roll) and keeping the palms flat, raise my hips as high as possible and walk toward the tripod. As my knees get close to my head (almost touching my chest) I can't crawl any further forward and my feet slowly lift off the floor. This is the point of balance that creates the headstand. Play with it for a moment—feet on the floor, feet off the floor—until I feel my torso balanced on the tripod. I'm now standing on my head, legs drawn into my torso with knees bent (looking something like a crab pulled into itself). If my feet do not leave the floor, my hips are either not high enough in the air or my tripod is no longer forming a broad triangle.

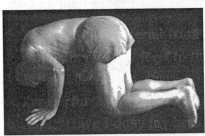

Note: K. says to check that my tripod has remained firmly in place, i.e., that the head did not roll forward as my legs walked toward it, and that my palms have remained flat. Also, when my feet leave the floor, fold them in close to my seat so the weight of my legs doesn't pull my torso back down.

4) Very slowly, adjusting my balance on the tripod, raise my legs in the air and straighten them. As I become comfortable in the headstand position over the days and weeks, I can begin to move my legs in various ways—doing splits, bicycling in the air, etc. That's when the headstand becomes fun.

Note: K. reminded me that when my weight is on the tripod and my feet are off the floor, I have in effect accomplished the headstand. Raising my legs over my head is the final flourish, and should be done only when I feel securely balanced. Shooting my legs up in the air too soon can make me fall, and repeated falls can be discouraging. If I fall, I won't hurt myself, because my body will roll. This means of course that the area must be free of furniture and other objects. I fell many times when first learning the headstand—but mainly when I didn't have my tripod or wasn't concentrating.

Balance, Not Strength

K. says the headstand requires no strength. It is all balance. So if I'm straining in any way, check all my positions as instructed above. This is where a partner can be especially helpful by giving me feedback each step of the way. When doing the headstand with a partner, start by standing back-to-back. In the tripod position we can watch each other through our legs, focusing our attention away from ourselves.

Standing On My Own

K. says some people learn to do the headstand with their legs up against a wall for added security, but using a wall for balance isn't necessary and just gets in the way. One of the benefits of the headstand is to demonstrate to myself that I can perform a task without the aid of props. The free-standing headstand is a metaphor for the idea of standing on my own, as I must do when performing.

Amy On My Head

The voice box opens when I'm upside-down, which enables me to focus my voice more clearly through my nasal passages. Voice teachers call this "speaking through the plate," a curious phrase that refers to the area between the palate and the forehead. K. calls it "Amy." The headstand is an excellent position for getting a feel of the most natural way of using the voice. *(Though it would probably appear bizarre to someone watching me sing or talk while standing on my head!).* K. says that feeling the sound vibrate through my body when upside-down makes it easier to replicate when standing up.

Standing on my head also deepens breathing and slows the heart rate almost immediately, creating a feeling of well-being. Thought processes slow down and muscles relax. Kumi says the feeling is so calming it will often induce a trance. At the very least I will get a brief and refreshing rest.

HATHA YOGA HEADSTAND

The Hatha Yoga headstand is a little trickier to get into, but more comfortable once I'm in it because my weight is almost entirely on my forearms. If I'm working with a partner, we start by standing with our backs to each other in an open uncluttered space.

l) Get down on all fours and place my forearms on the carpet, about eight inches apart and parallel to each other. Make sure the palms are facing each other, fingers curled, so that the fingertips of each hand are almost touching.

(Note: never lace the fingers. In case I unexpectedly roll over—which K. says is normal when learning any headstand—my hands and arms should be free to move naturally.)

2) Place my head in the oval space created by the curl of my fingers, with the head touching the carpet midway between my hairline and the center of my head.

3) Keeping my head and forearms held firmly in position, raise my hips high in the air and walk slowly toward myself.

4) As my legs draw closer to my body, my forearms—flat on the carpet—will naturally prevent me from going up smoothly onto my head. Therefore, K. recommends at this point a slight push-off to get my feet into the air. *(I found it helps to get one foot up at a time. This is the tricky part: if I push-off too much I'll roll over, and if I push too little my legs will fall back onto the carpet. This little push is what prompts some to think they need a wall to lean against, to keep them from falling over. When I get balanced in this headstand, though, I'll enjoy the ease of balancing on my forearms. I can stand longer in this headstand than in the three-point because there is less pressure on my head).*

5) When I'm balanced upside-down, immediately bend my legs and bring my feet toward my bottom for easier balance. *(When first learning, some people find it easier to bring one leg into position over the buttock, then the other.)* When I'm satisfied with my balance, slowly raise my legs and straighten them into the air.

BACK BEND

1) If done with a partner, we start by standing with our backs turned to each other, about ten feet apart. Kneel down with knees about one foot apart. Torso and thighs are in a straight line.

2) With arms hanging loosely at our sides, look at the ceiling and *slowly lower our heads backwards*, scanning inch by inch across the ceiling and down the wall behind us. Head and torso move slowly backward and down to the carpet. *(Avoid using the arms to brace myself against the floor.)* K. says to breathe normally and go only as far backward as I can control. I should be able to pull myself back up and forward at any point. Arch my torso as much as possible. *(K. says men will envy the muscular*

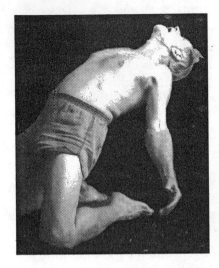

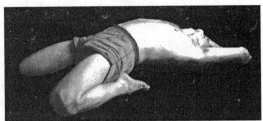

flexibility of women in creating this arch.)

3) When I'm arched completely backward with my head close to the carpet, I'll see Marion behind me. Reach out my arms and touch her hands. *(When we did this I felt a special connection with Marion—an intimate nonverbal greeting.)*

4) Using my thigh and stomach muscles, pull myself back to an upright position.

(Note: K. says keeping the thighs pressed forward as I lean backward is the secret to controlling the backbend. If I let go of my thighs my seat will collapse to the floor. The back bend is a great stretch for the thigh muscles.)

SOMERSAULT

1) From a standing position, go into a crouch.

2) Place my palms flat on the carpet and shift my weight onto my hands.

3) Using my arms for support, tuck my head between my legs as I lower my shoulder blades to the carpet and roll over forward.

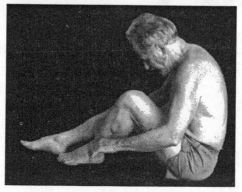

✓ *Note: K. likes it best when my head never touches the carpet. My back curls as my head goes between my legs; my shoulder blades are the first thing to touch the floor and I roll on the curve of my back.*

K. warns that if I have not done somersaults for a long time—or ever—I can get a little dizzy or nauseous after doing several. To regain my equilibrium quickly, crouch down and put my head between my legs, stare at one point on the floor, and breathe deeply for a few moments.

SHOULDER ROLL

This move is particularly cat-like—like a cat tumbling over when playing with a ball of string.

Sitting on the carpet, roll over backward on one shoulder, thrusting both arms and legs (bent) over that same shoulder as I go. Repeat the same action on my other shoulder. If I start from a standing position, I first drop to my seat, then roll over backwards all in one motion.

✓ *Note: the object is to roll over on my shoulder blade—not my neck or head—with my weight being borne completely on the broad blade of the shoulder. Legs should be curled. If I find I'm rolling sideways instead of over on the shoulder, I need more thrust from my hips to send me over. When I come out of the roll I can stay down on my knees or roll up on my feet, pushing off the floor with both hands.*

K. showed us that performing the whole action in reverse—rolling *forward* onto the shoulder and over—creates the forward shoulder roll commonly seen in the Asian martial arts.

SINGLE SHOULDER STAND

K. says this move comes from the ancient Chinese theater, where actors would give the illusion of turning into inanimate objects, like trees or rocks, to hide from their enemies.

1) Kneeling down, with knees about a foot apart, place my right forearm on the carpet, with the elbow about six inches in front of my right knee. Make sure my right hand, palm up and flat, is about a foot in front of my left knee.

2) Place my left hand, arm bent, palm down, a few inches to the left of my right hand, so that both hands are aligned.

3) Drop my right shoulder to the carpet in front of my right elbow. I'm now balanced comfortably on my right shoulder with the right side of my face resting on the carpet. *(I'm resting on the side of my neck, but avoid putting weight on the neck. The weight should be on my shoulder only.)*

4) Raise my seat as high as comfortably possible, and walk on my tip-toes slowly around to the left, until my right elbow is between both knees. (I'll be in somewhat of a scrunch now, but be patient.)

5) Tip-toe straight toward my right shoulder, along the line of my arm, keeping the left elbow between the legs, until I roll off the top of my shoulder onto the full support of the shoulder blade—not on the neck. I am braced by the left arm with the left palm flat down, and the right forearm with right palm flat up.

6) Slowly raise my legs in the air

Repeat the action in reverse for the left shoulder.

Note: The shoulder stand looks somewhat like a headstand that's slipped down onto one shoulder. The position of the legs and torso has an elegance all its own. Getting into the shoulder stand can be frustrating at first, but K. says to stick with it. The key to balance is how I place the arms and hands on the carpet: make sure they don't slip out of place as I walk my body into position, or else my support is lost.

K. warned repeatedly that no weight whatsoever should be borne by the neck, or else I might strain it. As in the backward shoulder roll, the shoulder itself is the weight-bearing part.

Kumi showed us how the backward shoulder roll, arrested in mid-roll (as if freeze-framing a video of the action) becomes a shoulder stand. Some like using the shoulder roll to get into the shoulder stand. For fun and variety in doing The Cat, Kumi recommends practicing both.

LEG CRAWL

1) I start by lying on my back, arms out to the sides, my body in a straight line. I draw the right knee up toward my chest, roll onto my left buttock, and then extend the right leg as far away from myself as possible in a "footward" direction. This is a lurching action, toes extended, which moves my body in the direction of my feet, as if someone were pulling me toward him by my leg, with my head and torso dragging behind.

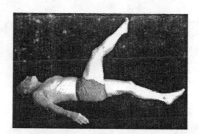

2) As my right leg extends footward, my left knee draws back to my chest, and I roll onto my right buttock, and then extend the left leg as far footward as possible with a lurch.

3) Continue this draw-back-and-extend-forward action of each leg alternately, until I've pulled my body across the floor. This is a great stomach exercise and gives the illusion of "swimming" across the floor on your back leading with your legs.

ROLL OVER

At the end of a Crawl, draw my right leg back to my chest as if I were going to continue the Crawl. But this time, as I roll over on the left buttock, lurch my right leg to the left and down to join the other leg, and my body will roll over and over. My arms are flopping freely on the carpet above my head as I roll over. *(This move reminds me of when I was a kid rolling down grassy hills in a park—or sometimes in the snow—a great feeling of abandon.)*

STALKING

Standing on my tip-toes and crouching, I stalk my imaginary prey slowly, then rapidly, then standing still with one foot poised in midair, always aware of stepping soundlessly, as if creeping up on an animal. With a partner, we stalk each other.

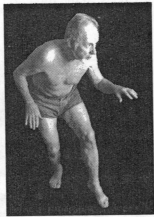

(Note: The Stalk represents a change of pace, from somersaulting and rolling to slower movements and balancing—as when I stand still on one foot. Stalking gives me the feeling of hiding from Marion and then suddenly springing toward her in a surprise move.)

THE WAKE-UP

When doing The Cat with a partner, K. likes us to begin by lying on the carpet, face down, as if asleep. Take this moment as a rest, perhaps after a period of work. My eyes open and slowly my body awakens. Keeping eyes focused

on my partner as much as possible, stretch my body in any way I enjoy: like raising myself up on my hands, stretching a leg out behind me, twisting my hips in a circle in a sit-up position, lowering myself toward the carpet in a "diving" motion with my nose like a stunt plane. Gradually go from these stretches into a seamless succession of Cat moves in any order and for any length of time I wish, always paying attention to my partner and playing "Cats" together.

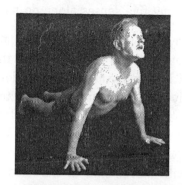

Imaginary Partner

K. suggests that, if I were learning these moves alone, I could visualize a partner to keep me company, helping me through The Cat. An imaginary partner also helps me direct my attention outward, enhancing The Cat as a metaphor for the performing state. This imaginary person could be a kind of guardian—someone I'd like to have with me at important moments—a friend, or perhaps a role model.

Vestibular System—"The Sixth Sense"

K. introduced us to something new today—the vestibular system, an organ in the inner ear which enables me to maintain physical balance, feel the space around me, and gauge distances for athletic, musical or verbal communication. Technically it's wrong to call the vestibular organ a "sense," but it's tempting to do so, because it creates an awareness of my surroundings in a way that my five senses alone do not, almost like a sixth sense.

K. says the vestibular system is made up of two parts: the static labyrinth, which detects linear movement, and the kinetic labyrinth, which detects angular and rotational movement (acceleration and velocity). He says my senses depend on highly sensitive hair cells connected to the vestibular nerve in the inner ear. These cells are stimulated by the flow of a fluid when I move my head. *(The dizziness in somersaults results from a disturbance of this fluid, until I get used to it.)* The vestibular nerve carries information to the brain to coordinate eye reflexes with movements of the head, trunk and limbs. This is what gives me physical balance.

Throwing Sound

Accuracy of vocal projection depends on finely-tuned coordination between the eyes and the vestibular organ, because I need to judge the distance between myself and the person or group I'm speaking to. Experienced musicians and actors continually adjust the distance they "throw" their sound depending on the size of their performance space and their distance from the audience. A ballet dancer needs to know exactly how far to leap in order to meet her partner, sometimes literally flying through the air. A football player throwing the ball needs to judge the distance and velocity of the ball against the direction and degree of acceleration of the receiver.

K. says these spatial judgments, common to athletes, dancers and musicians alike, depend on a highly developed vestibular system. Any exercise that sharpens this muscle-brain-voice coordination will improve performance. K. thinks The Cat is the best concise vestibular exercise he knows, because it conditions balance, sense of space and judgment of distance, while constantly changing velocity and acceleration.

Benefits Of The Cat

The Cat lets me know that I can perform under any conditions, so that virtually nothing can interfere with my fully focused state of mind. The Cat helps me:

- ❖ Tune my body and mind for performance.
- ❖ Concentrate my attention on the moment.
- ❖ Feel playful and uninhibited.
- ❖ Make a game out of muscle stretching.
- ❖ Open my larynx and improve my voice quality.
- ❖ Develop my sense of balance, space and distance.

Lesson 15

FREE OF SOUND

*"We create phobias by imagining something bad is
going to happen. Why not do it the other way
around and imagine something good is going to
happen?"*

Silent Performing With Hologram

This is a technique for separating sound from the action of producing the sound
and gives me a triple perspective on the result. I simply speak, sing or play a
musical instrument in the normal way but without making any sound. K. says it's
very important that I breathe normally so I feel and look like I'm really singing
or playing. And he wants me to perform with full energy, just as if I were making
the sound, so I can be fully aware of what I'm doing physically.

Exercise

1) Speak, read, play or sing a short piece of material.

2) Now perform the same material without sound while breathing as
   if I were making the sound, and making all the gestures and
   movements I would normally make to produce the sound.

3) Now perform it adding sound.

4) Notice the difference between the two performances from the three positions of the Hologram: Performer, Coach, Audience.

5) See myself using this technique for an upcoming presentation. Notice how my presentation will be different as a result.

Action Without Sound

Performing silently frees us from concerns about the quality (or content) of our vocal (or instrumental) sound and allows us to pay attention to the mechanics of producing the sound. After a trial run or two at silent performing I can add the sound, which then seems easy because I have gained control of the mechanics of making the sound. K. says this exercise is effective because it enables me to separate interpretation from mechanics and thus teaches me how to focus my concentration where I need it.

Free To Respond Instinctively

K. points out that vocal or instrumental sound production requires effort and we tend to worry about it, which inhibits our body from producing the sound in the most natural way. When we leave out the sound and the mind's worry about it, the body responds freely and does what it needs to create the sound. Once I know what it feels like to speak or sing naturally—without the distraction of the physical mechanics—I understand exactly what to do with my voice (or musical instrument) and feel more comfortable doing it.

Performing Music Silently

Marion says K.'s silent-performing technique would be very useful for playing a musical instrument. She says the trick to playing an instrument (she plays flute and piano) is that you have two things to think about: making a sound and working your fingers. Silent performing would free her from making the sound so she could pay attention to fingerings. Then when she added the sound she'd be free to think about tone quality and projection of sound alone, because the mechanical aspects of playing the instrument had already been worked out. This focuses attention on the *process* of producing the sound, rather than the result.

She says it would be very important to breathe when miming the playing exactly as she would breathe when really playing because her breathing determines her musical phrasing—where to pause and how many notes she should take in one breath. Paying attention to phrasing lays the groundwork for the coordination of sound and fingers. Also, since musical phrasing is linked to breathing, silent playing would help her hear the sound in her head.

Marion wants me to learn a musical instrument. *(I told her I already play an instrument—the computer—but she wasn't amused.)* She drew up an approach to playing an instrument using K.'s Silent Performing idea:

Exercise

1) **Play an imaginary instrument, using all the correct fingerings, breathing patterns, etc., as if I were actually making the sound.**

2) **Still playing on an imaginary instrument, sing the music exactly as I want to play it.** *(Marion says never mind that I have an untrained voice. The idea is to hear myself shaping musical phrases on my instrument with total ease, without being preoccupied by fingerings or bowings. I have no idea how somebody would do this, but then I have a tin ear.)*

3) **Pick up the actual instrument and play it normally in every way but make no sound.** *(Marion said string players could play with an imaginary bow or tape the bow to make it silent.)* **It will look like the musician is playing on film with the soundtrack turned off.**

4) **Play the instrument with sound.**

"What If"

K., Marion and I had more discussion about altering our beliefs about performance (and life) by imagining alternative circumstances and truly believing them. Fantasizing new possibilities gives me a chance to test my reactions to them. Marion mentioned an acting exercise called "what if," where you say, "What if this were true—what would I do then?" *(Actually I've done this when creating new computer programs. And K.'s exercises have had me imagining alternate circumstances to give me a new feeling about them. Testing alternatives at least gives me a feeling of choice, and choice is liberating. And I'll go with anything that brings results.)*

The More Fantastic, The Better

K. emphasized that the more fantastical the "what ifs," the better. The idea is not to actually carry out all these fantasies, but to get new *feelings* about my circumstances by imagining them in new ways—to loosen up a little bit and realize there's more than one way to think about my life. *(Put that way, I can accept the idea better. I do think I've made some progress in the "loosening up" department, but I think I could do a lot more.)*

Make Up Your Own

K. encouraged me to make up "what ifs" about presentations. The crazier the better to shake up my thinking.

- **What if I ordered a thousand roses and put them all over the stage, or hall, or conference room?**
- **What if I invited the audience to sit on stage with me?**
- **What if I invited the audience home for a party instead of giving my presentation?**
- **What if I mimed my presentation instead of singing, speaking or playing it?**
- **What if I drove on stage in an old convertible and gave my presentation standing up in the front seat?**

"A Rip-Roaring Good Time"

Marion told me a funny story about a great classical singer who was ready to give an important recital but her accompanist didn't show up. She received a telegram: "Flight grounded due to a snowstorm. Can't be there before nine o'clock." It was eight o'clock and the audience was waiting, so she walked on stage, explained the situation and said, "So, why don't we just talk until he gets here?" She actually sat on the stage with her legs dangling over the edge. The audience was delighted to be able to ask her questions about being a singer and hear her anecdotes about performing. She said they had a "rip-roaring good time." When her accompanist showed up all nervous and worried an hour later she waved him onto the stage and said, "Come on out and join us." He was surprised to find such an informal, friendly atmosphere, and told everybody about the snowstorm. Finally the singer said, almost as an afterthought, "How about we make some music now?"

Audiences Are Friends I Haven't Met

This singer's evening was a tremendous success and it changed her concept of recitals. From that day forward she thought of concerts as communal rather than formal. Audiences were now a group of friends she had yet to meet, and this new attitude made performing even more natural and spontaneous for her.

Fantasy And Reality

You could say this story is an example of a "what if" that really happened. She might have imagined the whole thing and gotten a similar result, if she had imagined it fully and with conviction. K. has said time and again that when we fantasize something strongly enough our brain can't tell if it's "real" or not. As he says, this is how we create anxiety—by imagining something *bad* is going to happen. Why not do it the other way around and imagine something *good* is going to happen? I guess it all comes down to what we want, and how strongly we want it—and then doing everything we can to make it happen.

Silent Performing Helps Me:

❖ **Practice new or difficult material without worrying about how I sound.**

❖ **Find and correct the flaws in my performance.**

❖ **Learn unfamiliar material more quickly.**

❖ **Practice without disturbing others.**

❖ **Develop a new perspective on my performance.**

❖ **Concentrate before a performance.**

Lesson 16

THE LAUGHING TRANCE

*"Pessimists' Warning: laughter can hurt your ribs,
cut off your breath, upset your stomach and make
you cry. Laugh at your own risk."*

When You Need A Release

K. said he learned The Laughing Trance (so-called because it makes you feel spaced out) from actors in an experimental theater group. They used it when work tensions became high and they needed release. *(It's also good for relieving tension after encountering a bear.)*

Find a space large enough for the group, which can be any number of people, from three up. Everyone lies on their back on the floor, each with his or her head on another's stomach, forming a closed circle. The action begins with each person crying "Ha!" loud enough to make the stomach muscles contract sharply. *(K. says the exercise will also work with people lying in a zig-zag, but to remember that if the line of bodies does not loop back and close, the outer two people won't be connected.)*

Exercise

Person 1) Ha!
Person 2) Ha, ha!
Person 3) Ha, ha, ha!
Person 1) Ha, ha, ha, ha! Etc.

Soon normal laughter takes over and the exercise becomes spontaneous.

Bouncing Heads And Laughter

Shouting 'Ha!' sharply activates the muscles and organs of the stomach area, which makes the heads jump. As the laughter builds, the stomach muscles lurch more violently and the heads bounce faster, which in turn increases the laughter. K. says that laughing makes us breathe deeply and releases endorphins in the brain, which is deeply relaxing—in fact, it often makes people feel delightfully woozy.

Slow To Ignite

K. says laughter is sometimes slow to ignite and may need a witty remark to touch it off. Recalling frustrating or scary experiences can fuel laughter, especially when heads start bouncing on stomachs. When Marion and K. and I were doing the Laughing Trance, Marion tried to describe how I looked with my pants falling off after the bear had shredded them, which sent us into paroxyms of laughter.

Laughter In Waves

A laughing session might last 15-20 minutes, with the laughter coming and going in waves. The idea is to let the group continue until the laughter is finished (or the people are exhausted).

"Zzt" The Experience

K. looked at me and squeezed his fingers after we finished laughing in his cabin, to further embed the memory of the experience. He says he can remind people years later about the laughing exercise, sometimes holding up his fingers and saying "Zz-zzt," and they will giggle, recalling the memory.

Pessimists' Warning

Laughter can hurt your ribs, cut off your breath, upset your stomach and make you cry. Laugh at your own risk.

Laughter And Health

K. mentioned the book, "Anatomy of an Illness," by the late Saturday Review Editor Norman Cousins. The book documents Cousins' return to health after developing a disabling and often fatal spinal disease that makes the joints and spine permanently rigid. Cousins had read Dr. Hans Selye's book "The Stress of Life," which explains how negative thoughts produce negative chemical reactions in the body. Seriously ill, Cousins reasoned that positive thoughts might release beneficial chemicals and hormones and he decided to experiment, especially since the doctors had given up on him.

Pain-Free Sleep

First, he checked himself out of the hospital, booked a hotel room, and had himself hooked up to a 24-hour intravenous supply of vitamin C (25,000 milligrams per day). Then he ordered a movie screen and a projector to see his favorite funny movies and laughed all day. Cousins found that laughter was a natural pain-killer. In his book he said, "I made the joyous discovery that ten minutes of genuine belly laughter had an anesthetic effect and would give me at least two hours of pain-free-sleep." Matt had explained that Cousins was talking about the secretion of endorphins from the brain and pituitary gland, having the effect of opiates. Cousins was eventually cured through this method.

Placebo Effect

Skeptical doctors said the cure was simply the result of a placebo effect— that Cousins just thought he was healthier because he was taking vitamins and laughing. But what difference does it make? This anecdote supports K.'s point that if we believe something deeply, and act *as if* it were true, the brain doesn't know the difference. If that's placebo, I'll take it. And no side effects!

Crazy Idea

Kumi told about a very successful use of The Laughing Trance with a football band that was in rehearsal for a Saturday half-time show. The rehearsal was going badly and tempers flared. The band director asked the musicians to put down their instruments and lie down in a circle on the field with their heads on each other's stomachs. The craziness of the idea, and the clumsiness of trying to get a hundred-and-fifty people to lie cross-ways on each other's bodies, already produced laughter. By the time the director ordered various individuals to start the "Ha-ha" process, they were already on a roll. The chain of laughter filled the stadium with sound. After ten minutes, the director asked the group to pick up their instruments and continue the band practice—now in a mellow and cooperative mood.

Laughter Helps Me:

- ❖ **Create a feeling of unity within a group.**
- ❖ **Release tension in an overworked or aggravated group.**
- ❖ **Increase blood circulation and release beneficial hormones.**
- ❖ **Create an atmosphere of optimism.**
- ❖ **Relax and feel good.**

THE CHARTING GAME

In the spirit of fun, Marion tried out a new idea with Charting in one of her acting classes that she calls "The Charting Game." She chose two people, called Hosts (one male, one female), and had them both define their inner "staff," writing down the names and functions of each of their parts on separate pieces of paper. Then she had members of their respective groups role-play these parts, complete with the job descriptions taped to their chests.

Taking Your Parts On A Date

The Hosts were then introduced to each other and told to go out "on a date," accompanied by their flock of parts. But first each Host was given a secret instruction: the man should try to persuade the woman to go away with him for a weekend, and the woman's role was to refuse. Each Host should keep this resolve to make the conflict unresolvable. The role of their parts—who are "invisible" to the Hosts—is to prompt and nudge their Hosts. For example, the woman's Health part might encourage her to accept the skiing invitation for the healthy out-of-doors experience, whereas her Protector might warn her that she doesn't know this man well enough to go away with him for a weekend. The

Lover in the man might come up with clever persuasive lines, whereas his Financial Advisor might tell him the weekend would be too expensive. The Hosts improvise their responses either following or ignoring the advice of their parts.

Marion said the exercise was hilarious, especially when a number of the parts spoke up at once, sometimes contradicting each other, and the Hosts started "arguing with themselves."

Exercise

Setting Up The Fun

Working with a group, here's how Marion set up The Charting Game:

1) Divide the group into two equal subgroups and choose a Host from each subgroup. Then in each group do the following:

2) Ask the Host to define the parts that carry out the main functions of his/her life.

3) Select someone to write down each part's function on separate pieces of typing paper.

4) As each part is defined, the Host asks who wants to play that part, and the Writer tapes that part's description to the volunteer's chest. *(Marion says it's very important that the participants choose the parts they want to play, so that the role is natural for them.)*

5) The parts are then asked to examine their job descriptions carefully. If they are at all unclear about the job they're supposed to do for the Host, they should speak up immediately, asking the Host for clarification.

6) The Host deals with the ensuing onslaught of simultaneous demands for clarification the best way s/he can.

✓   *Note: The point of this step of the game is to see if the Host has a way of managing conflict. If the Host gets angry or withdraws in frustration, this signals the need for creating an inner Manager. The Host then defines the kind of person he/she would like to have handle such a situation. Someone volunteers to be the Manager part and help the Host resolve the conflict.*

7) Each Host is secretly given an assignment that would automatically put the Hosts in conflict with each other. (Like Marion's boy/girl situation.)

8) The two Hosts are introduced and proceed to role-play their assignments.

9) As the Hosts interact, the parts secretly coach them, acting as advisors. (They are like the voices in each Host's head.)

10) Since the conflict is unresolvable the game initiator steps in to end the improvisation when it reaches a peak or plays out.

Charting Helps Me:

❖ Realize that I am a community of selves.

❖ Identify the main parts of myself and define their functions.

❖ Be aware of the relationship between all my parts.

❖ Coordinate different parts so they can work together.

❖ Assign tasks to parts of myself for specific outcomes.

❖ Learn to make decisions with full compliance of all my parts.

❖ Take the time to listen to myself.

❖ Understand how my unconscious mind functions and how to connect with it.

❖ Notice what's missing in myself and add new parts by modeling others.

❖ Grow by continually updating the functions of my parts.

❖ Understand that all my actions are based on positive intent, even when my behavior is negative.

❖ Identify the source of any difficulty within myself.

K. liked The Charting Game. He said it demonstrates that the outcomes of our goals depend on how well our parts work with each other and with the Host. Success depends on the clarity of the parts' job descriptions and on how accurately and respectfully we communicate with them.

Lesson 17

LIFE LEVELS ALIGNMENT

"If I fail in a task I don't fail as a human being. The only 'failure' is loss of self. I've been so concerned with succeeding—with answering to people outside of me—that I didn't realize the person I really have to satisfy is me."

The Magic Harp

K. asked me why Jack, in "Jack and the Beanstalk," would risk his life going back up the beanstalk for the magic harp when he already had the goose that lays the golden eggs. I had another question: Why did he climb the beanstalk in the first place? I think he was searching for something more than riches—some purpose for living.

Crossing The Threshold

K. gave me an exercise based on Jack's adventure. The beanstalk is a call to Jack to cross a threshold into a new life experience. The climb is a challenge to Jack's capabilities, and his encounter with the giant establishes his identity. The harp that plays by itself represents the mystery that gives his life meaning, the spiritual.

The Six Plateaus

K.'s metaphor of the beanstalk, with its roots in the earth and its branches in the heavens, roughly parallels the six main categories of life he says I need to define to keep my life in balance:

Environment: Where I live

Activity: What I do

Capabilities: How I'm able to do

Values/Beliefs: Why I do it

Identity: Who I am

Spiritual: Who I do it for, my life mission

Walking Through Your Life

Charles asked me to "Kumi" him through all six levels adding one new element—*a goal.* We placed six pieces of paper on the floor, marked with the words Environment, Activity, Capabilities, Values/beliefs, Identity and Spiritual. Then he added a seventh sheet—"Goal: To be a TV anchorman"—and taped this goal sheet on the wall. He kept his eyes on the goal as he stepped backwards, away from the wall, through all the levels, from his Environment to the Spiritual and back again. We agreed he could step outside any of these spaces as he went if he wanted to get an "outside" view of one or more levels. But while in the space he must be "inside himself," fully experiencing each level.

Exercise

Climbing Up The Beanstalk

With a clipboard in hand to write down my observations, and a Walkman on my belt to record his exact words, here's what we did:

1) **Environment:** I asked Charles to step into this space and see, hear and feel the people, places and things that would be available to him in his proposed life in television. Keeping his eyes on his goal, he felt himself in these places (school, TV stations). When we were both satisfied that he had defined his environment in relation to his goal, I asked him to step on to the next space.

2) **Activities**: Charles evaluated his courses and teachers at the university in relation to his long-term outcomes and decided to drop one course. He imagined developing mentors who could help him professionally, and he saw himself getting the degree he needed to apprentice at a network. When he was ready he moved on to the next category.

3) **Capabilities**: Here he reviewed his study habits, concentration skills, reading ability and computer skills, and general knowledge that enabled him to perform as a student. Then he related those skills to his desired goal as a TV reporter and realized he needed better research skills. He wondered what course would give him that knowledge.

4) **Values/Beliefs**: He expressed his feelings about the importance of responsible TV journalism and how appalled he was at some of the tasteless media reporting that invaded people's privacy. He wondered how he would be able to hold on to his journalistic ethics when working for a big network. He decided he had to talk about this question with some of the top reporters in the profession. (His eyes narrowed, his face became still and he stood up straight as he talked about this subject. I recognized his "determined" stance, which I first saw in him when he was four years old.)

5) **Identity**: When Charles moved onto this space, I asked him to get a feeling of his basic self, the self he was born with and that he knows by instinct is unique to him. I asked him what metaphor or analogy might best describe that self? He said, "I'm like a flashlight shining light in dark corners." (He shifted from right to left on the balls of his feet as he said this, looking like an athlete getting ready to run the 200 meters.)

6) **Mission/Spiritual**: On this level Charles closed his eyes and became quiet for some five minutes. His facial muscles relaxed, and when he opened his eyes they were defocused. He looked very calm. My only instruction to him was that this space represented his connection to something larger than himself—society, the world or a higher power—which would represent his mission. He didn't speak, but only looked at his Goal sheet for a long minute and nodded his head almost imperceptibly.

The Return

7) I told him to step into the **Identity** space when he was ready, taking the feeling of the **Mission/Spiritual** with him. As he did this I saw the quiet feeling blend with the athlete's stance.

8) Then he carried this combined state into the **Values** space, smiling as he continued staring at his Goal and nodding his head in a determined manner.

9) Keeping the combined feelings of these three levels, he stepped into his **Capabilities** area. As he moved to this piece of paper he said, "Oh, yeah, I sure do need that." I had no idea what he meant and he didn't volunteer any information.

10) Then he stepped into the **Activity** space and laughed. "Good evening, ladies and gentlemen, this is Charles Cole..." he said. He looked quite different in this space now than he had before, more confident, like he had already graduated and was a professional announcer.

11) Holding this accumulation of feelings from all the levels he stepped into his **Environment**, and just stood there looking at his Goal. Then he stepped out, stretched and walked around the room, nodding his head. "Very powerful," he said quietly.

The whole exercise took thirty or forty minutes. K. had said we should take all the time we need to fully experience all the categories and their relationships to our satisfaction.

What We Learned From The Climb

This exercise helped Charles answer basic questions:

- **What do I want?**
- **Am I in the right environment to do it?**
- **Am I doing what I want?**
- **What capabilities do I need to do what I want?**
- **How do my beliefs and values support my goals?**
- **Who am I?**
- **What's my mission in life, and what higher power guides me?**

Life Levels Alignment

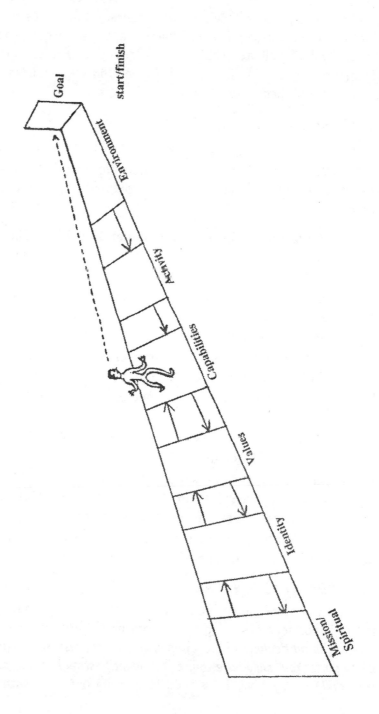

I told Charles that K. said most problems in life can be traced to a confusion of these six categories, and that we achieve our goals most easily when we clearly define all six levels and keep them clearly sorted and aligned. Every experience we have in life—in love, in work, in play—relates in some way to one or more of these categories.

Clarifying Thinking

He remarked on how the Alignment helps clarify thinking, because he can see exactly what level an issue is on. Here are typical examples Charles and I shared about people we know who were confused in relation to one or more of these levels:

- She trained to be a fashion model, but she's living in a small town with a population of only 5,000. (A mismatch of Capabilities and Environment.)
- He wants to be at the hub of the publishing business, but doesn't want to work in an urban area. (A discrepancy between Activity and Environment.)
- She wants to be a TV announcer, but has no public speaking skills. (A conflict of Activity and Capabilities.)
- He's dealing drugs to finance church programs. (A conflict of Mission and Values.)
- He's a corporate lawyer but thinks of himself as a guru. (A confusion of Activity and Identity.)
- She wants to do desktop publishing, but spent her savings on a new Mercedes instead of investing in state-of-the-art computer equipment. (A confusion of Activity and Values.)
- He's a playwright who gets easily depressed over a bad review. (A confusion of Activity and Identity.)

What I Do Is Not What I Am

K. says one of the key points I can learn from aligning my life categories is the importance of having an identity based on who I *am*, not what I *do*. (*Marion is particularly aware of this, maybe because she's an actor and plays many parts. You really have to get your identity straight if borrowing identities is your daily work.*) Many of us tend to identify ourselves with what we do—a conflict of Identity and Activity, not unnatural in a society where we are often identified with our job. But if I identify myself with my job and it suddenly becomes obsolete—as often happens today—I'm likely to think I'm obsolete. *(Which is exactly what I thought when Streicher cut me from Globalcom.)* I see now that my identity is deeper and more permanent than any activity I perform; my identity is what I'm born with. It is my very nature, and is the only security I have in life because it can never be taken away from me. Understanding my identity gives me a sense of psychological real estate, a self-assurance that underlies everything I do.

A Model Of Leadership

K. says former President Jimmy Carter is a stellar example of a man with a strong personal identity. Generally, when presidents finish their terms, they fade away, because their identity was in their presidential role. When Jimmy Carter lost his re-election his real identity came through and he started his own foundation for peace. He since became one of the world's great peace-makers and humanitarians, a model of leadership.

K. says I can't avoid labels given to me by others, but I must not believe those labels. *(Marion says she's seen actors deteriorate after receiving an Oscar or a Grammy because they came to believe that winning honors was more important than their innate creativity—a conflict of Values and Identity.)*

"Proclaim Your Rarity"

Maybe I should have a brief daily ritual where I remind myself of the core self I brought into this world. I understand Willie Nelson says to himself every day, "Proclaim your rarity."

Knowing my identity means I can stop thinking "me" all the time, because when I'm confident about who I am I needn't focus on it. *(What a relief that would be—will be, because I'm already doing it.)*

Your Body Tells The Story

K. encourages people to move and gesture freely while doing the Alignment. I learned as much or more from Charles' nonverbal responses as from his words. Sometimes he didn't speak, but his breathing, stance, gestures, voice tone, skin color, facial expressions and general comportment revealed his unconscious reactions to each level—like his "power stance" at the Values level.

Combining The Alignment With Triple Position

Then Charles and I got a great idea: to combine the Triple Position exercise (the variation I made on the Hologram) with the Alignment, and create an imaginary Mentor and Observer for each level.

Here's how it works:

Exercise

1) Place my six sheets of paper representing the life levels on the floor and my goal on the wall.

2) Step into my Environment. Ask myself, "Who would be the best person in the world to tell me what's needed in my environment in relation to my goal?" We decided we could use whoever inspires me—any person in the world from any period in time, even mythical figures. This person will be my mentor (and also my ally).

3) Place a piece of colored paper near the Environment space representing this Mentor.

4) Imagine what the Mentor would say. Then step out of the Environment space and into the Mentor space and play the role of the Mentor, giving myself advice on my environment in relation to the goal. Then step back into the Environment position and consider the Mentor's words.

5) Establish an Observer position with another piece of colored paper. *(Now I have two colored sheets beside the Environment position, representing the Mentor and the Observer.)* Step into the Observer space and see myself in my environment from the standpoint of this totally detached person, and speak my thoughts freely to myself. *(As the Observer I will have no personal interest in this Environment space or myself in it. My only job as the Observer is to report facts as they relate to myself in this environment: how I appear, what I'm saying or doing, how I'm reacting to others, etc.)*

6) Step back in my Environment, becoming myself again, and consider the response of the Observer.

7) Discuss freely with the Mentor and Observer as needed, switching positions in this three-way role-play.

8) Create a Mentor and Observer for each of the subsequent five levels. On the Activity level, I will be discussing my main activities—professional, family, social—with another Mentor of my choice and getting the disinterested response of yet another Observer. On the Capabilities level I will be mentored and observed on my education, my knowledge, my experience. On the Values/Beliefs level I will get advice from a Mentor whose morals and ethics I admire. On the Identity level I will choose someone with a strong identity whose nature relates closely to my own. In the Spiritual realm I will select a Mentor who has achieved the peace of mind I'd like to have, or has fulfilled a life mission similar to the one I want for myself. I can have Buddha, Deepak Chopra, Mother Teresa—whoever I want.

ALIGNMENT WITH TRIPLE POSITION

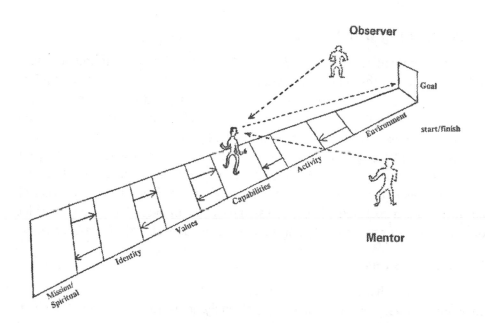

A Walking Resource Center

When I'm finished I have a Mentor and an Independent Observer for each of the six levels—a total of 18 positions. When I walk back down the levels I can take with me any of these helpers, deciding which ones I'd like to have as my daily consultants. With such a team of mentors and observers, I'm like a walking resource center.

Alignment With Partner

Then we went "ape" inventing variations of the Alignment. For example, a couple (lovers, roommates, business partners) can go through their alignments simultaneously, lining up two rows of levels and cross-relating their responses. This way they can quickly see what matches and what doesn't in their individual needs at each of the six levels. Turning it into a game makes these comparisons less threatening.

Aligning Yourself With Your Job

We decided you can also do a double alignment: with yourself and your job. First, step through the six levels of your job, defining the location, skill requirements, values, job identity (how others think about it) and any mission it might have. Then, beside it, set up a second set of levels representing yourself and step through these, cross-relating your six categories with the job's categories at each level. This way you might see, for example, that a frustration with your job that you thought was on the Activity level (long hours), might really be on the Values level (lack of communication). Seeing and feeling the six levels of your life and the six levels of your job side by side can help identify any conflict between yourself and your job, and perhaps also suggest ways to resolve it.

Think Like A Leader

Charles and I discussed how well-organized people often seem to align themselves instinctively, because they are so strongly goal-oriented. Where they live, their skills and values, their personal identity all seem to be inextricably linked to their goal. Maybe that's why they make fast decisions, because they notice an immediate discrepancy in any category of their lives between what they want and need and what they're doing. These people are in fact the models from which this exercise was formed. The Life Levels Alignment teaches us how to think like leaders.

Living Through The Experience

Even though a person may have visual clarity about his or her life, the Alignment offers a *kinesthetic* experience—the chance to *feel* what it's like on each of the major life levels. For example, a person might think that she'd like to take a particular job in a new location, but then find that when she actually steps into the Environment or Activity spaces that represent that job, she feels an uneasiness that was not apparent when talking about it or visualizing it. The Alignment offers us the chance to make a triple-channel decision on all the levels because we can actually walk and talk through the experience, living it as we go.

✓ *An unexpected bonus from doing all these alignments was that Charles and I felt very close afterward. In fact, Charles became a kind of Mentor for me—for the spiritual level, though he doesn't know that. We embraced before parting, the way two men will when they're feeling good, and I realized I hadn't hugged him since he was a child. We seemed to have stepped onto a new level now with each other, the beginning of a friendship that I think will continue to grow.*

The Life Levels Alignment Helps Me:

- ❖ Decide what I want to do in life.
- ❖ Choose where I want to live.
- ❖ Identify the skills I need.
- ❖ Define what I value and believe.
- ❖ Understand who I am as opposed to what I do.
- ❖ Clarify my sense of purpose in life.
- ❖ Understand how I relate to the rest of the world.
- ❖ See the connection between all the levels of my life.
- ❖ Develop allies in the important areas of my life.

Answering To Yourself

Going through the Life Levels Alignment by the river with K. made me realize that I do in fact have a "self," a basic nature that's unique to me, regardless of my abilities or accomplishments. If I fail in a task I don't fail as a human being. The only "failure" is loss of self. I've been so concerned with succeeding—with answering to people outside of me—that I didn't realize the person I really have to satisfy is me. I think my parts have been trying with increasing desperation to tell me this for years, which may explain the rage I'd been feeling. I couldn't respond to them because I didn't know who "I" was. I guess this is what is called "answering to yourself."

Lesson 18

CIRCLE OF EXCELLENCE

"No one has my hand print, or my voice print, and that's only the beginning of a thousand million ways in which I differ from anyone else on this planet..."

Charging My Battery

The idea of The Circle of Excellence is to step into a circle that represents my personal power and will fill me with strength and energy. I can expand the Circle to include everything around me and carry that feeling of connectedness into any situation where I may need it. Put simply, it's a way to "charge my battery."

Exercise

Steps For The Circle Of Excellence

l) Cut a piece of yarn, about 9 feet long and place it on the floor in a circle. It will be about one yard in diameter. (I used string at the conference because it was all I had. Yarn is thicker and I can choose my favorite color.)

2) **Standing outside the Circle, look at the center and see, hear and feel myself there with the memories of my best accomplishments.**

3) **When I'm ready, step into the Circle and let that feeling of strength fill me.**

4) **As I stand in the Circle, increase this resourceful feeling by re-living the memories of past successes. If, for even a second, I feel less than excellent, I step out of the circle.**

5) **Outside the Circle, quickly restore the full feeling of excellence and step back into the Circle.**

6) **Remain in the Circle until I feel my full strength, then step out and go on to my appointed task.**

When To Use It

The Circle can help me concentrate for an exam, a speech, an interview or audition, an athletic event, a concert, a presentation to a group, or any other kind of special situation where I want to be at my best. The more I practice stepping into the Circle, recalling past successes, the more quickly I'll be able to retrieve those resourceful feelings at crucial moments.

Realm Of The Right Brain

The Circle is a place to *feel*, it's not for analyzing or questioning. My goal is to achieve a strong feeling of resourcefulness, which I find through inspiring imagery and rich memories. The Circle is a natural place to rely on my instincts. Reading about the mythology of circles, I've learned they have always been a symbol of creativity (the navel of the world) and can sometimes even spark psychic experiences. It is the realm of the right brain.

No One Can See It

A nice touch about the Circle is that, after enough practice I don't need the yarn anymore. I carry the Circle in my mind, invisible to anyone but myself. Just knowing this gives me a feeling of security.

Mix And Match

I can combine the Circle with many of K.'s techniques:

The Hero Image: Stand in the Circle and visualize my hero or favorite animal with myself and zoom the pictures into me.

Zzt-Squeeze: When I achieve a feeling of exhilaration in the Circle, squeeze the fingers and take it with me.

The Hologram: Stand in the Circle and imagine an upcoming performance, exam, interview or audition. Then step out of The Circle and coach myself in this presentation and step back in and perform it again. Then step out on the other side of the Circle and notice how I look and sound to the audience.

Modeling: Stand in my Circle when identifying with someone I want to model.

Walk-On: Stand in the Circle when preparing to walk on stage.

Physical and vocal work. Stand in the Circle when doing The Tuning Dance or Amy. (Enlarge the Circle for movement.)

Life Levels Alignment: Place the Circle on any of the six levels. It can be especially inspiring when using the levels for goal-setting, where I visualize my goal from each of the six levels. It can help me solidify my Identity and deepen my experience of the Spiritual level. I might even place six little pieces of colored paper inside the Circle representing each of the six levels and do the whole Alignment inside the Circle.

Verbal Silence

I prefer not to talk while standing in the Circle, at least not at first. Silence helps me create the feeling that I'm on a special plane, in my own world. When Marion or Charles or Matt speak to me in the Circle, I hear their voices as if they were a memory or a thought process going on in my head. Maintaining verbal silence allows me to monitor my own feelings and thoughts. The main thing is to make sure nothing disturbs my concentration or minimizes the feeling of power I have in the Circle.

"You're Gonna Screw Up"

Once I have established a strong feeling of presence in the Circle, I like to be challenged to help me strengthen my resourceful state of mind. The challenges should be designed to anticipate and flush out any fears or insecurities I might have about myself or about performing. Hearing my fears spoken aloud by someone else while I'm in the Circle enables me to face them while in this highly resourceful state. Should these fears arise again during or prior to a performance, I will have a feeling of strength associated with the Circle that can kick in and energize me, bypassing the fear and switching me to a new source of energy.

Here are some challenges Charles and I fire at each other once we're securely grounded in the Circle.

- **"Someone close to you says something discouraging."**
- **"You're gonna screw up."**
- **"You don't deserve to succeed."**
- **"Maybe you're not as good as you thought you were."**
- **"People with knowledge superior to yours are judging you."**

From Fear To Strength

The partner's role in challenging is very sensitive. The challenges are intended to help me build strength, not frighten me. Therefore my "Kumi-ing" partner should use challenges that are strong enough to touch on fears that are relevant to me, but not jeopardize my confidence. If at any point I feel a pang of insecurity in response to the challenges, I quickly step out of the Circle, retrieve my resourceful state (with encouragement from my partner if needed), and then step back into the Circle.

Embedded Commands

I learned from K. that embedded commands are very effective in helping a person build strength and confidence. Embedded commands are sentences within a sentence. They occur frequently, though often unnoticed, in everyday conversation. For example, someone might say "You're going to be a big success tonight." This sounds like a typical comment from a well-wisher. In fact, the sentence contains two direct but hidden commands: "Be a success," and "Be a big success tonight." I remember from reading Will Strunk Jr.'s English book, *Elements of Style*, that the most important word or clause in a sentence is the last, the second most important word or clause is the first. So, embedded commands at the end or beginning of a of sentence are the most effective.

Slipping Into The Unconscious

K. always lowers his voice slightly on embedded commands to give them a subtle emphasis. He says the hidden sentences slip into the unconscious unnoticed this way and are therefore more effective. When he writes an hypnotic script the embedded commands are italicized.

Ethics Of Embedded Commands

Marion and I discussed the ethics of speaking covert or subliminal messages. For K., ethics are essential and are decided by intent. *("Do you want to help the person or manipulate him to your advantage?")* But K. was quick to add that, contrary to popular belief, you rarely create an emotion or affect the behavior of another person by the spoken word; people do what they want to do, and they create their own states of mind. But he admits that when a person allows me to influence him—in fact requests it—and then opens up his heart and mind to me, he is then vulnerable to influence. *(See Counterbuttons on p. 302.)* This voluntary openness requires the utmost respect on my part for his integrity. I remember challenging K. in our last conversation on the subject:

"We talked about this before and you said that words will never brainwash someone. But isn't it possible that a person who has not given you permission to influence her might be, say, a little tired, or in a state of doubt about something, and that a cleverly placed embedded command might work its way into her mind and tip the balance?"

"Possibly. But the spotlight then is on you, not her. Do you want to help the person or take advantage of her? If it's manipulation you're after, don't bother with embedded commands, just lie. That's the easiest thing in the world, and people do it all the time. Inserting sentences within sentences is a gentle and very thoughtful way of helping a person accomplish something that she might otherwise have found difficult."

"But Kumi—just for the sake of argument—what if you're wrong? What if your words could control a person's behavior in an important way?"

"Then all the more reason to examine your own motives. You have the choice in life to be a good person. If you want to hurt someone you can do it very easily. It takes a split second to snip off the head of a flower. It takes patience and nurturing to grow one."

The Circle Helps Me:

- ❖ Recall my successes and accomplishments.
- ❖ Reinforce my best qualities.
- ❖ Focus my attention for an upcoming task.
- ❖ Prepare myself for performances, interviews and exams.
- ❖ Stimulate my imagination for creative work.
- ❖ Boost my spirits when I'm down.
- ❖ Energize my body when I'm tired.
- ❖ Tune out interfering thoughts.
- ❖ Stabilize my sense of self.

Priming Myself For The Circle

A good way to prime myself for the Circle of Excellence is to do a series of movements, especially The Tuning Dance or The Cat, since they are associated with the idea of performing. When I'm in my performance state of mind, I look into the Circle and see, hear and feel my performance as I want to give it. The excitement and adrenaline rush of physical exertion helps create a feeling of readiness, and visualizing my performance helps me concentrate. When this mind/body state is firmly established I can step into the Circle.

Create A Text

The quality of the instructions given to me while in the Circle is critical to the successful creation of a state of personal excellence. Marion and I wrote out a sample text (edited by K.) to read aloud to a person standing in the Circle. This script can also be recorded for playback if the person prefers to be alone. Scripts can be designed to personal taste, depending on the kind of encouragement needed. My partner may also recite an appropriate myth, parable or metaphor, or I can also use music to enhance my state of mind while in the Circle.

My partner has just done The Tuning Dance (K.'s or her own) and is now standing still with her eyes closed, her weight balanced equally on both feet, arms hanging freely at the sides. I take a piece of yarn about nine feet in length and curl it into a circle about one yard in diameter on the floor in front of her.

Then I begin reading the script. As I start, I am aware of my voice tone, modulating it appropriately for the intended mood.

OUR SCRIPT FOR THE CIRCLE

(by Marion and Nick)

Performance State

"You're performing now at an upcoming event. All *your energy is going into this performance.* You are *concentrating so deeply* that I could pinch your arm and you would barely feel it. As you *continue to perform*, you're already *thinking ahead* to the main *challenges* awaiting you in this presentation, and you are *feeling your energy and confidence* as you *sail* through each of them *with ease."*

Stepping Into The Circle

(Speaking slower)

"And...as you continue to...*enjoy this performance*...very, very slowly allow your eyes to open (if they were closed)...and ...you will *begin to notice* something of particular *interest...to you*...(pause)...and you...*become aware*...that you are looking at ...your own personal *circle of excellence*...(pause)...inside that circle is *your best performing self...feeling* the *comfort*...and *energy*...you *enjoy*...when *at your finest*...when you step into that circle you will...*feel completely at ease*...step in when... *you're ready. Take* all the *time...you need* to *step into the circle..."*

Inside The Circle

"...and you can...*feel the energy* of the circle filling you...as if a *powerful radiance* were *shining through your body*...enclosing you in an impenetrable beam of light...this is the force field of *your energy*...surrounding and protecting you...in this circle...*you feel the energy...you're strong...ab-so-lute-ly safe...*(speaker continues speaking encouraging words until noticing that a resourceful state has been firmly established, then begins challenges)...and if you feel, even for a split second, your concentration begin to fade, step out of the circle immediately, quickly *retrieve* the *feeling of strength*, and step back in again (pause)..."

Preparation For Challenges

"...prepare yourself for any challenges or interruptions to this resourceful state that I might make..."

"Someone close to you says something discouraging."

(If the person steps out say the following:)

"Don't indulge it...bring back the *strong feeling...now...*(When the person steps back in:) That's it, good. (Pause, then repeat the same challenge as a check:) *"Someone close to you says something discouraging."* (If person steps out again:) Only you can discourage, or...*encourage yourself...nowww...*(Steps back into the circle). Good! That's *behind you...for good!*

(With an unpleasant voice tone:) *"I've been watching you, and you're not really as good as you think you are."*

(If person steps out:)

"Get the feeling of The Circle back quickly...*quickly...*(steps back in)...(pause)..."*You're still no better than you were. Nothing's changed."* (If person maintains resourceful state) Good! *That's in the past!"*

"Oh-oh, memory slip...you're going to make a fool of yourself."

(If person remains in a resourceful state:)

*"Wonderful! Double that strong feeling...now...remember...you are cre-*ating this state...with *your energy...*this...*confidence is yours...*and no one can ever take it away from you...(pause)...and you can...*place this circle wher-ever you wish...*on stage...at an audition...an exam...giving a speech...or in a sudden moment of unexpected challenge...and only *you will know it's there...*and you can *allow it to expand* to include the room...the building...the environment and the people in it...and others will see and *feel your confidence...*and *your poise...* (pause)...in the circle you can...*feel what makes you unique...*no one has your hand print... or your voice print...and that's only the beginning of a thousand million ways in which you differ from any-one else on this planet ...at the same time there's a paradox...because *you are vital*, yet unimportant...self-importance produces a strange kind of

fatigue...but *you are extremely valuable*...and as you *discover what makes you unique,* you will begin to *sense your true value*...and to *understand* where...*you fit into the overall picture of life*...this *discovery energizes you* and gives you *faith*...the greatest *gift* you can *give* yourself..."

The Choice Is Yours

"...the choice is yours to...*be what you want to be*...and this may mean to...*have the courage* to...*take a new direction*...and as we know from the myths of people everywhere and all through time...when you...*venture into the unknown*...although you will encounter challenges...you will also *have a guardian*...who *goes with you*...and *takes care of you*...think back on the biggest *changes in your life*...and how overwhelming they might have seemed at the time...and you may recall that...*someone helped you*...it's a nice thought, is it not?...that when you really need help...*you're not alone*...and that may be the most significant thing of all to remember..."

THANKS

My Lessons With Kumi is a novel based on ideas I've gathered from experts in many fields over a period of three decades.

Special credit goes to John Grinder and Richard Bandler, the original co-creators of neuro-linguistic programming (NLP), whose ideas are woven into this teaching tale. I have learned much from NLP developers Steve and Connirae Andreas, Leslie Cameron, Judith DeLozier, Robert Dilts, David Gordon, Michael Grinder and Steve Lankton. The ground-breaking work of family therapist Virginia Satir and hypnotherapist Milton H. Erickson also inspired me.

Affectionate thanks to Toronto psychiatrist Raymond D. Leibl, M.D., in whose study group I first experimented with many of the ideas that led to this book. Also to Paul Madaule, director of The Listening Centre in Toronto, for his speech therapy techniques. My worldwide theater studies have shaped much of *My Lessons With Kumi*. I want to thank Stanislaw Brozowski of the Polish Mime Theater, and Richard Cieslak and Jerzy Grotowski of the Polish Theater Laboratory for their techniques in physical training. To actor/teacher Bill Hickey and voice teacher Eugene Brice of the H-B Studio in New York I owe my acting and vocal training. Thanks also to the actors of New York's Open Theater for teaching me the laughing exercise.

My sources for natural healing through nutrition are numerous, including Adele Davis, Lavon J. Dunne, Julian Whitaker, M.D., and James and Phyllis Balch. From my wife, Ulla, I learned how to translate their nutritional knowledge into delicious meals.

Many professionals and friends read my manuscript and gave valuable suggestions or technical information: computer specialist Alan Hahn; violinist and student of psychotherapy Janie Kim; actor/theater manager Jens Kohler;

composer and teacher David Maslanka; computer software manager Bruce Anderson; graphologist Gloria Lokay; occupational therapist Roula Makhlouta; neurosurgeon Samuel Brendler, M.D; performer/teacher/educator Kenneth Radnofsky and book producer/literary agent, Sandra J. Taylor.

Special thanks to editor Steve Andreas for his incisive edits and suggestions, and for understanding what this book is about.

I enjoy the mixed blessing of living in a family of professional editors. I am grateful to my wife, Ulla, whose ruthless red pen made this book more readable, and to the laser-eyed scrutiny of my screenwriter son, Neal, whose suggestions added life to *My Lessons With Kumi*. Most of all, my appreciation for Ulla's patience in sharing her life with this book for eight years.

A Guide to Sources

Footnotes would be inappropriate in a novel such as *My Lessons With Kumi*. In order to help the reader quickly find the origins of some key techniques in my book, I offer the following information (a complete bibliography is on page 410.)

- Visualizations (Chap. 1). See "submodalities" in *Using Your Brain—for a Change* (Bandler).
- Zzt-Squeeze (Chap. 2). See "anchoring" in *Frogs into Princes* (Bandler and Grinder).
- Hologram and triple position (Chap. 3). See "perceptual positions" in *Turtles all the Way Down—Prerequisites to Personal Genius* (Grinder & DeLozier).
- Kumi's stage fright technique with cellist (Chap. 3, p. 38). See "The phobia cure" in *Using Your Brain—for a Change* (Bandler), and *Heart of the Mind* (Andreas & Andreas).
- Modeling (Chap. 4). See modeling genius in *Turtles all the Way Down—Prerequisites to Personal Genius* (Grinder & DeLozier).
- Sequencing (Chap. 5). See "strategies" in *Neuro-Linguistic Programming: The Study of the Structure of Subjective Experience*, by Dilts, Grinder, Bandler, Bandler & DeLozier; and in *Practical Magic* by Lankton.

- See-Hear-Feel-Do technique (Chap. 7). See Betty Erickson's exercise from Grinder & Bandler's *Trance-formations: Neuro-Linguistic Programming and the Structure of Hypnosis*.

- The Microphone Hand (Chap. 10). See *When Listening Comes Alive* (Madaule).

- Placing time in space (Chap. 13). See "Personal Timelines" in *Heart of the Mind* (Andreas & Andreas), and "Timelines" in *Change Your Mind-- And Keep the Change* (Andreas & Andreas).

- Vestibular organ (Chap. 14). See "The Vestibular System in NLP" by Cecile A. Carson, M.D. in *Leaves Before the Wind*, edited by Charlotte Bretto, Judith DeLozier, John Grinder and Sylvia Topel.

- Charting (Chap. 16). This technique I devised from Virginia Satir's "parts parties"— see *Virginia Satir: the Patterns of Her Magic* (Andreas), and from *Reframing: Neuro-Linguistic Programming and the Transformation of Meaning* (Bandler & Grinder).

- Life Levels Alignment (Chap. 17). "Neuro-logical levels" was created by Robert Dilts and can be found in his *Tools of the Spirit*.

- Circle of Excellence (Chap. 18). Created by Grinder and Bandler in their workshops.

- Embedded commands (Lesson 18). See *Patterns of the Hypnotic Techniques of Milton H. Erickson, M.D.* (Vol. I) (Bandler & Grinder).

BIBLIOGRAPHY

Andreas, C. & Andreas, S. *Change Your Mind and Keep the Change.* Moab, Utah: Real People Press, 1987.

Andreas, C. & Andreas, T. *Core Transformation: Reaching The Wellspring Within.* Moab, Utah: Real People Press, 1994.

Andreas, C. & Andreas, S. *Heart of the Mind.* Moab, Utah: Real People Press, 1989.

Andreas, S. *Virginia Satir: the Patterns of Her Magic.* Moab, Utah: Real People Press, 1991.

Balch, J.F., M.D. & Balch, P.A., C.N.C. *Prescription for Nutritional Healing.* Garden City Park, New York: Avery, second edition, 1997.

Bandler, R. & Grinder, J. *Patterns of the Hypnotic Techniques of Milton H. Erickson, M.D.* (Vol. I) Cupertino, CA: Meta Publications, 1975.

Bandler, R. & Grinder, J. *Frogs into Princes.* Moab, Utah: Real People Press, 1979.

Bandler, R. & Grinder, J. *Reframing: Neuro-Linguistic Programming and the Transformation of Meaning.* Moab, Utah: Real People Press, 1982.

Bandler, R. *Using Your Brain--for a Change.* Moab, Utah: Real People Press, 1985.

Campbell, J. *Hero With A Thousand Faces.* Princeton, New Jersey: Princeton University Press, 1949.

Carson, C.A., M.D. "The Vestibular (VS) System in NLP" in *Leaves Before the Wind*. Santa Cruz, CA: Grinder, DeLozier & Assc., 1991.

Castaneda, C. *Journey to Ixtlan: The Lessons of Don Juan*. New York: Simon and Schuster, 1972.

Cousins, N. *Anatomy of an Illness*. New York: W.W. Norton & Co., 1979.

Cummings, E.E. *Six Nonlectures*. Boston: Harvard University Press, 1951.

Davis, A. *Let's Eat Right to Keep Fit*. New York: Harcourt, Brace Jovanovich, Inc. 1970.

DeLozier, J., & Grinder, J. *Turtles all the Way Down: Prerequisites for Personal Genius*. Santa Cruz, CA: Grinder, DeLozier & Associates.

Dilts, R.B., Grinder, J., Bandler, R., Bandler, L.C. & DeLozier, J. *Neuro-Linguistic Programming: The Study of the Structure of Subjective Experience*. Cupertino, CA: Meta Publications, 1980.

Dilts, R.B., Dilts, R. W. & Epstein, T. *Tools For Dreamers--Strategies for Creativity and the Structure of Innovation*. Cupertino, CA: Meta Publications, 1991.

Dilts, R.B. & McDonald, R. *Tools of the Spirit*. Capitola, CA: Meta Publications, 1997.

Dilts, R.B., *Visionary Leadership Skills: Creating A World To Which People Want To Belong*. Capitola, CA: Meta Publications, 1996.

Dunne, L.J., *Nutrition Almanac* (third edition). New York: McGraw-Hill, Inc., 1990.

Erickson, M.H. & Rossi, E.L. *Hypnotherapy*. New York: John Wiley & Sons, 1979.

Feldenkrais, M. *Awareness Through Movement*. New York: Harper & Row, 1977

Grinder, M. *Righting the Educational Conveyor Belt*. Portland, OR: Metamorphous Press, 1989.

Grinder, J. & Bandler, R. *Trance-formations: Neuro-Linguistic Programming and the Structure of Hypnosis.* Moab, Utah: Real People Press, 1981.

Haley, J. *Advanced Techniques of Hypnosis and Therapy: Selected Papers of Milton H. Erickson, M.D.* New York: Grune and Stratton, 1967.

Jung, C.G. *Memories, Dreams, Reflections*. New York: Random House, 1961.

Lankton, S. *Practical Magic*. Cupertino, CA: Meta Publications, 1980.

Lopez, B. *Arctic Dreams*. New York: Charles Scribner's Sons, 1986.

Madaule, P. *When Listening Comes Alive*. Norval, ON, Canada: Moulin Publishing, 1993.

Pauling, L. *How to Live Longer and Feel Better*. New York: Avon Books, 1986.

Satir, V. *Peoplemaking*. Palo Alto, CA: Science & Behavior Books, 1972.

Selye, H. *The Stress of Life*. New York: McGraw-Hill, 1956.

Stanislawski, K. S. *The Stanislawkski Method*. New York: The Viking Press, 1960.

Whitaker, Julian, M.D. *Dr. Whitaker's Guide to Natural Healing*. Rocklin, CA: Prima, 1995.

INDEX

Birgitte Nielsen

MICHAEL COLGRASS

Michael Colgrass is a composer, writer and lecturer, who gives personal development workshops all over the world for performers, students and professional groups. A graduate of the University of Illinois, he is a Tanglewood scholar, twice Guggenheim Fellow, and winner of the Pulitzer Prize for Music. He won an Emmy for the PBS documentary "Soundings: The Music of Michael Colgrass," which features his unique teaching methods.

The Rockefeller Foundation created a special program for Colgrass called "Artist in the Theater at Large," which led to studies in mime, acting, dance and directing in New York, *commedia dell' arte* in Milan and avant garde theater with Jerzy Grotowski's Polish Theater Laboratory in Wroclaw, Poland. In 1985 Colgrass became a certified trainer of neuro-linguistic programming (NLP) and today combines these techniques with his 45 years of professional performing experience in his "Excellence In Performance" workshops. He has trained more than 25,000 people in Europe, Britain, South America, South Africa, Indonesia and throughout the United States and Canada.

Colgrass' strategies for creativity were modeled by NLP co-founder John Grinder and also by Robert Dilts and David Gordon, and were described in Dilts' book, *Tools For Dreamers* (Meta Publications, 1991). Colgrass originated "Deep Listening," a technique for using hypnosis with audiences to heighten concentration, which is featured in the book *Leaves Before The Wind* (Grinder DeLozier & Associates, 1991), a collection of innovative NLP ideas edited by Charlotte Bretto, Judith DeLozier, John Grinder and Sylvia Topel. His articles on creativity and life skills have appeared in *The New York Times, The Christian Science Monitor* and *Music Magazine*. His first book, *My Lessons With Kumi*, is the summation of his work as a trainer and performer. For more details visit: www.michaelcolgrass.com